Brian Fleming Research & Learning Library
Ministry of Education
Ministry of Training, Colleges & Universities
900 Bay St. 13th Floor, Mowat Block
Toronto, ON M7A 1L2

D1801588

GLOBALISATION, TRADE LIBERALISATION, AND HIGHER EDUCATION IN NORTH AMERICA

HIGHER EDUCATION DYNAMICS

VOLUME 4

Series Editor
Peter Maassen, *University of Oslo, Norway, and University of Twente, Enschede, The Netherlands*

Editorial Board
Alberto Amaral, *Universidade do Porto, Portugal*
Akira Arimoto, *Hiroshima University, Japan*
Nico Cloete, *CHET, Pretoria, South Africa*
David Dill, *University of North Carolina at Chapel Hill, USA*
Jürgen Enders, *University of Twente, Enschede, The Netherlands*
Oliver Fulton, *University of Lancaster, United Kingdom*
Patricia Gumport, *Stanford University, USA*
Glen Jones, *University of Toronto, Canada*

SCOPE OF THE SERIES

Higher Education Dynamics is a bookseries intending to study adaptation processes and their outcomes in higher education at all relevant levels. In addition it wants to examine the way interactions between these levels affect adaptation processes. It aims at applying general social science concepts and theories as well as testing theories in the field of higher education research. It wants to do so in a manner that is of relevance to all those professionally involved in higher education, be it as ministers, policy-makers, politicians, institutional leaders or administrators, higher education researchers, members of the academic staff of universities and colleges, or students. It will include both mature and developing systems of higher education, covering public as well as private institutions.

GLOBALISATION, TRADE LIBERALISATION, AND HIGHER EDUCATION IN NORTH AMERICA

The Emergence of a New Market under NAFTA?

Edited by

CLYDE W. BARROW

*University of Massachusetts,
North Dartmouth, U.S.A.*

SYLVIE DIDOU-AUPETIT

*National Polytechnical Institute,
Mexico City, Mexico*

and

JOHN MALLEA

*Brandon University,
Manitoba, Canada*

KLUWER ACADEMIC PUBLISHERS
DORDRECHT / BOSTON / LONDON

A C.I.P. Catalogue record for this book is available from the Library of Congress.

ISBN 1-4020-1791-X (HB)
ISBN 1-4020-1862-2 (PB)

Published by Kluwer Academic Publishers,
P.O. Box 17, 3300 AA Dordrecht, The Netherlands.

Sold and distributed in North, Central and South America
by Kluwer Academic Publishers,
101 Philip Drive, Norwell, MA 02061, U.S.A.

In all other countries, sold and distributed
by Kluwer Academic Publishers,
P.O. Box 322, 3300 AH Dordrecht, The Netherlands.

Printed on acid-free paper

All Rights Reserved
© 2003 Kluwer Academic Publishers
No part of this work may be reproduced, stored in a retrieval system, or transmitted
in any form or by any means, electronic, mechanical, photocopying, microfilming, recording
or otherwise, without written permission from the Publisher, with the exception
of any material supplied specifically for the purpose of being entered
and executed on a computer system, for exclusive use by the purchaser of the work.

Printed in the Netherlands.

TABLE OF CONTENTS

	Figures and Tables	vii
	Acknowledgments	ix
	Preface	xi
1	Globalisation, Trade Liberalisation, and the Knowledge Economy	1
2	The Premise and the Promise of North American Higher Education	23
3	Globalisation, NAFTA, and Higher Education in the USA	43
4	Globalisation, NAFTA, and Higher Education in Canada	95
5	Globalisation, NAFTA, and Higher Education in Mexico	123
6	The Triumph of the Market Model in North American Higher Education	165
	Appendix A The Wingspread Statement	187
	Appendix B The Vancouver Communiqué	191
	Appendix C Members of the North American Consortium for Higher Education Collaboration	195
	Appendix D USAID/ALO Higher Education Linkage Project	197
	References	213

FIGURES

1. U.S. Percent of World International Student Market — 11
2. North American Gross Domestic Product, 2000 (US$) — 25
3. GNP Per Capita: USA, Canada, Mexico (1997) — 25
4. Percentage of Total World Trade Among NAFTA Partners, 1998 — 25
5. Modern Foreign Language Registrations, 1960 to 1998 — 68
6. Share of U.S. Total World Trade with NAFTA Partners, 1983 to 1998 — 70

TABLES

1. SCANS Competencies and Foundation Skills — 48
2. Registrations in Ten Leading Modern Foreign Languages, 1998 — 68
3. Foreign Students and Total U.S. Student Enrollment in Higher Education, 1954/55 to 1996/97 — 69
4. Leading Places of Origin for Foreign Students in the United States — 70
5. Host Countries of U.S. Study Abroad Students — 72
6. Origins of Foreign Visiting Scholars at U.S. Higher Institutions — 72
7. Cross-Border Participation in U.S. Academic Conferences by NAFTA Partners, 1998-1999 — 74
8. Summary of USAID Institutional Higher Education Linkage Project — 83
9. Federal Contributions for Post-Secondary Education in Canada — 98
10. Students in Canada from Mexico and USA — 118
11. Estimated Academic Year Foreign Student Expenditures and Job Creation by State, 1994 — 171

ACKNOWLEDGMENTS

The research project leading to this book was conceived by the authors in 1997 in response to a request for proposals from El Colegio de Mexicoís North American Fund for Studies of the North American Region. This Fund supports El Colegio de Mexicoís Inter-Institutional Research Program in North American Studies, which has been one of the most significant initiatives since NAFTA's ratification to promote the development of tri-lateral cooperation in the social sciences and the creation of a knowledge-base in North American Studies. We owe an exceptional debt of gratitude to the Fund for its financial support. Dr. Blanca Torres and Dr. Carlos Alba, secretary generals of the Fund have provided unwavering support for the project. We also thank Dora, Luis Nava, and Adriana Carrillo for their assistance with the Fund.

Dr. Meir Serfaty, a Professor of Political Science and Spanish at Brandon University, translated Chapter 5 from Spanish into English.

PREFACE

Since the mid-1970s, economic and educational developments in Canada, Mexico, and the USA have been influenced by two parallel trends: (1) the resurgence of global economic competition and (2) the active promotion of knowledge-intensive, service based economies. Both trends have been reinforced by the liberalisation of international trade under the rubric of the General Agreement on Tariffs and Trade (GATT) and the World Trade Organisation (WTO). The North American Free Trade Agreement (NAFTA) has accelerated these trends in all three countries by providing the framework for an integrated regional economy in North America designed to compete against comparable trading blocs centred in Japan and the European Union. The purpose of this study is to examine the developing relationship between trade liberalisation, post-industrialisation, and higher education in Canada, Mexico, and the USA.

The larger trends and linkages that we identify are by no means confined to these three countries. We have chosen to focus on Canada, Mexico, and the USA, because the adoption of the North American Free Trade Agreement has accelerated the development of economic policies in these countries, which identify higher education as a central component of each country's new competitiveness strategy. As a consequence, government policy-makers and higher education decision-makers are responding with targeted initiatives to promote the internationalisation of higher education generally and to promote trilateral co-operation among North American higher education institutions specifically. This book examines the origins, rationale, and implementation of these initiatives with three national case studies that are carried out within a common theoretical and analytical framework.

The common framework identifies economic globalisation, trade liberalisation, and post-industrialisation as common structural factors exerting a significant, if often indirect, influence on higher education in the three countries. Therefore, the central concepts that organise the analysis are drawn from the "neo-liberal" economics literature that has come to exert a powerful influence on the thinking of policy-makers in all three countries. This literature points to the emergence of a global economy structured by competition among three regional trading blocs in Europe, North America, and the Asia-Pacific. This literature also emphasises the importance of higher education in the promotion of knowledge-intensive service-based economies. The authors have adopted this analytic framework because it is the dominant policy paradigm for higher education initiatives in all three countries and, therefore, the authors consider it a crucial framework for understanding contemporary higher education policy in North America. However, our references to this framework should not be read as an uncritical acceptance of its assumptions, policy implications, or practical results.

For better or worse, over the last twenty-five years, Canada, Mexico, and the USA have each struggled with their own policies of structural readjustment designed to reconfigure each country's domestic economic base, while simultaneously opening their economies to international competition through trade liberalisation. The three countries' political and business leadership, as epitomised by NAFTA, have each gravitated toward the adoption of neo-liberal economic principles as the basis for both national and continental economic strategies. Yet, each country has arrived at this common point by a different path and from a different starting place. As a result of global trade liberalisation, Canada has gradually abandoned the "comfortable insularity" of a prosperous resource-based economy that was buffered against international competition by high tariffs, import quotas, and state industrial subsidies. Mexico has taken even more dramatic strides to abandon an autarkic policy of economic nationalism based on import substitution, state ownership, and the regulation of foreign investment. In contrast, the USA has long been a proponent of "free trade," but in pursuing this policy it has ceded large segments of its mass manufacturing base to developing countries, including Mexico. Furthermore, the relative erosion of the USA's dominant position in the world economy has forced policy-makers to gradually recognise that in the new global economy, the USA can no longer dictate the terms of international trade. It must compete against powerful economic blocs in Japan and the European Union, while being challenged in many industries by imports from developing countries.

In each instance, policy-makers and business leaders have identified higher education as a central component of an economic strategy designed to meet the challenges of economic globalisation, while building a knowledge-intensive economy. However, the higher education systems in these countries have different relationships to the federal government, different institutional and funding arrangements, and different academic cultures. Consequently, higher institutions in the three countries have exhibited different capacities for responding to economic globalisation and post-industrialisation. The three case studies, while adopting a common analytical framework, have allowed the authors to examine how these asymmetries mediate the linkages between higher education institutions and competitiveness policies in the three countries. These linkages include the motivations of various stakeholders, the degree of involvement of the private sector, the different roles of the federal governments, and higher education's institutional capacity to respond to opportunities for trilateral co-operation. There are numerous obstacles to trilateral co-operation and many of these obstacles are specific to individual countries. Nevertheless, in Canada, Mexico, and the USA a range of initiatives are being introduced to promote the internationalisation of higher education and, more specifically, to encourage trilateral co-operation among the three country's higher education institutions at the level of policy, structure, programs, and curricula.

While it is certainly premature to suggest that the three countries' higher education systems are converging into a North American model, there are several reasons why such a study is timely and important. First, most scholars and higher education administrators have failed to recognise that NAFTA contains provisions directly relevant to higher education with respect to the mutual recognition of credentials, accreditation, and the harmonisation of professional standards. Furthermore, in their myopic tendency to view colleges and universities as merely "cultural" or "educational" institutions, these same individuals have often failed to recognise that policy-makers and business leaders view higher education as a "service industry." Indeed, in the new North American Industrial Classification System (NAICS), which was created to harmonise economic and trade statistics among the three NAFTA countries, higher education institutions are classified under "Educational Services" for statistical purposes. Thus, even if NAFTA contained no provisions directly affecting higher education in the traditional sense of the term, its provisions liberalising international trade in "services" will have a significant impact on higher education *as an industry.*

Educators, business leaders, and government officials in North America are only starting to explore these impacts after a decade of rhetorical flourish and heightened expectations generated by NAFTA's ratification in 1993. The governments of Canada, Mexico, and the USA have convened three major trilateral conferences on higher education co-operation since 1992 as a direct response to the possibilities and challenges posed by NAFTA. There have been official statements, communiqués, and action agendas issued by these conferences. There have been many other policy statements about the importance of "internationalising" higher education issued by various higher education associations. This study evaluates the actual impact of such statements and policies over the last ten years in each of the three countries.

Our study begins that process of exploration as the first *comprehensive comparative analysis* of NAFTA's impact on higher education in North America. It is also one of the few efforts to link the political economy of global and regional development to the development of higher education in North America specifically. In addition, because NAFTA is the first free trade agreement between developed countries and a developing country, this study is the first to explore the *asymmetrical impact* of globalisation on higher education in North America. There are numerous commonalties between the three countries, such as the forces of globalisation, the impact of trade liberalisation, the emergence of post-industrial or knowledge-based economies, and domestic fiscal constraints in higher education, which combine to structure the issues confronting higher institutions and the realistic options available for addressing those issues. Despite these structural similarities, and the common analytical framework it provides for the authors, the impact of these forces on higher education in the three countries is quite different. The different resources available to higher institutions, their relation to political institutions, and the different structure of higher education institutions mean that local differences remain important factors in decisions about how educational, political, and business leaders seek to implement solutions to the challenges facing higher education at its interface with the global and domestic economies.

This study, which was itself the result of trilateral co-operation between three scholars in Canada, Mexico, and the USA, is the first effort to document the extent, if any, of NAFTA's impact on higher education. In presenting our findings, the book starts with an introductory chapter that describes the processes of globalisation and trade liberalisation and that identifies the role of higher education in the competitiveness strategies of Canada, Mexico, and the USA. This chapter is followed by a description and evaluation of trilateral initiatives in higher education developed in response to NAFTA at the international level. This survey of trilateral initiatives is followed by three national case studies of higher education – Canada, Mexico, and the USA – which use a common analytical framework to document, describe, and analyse national and institutional responses to economic globalisation and trade liberalisation. The book concludes with a comparative chapter that includes an analytical overview of the differences and similarities observed in the three case studies.

We conclude that expectations about North American higher education co-operation have been organised around two competing models of international higher education. A traditional liberal model has been articulated that emphasises the social role of international higher education in creating a regional identity based on an appreciation of the cultural differences and economic asymmetries of the three countries. These expectations have been largely deflected by the triumph of a market model of international higher education, which emphasises higher education's role in regional economic development. For the time being, the market model of trilateral co-operation has triumphed in North America in distinct contrast to the model of international co-operation being implemented in the European Union. However, the debate about higher education's role under NAFTA is far from finished and we hope that this book will stimulate that debate anew.

CHAPTER I

GLOBALISATION, TRADE LIBERALISATION, AND THE KNOWLEDGE ECONOMY

THE DIMENSIONS OF GLOBALISATION

The term globalisation is now widely used to capture a variety of economic, cultural, social, and political trends that are each extending the boundaries of the world's social systems beyond the borders of its nation-states (Steger 2002; Waters 2001; Leyton-Brown 1996, 11). Globalisation, as we now understand it, has become possible as a result of technological changes that are literally making the world smaller with improvements to transportation and communication. International voyages that once took days or even weeks to complete at the turn of the century are now completed in a matter of hours through air transportation. The improvements to transportation and shipping technology have reduced average ocean freight charges from $95 per short ton in 1920 to $29 in 1990. Between 1930 and 1990, the average air transport revenue per passenger-mile fell from 68 cents to 11 cents, while the cost of a 3-minute telephone call from New York to London dropped from $244.65 to $3.32 (Office of the U.S. President 1997, 243).[1] Communications and other transactions that once took days are now completed in a matter of seconds through computer networks. This same computer technology has placed global information storage, retrieval, and processing capabilities in the hands of individuals at a cost of a few hundred dollars, when it previously required millions of dollars in hardware, technical support, and personnel (Leyton-Brown 1996, 11).

Globalisation is perhaps most pronounced in the economic sphere where production and marketing by multinational enterprises (MNEs) is giving way to globally integrated transnational enterprises (TNEs) (Reich 1991; Gilpin 2001). The ability to move capital, raw materials, components, manufactured products, and information inexpensively and quickly has transformed, and sometimes disrupted, the old relationship between trade, investment, and domestic economic policy. The nation-state has lost much of its ability to control the pace of domestic savings, business investment, and inflation through macro-economic fiscal and monetary policies, because the spatial horizon for economic decision-making is now wider than the territorial boundaries of nation-states. There are real tensions between the market imperatives of an open global economy, the international mobility of capital, and globalised systems of production, on the one hand, and the nation-state's exercise of its traditional sovereign authority on behalf of citizens (Leyton-Brown 1996, 12). Thus, political scientists now routinely refer to "the crisis of the nation-state" and even to "the end of the nation-state" (Poggi 1990, 184-88).

Cultural globalisation is a highly visible component of the same developments in communications and transnational economic relations (Ibid., 12). A large percentage of the global economy consists of news and information, advertising images, corporate logos, entertainment, sports, food, fashion, and other cultural commodities. It is increasingly common for the citizens of different countries to watch the same movies, television programs, and newscasts. They read translated versions of the same magazines and books, listen to much of the same music, and are subject to global advertising campaigns that seem to attract different peoples toward homogeneous cultural tastes and values while at the same time provoking a "clash of civilisations" (Huntington 1996; Waters 2001, Chap. 6). Moreover, because the United States remains the single most powerful economic and political entity in the world, English is rapidly becoming the language of commerce, tourism, and diplomacy, much as Latin was the language of the medieval literati. These cultural developments are a further source of tension within many nation-states, because large segments of their populations identify with cultural tastes and values that are defined outside the historical national culture.

The social manifestations of globalisation are often less highly developed than in other areas, but they are having significant repercussions in states throughout the world. The changes in communication and transportation have both encouraged and facilitated greater international mobility for purposes of business, tourism, temporary employment, and permanent migration. Once homogeneous national societies must deal increasingly with the tensions and dislocations of multiculturalism due to official and unofficial population movements across borders.

Finally, there is a new range of political problems that stem from the incongruity of having to deal with economic, cultural, and social policy issues that extend beyond the territorial boundaries of individual nation-states. The term interdependence is often used to describe the trend toward political globalisation. Interdependence is a policy relationship between nation-states where (1) the domestic policy actions of one government inevitably have effects in other countries, whether intended or not, and (2) there are many issues where one government is unable to achieve its domestic policy objectives unilaterally and must seek the co-operation of other governments. The growing interdependence of nation-states has resulted in the strengthening of international institutions such as the International Monetary Fund (IMF), the World Bank, the Group of 7, the Organisation for Economic Co-operation and Development, the World Trade Organisation, the United Nations, and the North Atlantic Treaty Organisation (NATO), to name a few (Gilpin Chap. 15). International institutions are assuming more responsibility for co-ordinating and implementing international policy initiatives even in areas once considered the sacrosanct sphere of domestic sovereignty and national independence (Leyton-Brown 1996, 14-15).

WHAT IS "NEW" ABOUT THE NEW GLOBAL ECONOMY?

The Knowledge Economy

At the same time, the emergence of post-industrial economies in the world's most developed nations has stimulated new theories of economic growth, which suggest that faster technological change is crucial to increasing the long-run economic growth rate of the most advanced economies. However, the pace of technological change can increase only to the extent that basic research is transferred into technological applications and only if workers are skilled in the flexible application and use of new technologies or processes. According to one of these theories, it is the accumulation of "human capital" that facilitates the development of new technologies and is the source of self-sustaining growth for post-industrial economies (Becker 1993; Bell 1976; Roemer 1986; Azariadis and Drazen 1990; Barro 1991; OECD 1996b, 18; OECD 1996d). Human capital is the knowledge that individuals acquire during their lifetime and use to produce goods, services, or ideas in market or non-market circumstances. Despite the absence of generally accepted standards for the measurement of human capital, there is growing agreement that the knowledge embodied by workers is gradually becoming a larger proportion of the overall productive capacity of firms in comparison to raw materials, fixed capital, and even managerial skills (OECD 1996b, 15-22).

A major firm-level effect of the transition from industrial to post-industrial economies has been the shift from high-volume mass production to high-value enterprise (Reich 1991; Piore and Sabel 1984). The high-volume mass production model of business enterprise was based on a labour process geared to the standardised manufacture of low-cost consumer goods. Carnevale (1991, 2) observes that in the industrial economy an individual firm's success depended largely on its ability "to produce higher volumes of goods and services with the same or fewer resources." A particular firm's competitiveness depended on its ability to mass-produce goods at a low unit-cost (i.e., total costs divided by the number of units produced). The classic example of this production model is the automobile assembly line that relied, for the most part, on unskilled and semi-skilled labour to perform routine, monotonous, and repetitive tasks. In this high-volume production regime, the economic value of a business enterprise was identified with its cash reserves and physical capital (e.g., land, mineral rights, and machinery).

The new model of business enterprise is not simply a change in business organisation, but rests on a fundamental transformation of the production process and its underlying value-form. It consists of shifting from a production process where value is a function of investments in financial and physical capital to a production process characterised by the predominance of intellectual property and human capital (Davidow and Malone 1992; Hammer and Champy 1993). A firm's value has come to depend increasingly on the intellectual skills, knowledge, and intelligence of its human capital and its patented, licensed, or copyrighted intellectual property. Indeed, Robert Reich (1991, 105), the former U.S. Secretary of Labour observes that "intellectual capital continues to overtake physical capital as the key asset of corporations" in one industry after another. Consequently, the nature of the workforce is also changing and the types of skills needed by the post-industrial workforce are determined by the structural requirements of the new high-value model of business enterprise.

The high value model is a response to simultaneous but contradictory tendencies in the restructuring of markets: (a) market globalisation and (b) market fragmentation. On the one hand, business firms must increasingly compete in a global marketplace. In the United States, for instance, a consumer is as likely to purchase a shirt made in Jamaica, a car made in Japan, and a television made in Korea as they are to purchase an "American-made" good or service (to the extent that these national identifiers still have any meaning). Yet, even as markets assume global dimensions, there is a simultaneous fragmentation of mass markets into niche markets that are often dominated globally by one or a few firms. The development of television programming is an example of the growth of global niche markets where the dominance of two or three networks in each country has given way to hundreds of specialised channels delivered through cable and satellite networks. Thus, while globalisation requires companies to compete on an international basis, niche marketing requires them to serve the unique needs of particular types of customers, rather than the standardised needs of the average mass consumer.

Importantly, as Reich (1991, 82-83) also points out, niche production can offset the competitive cost differentials of a high-wage economy, since "customers are willing to pay a premium for goods and services that exactly meet their needs and because these high-value businesses cannot easily be duplicated by high-volume competitors."[2] Thus, he (1991, 84) observes that "successful businesses in advanced nations are moving to a higher ground based on specially tailored products and services." This means that the new barrier to market entry and global competitiveness is no longer the volume or price of production, but the skills of a highly trained and well educated workforce that can repeatedly discover the right fit between particular technologies or services, specialised markets, and individual clients. Thus, in the developed nations, strategies for post-industrial economic development directly or indirectly rely heavily on higher education as a policy instrument, particularly in the areas of workforce development, applied research, and technology transfer.

Transnationalisation

The geographic distribution of economic activity is also being transformed on a global scale by the emergence of post-industrial economies anchored by knowledge-intensive high technology and service industries (OECD 1996b). In many respects, capitalism has always been an economic system with a significant volume of international exchange and numerous multinational enterprises (Wallerstein 1980). The trend toward transnational business consolidation and the emergence of regional trading blocs was noted by critical political economists in the first half of the twentieth century (Beard 1934; Lenin 1939). More recently, economist Paul Krugman

(1994a, 1994b, 1994c, 1994d) has pointed out that the ratio of United States Gross Domestic Product (GDP) attributable to international trade has not changed substantially since the 1940s. For instance, exports accounted for approximately 10 percent of U.S. Gross National Product (GNP) in 1940 and had increased to only 10.6 percent by 1992.

The new global economy is not fundamentally "new" due to any increase in the relative volume of international trade, but the composition and structure of that trade is substantially different than it was at the end of the Second World War. In earlier stages of capitalist development, trade between nations consisted primarily of trade in finished goods between the developed countries who had a comparative advantage in the production of a particular good. Trade between developed and undeveloped countries consisted mainly of the exchange of finished manufactured goods for agricultural products and natural resources.

When compared to this historical pattern, two aspects of international trade distinguish the new global economy from its predecessor. First, an increasing proportion of international trade consists of intra-industry and intra-firm trade, rather than the exchange of goods and resources between firms and nations (Lawrence 1996). For example, it is estimated that in 1989 nearly 40 percent of U.S. merchandise exports and more than 60 percent of its imports were intra-firm transactions (Ostry 1996, 147). This change in the structure of international trade has made inter-firm competition truly global, rather than inter-national. International trade is less and less an exchange of one good for another as compared to a transnational production process that takes place within a single firm across multiple national boundaries. Transnational enterprises rationalise their operations on a global scale by locating different aspects of the firm – research and development, manufacturing, data processing, warehousing, and marketing – in the most advantageous locations throughout the world (Helpman and Krugman 1985). Thus, the movement of goods and labour is occurring more and more within firms, rather than between firms.

The expanding and changing role of foreign direct investment (FDI) is directly linked to this new form of global economic competition. In 1997, 151 changes in FDI regulatory regimes were made by 76 countries and 89 percent of these changes created a more favourable or liberalised environment for FDI (UNCTAD 1998, xix). The value of international production attributable to some 53,000 transnational enterprises (TNEs) and their 450,000 foreign affiliates was $3.5 trillion in 1997, while the estimated global sales of these foreign affiliates was $9.5 trillion. Total FDI stocks are now equal to 21 percent of global GDP, while foreign affiliate exports account for one-third of world exports. The sales of foreign affiliates are currently growing faster than total world exports of goods and services. The ratio of total world FDI stocks to world GDP has also grown twice as fast as the ratio of world imports and exports to world GDP. These developments suggest that the expansion of transnational production is deepening the interdependence of the world economy beyond that achieved by international trade alone (Ibid., xvii).

As developing countries have begun lowering their trade barriers, trade liberalisation has facilitated a trans-border rationalisation of production as firms seek to maximise the use of local factors of production to achieve competitive advantages on a global scale. As firms increasingly pursue global competitive strategies, foreign direct investment has been motivated more by the desire to service export markets around the world, rather than to produce goods for the domestic market of the host country. In many industries, a significant production and distribution presence in each of the world's major markets has become an essential ingredient of competitive success. Not surprisingly, the developing countries that provide a strategic "export platform" for TNEs have become the most successful at attracting FDI. Between 1980 and 1990, the developing economies receiving the largest inflows of FDI were Singapore ($ 2.3 billion), Mexico ($1.9 billion), Brazil ($1.8 billion), China ($1.7 billion), Hong Kong ($1.1 billion), and Malaysia ($1.1 billion) (Lawrence 1996, 28). These same countries were among the leading recipients of FDI during the 1990s (Ibid., 254-263).

TRADE LIBERALISATION

A fundamental premise of our approach to the impact of globalisation on higher education is that globalisation is a *policy process* and not an inexorable technologically determined event. The global economic system is structured both by national laws and by international treaties that govern cross-border economic transactions. There are a variety of trade and economic policies established by each of the world's 190 countries, including tariffs, import quotas, foreign exchange rationing, domestic monetary policies, and many other national laws that affect international trade. There are also numerous bilateral and multilateral agreements between countries that establish an international legal framework limiting tariff protection, prohibiting certain trade policies (e.g., export subsidies), providing safeguard measures (e.g., anti-dumping), and establishing dispute resolution procedures (e.g., binding arbitration) (Whalley 1989, 7).

The World Trade Organisation

The General Agreement on Tariffs and Trade (GATT) has long been the most important treaty governing the global economic system. The GATT was established by 23 countries in 1947, including the United States, Canada, Great Britain, Western Europe, Japan, Australia, and New Zealand. Article I of GATT establishes most-favoured-nation (MFN) status as the trading system's basic principle of non-discrimination against imports on the basis of national origin. This principle of non-discrimination requires each country participating in GATT to grant other parties to the agreement no less favourable treatment than is granted to the country receiving the most favourable treatment under its trade laws. If a participating country decides to grant the imports of one country better or more favourable treatment than required by GATT, the better treatment is automatically extended to the same goods imported from all countries that are parties to GATT (Graham 1996, 46). GATT was given an institutional existence through its Secretariat, which provided technical assistance, dispute settlement, and enforcement of the Agreement.

GATT provided the framework for eight rounds of multilateral trade negotiations after World War II. The first round in Geneva (1947) resulted in significant tariff reductions, particularly by the advanced industrial countries that initiated the Agreement. Subsequent negotiations failed to produce any significant breakthroughs until the Kennedy Round (1963-1967) resulted in a single tariff cutting formula that led to a 35 percent overall reduction in the average tariff level among participating nations. The Tokyo Round (1973-1979) resulted in another overall reduction of 34 percent in average tariff levels. By the early 1980s, the average tariff on most goods imported by the advanced industrial countries was under 10 percent, although GATT permitted higher tariffs for import-sensitive areas such as agriculture, textiles, and apparel (Schott 1994, 60). In the Tokyo Round, governments also began negotiating new and improved rules on the use or removal of non-tariff barriers (NTBs) (Whalley 1989, 9).[3]

However, in GATT's first seven rounds, multilateral negotiations mainly liberalised trade regimes for the trade in goods among developed countries. During this time, there was very little trade liberalisation by developing countries that could be attributed to GATT. For the most part, developing countries continued with import substitution strategies that relied on high tariffs, import licensing, foreign exchange rationing, and balance-of-payment restrictions as allowed under Article 18-B of the GATT. Furthermore, international trade in services, a key growth sector in the new post-industrial economies, was not covered by previous iterations of GATT.

However, by the mid-1980s, many developing countries unilaterally abandoned import substitution policies or moved toward trade liberalisation through a variety of bilateral and regional trade agreements negotiated with other developing countries. This movement was stimulated partly by dissatisfaction with the results of import substitution strategies, the Latin American debt crisis, and a growing conviction that the export oriented policies of the "Asian tiger" countries were proving more successful in promoting economic development (Ibid., 15-16, 32). Consequently, in reaction to a perceived movement toward "closed regionalism" by Europe, Japan, and the developing countries, the United States initiated the Uruguay Round (1987-1994) as the eighth round of multilateral trade negotiations held under the auspices of the General Agreement on Tariffs and Trade. After seven years of negotiations, the Uruguay Round culminated in the World Trade Organisation (WTO) treaty, signed in Marrakesh, Morocco (April 1994), which became effective on January 1, 1995. The Uruguay Round cut the developed countries' tariffs by an average of 38 percent and lowered their average tariff to only 3.9 percent (Schott 1994, 9, 61), while the WTO's membership has grown to 144 of the world's 190 countries (WTO 2002).

Trade Liberalisation and Regionalisation

A potentially paradoxical consequence of global trade liberalisation was the simultaneous proliferation and expansion of regional free trade agreements in Europe, the Pacific Rim, Latin America, Africa, and North America. World trade is already highly regionalised, but it is becoming increasingly concentrated within three regional trading blocs organised around the European Union (EU), the Pacific Rim (APEC), and North America (NAFTA) (Hinojosa-Ojeda 1996, 89; Thurow 1992). Regional trading arrangements are an exception to the GATT's most-favoured nation principle authorised by Article XXIV, which allows the establishment of free trade areas and customs unions.

In the 1990s, economic regionalisation accelerated with 34 different regional trading agreements reported to GATT from 1990 to 1994 alone (Safadi and Nicholas 1996, 4; de la Torre and Kelley 1992). The most important regional trading areas are the Asia-Pacific Economic Co-operation Forum (APEC), the European Union, Australia-New Zealand, the Common Market of the Southern Cone (Mercosur),[4] the Caribbean Community (Caricom),[5] the Andean Group,[6] the Central American Common Market, and the North American Free Trade Agreement (NAFTA). In addition, a complex overlapping network of bilateral free trade arrangements has been established in each of these areas between individual countries and between individual countries and other regional trading blocs. Most of the Latin American free trade arrangements are now patterned on the Canada-U.S. Free Trade Agreement (1989), which provided the basic framework for NAFTA (Hufbauer and Schott 1993b; Hinojosa-Ojeda 1996, 87, 99-100; Laird 1996, 187).

Transnational enterprises (TNEs) have played a leading role in promoting regional free trade agreements for several reasons. In the short-term, regional trade arrangements secure continued preferential access to markets among trading partners that historically conduct large volumes of trade with each other. Furthermore, regional trade liberalisation and regional free trade arrangements have generally been adopted and implemented on a much faster track and have covered more sectors of economic activity than the more complex arrangements of the GATT and WTO. Thus, in a context of economic globalisation, regional free trade areas can enhance the competitiveness of transnational corporations by lowering the costs of operating across national borders, particularly where the parties to a regional arrangement provide access to different strategic assets such as labour, natural resources, and technology. Economic regionalisation allows transnational enterprises to rationalise operations with asset deployment strategies that strengthen their global competitiveness against similarly situated firms elsewhere in the world (Hufbauer and Malani 1996; Safadi and Nicholas 1996, 17-18).

For example, Canada and Mexico were drawn to the North American Free Trade Agreement by the prospect of securing preferential market access to the large domestic markets of the United States, which historically is both countries' leading export destination. Both countries also hoped to attract additional foreign direct investment (FDI), particularly from U.S. firms seeking access to Canada's vast natural resources and to Mexico's low-cost labour supply. Conversely, U.S. firms were attracted to NAFTA by the prospect of liberalised investment policies in Canada and Mexico and by the possibilities of rationalising their operations with continental strategies that use the Mexican labour force and Canadian natural resources to competitive advantage (Grayson 1993, 48; Lawrence 1996, 30). Similarly, within the European Union, German producers benefit from comparatively low wages in

Southern and Eastern Europe, while Japanese firms have access to inexpensive manpower in Malaysia, the Philippines, Thailand, and other Pacific Rim countries.

THE GENERAL AGREEMENT ON TRADE IN SERVICES

The Uruguay Round established a framework for trade liberalisation in services that has the potential to extend GATT's provisions to large sectors of the post-industrial economy that were not covered by previous iterations of the agreement. The General Agreement on Trade in Services (GATS) is the first multilateral agreement to establish guidelines governing international trade and investment in the service sector. The GATS covers service industries that "conduct international transactions either by sending highly skilled personnel, technical information, or currency across national borders or by performing services for foreign entities through affiliates located overseas" (USITC 1994, IX-5). This definition includes education, finance, insurance, travel, film rentals, payments by governments abroad, business and professional services (e.g., legal, engineering, management, and information systems), telecommunications, and payments on franchises, patents, copyrights, trademarks, broadcast rights, and other intangible property rights.

For purposes of this study, we have adopted the World Bank (1994, ix) definition of "higher education," which encompasses all post-secondary institutions with degree-, diploma-, and certificate-granting programs. These institutions produce new scientific and technical knowledge through research and advanced training and they serve as conduits for the transfer, adaptation, and dissemination of knowledge (World Bank 1995, 23). This comprehensive definition includes "traditional" public and private post-secondary institutions, as well as virtual universities, corporate universities, and for-profit institutions that are also covered by the GATS.

The GATS is fully integrated into the World Trade Organisation, which has established a Council for Trade in Services to oversee the implementation of service agreements, to monitor on-going negotiations within the GATS framework, and to organise working groups on outstanding issues involving trade in services. The General Agreement on Trade in Services (GATS) consists of three major components: (1) a framework of rules intended to discipline government regulation of trade and investment in services, (2) a set of schedules where each WTO member commits itself to apply these rules to specific service sectors, subject to defined exceptions, and (3) a series of annexes and ministerial decisions that supply additional sector-specific detail and that identify follow-up activities required by the schedule. The framework for trade in services obligates WTO members to respect fifteen general principles that apply to all services except those supplied "in the exercise of governmental authority."[7] The GATT's most fundamental principles, including transparency of laws and regulations, recognition of operating licenses and qualifications to practice a profession, and most-favoured-nation treatment, are extended to the service sectors in principle at least. Governments can exempt themselves from the MFN obligation on a sector-by-sector basis, but the exemption is not to exceed 10 years and is subject to review within five years. Other principles, including market access and national treatment, are binding only to the extent that each member country commits itself to those particular principles for selected service sectors.

Once a country commits itself to a GATS principle, it may choose to apply that principle to one or more of four modes of supply: commercial presence, consumption abroad, cross-border supply, and presence of individuals.[8] A country may also include "horizontal commitments" in its schedule, which limit the principle's applicability to trade in a limited number of service sectors, or it may be specific to only one mode of supply across a broad range of service sectors. Once a country has made a partial or complete commitment on market access or national treatment, the other GATS rules automatically apply to that sector.

Most of the initial commitments submitted by individual countries with respect to market access and national treatment are "standstill" commitments that merely promise to not impose new trade restrictions on foreign service providers. Hence, at this point, GATS merely provides an institutional framework for pursuing future liberalisation in the service sector (USITC 1994, IX-5-6). The GATS has potentially significant implications for higher education, since education services is one of the most significant areas of growth in the global service sector. Under the GATS, trade in education services is classified in five categories: Primary Education, Secondary Education, Higher Education, Adult Education, and Other Education Services (WTO 1998a, 1, 25-26). The GATS will have its most significant impacts on trade in higher education, adult education, and other education services, since the agreement exempts "services supplied in the exercise of governmental authority." It is widely accepted that primary and secondary education are covered by this exemption (WTO 1998b, 4). However, by 1998, thirty countries had made specific commitments in the education services sector with 21 commitments in the area of higher education services. The countries making commitments to liberalise trade in higher education services include all but 2 (France and Russia) of the world's ten largest exporters of higher education services (WTO 1998b, 20).

In 1999, the international market for global higher education was conservatively estimated at $30 billion (Larsen et al. 2002, 1). Higher education services are traded primarily through student mobility across borders (consumption abroad) and, therefore, the largest current source of receipts for higher education services is student fees paid to attend traditional colleges and universities in host countries. Currently, more than 1.5 million students study abroad and this number is continuing to grow each year.

The comparative advantage of the OECD countries in the higher education service sector is evident in the fact that collectively they receive more than 80 percent of the 1.5 million international students who study abroad each year (Skilbeck and Connell 1996, 73). The ten main receiving countries of international students are the USA, France, Germany, the United Kingdom, Russia, Japan, Australia, Canada, Belgium, and Switzerland (WTO 1998b, 20). Significantly, the impact of globalisation has stimulated a great deal of discussion about the need to internationalise higher education in these countries, partly to retain their competitive advantage in this sector and partly to capitalise on this global advantage to support the competitive strategies of transnational enterprises in other sectors of the post-industrial economy.

Figure 1. U.S. Percent of World International Student Market.

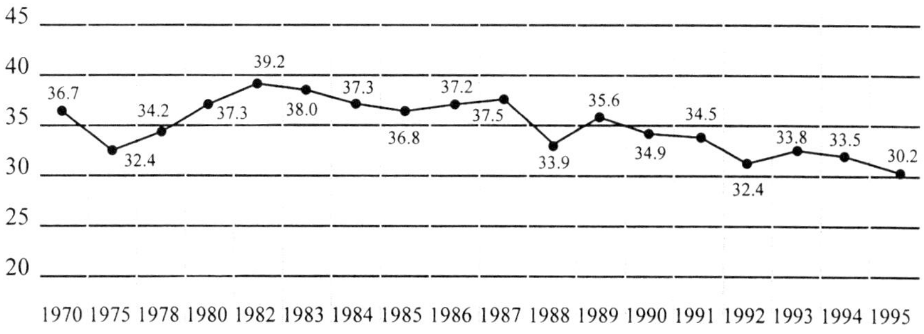

```
45
40          39.2
   36.7          37.3    37.2
35 •   34.2  37.3  38.0  •     •    35.6
        •    •     •     37.5   •    34.5
                     36.8            •       33.8  33.5
30       32.4                   34.9   •      •    •
              •              33.9  •                  30.2
                                      32.4
25
20
   1970 1975 1978 1980 1982 1983 1984 1985 1986 1987 1988 1989 1990 1991 1992 1993 1994 1995
```

Source: Open Doors, 1994-1995, 79.

The USA is the leading exporter of higher education services and commands approximately one-third of the total world market for higher education services supplied by consumption abroad (see Figure 1; Davis 1995, 79, 103-110). In 1998, the USA exported nearly $9 billion in higher education services and recorded a trade surplus in higher education services of about $7.4 billion (U.S. Department of Commerce 2001, D-56). Higher education is now the USA's fifth largest service export and in 2000 the higher education services provided to foreign students (tuition, fees, dormitories) generated approximately $8.1 billion in net economic impacts on local and state economies. When one accounts for travel by students and parents and miscellaneous living expenses estimates by the National Association of Foreign Student Advisors (NAFSA) and the Institute for International Education (IIE) place the direct economic impact of U.S. higher education exports at nearly double this figure (Davis 1997, 96). The U.S. Department of Commerce estimates that expenditures by foreign students in the USA generate approximately 80,000 to 100,000 jobs each year with most of these jobs concentrated in the higher education sector.

The global market for higher education services delivered through traditional institutions of higher education continues to expand as measured by the increasing number of students studying abroad (consumption abroad), the number of foreign visiting scholars travelling abroad to teach and conduct research (presence of individuals), international marketing of curricula, textbooks, and academic programmes (cross-border supply), and the establishment of branch campuses in foreign countries (commercial presence). However, education services is a growing industry that is also branching out into new institutions such as for-profit education and training facilities, and corporate-sponsored universities; into new methods of delivery, such as distance learning via the internet, radio, and television; and into new activities, such as educational exchange services and educational testing services. Changes in the domestic and international structure of higher education services markets are also promoting the development of "other" education services, such as educational management consulting, educational testing services, student exchange services, and study abroad facilitation services (WTO 1998a).

Unfortunately, official trade data on higher education services woefully underestimates the actual levels of cross-border activity, since official trade statistics at the national and international level only estimate the value of the tuition and living expenses of students enrolled in foreign colleges and universities (consumption abroad). The official statistics on trade in higher education services, including those of governmental and international organisations, do not capture fees paid by students enrolled in any form of electronic or distance education (cross-border supply), the fees paid by students receiving instruction in their home country from foreign providers (commercial presence), or those being instructed in their home country by visiting foreign teachers or trainers (presence of individuals) (WTO 1998b, 7). The official statistics also do not capture the international trade in higher education services conducted by for-profit educational institutions (e.g., language institutes) or by corporate universities and training facilities in foreign countries (commercial presence), because these activities are recorded by the host countries as part of their gross "domestic" product (Ibid., 1).

Despite the fact that few countries have made serious commitments on higher education under the GATS, the World Bank's (1995, 23-24) policy on higher education promotes the development of higher education in those countries which already enjoy a competitive advantage in the sector. The World Bank's higher education policy is based on the social investment principle that the economic value of higher education, and its contribution to national economic growth, increases with the level of technological development and as countries achieve universal primary and secondary education. Thus, despite an increasing number of post-secondary graduates in the post-industrial societies, the empirical evidence suggests that rewards to higher education for individuals and society are still increasing in the developed countries (Davis 1992). This correlation alone provides a significant rationale for continuing investment in higher education in those societies, which certainly include Canada, the USA, and the other OECD countries (World Bank 1995, 43).

However, at a time when many of the OECD countries have surplus capacity in their higher education systems, the World Bank (1995, 2-32) concludes that on a global scale "the demand for higher education is in general increasing faster than the supply." Much of this global demand is being generated by growth outside the OECD, particularly in Asia, the Middle East, and Latin America. The World Bank's and IMF's structural adjustment policies grant priority to primary and secondary education, because its estimated social rate of return is higher in countries that have not yet achieved universal literacy. Consequently, higher education is considered a much higher priority in the developed countries, where its linkage to economic development and global competitiveness is more immediate. The impact on higher education of World Bank and IMF structural adjustment policies, when coupled to the developing countries' preferential investment in elementary and secondary education, is to institutionalise a global asymmetry in the provision of higher education services and to privilege the developed countries as suppliers of higher education services. In this respect, higher education is becoming an increasingly important service export for the OECD countries, both in terms of exporting educational services directly to foreign countries and by attracting foreign students, scholars, and international research grants to a country's colleges, universities, and research institutes.

The resulting internationalisation of higher education in the OECD countries is also considered increasingly important because of its potential contribution to the competitive advantage of nations (Porter 1990). Students educated in a developed country often become political and business leaders in their home countries, but they are likely to maintain professional contacts in the country where they received their higher education (Davis 1997, 81). Individuals and transnational corporations are also beginning to recognise the competitive advantage of employees with multicultural competencies and international skills. Thus, many firms are starting to recruit professional employees who can operate in foreign or multicultural workplace environments (Davis 1997, 4).

In this context, government and higher education officials in many of the OECD countries have begun to recognise that higher education is a knowledge-intensive export industry with a positive balance of trade, which simultaneously supports post-industrial development and the global competitiveness of transnational enterprises based in their own countries. Globalisation of the world economy, the pursuit of competitive advantage, and the investment policies of international organisations are each promoting the internationalisation of higher education in the advanced countries, especially as excess demand for higher education in the developing countries is shifted into the OECD countries.

THE USA IN THE NEW GLOBAL ECONOMY

The USA's strategic economic development policies have evolved over the last two decades as an explicit response to economic globalisation and the shift to post-industrialism (Reich 1991; Porter 1990, 1991a; Thurow 1992). The USA's dominant position in the world economy was eroded over the last two decades as Japan and the European Union (EU) captured larger shares of the world market for high technology and medium technology and even penetrated the U.S. domestic market. For example, import penetration for high technology increased from 4.2 percent of the U.S. domestic market in 1970 to 18.4 percent in 1990. Likewise, import penetration for medium technology (e.g., automobiles) increased from 5.6 percent of the U.S. domestic market in 1970 to 18.5 percent in 1990 (Ostry 1996, 165).

During the same period, the developing economies of the Pacific Rim – China, South Korea, Taiwan, Hong Kong, Malaysia, and Singapore – capitalised on low-cost labour to pursue export strategies that allowed them to capture growing shares of the world market for consumer electronics, apparel, and textiles, among other industries (Lawrence 1996, 27). The net result of these combined trends is that the U.S. share of world gross domestic product fell from more than 55 percent in the late 1940s to about 25 percent in the late 1990s (World Bank 1999). Between 1975 and

2000, the U.S. balance of trade went from a $12.4 billion surplus to a $369.7 billion deficit (U.S. Department of Commerce 2001). Thus, for the first time since the end of World War II, the USA has been forced to respond to trends in the world economy, rather than dictate them unilaterally.

In the USA, economists, corporate executives, and government officials attributed much of the nation's competitive decline after 1973 to a slowdown in domestic productivity growth. From 1889 to 1937, for example, when the USA was emerging as one of the world's leading industrial powers, productivity growth averaged 1.9 percent a year. From 1937 to 1973, when the USA was the world's dominant economic power, total factor productivity grew at 3.0 percent per year. However, between 1973 and 1992, as the USA's economic dominance was slipping, productivity growth averaged only 0.9 percent per year and only 0.6 percent annually from 1992 to 1997 (Office of the U.S. President 1993, chap. 1:1; USBLS 2000).

There is still a great deal of disagreement among experts about the specific reasons for the collapse of productivity after 1973 and there are still important ideological debates over the types of policies that are necessary to solve this "productivity paradox." Indeed, the USA still has the highest level of productivity in the world, but other countries have had higher productivity growth in recent decades and this development was viewed as a growing challenge to the USA's competitive advantage in many areas of the global economy. Thus, over the last two decades, a broad consensus has developed among neo-conservatives (Republicans) and neo-liberals (Democrats) that "the major long-run challenge confronting the American economy is to increase the Nation's rate of productivity growth – that is, growth in output per worker (Office of the U.S. President 1993, chap. 1:1). Within this consensus, there are three broad classes of explanations for the collapse of U.S. productivity growth after 1973: (1) a reduction in the rate of capital accumulation by private businesses, (2) a slowdown in the rate of technological advance, and (3) a slower rate of improvement in the skill levels of the U.S. labour force (Ibid., chap. 3:2).

Each of these explanations has been particularly troubling to economists, business leaders, and policy makers, because the USA has been shifting simultaneously from an industrial to a post-industrial economy anchored by information-, service-, and technology-based industries (Bell 1976). These sectors are particularly dependent on high rates of capital investment, technology transfer, and improving workforce skills. Yet, the productivity paradox emerged as an economic policy concern just as U.S. trade policy (i.e., GATT, WTO, and NAFTA), as well as many state economic development strategies (e.g., Dukakis and Kanter 1988; Porter 1991a), were ceding low technology and low-wage mass manufacturing industries to the developing countries.

Most business leaders and government officials have embraced a strategic response to globalisation designed to compete in the more advanced post-industrial sectors of the global economy, such as high technology and services, where U.S.-based companies often still have a competitive advantage (Porter 1990, 1991a; Reich 1991; Tsongas 1991). For example, despite rising import penetration in the high technology sector, the USA has maintained an average trade surplus in "advanced technology" of approximately $30 billion annually since 1989 (U.S. Department of Commerce 2000). Similarly, despite a total trade deficit of more than $369 billion, the United States consistently records a trade surplus in services.

In 1998, the United States exported $260.3 billion in services. As service sector exports have risen over the last two decades, the U.S. trade surplus in services has ballooned from $0.1 billion in 1985 to $79.4 billion in 1998 (U.S. Department of Commerce 2001, D-51). Consequently, the USA strongly favours the liberalisation of trade in services, where U.S. firms are among the largest and most successful global service providers (USITC 1994, IX-3). Thus, the strategic objective of U.S. competitiveness strategies is to facilitate and support the continued development of domestic high-wage sectors such as financial, professional, and business services and advanced technology in telecommunications and information processing, computer-assisted manufacturing, and other high technology industries (Bartell and Lichtenberg 1987; Johnston 1991).[10]

CANADA IN THE NEW GLOBAL ECONOMY

In 1985, President Ronald Reagan and Prime Minister Brian Mulroney signed a Declaration on Trade in Goods and Services only one year after Mulroney had won the Canadian federal election on an anti-free trade platform. The 1985 Declaration on Trade signalled an end to "the comfortable insularity" of Canada's old economic order (Porter 1991b, 5-7) by opening talks on a broad free trade agreement between Canada and the USA, which concluded in the Canada-United States Free Trade Agreement (CUFTA) that became effective on January 1, 1989. CUFTA required the phase-out of all tariffs between the two countries over a ten-year period (by January 1, 1999) and it also mandated the elimination of many non-tariff barriers (e.g., quotas). Foreign direct investment between the two countries was liberalised by extending national treatment to most private investment, although Canadian restrictions on energy and culture remained in place. Unlike the European Union, there was no requirement for a co-ordinated fiscal and monetary policy.

Canada's industrial economy was built on its abundant natural resources, which allowed many Canadian firms to export highly profitable, but unprocessed commodities, including timber and wood pulp, minerals, petroleum, coal, and agricultural staples. A large proportion of the Canadian economy was insulated from international competition, because a major objective of Canada's foreign policy was to safeguard national autonomy by protecting Canadian firms from international rivals. These policies included high tariffs, subsidised inputs to private firms such as transportation, hydroelectric power, and agriculture, and the operation of key state-owned enterprises (Ibid., 43-44, 61-62).

The export sector has long been a vital component of Canada's economy and is roughly two and a half times larger than the USA's export sector as a proportion of GDP. When CUFTA became effective in 1989, exports accounted for 25.2 percent of Canada's GDP, which was second only to Germany among the G-7 nations.

However, in contrast to Germany, the distinguishing feature of Canada's export sector was its dependence on natural resource exports, which in 1989 accounted for 45.8 percent of the nation's exports and 8.3 percent of the world's total resource exports.[11] More than one-third of Canadian exports were unprocessed or semi-processed resources that left the country's economy vulnerable to commodity price fluctuations, technology substitution, and the emergence of low-cost producers in the developing countries (Ibid., 10-11).[12]

Another important feature of Canada's economy is the relatively high level of foreign ownership, despite trade and domestic economic policies designed to insulate Canadian industries and protect national autonomy. Approximately 45 percent of Canada's manufacturing assets are held by foreign owners, particularly by parent firms based in the USA. In 1989, when CUFTA was adopted, U.S. parent companies controlled 71 percent of the assets in Canada's transportation equipment industry (mostly trucks and automobiles), 59 percent of the assets in the rubber products industry (tires), 51 percent of the assets in chemicals and chemical products, and 33 percent of the assets in petroleum and coal. U.S. ownership accounted for 12 to 25 percent of the assets in several other industries such as wood, paper, primary metals, food and beverages, and mining. Thus, the Canadian economy was already highly dependent on foreign direct investment, particularly U.S. investment, which means that many of the strategic business decisions affecting key sectors of the Canadian economy are increasingly tied to the global competitiveness strategies of transnational companies based in the USA (Ibid., 15).

At the same time, like the USA and many other developed countries, Canada's employment base had been shifting from goods-producing sectors to the service sector for several decades (Minister of Supply and Services 1991c, 4). The service sector now accounts for 68 percent of Canada's GDP and approximately 70 percent of the nation's employment. Canada is second only to the USA in the relative size of its service sector among the G-7 nations. Furthermore, as in other countries making the transition to a post-industrial economy, the structure of Canada's manufacturing sector has been shifting to more sophisticated end products such as transportation equipment, high-tech industrial machinery, and electrical products.

However, with the onset of the 1990-91 recession, prominent corporate executives in the Business Council on National Issues (now the Canadian Council of Chief Executives) and Canadian government officials became increasingly concerned about the nation's declining competitiveness. Canada already had rising trade deficits in most of its non-resource industries, which many economists argued were the result of structural weaknesses in the competitive profile of Canada's growing service sector (Porter 1991b, 17-18). Indeed, very few of Canada's service industries had attained international standing as demonstrated by the fact that its service exports, as a percentage of total exports, was the lowest of the G-7 nations, despite the growing importance of these sectors to the nation's economy. Similarly, only 3.3 percent of Canada's total exports could be strictly classified as "high-tech," such as computers, semi-conductors, telecommunications equipment, and health care products (Ibid., 11).

Given the importance of exports to Canada's economy, business and government concerns about these sectoral trade deficits were magnified by the realisation that growth in manufacturing labour productivity had been slower in Canada than in any other G-7 nations during the previous decade with an average annual growth rate of 1.8 percent per year (Ibid., 7). Total Factor Productivity (TFP) – which measures the growth in the productivity of both labour and capital inputs – rose by only 0.4 percent per year in Canada, which tied it with the USA as the worst performer among the G-7 nations. CUFTA's implementation raised the particular concern that productivity growth in Canadian manufacturing was lagging behind the USA, the country's largest trading partner, especially in sophisticated high productivity-growth areas such as electrical products (one of Canada's only high-tech export industries) and even in Canada's basic export industries such as paper products, petroleum, and coal (Minister of Supply and Services 1991c, 4-8). The Canadian Ministry of Supply and Services (1991c, 6-8) released an industry sector analysis in 1991 which concluded that solutions to the nation's "productivity problem are likely to reside in a broad range of factors rather than in narrow conditions specific to particular industries."

Business leaders and federal government officials were increasingly convinced that Canada's competitive position in the world economy was being eroded by the continued insularity of its economic policies.[13] Business elites and the Progressive Conservative party's leadership agreed that Canada's future prosperity "must be driven by a new paradigm, based on productivity and innovation" in order to meet the challenges of economic globalisation and world trade liberalisation (Porter 1991b, 65). At the same time, Governor John Crow led the Bank of Canada in implementing a tight monetary policy that aimed to lower inflation to zero. This policy was maintained right through the 1990-1991 recession (Hufbauer and Malani 1996; Porter 1991b; Ministry of Supply and Services 1991). The high interest rates caused unemployment and general hardship for many Canadians, while many critics blamed the Bank's policy for exacerbating the government's burgeoning debt and deficit problems (Bradford 2000).

Consequently, in 1993, after four years of CUFTA, tight monetary policy, and a controversial vote to ratify NAFTA (1993), Mulroney's Conservative government was badly beaten at the polls and reduced to holding only two seats out of 301 in the Canadian Parliament. The Liberals won an overwhelming majority largely because of their campaign promise to either abrogate or renegotiate NAFTA. Many voters also hoped that a new Liberal Government would reverse or modify the wide-ranging neo-liberal policies of the previous government.

Only a few months after the election, however, the Liberal Government led by Prime Minister Jean Chrétien reversed itself and agreed to implement NAFTA in 1994. Moreover, when faced with slow economic growth and a burgeoning budget deficit, the Liberals also proceeded to cut social programs, lower taxes, and lay off thousands of civil servants. Moreover, it was not by coincidence that in 1994 the International Monetary Fund (IMF) had told Canadian officials that these exact measures were needed to restore business vitality in Canada; nor was it coincidental that Wall Street was musing about lowering the country's credit rating if it did not get its financial house in order. These pressures, combined with the Mexican peso crisis of 1994, were largely responsible for producing the tightest federal budget in Canadians' living memory. Indeed, despite the Liberals' campaign promises, Canada's 1995 federal budget adhered so closely to neo-liberal principles that even the Fraser Institute, one of the most conservative think-tanks in the country, observed that Canada now had one of "the most extreme free-market, pro-business economic policies" in the world (Stanford 1999, 89).

In 1996, when a new Governor of the Bank of Canada, David Dodge, was faced with the overall costs of the Bank's anti-inflation policy ($45-77 B) did officials finally conceded that a zero inflation monetary policy was excessive (Bradford 2000). Yet, for the remainder of the 1990s, the Liberal Government was unwavering in its fiscal policy of reducing the federal deficit by cutting public spending, restoring business vitality by reforming corporate taxation and reducing marginal tax rates, broadening the tax base, deregulating key sectors of the economy (e.g., energy, financial services, transportation), liberalising foreign direct investment rules, and privatising state-owned industries. Notwithstanding that the political spectrum in Canada is broader and more complex than in the USA, both neo-conservatives (Progressive Conservatives) and Liberals now largely agree with business leaders that Canada's major long-run economic challenge is to increase its rate of productivity growth by upgrading the technical foundations of its resource-based industries, while promoting the development of an internationally competitive service sector.

Consequently, since NAFTA's implementation, Canada's strategic economic development policies have closely paralleled those of the USA, despite important differences between the two countries' economies and political traditions. Moreover, Canada's dependence on the USA has increased markedly in terms of trade and investment. Two-way trade between the countries has more than doubled since 1994. In 2000, Canada sent 87 per cent of its exports to the USA, which is up from 70 percent in 1990 (Yalnizyan 2002).

In addition, the sale of Canadian assets and companies to foreign corporations has become so pervasive that even ultra-conservative business organisations like the CCCE are talking about the "hollowing out" of Canada's industrial sector and are speaking heretically of the possible need for protection from this invasion of foreign take-over capital (Reguly 2002). Between 1985 and 2002, there were 9,948 corporate take-overs in Canada with 6,381 of these by U.S. corporations. Industry Canada estimates that of the $473 billion spent on corporate take-overs and new investment during that time about 96.6 per cent was for take-overs (Ibid.). By some accounts, in 1997 Americans owned 25 per cent of the Canadian economy or five times the level of foreign ownership in most other developed countries and this ratio has been growing at unprecedented rates since CUFTA and NAFTA (Saul 1997).

MEXICO IN THE NEW GLOBAL ECONOMY

Historically, Mexico has relied heavily on import-substitution and managed trade policies that emphasise industrialisation, infrastructure development, and domestic economic diversification. Mexico's emerging industries were protected from import competition through tariffs, quotas, and licensing, while the costs of protection were borne by established economic activities, particularly the agricultural and oil sectors (OECD 1996e, 9). These policies were sustained by the state-owned monopoly in oil and petrochemical products, which allowed the government to use super-profits from high world-wide oil prices in the 1970s to modernise infrastructure and subsidise other sectors of the economy. While this policy established an industrial base and allowed Mexico to modernise much of its economy, the policy reached its limits in the small size of the country's domestic market, the growing inefficiency of many state enterprises, a large trade management bureaucracy, and the lack of international competitiveness in protected sectors of the economy. The government's ability to subsidise inefficient and non-competitive sectors of the economy collapsed with the decline in oil prices during the 1980s.

The Mexican government began unilaterally liberalising its trade and investment regimes in the early 1980s under the Presidency of Miguel de la Madrid. A recent OECD (1996e, 9) report on the country's continuing trade liberalisation concludes that "Mexico has undergone an economic transition in the last decade and a half that is extraordinary by any standards. In its pace, breadth and depth, Mexico's reform process has surpassed those of most other developing countries that have undergone similar economic adjustments in recent years." Moreover, a great deal of economic integration between Mexico and the United States had already occurred in the decade prior to NAFTA as transnational enterprises (TNEs) began rationalising production across the United States-Mexico border.

President Miguel de la Madrid (1981-1988) began unilaterally liberalising Mexico's trade and FDI regimes as part of the government's solution to the 1982 debt crisis (Gestrin and Rugman 1996, 65-70). The debt crisis emergency softened political resistance to policy change and Madrid used this window of opportunity to initiate a sustained and far-reaching program of economic reform. Madrid's short-term strategy for dealing with the debt crisis included a large devaluation of the peso, a reduction of real wages in the public sector, and a privatisation program that reduced the number of state-owned enterprises from 1,214 to 468 during his presidency. These policies were designed to restore macroeconomic stability by increasing exports and reducing the federal budget deficit.

De la Madrid's reforms explicitly rejected Mexico's history of import substitution as the theoretical basis for a viable model of long-term economic development. However, it was not until 1984 that the de la Madrid Administration reached a consensus that trade restrictions were an additional obstacle to further economic recovery (OECD 1996e, 13-15, 86-89; Ramirez de la O 1993, 61-68, for background). In 1979, 60 percent of the total value of imports to Mexico was subject to licensing requirements and by December of 1982 this coverage had been extended to 100 percent. This policy was softened in December of 1984 when licensing requirements were eliminated for 17 percent of the total value of all imports to Mexico. After several months of negotiations, Mexico joined the GATT in June of 1986 and, as part of its accession commitments, Mexico eliminated import licensing requirements on all but 27.8 percent of the value of its imports. In addition, the trade weighted average tariff on imports was reduced from 16.4 percent to 13.1 percent and tariff dispersion was reduced.

President de la Madrid also challenged Mexico's highly nationalist view of foreign direct investment (FDI), which is partly ensconced in the Mexican Constitution (petroleum and land) and partly in federal legislation. In particular, President de la Madrid's abandonment of the import substitution regime was accompanied by modifications to the 1973 Law to Promote Mexican Investment and Regulate Foreign Investment. The 1973 Foreign Investment Law limited foreign equity in Mexican firms to a maximum of 49 percent, subject to exceptional case-by-case rulings by the National Foreign Investment Commission (NFIC). In 1984, President de la Madrid issued new "Guidelines for Foreign Investment and Objectives for Its Promotion," which stipulated that foreign ownership shares up to 49 percent in private firms would no longer need to be authorised, but simply registered (excluding numerous sectoral exemptions). The new Guidelines also included a list of sectors where foreign investors could hold shares in excess of 49 percent subject to approval by the NFIC. The new guidelines did not guarantee automatic approval, but the change was designed to encourage the expectation that approval would be expedited in the pre-approved areas. Importantly, the new Guidelines did not change the 1973 law, but only altered its administration and implementation (Ramirez de la O 1993, 67).[14]

The liberalisation of trade and foreign direct investment accelerated under President Carlos Salinas de Gortari (1988 - 1995) (Grayson 1993, 7-15). In 1989, the trade weighted average tariff on goods imported into Mexico was reduced from 13.1 percent to 9.7 percent and tariff dispersion was again reduced. Import licensing was again reduced from 27.8 percent to 20.0 percent of the value of imports. By 1993, less than 2 percent of Mexico's tariff lines were subject to licensing requirements (OECD 1996e, 86).

President Salinas also changed the 1973 Foreign Investment Law in 1989 to grant automatic approval to foreign ownership shares in excess of 49 percent, if six criteria were met. These criteria included an investment ceiling of $100 million, full compensation of imports by exports, location outside the main urban areas, and technology "suitable" for Mexico. In lieu of meeting these criteria, the 1984 Guidelines requiring approval by the NFIC still applied to foreign majority ownership. In December of 1993, even the watered-down version of the Foreign Investment Law was replaced with a completely new and far more liberal legal framework.

A major result of trade liberalisation is that imports into Mexico rose from 9.5 percent of GDP in 1985 to 12.5 percent in 1989, 15.3 percent in 1993, and 30.2 percent in 1998 (Ramirez de la O 1993, 63; Banco de Mexico 1999). Mexico has recorded a balance of trade deficit since liberalising its trade policies, but Mexican officials anticipated this situation at the time (Banco de Mexico 1999, 258). More importantly, the rate of growth in Mexico's exports has accelerated from an 11.9 percent average annual rate of increase from 1987 to 1994 to 18 percent between 1994 and 1998 (Banco de Mexico 1993-1999).

The main source of export growth during the first decade of liberalisation (1984 – 1993) was the maquiladora industry, which recorded export growth rates well in excess of the national average. However, both within and outside the maquiladora industry, export growth was supported mainly by U.S. investment in the automobile, auto parts, and electronic equipment manufacturing sectors. In 1982, the leading manufactured exports from Mexico to the USA were in food processing (food, drink, and tobacco), petroleum derivatives, and chemicals, (i.e., primarily agricultural and petroleum products). By 1993, transportation equipment (automobiles) and electronic equipment had become Mexico's leading exports to the USA. By 1994, fully 78 percent of Mexico's total exports were machinery and transportation equipment, i.e., mainly automobiles, panel trucks, and auto parts as Mexico shifted from an agricultural and resource-based economy to an industrial economy (OECD 1996e, 25).

The investment liberalisation reforms also had the expected effect of increasing foreign direct investment in Mexico. The flow of FDI into Mexico quadrupled from an average of $3.1 billion in 1986-1991 to $4.4 billion in 1992-1993 to $12.1 billion in 1997, with the most dramatic increases occurring after NAFTA's adoption (UNCTAD 1998, 363). The flow of FDI into Mexico increased from 8.3 percent of gross fixed capital formation in 1986-1991 to 14.2 percent in 1996 (UNCTAD 1998, 391). As a result of increased foreign investment, Mexico's total stock of FDI nearly tripled from $24.1 billion in 1989 to $65.8 in 1993. In 1990, 68 percent of the developed countries' FDI in Mexico came from the USA and Canada (Gestrin and Rugman 1996, 66).[15] Mexico's share of the total FDI flows into Latin America and the Caribbean increased from 26 percent (1975 to 1980) to 36 percent (1987 to 1991) after investment liberalisation (UNCTAD 1998, xxiv).

The increasing depth of the cross-border economic integration stimulated by this new investment is most apparent in the growing intra-firm trade between U.S. majority-owned foreign affiliates (MOFAs) in Mexico and their parent companies in the USA. Intra-firm trade between MOFAs in Mexico and their U.S. parents accounted for 24 percent of total U.S.-Mexican trade in 1989 compared to a hemispheric average (excluding Mexico) of only 15 percent. By 1992, intra-firm trade between MOFAs in Mexico and their U.S. parents had increased to 30 percent of total U.S.-Mexican trade or double the Latin American and Caribbean share, which remained at 15 percent (Gestrin and Rugman 1996, 66). The main destination industries for United States FDI in Mexico are automobiles, electronics, and food processing (Ibid., 245, 338). The largest foreign affiliates in Mexico are Chrysler, General Motors, Ford, and Pepsi (Ibid., 249).

Just prior to the ratification of NAFTA, more than half of Mexico's manufactured exports to the USA were intra-firm transactions and the same was true of Canada's manufactured exports to the USA (Weintraub 1993, 24; UNCTAD 1998, 258). Hence, when Mexico initiated discussions on a free trade agreement with the USA in 1991, it was a logical extension of the nation's trade and investment liberalisation policies. NAFTA institutionalised the liberalising reforms of previous presidential administrations, who believed that Mexico's future economic growth and political stability depended on access to foreign export markets and foreign direct investment (Rubio 1999).

CHAPTER 2

THE PREMISE AND THE PROMISE OF NORTH AMERICAN HIGHER EDUCATION

THE NORTH AMERICAN FREE TRADE AGREEMENT

The North American Free Trade Agreement (NAFTA) was passed by the legislative bodies of Canada, Mexico, and the USA in 1993 and it became effective on January 1, 1994. NAFTA is the most comprehensive free trade and investment pact, short of a common market, ever negotiated between regional trading partners (Hufbauer and Schott 1993; Weintraub 1993). It is also the first regional trade agreement between advanced industrial nations and a developing nation.

The North American Free Trade Agreement mandates the elimination of tariffs and non-tariff barriers (NTBs) on substantially all trade among the three signatories over a ten-year period concluding December 31, 2003.[1] The cornerstone of NAFTA's investment provisions is Article 1102.1, which requires that each party to the Agreement accord the investors and investments of other NAFTA parties "treatment no less favourable than it accords, in like circumstances, to its own investors." NAFTA's national treatment clause for foreign direct investment (FDI) goes beyond the General Agreement on Tariffs and Trade's (GATT) most favoured nation provisions by establishing *common norms* for the treatment of international investments among the three countries.[2] NAFTA further modifies Mexico's Foreign Investment Law by removing the requirement that foreign majority ownership by a NAFTA-based parent company receive government approval.

The Agreement also strengthens the Mexican government's 1987 reforms on intellectual property rights by subjecting intellectual property disputes to the Agreement's dispute settlement process. In addition, NAFTA's provisions on intellectual property rights go beyond those adopted in the GATT Uruguay Round, mainly by extending better protections to products that are still under development. This provision is particularly important to high-technology industries where up-front research and development costs are high, lead times to market are long, and product life-cycles are short (Gestrin and Rugman 1996, 69-70). As a result of subsequent side agreements, the treaty has catalysed efforts to establish cross-border policies on working conditions and environmental standards among the three countries.

The United States, Canada, and Mexico are the 1st, 9th, and 16th largest economies in the world, respectively, with a combined gross domestic product of $8.7 trillion, and a combined population of more than 392 million persons. The three North American economies account for approximately 29 percent of world gross national product. The United States accounts for 89 percent of the North American regional economy, Canada for 7 percent, and Mexico for 4 percent (see Figure 2). The GNP per capita is $35,095 in the USA, $22,459 in Canada, and $5,862 in Mexico (World Bank 1999, 1-3, see Figure 3). Canada and Mexico have long been among the United States' top three trading partners. In 1998, Canada and Mexico accounted for 34.3 percent of the USA's total world trade (i.e., the combined dollar value of exports and imports) compared to 28 percent in 1993.[3] The ratios of regional trade concentration are much higher for Canada and Mexico. In 1998, 80.4 percent of Canada's total world trade was conducted with the USA alone, while 82.4 percent of Mexico's total world trade occurred with its two NAFTA partners, mostly with the USA (see Figure 4).

There are significant asymmetries among the three countries in terms of population and culture (especially language), the size of their economies, standards of living, the degree of trade concentration with NAFTA partners, and the extent of post-industrialisation, to name a few. Consequently, NAFTA has a very different look in the USA than in Canada or in Mexico, since its visible impact and relative importance to the national economy is much less dramatic in the United States than in the other two countries (except perhaps in the south-western "border states"). However, many U.S. firms were attracted to NAFTA by the prospect of liberalised investment policies in Canada and Mexico and the possibilities of further rationalising their operations on a continental basis by drawing on Canadian natural resources and the Mexican labour force to achieve global competitive advantages (Hufbauer and Schott 1992, 1993a, 3-4; Lawrence 1996, 30). These firms were less interested in the prospects of increasing sales and exports to Canada and Mexico, which remain relatively small markets from the perspective of major U.S. corporations, than in the possibilities of developing continental advantages to support global competitiveness strategies.

The most significant inflows of Foreign Direct Investment (FDI) into Mexico are from the United States and Canada, which in 1990 accounted for 68 percent of the FDI flows into Mexico from all developed countries (Gestrin and Rugman 1996, 66). The largest share of FDI in Mexico has historically come from the United States. In 1995, the United States accounted for 59 percent of all foreign direct investment in Mexico and U.S. owners had a cumulative direct investment in Mexico of nearly $32 billion (or about 59 percent of the nation's cumulative foreign direct investment). In 1995, Canada accounted for another 2.5 percent of foreign direct investment in Mexico and Canadian owners had a cumulative direct investment in Mexico of $1.3 billion (or 2.5 percent of the nation's cumulative foreign direct investment) (Banco de Mexico 1997). The percentage of new foreign direct investment in Mexico coming from Canada and the United States has increased from 63.5 percent in 1992 to 74.8 percent in 1996, which suggests that NAFTA is promoting greater regional concentration of investment as many U.S. and Canadian firms rationalise their operations on a continental basis (Banco de Mexico 1997).

Figure 2. North American Gross Domestic Product, 2000 (US$).

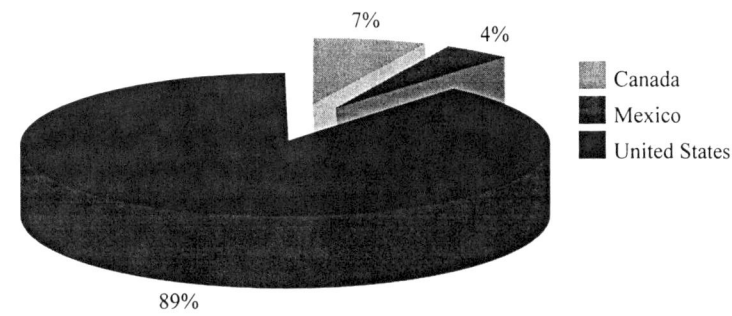

Figure 3. GNP Per Capita: USA, Canada, Mexico (1997).

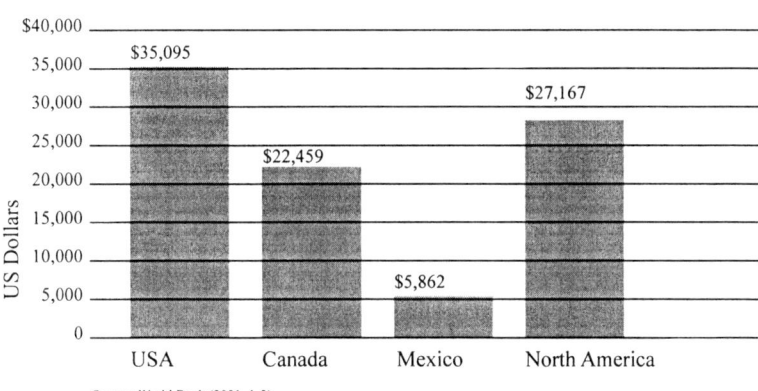

Source: World Bank (2001, 1-3).

Figure 4. Percentage of Total World Trade Among NAFTA Partners, 1998.

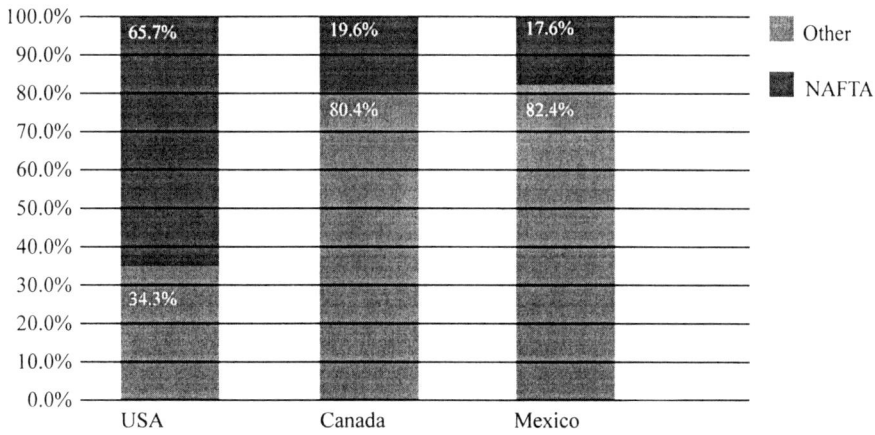

WHICH NORTH AMERICA?

The North American Free Trade Agreement has certainly liberalised *trade and investment* among the three North American countries, but in this respect it has merely facilitated a process of regional economic integration that was already well underway before 1994 when the treaty became effective. Yet, it is important to emphasise that NAFTA is not a finished body of rules and agreements, but a framework for making decisions and resolving disputes between the three countries. NAFTA's future impact on the three countries will depend on the recommendations of numerous committees and working groups established by the agreement, as well as the decisions of dispute resolution panels, which means that its actual impact will continue to evolve over time. For example, committees and working groups are setting standards or establishing dispute resolution procedures on sanitation, small business, financial services, customs, rules of origin, agricultural subsidies, trade and competition, temporary entry, and professional certification, to name a few (Weintraub 1994, xxi).

This "political" aspect to the implementation of all trade agreements means that NAFTA does not have any foreordained consequences for Canada, Mexico, or the USA. Economic globalisation and regional integration are not inexorable events, but multi-dimensional processes that can be facilitated, modified, or obstructed at many levels by government policies, supra-national institutions, non-governmental organisations, and local forms of association. Depending on how various issues are addressed in the implementation process, NAFTA can provide the framework for a "weak integration" of North America – limited merely to free trade and investment – or it can become a framework for "strong integration" that goes beyond simple trade and investment preferences (Ibid., 1). In this respect, NAFTA should be viewed as a range of options – a work in progress – that does not have any foreordained consequences for Canada, Mexico, or the USA.

There are at least three major trajectories that the Agreement could take in future years and these three trajectories are all in play simultaneously (Weintraub 1994). First, it is entirely conceivable that NAFTA will never be more than it is right now: a free trade agreement that promotes an increase in the regional concentration of trade and investment between Canada, Mexico, and the United States. One of the significant differences between NAFTA and the Treaty of Rome, which laid the foundation for the European Union (EU), is that the latter treaty envisioned the free movement of capital and labour across national boundaries. NAFTA's architects purposely excluded labour migration from the treaty, and with the exception of professional services, confined the treaty to the cross-border movement of commodities (trade) and capital (investment). In fact, many of NAFTA's supporters in the U.S. Congress view the treaty as a long-term solution to the "problem" of undocumented Mexican immigration to the USA (Grayson 1993, 48). In other words, many of NAFTA's proponents in the USA do not see the treaty as a vehicle for increasing mobility and interaction between citizens of the three countries, but as a mechanism for *limiting* cross-border movement to goods and capital. There is only a marginal role for international higher education (IHE) and trilateral collaboration among colleges and universities in this version of the agreement. In this version of NAFTA, higher education is merely another professional service export along with engineering and management consulting, architectural, accounting, medical, and dental services, among others (Cf. Barrow 2002; Mallea 1997, 1998a).

A second possibility is that this same pattern of weak integration may eventually be widened to include the entire Western Hemisphere through the accession of individual countries or the accession of other hemispheric trading blocs. NAFTA explicitly anticipates a widening of the North American free trade area, since it includes provisions for the accession of new partners to the Agreement. Many advocates of NAFTA's widening view the agreement as merely the first step toward creating a Western Hemispheric Free Trade Area (WHFTA) (Hufbauer and Schott 1993b). This second trajectory is merely an expanded version of the first, since it anticipates that the greater the number of countries encompassed by the free trade area, the more difficult it will be to resolve differences and to reach agreement on the many intricate details that would allow a "deepening" of NAFTA. Despite the persistence of strong opposition to NAFTA in all three countries, leaders at the 2000 Summit of the Americas meeting reaffirmed their previous commitment to create a Free Trade Area of the Americas (FTAA) by 2005. As preliminary first steps in that direction, Canada and Mexico have each negotiated NAFTA-like free trade agreements with Chile, while the USA has granted "NAFTA-parity" to the Caribbean island nations (2000).

A third option is that NAFTA will be gradually deepened through the initiatives of government, business, educational, and other institutions to promote a strongly integrated North American economy, society, and culture (Laird 1996, 175-183).[4] There are even suggestions that NAFTA may become the institutional foundation for the emergence of a new North American community with a distinctively multicultural identity (Wirth and Earle 1995; Wirth 1996). The deepening of North American integration will involve the movement of people across national boundaries as well as an increased exchange of cultures and ideas. It is this vision of using NAFTA as a platform to go beyond NAFTA that has captured the imagination of many in higher education. There are numerous institutions and activities that can play a significant role in creating "North America," including transnational corporations, immigration, tourism, and the mass media, but as one of the most important cultural and intellectual institutions in all three countries, higher education is certainly positioned to play a significant role in this process. The internationalisation of higher education can contribute to the creation of a continental identity that both reinforces and goes beyond NAFTA.

There are multiple and overlapping definitions of "internationalisation" in higher education and the concept is often used by scholars with the same plasticity as the concept of globalisation (Laxer 1993). In our analysis, the internationalisation of higher education is viewed as an on-going *process* that can be measured to the extent that systems and institutions of higher education engage in specific activities, including (Harari 1992a, 1992b; Knight 1993; ACE 1996; OECD 1996f):

1) the study of foreign languages by enrolled students;
2) the inclusion of an international component in the general education curriculum;
3) the availability of area studies programmes and enrolment in area studies programmes;
4) the availability of study abroad and work abroad opportunities for students and the extent to which students participate in such programmes;
5) the enrolment of international students in higher education institutions;
6) the availability of extra-curricular activities and institutional services for foreign students;
7) the availability of faculty and staff exchange programmes and the extent to which faculty and staff participate in such programmes;
8) the participation in international development assistance programmes by higher education institutions;
9) the participation in transnational institutional co-operation agreements by higher education institutions;
10) joint research projects by faculty with transnational partners;
11) the provision of cross-cultural skills training and cross-border job training programmes by higher education institutions.

While NAFTA's effect on trade and investment between Canada, Mexico, and the USA is the treaty's original *raison d'etre*, many of NAFTA's proponents have always articulated implicit objectives that extend beyond free trade and investment (Weintraub 1994, xxi). However, this vision has also led to increasingly frequent and vocal disputes between international educators, who view higher education as a mechanism for promoting a North American social and cultural identity, and most political and economic elites, who view higher education as merely "just another industry" within NAFTA.[5]

TOWARD AN ACADEMIC COMMON MARKET?

The debate over NAFTA was acrimonious in all three countries with advocates insisting that it will improve the standard of living and quality of life for the citizens of all three countries and critics pointing to an especially negative effect on the employment and safety of unskilled workers. However, a similar debate is now occurring over the agreement's potential impact on higher education. The agreement's advocates hope that NAFTA will stimulate cross-border collaboration in higher education equal to that in the European Union. The long-term aspiration of these proponents is for students, graduates, and faculty to become internationally mobile, bi-lingual, and multi-culturally proficient. It is also hoped that the international component of faculty professional development will be strengthened on a regional basis and that multiple forms of bi-lateral and trilateral co-operation in scientific research, economic development, the environment, public health, and job training will address common concerns in all three countries. On the other hand, the agreement's critics contend that NAFTA is increasing the pressure to restructure higher education for primarily economic purposes, which will divert funding towards academic programs and research topics of interest to transnational corporations to the exclusion of more humanistic cultural values (Calvert and Kuehn 1993). Many critics in Canada and Mexico, especially, are concerned about NAFTA's potential to erode national cultural identities and political sovereignty, which are partly supported by the cultural and civic activities of their higher education institutions.

Whatever the long-term merits or demerits of the North American Free Trade Agreement, there is little doubt that it has catalysed a new and important continental project to internationalise higher education (Barrow 1999, 2000). One impetus for a regionally-oriented internationalisation policy stems from the agreement's provisions on professional services. These provisions have stimulated a great deal of discussion about creating an "academic common market" that would rationalise higher education on a regional basis in North America in ways comparable to that taking place in other industries (Adelman 1990, 1992; Katz 1996; Santillanez 1995, 11-13). Under NAFTA, cross-border service providers from other NAFTA countries must receive national treatment as in other industries (Articles 1201 - 1204). The three countries are prohibited from requiring a service provider from another NAFTA country to establish a residence or place of business in its territory as a condition for providing a service (Article 1205). In addition, licensing and certification procedures for service providers must be based on clear standards, objective criteria, and administrative decisions that are open to public scrutiny (Article 1210). Hence, NAFTA's provisions on trade in professional services have raised issues about the "higher education industry" that are not substantially different from those being considered by working groups, implementation committees, and dispute resolution panels in other industries. In economic terms, these issues involve the free movement of inputs (students and faculty), the standardisation of outputs (graduates and degrees), product content (curriculum), industry standards and product quality (accreditation, testing), and the role of government subsidies in sustaining domestic producers (privatisation).

The potential impact of these provisions on the delivery of higher education services is only starting to be explored by scholars, administrators, and government officials, but their future impact probably extends far beyond anything that is currently understood by most educators (Barrow 2002). NAFTA established a mechanism (Annex 1210) to address a range of what appear to be technically narrow trade issues involving negotiations over the "development of mutually acceptable professional standards and criteria" among the three countries, although it *does not require* the mutual recognition of professional standards and criteria by the North American countries. However, the parties to the agreement are required to "encourage the relevant bodies" in each country "to develop mutually acceptable professional standards and criteria for licensing and certification of professional service providers and to provide recommendations on mutual recognition to the Commission." In some rather vague passages of Annex 1210, NAFTA authorises the development of mutually acceptable standards and criteria on:

" (a) education – accreditation of schools or academic programs where professional service providers obtain formal education;
(b) examinations – qualifying examinations for the purpose of licensing professional service providers, including alternative methods of assessment such as oral examinations and interviews."

Annex 1210 extends this authorisation to include standards and criteria regarding professional experience, conduct and ethics, professional development and re-certification, the scope of professional practice, requirements for territory-specific knowledge, and consumer protection. In the USA and Canada, the professional standards and criteria covered by NAFTA are largely under the jurisdiction of non-governmental organisations, which exercise delegated sovereignty, such as individual higher education institutions (e.g. admission and graduation requirements), professional associations (curriculum, certification, licensing, accreditation), regional accreditation agencies, private testing boards (Education Testing Service), and sub-national licensing boards (the professions). In Mexico, where professional associations are weak and accreditation agencies have been non-existent until recently, the professional standards and criteria covered by NAFTA have been controlled almost exclusively by individual higher education institutions.

The agreement requires the parties to convene negotiations on these matters every two years, but it does not mandate a time line for reaching an agreement, nor does it mandate that the three countries reach any agreement on these matters. Trilateral working groups were established in twelve professions, including actuarial sciences, accounting, agronomy, architecture, dentistry, engineering, law, medicine, nursing, pharmacy, psychology and veterinary sciences. The primary purpose of each working group is to develop a Mutual Recognition Agreement (MRA) on professional standards and certification that would facilitate greater cross-border mobility of professionals and more cross-border professional practices.

NAFTA only requires these working groups to make periodic recommendations to governmental agencies on the cross-border harmonisation of professional standards and practices. There has been little progress and even fewer agreements on this set of issues since NAFTA's passage (see Chapter 3). However, the pressure to reach agreements on mutually acceptable standards has intensified with the World Trade Organisation's General Agreement on Trade in Services (GATS), which requires participating countries to accept international applications (in those majority of cases where they did not before), which opens the possibility that higher education institutions, programs, and professional graduates may seek multiple accreditations, certifications, or licenses based on national or MFN treatment (Lenn and Campos 1997, 1998).

TRILATERAL COOPERATION IN NORTH AMERICAN HIGHER EDUCATION

The three federal governments of Canada, Mexico, and the USA have also provided joint leadership for continental initiatives in higher education that extend far beyond the narrow technical negotiations on mutual recognition agreements. Governmental interest in trilateral higher education co-operation was triggered in 1991 by Mexico's request to begin negotiations on the North American Free Trade Agreement and the explicit understanding that NAFTA would go further than the Canadian-United States Free Trade Agreement. In response to the prospect that the USA would become the hub of a North American Free Trade Area, federal officials in the USA invited their counterparts in Canada and Mexico to consider the possible benefits of greater North American co-operation in higher education. The invitation was extended by the U.S. Information Agency (USIA)[6] and the invitation resulted in each country appointing a senior official to a Trilateral Steering Committee (TSC). The Steering Committee consisted of the Director General of Canada's International Cultural Relations Bureau (Department of Foreign Affairs and International Trade), the Associate Director of USIA's Bureau of Educational and Cultural Affairs, and Mexico's Director General of Higher Education.

The Wingspread Statement

In 1992, the Trilateral Steering Committee initiated a series of conferences that opened a dialogue between government officials, business executives, and higher education leaders about ways to increase North American co-operation in higher education, research, and workforce training. The first *Conference on North American Higher Education Co-operation: Identifying the Agenda* was convened on September 12 to 15, 1992 at the Wingspread Conference Centre in Racine, Wisconsin. The "Wingspread Conference" brought together sixty high-level government officials and higher education administrators from the three countries "to chart a course of higher education co-operation in North America for the coming decades" (CONAHEC 1999a).[7]

The North American Free Trade Agreement, which had been completed but not approved at the time of the conference, provided "a clear and positive reference point" for the proceedings (CONAHEC 1999b), especially since free trade in professional services and the mutual recognition of professional credentials had been included in the agreement. The most significant outcome of the conference was the Wingspread "Statement of Purpose, Objectives and Recommendations" that was approved unanimously by conference participants (See Appendix A). The Wingspread Statement was commended "to the urgent consideration of our respective authorities as a constructive trilateral contribution to the development and implementation of appropriate public policies that support and promote the internationalisation of higher education."

The Wingspread Statement affirms that trilateral co-operation in higher education has merit in its own right, although in affirming the statement's basic principles, conference participants took explicit "note of the North American Free Trade Agreement" as a platform for initiating trilateral co-operation in higher education. In this context, the Wingspread Statement identifies the internationalisation of higher education as a key to improving the standard of living and the quality of life in the three countries, particularly if trilateral collaboration builds on existing relationships that mutually benefit the three countries and their higher education institutions. However, the Statement also observes that stronger trilateral partnerships in higher education must acknowledge the three countries' asymmetries, respect the national sovereignty of each country, and not threaten the autonomy of their higher education institutions. Finally, the Statement suggests that trilateral collaboration be pursued in the spirit of open regionalism – as one facet of a larger process of globalisation – and not to the exclusion of bi-lateral co-operation with non-NAFTA countries and multilateral organisations.

Consistent with these basic principles, the Wingspread Statement proposed seven mutually reinforcing objectives for trilateral initiatives in higher education:

1. The development of a North American dimension in higher education,
2. The exchange of information on common issues and on experiences of common interest,
3. The promotion of collaboration among higher education institutions,
4. The facilitation of student mobility,
5. The mutually satisfactory removal of impediments to academic and professional mobility,
6. The promotion of stronger collaboration among higher education institutions, government, business, and other organisations that have a stake in the quality of higher education,
7. The exploration and exploitation of the full potential of current and emerging information management and transmission technologies in support of the foregoing objectives.

The first major action to come out of the Wingspread Conference was the call for an inventory of existing resources and partnerships that could provide the basis for expanding North American co-operation in higher education. The responsibility for conducting national inventories of existing linkages between higher education institutions in the three countries was delegated to the Institute of International Education (IIE), the National Association of Universities and Institutions of Higher Education (ANUIES), and the Association of Universities and Colleges of Canada (AUCC). The three NGOs were each charged with preparing a "national inventory of existing resources and priority needs" in North American higher education for distribution and discussion at a second conference the following year.

The second major action to emerge from Wingspread was the creation of a "Trilateral Task Force on North American Higher Education Collaboration." The 18-member Task Force, with six members from each country, was appointed by the three governments and consisted mainly of university and higher education association presidents. The Task Force developed a strategic plan, supported and monitored the three countries' progress on the Wingspread Statement objectives, commissioned research papers, and organised the Vancouver Symposium in September 1993.

The Vancouver Communiqué

The second trilateral *Conference on North American Higher Education Co-operation: Implementing the Agenda* was held in Vancouver, Canada. By the time the "Vancouver Symposium" convened on September 10 to 13, 1993, the North American Free Trade Agreement had been ratified by the three countries. Consequently, the Vancouver Symposium focused on "implementing the agenda" agreed to at the Wingspread Conference and, accordingly, participation was expanded to include more than 300 representatives from business, state and provincial governments, professional associations, and private foundations.

As a basis for building on existing relationships and linkages, the Symposium discussed the results of the three national inventories conducted by IIE, ANUIES, and the AUCC. In the USA, the survey data revealed that in 1993 at least 109 or 3.2% of U.S. higher education institutions had linkages with Canadian higher institutions and 182 or 5.3% of U.S. higher education institutions reported linkages with Mexican higher institutions. Only 56 or 1.6% of U.S. higher education institutions reported linkages with both Canada and Mexico. In sum, the IIE survey found that approximately 235 or 6.8% of U.S. higher education institutions had some type of bi-lateral or tri-lateral linkage to counterparts in Canada and Mexico (CONAHEC 1999b).

The vast majority of bi-lateral and tri-lateral collaborations consisted of traditional student and faculty exchange agreements and study abroad programs. Most students participating in exchange relations with Canada (67%) and Mexico (90%) were in programs sponsored by their home campus, rather than in programs sponsored by government agencies, non-profit foundations, or private business. Thus, not surprisingly, the IIE inventory found that university support and individual self-funding are the leading sources of financial support for current faculty and student exchanges. Yet, for this reason, the IIE report calls attention, quite correctly, to the much higher level of exchange that probably "occurs through informal linkages and on an individual basis, with students and faculty members applying on their own to study, teach or conduct research in a neighbouring country" (CONAHEC 1999b). However, the IIE also found that a "lack of interest" and "financial constraints" were the major obstacles to increased linkages between U.S. and Canadian higher education institutions, while "financial assistance" and "language problems" were the main obstacles to increased linkages with Mexican higher education institutions (IIE 1997).

The asymmetrical impact of NAFTA on the three countries' higher education systems is evident in the much higher density of relationships reported by Mexico and Canada. Given the sheer size of the U.S. higher education system, which consists of nearly 4,100 post-secondary institutions, it is not surprising that NAFTA's immediate impact would be comparative small and diffuse when compared to the density of arrangements emerging in Mexico and Canada.

In Mexico, ANUIES conducted a survey of 77 public and private higher education institutions and found that thirty (39%) of the institutions reported various types of collaborative agreements with counterparts in the USA and Canada. These institutions reported 193 agreements with U.S. higher education institutions and 22 agreements with Canadian higher education institutions. At the time the survey was conducted (1993), over 50 percent of the exchange and collaborative agreements had been initiated within the previous year, but disappointingly less than 40 percent of the agreements were actually being implemented by the institutions. NAFTA generated a flurry of new collaborative agreements in Mexico, but the results of many of these agreements are still doubtful. The most frequently cited objectives for co-operation by Mexican higher education institutions were faculty and student exchanges with a secondary emphasis on joint research, curriculum development, and pedagogy (CONAHEC 1999b).

The AUCC also presented the results of an analysis of its Canadian University International Exchange Agreements Database (CUE) and its Canadian University Projects in International Development Database (CUPID), which includes government economic development projects with Mexico. The CUE database revealed that 36 (40%) of 89 Canadian colleges and universities had a total of 68 agreements with the USA and 33 agreements with Mexico. The CUPID database showed that 18 (20%) Canadian universities were involved in 29 international development projects with Mexico. A survey of AUCC members found that half of the faculty exchange agreements with the USA had been active for only two to four years, while almost 30 percent of the linkages with Mexico had been active for one year or less (CONAHEC 1999b).

The evident increase in bi-lateral and tri-lateral co-operative agreements stimulated by NAFTA encouraged the Vancouver Symposium to issue a Communiqué reaffirming "the spirit of Wingspread," but the Symposium went further by calling for "a new sense of North American community" based on the acceptance of each country's cultural identity and an acknowledgement of the significant asymmetries between them (Wirth and Earle 1995; Wirth 1996; see Appendix B). The Vancouver Symposium agreed to six action initiatives aimed at implementing the Wingspread agenda and stimulating further North American co-operation in higher education.

These six action initiatives included:

1. The establishment of a North American Distance Education and Research Network (NADERN),
2. The formation of a trilateral mechanism (through the existing professional associations) to examine issues related to mobility, portability, and certification of skills across national borders,
3. The establishment of programs to enable faculty and administrators from the three countries to meet and develop trilateral higher education collaborative activities,
4. The establishment of an electronic information base with co-ordinated sharing of information on initiatives and resources relevant to trilateral co-operation,

5. The strengthening and expansion of North American studies programs,
6. The establishment of a program to support trilateral exchange, research, and training for students.

The Vancouver Communiqué embraced the immense possibilities of NAFTA, but it was issued against the backdrop of a major U.S. and Canadian recession (1990-91), fiscal crises in state and provincial governments, declining government support to higher education institutions, and the first serious efforts to balance the U.S. and Canadian federal budgets (Barrow 1993). Consequently, the Vancouver Communiqué explicitly acknowledged that trilateral initiatives in higher education had to accept a fiscal reality where additional resources from government would not be available for the foreseeable future. This meant that financing new trilateral initiatives would necessitate fiscal "reallocation and the establishment of international education priorities" within existing higher education budgets (CONAHEC 1999b). Given the limited or declining resources available through reallocation, the Communiqué concluded that a key to the success of the proposed collaborative projects would be their ability to leverage resources from the private sector (Mallea et al. 1997, 6-7).

CONSORTIUM ON NORTH AMERICAN HIGHER EDUCATION COLLABORATION

The Consortium for North American Higher Education Collaboration (CONAHEC) is one of the more significant trilateral initiatives to emerge from the Wingspread Conference and the Vancouver Symposium.[8] CONAHEC is a trilateral partnership founded in 1994 by the Western Interstate Commission on Higher Education (WICHE), the Mexican Association for International Education (AMPEI), the University of Arizona, the Autonomous University of Baja California, the University of British Columbia, and the California State University System. CONAHEC's strategic goal is to remove the obstacles to North American educational interchange and to increase opportunities for collaboration between Canada, Mexico, and the USA.

The Consortium grew to 35 institutional and association members by 1998 and it currently has 60 members in Canada, Mexico, and the USA (CONAHEC 1999c; CONAHEC 1999d; see Appendix C).[9] CONAHEC is based at the University of Arizona and receives financial support from the Ford Foundation, the USIA, Canadian Department of Foreign Affairs, member institutions, and private corporations. The Consortium has implemented several programs and initiatives over the last nine years, including conferences and seminars, a web site and list serve, publications, a mobility program, and BORDER PACT.

CONAHEC has held an annual conference since 1994 that now brings together more than a hundred government, foundation, and academic leaders from the three countries to discuss North American co-operation in higher education. The Consortium has sponsored yearly Educational Leadership Seminars since 1994 for the purpose of encouraging new collaborations and opportunities for academic exchange among North American higher education institutions and for discussing obstacles to increased collaboration (WICHE 1994; Villa-Prezelski and Navarro 1996). In 1997, CONAHEC started the Institute for North American Higher Education, an intensive three-week training program, to provide "leadership development opportunities with a North American perspective for campus administrators" (Villa Prezelski and Navarro 1996, 20).

In addition to the numerous opportunities for face-to-face interactions, the Consortium has positioned itself as the most important information clearinghouse on issues related to North American higher education collaboration. The El Net Information Clearinghouse is a trilingual web site (English, Spanish, French) that provides convenient access to information about resources and collaborative research opportunities in North America. The web-site includes a bibliography of publications on North American higher education, online manuscripts for review and discussion, related newsletter and journal links, announcements of government actions that affect North American academic mobility, summaries of past conference proceedings, and descriptions of model "best practice" programs in bilateral and trilateral co-operation. The Clearinghouse facilitates mobility and collaboration by providing links to government and foundation funding sources in the three countries that support academic exchange and collaborative research. A calendar of events in the three countries related to international education, regional integration, and related topics is part of the Clearinghouse web site. The Consortium sponsors ELNET-L (Educational Leadership Network), which is a closed moderated list-serve for the exchange of information, research, and discussion about North American higher education collaboration.[10] CONAHEC also sponsors a series of research publications on "Understanding the Differences" between the three countries' higher education systems to advance the Wingspread goal of establishing a continental identity that respects the "distinctive realities" of each country (Gill and Testa 1995; Wirth and Earle 1995).

The emerging institutional network in North American higher education has taken a considerable step forward with the establishment of BORDER PACT (Ponton et al 1997). BORDER PACT was launched by CONAHEC in 1997 with financial support from the Ford Foundation ($80,000) and the endorsement of the American Council on Education (ACE) and ANUIS. The pact was created through a memorandum of understanding signed by CONAHEC, ACE, ANUIS, and 65 higher education institutions in the U.S.-Mexico borderlands to "focus attention on border issues and to collaborate and share resources in response to the region's needs." The Pact includes 24 Mexican higher education institutions and research institutes and 34 U.S. higher education institutions (19 in southern California, 9 in Texas, 4 in Arizona, and 2 in New Mexico), as well as other scholarly and higher education associations.

The new pact extends and builds on several earlier cross border pacts dealing with economic development, the environment, job training, and cross border enrolments (BORDERLINK 1994) that were initiated by various consortia of higher education institutions in California, Arizona, New Mexico, and Texas (BORDER PACT 1999;

Santillanez 1995, iv, 8-10;). The pact focuses specifically on issues related to education, health care, housing and community development, social services, regional planning, business development, transportation, the environment, and regional economic development. As with similar bi-lateral arrangements, the pact seeks to mobilise and reallocate the resources of border institutions for the purpose of leveraging additional resources from community-based organisations, foundations, and local governments to implement BORDER PACT initiatives (CONAHEC 2002).

THE ALLIANCE FOR HIGHER EDUCATION AND ENTERPRISE IN NORTH AMERICA

Following the Vancouver Symposium and the establishment of CONAHEC, the Trilateral Steering Committee convened a third conference on April 28-30, 1996 in Guadalajara, Mexico. The "Partners for Prosperity" meeting built on the previous conferences, which focused on promoting trilateral co-operation among higher education institutions, but the Guadalajara conference emphasised the idea that tri-lateralism also means co-operation between higher education, government, and private business. The conference was attended by more than 1,000 individuals and, not coincidentally, it was the first trilateral conference where business executives took the lead in conference discussions.

Consequently, most of the conference discussions revolved around issues involving the construction of strategic alliances between corporations and higher education institutions. In his opening remarks, Dr. John P. Loiello (1996), Associate Director for the USIA's Educational and Cultural Affairs Bureau, called on conference participants to adopt a new paradigm which focused on the "commonalities of interests and shared goals" between the public and private sector and "to eschew stereotypes which…questioned one another's motives." In promoting this neo-liberal paradigm, Loiello reiterated two fundamental themes from the Vancouver Symposium. First, the role of government in this new paradigm of trilateral co-operation was not merely to provide financial resources for new initiatives, but to focus limited resources in ways that catalyse and facilitate greater co-operation between business and higher education. Second, the funds appropriated for international exchange programs were facing "major reductions" in all three countries and, consequently, limited resources would be targeted at international programs with demonstrated effectiveness. The Guadalajara conference arrived at a vague consensus that more needed to be done to promote North American higher education co-operation and to build strategic alliances between business and higher education. However, the conferees were not able to specify what steps should be taken next to promote these goals. Thus, the Trilateral Steering Committee invited the North American Institute, which had participated in the conference to recommend options for further action.

The North American Institute (NAMI) is a private non-profit organisation with a secretariat in Santa Fe, New Mexico and branches in Ottawa and Mexico City. The North American Institute was founded in 1988, well before NAFTA's adoption, by political leaders from the USA, Canada, and Mexico "to examine all aspects of the

North American regional relationship" (North American Institute 2000). In contrast to CONAHEC, whose members are mainly higher education administrators and international educators, NAMI's core members and directors include business executives, former state, provincial, and federal government officials, foundation officials, and academic specialists on North America. While CONAHEC is primarily a trilateral alliance of higher education institutions and international educators emphasising academic mobility and international education, NAMI is concerned with a much broader set of issues related to the development of a North American community.

NAMI has sought to promote this goal mainly by organising small workshops, conferences, and other forums where "people from North America can share ideas and discuss ways to work together, while also acknowledging the social and political differences between the countries" (Ibid.). NAMI has sponsored events in the three countries on issues such as energy, the environment, the role of NGOs in North America, the history and national identities of the three countries, and North America's relation with the Caribbean. In addition, NAMI's publications are designed to promote thinking about issues in continental terms and they are routinely disseminated to the three countries' public policy communities.

The North American Institute initially proposed "a broad-based agenda of continental identity-building," but after discussions with the Trilateral Steering Committee a narrower action agenda was approved by the governments of Canada, Mexico, and the USA. In April of 1998, the three governments endorsed the Alliance for Higher Education and Enterprise in North America (AHEENA), a NAMI initiative aimed at building a network of strategic alliances between business and higher education throughout North America. The Alliance was launched with seed money from the three governments on the expectation that NAMI would secure matching funds from private businesses and foundations in each of the three countries. The total budget for AHEENA is estimated to be approximately $6.2 million from all sources over five years (1997-2002) compared to the $1.6 billion that the European Union will spend on similar programs over the same period of time (Ibid.).

The Alliance for Higher Education and Enterprise in North America operates two programs: the Strategic Partnership Program and the Dialogue Program. The Strategic Partnership Program (SPP) was created to broker partnerships between transnational corporations with continental interests and higher education institutions in the three countries. The SPP brokers partnerships with higher education institutions that can meet a company's specific needs in a particular country, such as job training, management skills development, and other forms of long-term human capital development. The inter-governmental agreement endorsing the Alliance left open the possibility that AHEENA's agenda may eventually expand to include academic and professional mobility issues, mutual recognition of credentials, human resource curriculum development, and technology transfer. The Dialogue Program is an information clearinghouse for best practices developed through AHEENA's strategic alliances (The Alliance 1998).

The Strategic Partnership Program differs from CONAHEC's BORDER PACT in several important respects:

1. AHEENA's strategic alliances are fully national in scope, rather than focused on border issues.
2. AHEENA's strategic alliances are rigorously trilateral, rather than bilateral, with governance structures equally reflecting the higher education institutions, associations, business communities, and governments of the three countries.
3. AHEENA's strategic alliances will aim to achieve measurable targets established by NAMI with substantial involvement by private sector business leaders.

Yet, in other respects, the focus of Alliance projects is much narrower than BORDER PACT and other bilateral programs stimulated by the trilateral conferences on higher education co-operation. The Strategic Partnership Program was originally expected to implement much of the Wingspread agenda by sponsoring programs in business administration, management science, public administration, economics, teacher training, human resource development, language studies, cultural acclimatisation, urban studies, public health, sustainable development, and North American studies. However, in April of 1999, the Alliance's board of directors concluded that the full Wingspread agenda was beyond its current capabilities and, consequently, it conducted a "scoping study" to identify immediate priorities for Alliance projects and partnership building. Following several months of study, the Alliance's board decided to concentrate on the financial services and environmental management sectors. The priorities identified in the financial services sectors include diversity management training, the role of the Internet in cross-border commerce, and the regulatory complexities of operating across a tri-national regional economy. The priorities identified in the environmental management sector include the development of environmental audit and risk assessment systems for operating in a tri-national economy and the standardisation of training and accreditation of environmental professionals working in Canada, Mexico, and the USA (Harvey 1999).

THE NORTH AMERICAN PARTNERSHIP

As a follow up to NAFTA's preliminary success, the Foreign Ministers of Canada, Mexico, and the USA met in New York City in September of 1998 for what became their first annual Trilateral Ministerial Meeting. The purpose of the meeting was to establish the framework for moving beyond NAFTA and building a "North American Partnership." The North American Partnership was formally established at the foreign ministers' second annual meeting in September of 1999, where they agreed to a framework statement and signed a memorandum of understanding on international development co-operation.

In the formal statement released jointly by U.S. Secretary of State Madeleine Albright, Mexican Foreign Secretary Rosario Green, and Canadian Foreign Minister Lloyd Axworthy, the foreign ministers declared that:

"The North American Partnership is becoming a reality, as the economies and societies of Canada, the United States and Mexico grow increasingly interdependent. Trans-boundary trade, culture, travel, family ties and cyberspace bring our societies ever closer together...Our strength as a North American partnership resides in democracy, transparency, plurality, and healthy economic conditions that provide for longer-term growth prospects and ensure that none of our citizens are left behind" (U.S. Department of State "Statement" 1999b).

The framework statement commits the partnership to "support and promote new and existing co-operative efforts" among the three countries in areas of mutual interest that go beyond the trade and investment regimes established by NAFTA. The framework statement was immediately followed by a nine article memorandum of understanding (U.S. Department of State 1999c). Article 1 states that the purpose of the North American Partnership is "to enhance the relations between the Participants in the area of international development co-operation," by identifying "new areas for joint or complementary activities in the fields of international development co-operation and, wherever they deem it appropriate, to strengthen, extend or expand existing programs" (Article 3). However, the MOU was scheduled to expire in September of 2002 and leaves funding of the Partnership's activities to "the sole discretion of the Participant involved" (Article 2).

The North American Partnership also anticipates the creation of a Free Trade Area of the Americas by committing the partners "to work together and with other nations in the Hemisphere in international development activities" to achieve the objectives listed in the Declaration of Principles and the Plan of Action adopted at the Second Summit of the Americas, held in Santiago, Chile (1998). Furthermore, the Partnership's activities will be undertaken "without prejudice to activities provided for in arrangements or agreements between the Participants, third countries, and regional institutions regarding educational, cultural, scientific, or technical co-operation" and the Participants are encouraged to "work together on bilateral, trilateral, or multilateral activities" that support the objectives of the MOU. The MOU designates the lead agencies for the North American Partnership as the United States Agency for International Development, the Canadian International Development Agency, and the Mexican International Co-operation Institute as a clear declaration that the Partnership is primarily an instrument of foreign policy and international economic development.

Nevertheless, the third annual meeting, which was held in Santa Fe, New Mexico in August of 2000, reaffirmed that "the three North American nations should deepen and widen their relationship, and should seek to play a constructive international role, particularly within the hemisphere" (U.S. Department of State August 16, 2000). This meeting identified "civil society as an area where much more can be done to take advantage of the growing synergies that North American interconnectedness has generated." The three governments' defined their joint role as facilitating the trilateral development of civil society organisations (CSOs) within the framework of the Parternship, rather than sponsoring major new programs funded and controlled by government. The governments' role is to serve only as a "repository for information on the North American Partnership," but with the clear understanding that trilateral initiatives are to be generated directly by CSOs (which includes higher education institutions).

The North American Partnership is designed to promote more trilateral co-operation in a wide range of areas mainly by serving as an information clearinghouse on trilateral programs sponsored by non-governmental and civil society organisations. The three countries' foreign ministries have developed a Partnership webpage with an extensive "trilateral inventory" on initiatives in higher education, culture, the environment, health, industry and professional associations, labour, politics, science and technology, tourism, trade, transportation, and youth (U.S. Department of State 1999d). In the field of higher education, the foreign ministries have identified CONAHEC and NAMI as the continent's leading CSOs promoting trilateral co-operation among the region's post-secondary institutions. Consequently, in 2000, the three foreign ministries agreed to fund an upgrade to the El-Net mainly for the purpose of providing easier and more extensive access to information on trilateral projects in higher education. However, the North American Partnership has not resulted in any major new government programs, nor any significant expansion of existing programs, to promote North American collaboration in higher education. The main goal is to build collaboration from the ground up by removing obstacles (i.e., trade barriers) that obstruct mutually advantageous co-operation among non-governmental and civil society organisations and it is this vision that goes beyond NAFTA.

CHAPTER 3

GLOBALISATION, NAFTA, AND HIGHER EDUCATION IN THE USA

COMPETITIVENESS POLICIES IN THE USA

Over the last two decades, state and federal governments in the USA have adopted numerous economic policies and regulatory reforms designed to solve the "productivity paradox" in the U.S. economy (see Chapter 1). A major component of these policies, whether neo-conservative or neo-liberal, Republican or Democratic, has been to foster the development of intellectual and human capital to support the growth of globally competitive knowledge-intensive industries in high technology and specialised services. Not coincidentally, the current thinking of government economic policy-makers and business leaders is virtually dominated by concerns with human capital development, technology transfer, and international competitiveness (Newman 1985).

The new emphasis on human capital development and technology transfer has drawn higher education into the maelstrom of economic policy debates at all levels of government in the USA (Johnson 1984; Crawford 1991). Yet, despite recognising the increasing importance of higher education to national and state economic development strategies, governments have simultaneously restrained the growth of higher education budgets (Johnstone 1993; Massy and Meyerson 1992; Finifter, Thelin, and Baldwin 1991). The fiscal restraints, when coupled to new demands on curriculum and research, have generated intense pressures to restructure higher education institutions, first, by reallocating existing resources toward programs targeted at economic competitiveness and, second, by seeking additional resources from private businesses through a variety of new university-industry partnerships. Thus, fiscal restraints are inducing the construction of a "post-industrial university" as higher education administrators and faculty seek out new resources through stronger corporate-university relationships and from mission-driven government programs.

Neo-Conservatism and the Productivity Paradox

During the 1980s, macro-economic fiscal and monetary policies in the USA were largely guided by neo-conservative principles. The Presidential administrations of Ronald Reagan (1980-1988) and George H. Bush (1988-1992) were broadly committed to a set of policies that sought to stimulate new private investment in the U.S. economy and to minimise the role of government in economic regulation and the provision of social welfare. The neo-conservative economic agenda of "rolling back the welfare state" consisted of five major policies, including:

(1) a fiscal policy designed to reduce the federal government's structural budget deficit (and, hence, free up capital for savings and private investment),
(2) a trade policy designed to promote U.S. economic growth by liberalising world markets and opening foreign economies to U.S. products and services (e.g., GATT, CUFTA, and NAFTA),
(3) a deregulation policy designed to reduce unnecessary burdens and costs on private business,
(4) a human capital investment policy focused on improving education, training, and preventive health care, and
(5) an anti-inflationary monetary policy designed to stimulate increased private investment through lower interest rates (Office of the U.S. President 1993, chaps. 1:2–1:4)

The Reagan and Bush Administrations both considered budget discipline the centrepiece of their fiscal policy with the assumption that federal fiscal restraint would foster long-term economic growth by encouraging private savings and investment. Despite a great deal of rhetoric about "balancing the budget" during the 1980s, the first real progress toward achieving a balanced budget was the Omnibus Budget Reconciliation Act of 1990 [OBRA 1990], which combined selective tax increases with reductions in entitlement spending (Ibid. 1993, chap. 1:3). However, the Bush Administration's budgets did not merely slow growth in federal spending during the early 1990s, it also shifted selected spending from social consumption (i.e., social welfare entitlements) into social investment. These expenditure shifts were designed to stabilise federal spending for research and development, which had fallen during the Reagan Administration, and to make selective new investments in public infrastructure (e.g., airports, roads, seaports, and the Internet) that had been severely neglected in favour of tax cuts during the previous administration.

In the area of trade policy, the Reagan and Bush Administrations pushed aggressively for global trade liberalisation by promoting the Uruguay Round of the GATT (1987-1993), by signing the Canada-United States Free Trade Agreement (1989), and by agreeing to negotiate a free trade agreement with Mexico (1990). As part of the Bush Administration's trade liberalisation strategy, the President also persuaded the U.S. Congress to begin a national dialogue about U.S. "competitiveness policy" against the backdrop of the 1990-1991 recession and established a bi-partisan Competitiveness Policy Council (CPC). The CPC's creation symbolised the emergence of a broad ideological and political consensus among U.S. policy leaders about the need to re-establish the international competitiveness of U.S. firms in the context of global and regional trade liberalisation.

The Competitiveness Policy Council is a 12-member federal advisory committee that includes leaders from government, business, labour, and education.[1] Its purpose is to "develop recommendations for national strategies and on specific policies intended to enhance the productivity and international competitiveness of United States industries." In its first annual report, the CPC concluded that "the time has come for the United States to establish a serious 'competitiveness strategy' through both sector-specific and generic policies" (CPC 1992, 32; Cuomo Commission 1992). The CPC recommended that sector-specific policies be devised for twenty "critical technologies" deemed essential to long-term national security and economic prosperity (CPC 1992, 33). Drawing on previous reports from the Department of Defence and the Office of Science and Technology Policy, the CPC's critical technologies list includes aeronautics, computing, genetic engineering, speciality and composite materials, electronics, computer software, trucks and automobiles, medical technology, optics, high performance metals and alloys, pharmaceuticals, and other high technologies.

In answering domestic critics, the CPC explicitly rejected claims that trade liberalisation and labour market globalisation were responsible for the loss of U.S. jobs to low cost producers or for the declining real wages of unskilled workers (Mishel and Bernstein 1992). Rather, the Competitiveness Council concludes that high U.S. wages are the result of high productivity, which in turn is the product of work skills and sophisticated capital equipment and technology. Thus, in defending trade liberalisation, the CPC (1992) concluded that the USA needed to solve its productivity paradox by increasing public and private investment in basic and applied research, advanced technology and capital equipment, and enhanced lifelong worker training.

The Office of Technology Assessment (1992), which formerly advised Congress on technology issues, also concluded that liberalised trade between the USA and other nations, particularly Mexico, would promote an increased standard of living for U.S. workers, but only if pro-active policies were implemented to improve the nation's competitiveness in the global economy. The OTA emphasised that a high wage future for the USA could not be achieved by competing directly against low-wage developing nations in labour-intensive industries. Instead, the OTA also recommended a policy of improving worker skills and strengthening the nation's research, innovation, and technology transfer process. Thus, the OTA's policy recommendations did not revolve around "labour cost issues" such as wages, benefits, taxes and government mandates, but called for additional government investment in education and training at all levels – from kindergarten to graduate school – as well as more emphasis on applied research and technology transfer.

The Bush Administration's economic advisers (Office of the U.S. President 1993, chap. 1:5) agreed that the USA could not "remain the world's leading economy without the world's leading labour force." Hence, the Bush Administration came to regard job training programs, especially those designed to retrain displaced workers for the new economy, as a key to increasing productivity and remaining internationally competitive in the future (Becker 1993, 30-51). The Bush Administration's general training objectives targeted the nation's elementary and secondary education systems through the "America Goals 2000" initiative, which set the agenda for state and local education reform throughout the country (National Education Goals Panel 1997).

As an economic policy initiative, America Goals 2000 was a response to several studies of the U.S. labour market, which called attention to a "skills gap" between the existing labour force and the demands of a post-industrial economy. The skills gap was first identified by the Hudson Institute's *Workforce 2000* report in 1987 (Johnston 1987). However, between 1987 and 1990, labour market projections by the U.S. Department of Labour, private foundations, and various think-thanks all agreed that by the year 2000, nearly two-thirds of the new jobs being created in the USA would require some level of post-secondary education. Approximately one-third of the new jobs were expected to require at least a baccalaureate degree, while another one-third were expected to require a two-year associate's degree or certification by a technical-vocational institute (Silvestri and Lukasiewicz 1987; Mangum 1989; Commission on the Skills 1990).[2]

The concern about the relationship between general levels of educational attainment and the national standard of living was reinforced by a growing recognition among academics and policy-makers that the correlation between high incomes and formal education had been growing stronger during the last two decades (USDOE 1989, 98-99; Office of the U.S. President 1997). In 1980, the average college graduate earned approximately thirty percent (30%) more than a high school graduate in the USA. By 1993, the "wage premium" attached to a college degree had more than doubled with the average college graduate now earning seventy percent (70%) more than a high school graduate. The single most important factor in this wage premium is the "skill-biased" structure of jobs in the new economy, which has increased the demand for more highly educated employees.

At the same time, the globalisation of production has put downward pressure on the wages of unskilled workers as labour-intensive industries shift their unskilled manufacturing operations to lower-cost areas of the world. A major implication of such findings was that the USA would not be able to re-establish or maintain its competitive advantage in the new global economy unless the entire education system was mobilised to close the projected skills gap. One facet of closing the skills gap was to improve high school graduation rates and to increase the number of students prepared to attend post-secondary institutions (Business-Higher Education Forum 1983, 1984, 1997; Reich 1991; Thurow 1994; Zemsky and Oedel 1994).

However, these same studies concluded that merely graduating more students from high schools, technical institutes, colleges, and universities was not sufficient to close the skills gap, because a globally competitive post-industrial workforce not only requires more education skills but different types of skills (Brazziel 1981; Piore and Sabel 1984; Carnevale 1991). Consequently, in 1990, the former U.S. Secretary of Labour, Lynn Martin, charged the Secretary's Commission on Achieving Necessary Skills (SCANS) with the task of specifying the new skills and identifying their linkages to particular types and levels of occupations (SCANS 1991). The Secretary's Commission included distinguished individuals from education, business, labour, and government and, after two years of intensive data collection and analysis, the Commission released its final report, *Learning a Living: A Blueprint for High Performance* (SCANS 1992). SCANS (1993, 6, 21-53) concluded that "workplace know-how" in the new economy consists of five Competencies and a three-part Foundation of skills and personal qualities that support workplace competencies (see Table 1). The authors of the SCANS report were seeking "to encourage a high-performance economy characterised by high-skills, high-wage employment" and, in so doing, it articulates another component of the bi-partisan consensus on competitiveness in the same way that the Competitiveness Policy Council forged a leadership consensus on trade liberalisation.

However, in contrast to popular misrepresentations, the SCANS workplace competencies and skills do not consist of traditional "vocational" or job-specific training. This fear is often voiced by educators and academicians in the USA who feel that humanistic learning is threatened by the new emphasis on skills, but such concerns are based on a false dichotomy between cultural and vocational education or between general and professional education inherited from an earlier period in the history of U.S. education. Furthermore, this false dichotomy is reinforced by a long-standing separation of the "two cultures" of business and academia (Business-Higher Education Forum 1984, 1986, 1997, 1998). For instance, recent survey findings by the Business-Higher Education Forum of the American Council on Education suggest that once educators and business leaders begin to interact with one another directly on the problems of curriculum reform, both sides begin to recognise that the types of competencies and foundational skills demanded by employers look remarkably similar to innovative curriculum initiatives advocated by academicians. The traditional dichotomies between general and vocational education are breaking down under the weight of new forms of social and business organisation, computer assisted production, and the new high-quality service orientation of businesses.

It is now generally agreed, at least outside academia, that curriculum at all levels of the education system must develop students' symbolic skills (conceptual, mathematical, and visual), research skills, and communications skills (oral and written), since post-industrial workers are involved primarily in assembling ideas (rather than things) and in transferring ideas from one arena to another to solve problems (Schultz 1975; Bailey 1990; Carnevale, Gainer, and Meltzer 1988; Rodriquez 1992; World Bank 1995, 24).

Neo-Liberalism and The Productivity Paradox

When William Jefferson Clinton was elected President in 1992, the new administration distanced itself from the "state-centred" policies of New Deal liberals by referring to themselves as "New Democrats" committed to the philosophy of American "neo-liberalism."[3] On the one hand, neo-liberals in the USA reject "traditional liberalism" which claims that government is primarily responsible for citizens' economic welfare through economic regulation and income redistribution. On other hand, neo-liberals also reject the neo-conservative view that a "free market" will automatically provide economic welfare for most citizens. Thus, the New Democrats define neo-liberalism as an economic philosophy that "recognises both the market's efficiencies *and* its imperfections. The government can sometimes make markets work better, but

Table 1. SCANS Competencies and Foundation Skills.

COMPETENCIES.
Effective workers can productively use:

Resources: Allocating Time, Money, Materials, Space, Staff;
a. *time* – selects goal-relevant activities, ranks them, allocates time and prepares and follows schedules.
b. *money* – uses or prepares budgets, makes forecasts, keeps records, and makes adjustments to meet objectives.
c. *material and facilities* – acquires, stores, allocates, and uses materials or space efficiently.
d. *human resources* – assesses skills and distributes work accordingly, evaluates performance, and provides feedback.

Interpersonal Skills: Working on Teams, Teaching Others, Serving Customers, Leading, Negotiating, and Working Well with People from Culturally Diverse Backgrounds;
a. *team work* – contributes to group efforts.
b. *teaches others new skills* – transmits knowledge and skills to others.
c. *customer service* – works to satisfy customers' expectations.
d. *leadership* – communicates ideas to justify position, persuades and convinces others, responsibly challenges existing procedures and policies.
e. *negotiates* – works toward agreements involving exchange of resources, resolves divergent interests.
f. *works with diversity* – works well with mean and women from diverse back grounds.

Information: Acquiring and Evaluating Information, Organizing and Maintaining Files, Interpreting and Communicating, and Using Computers to Process Information;
a. *acquires and evaluates information* – analyzes questions/problems to determine what information is needed; selects and evaluates information; determines when new information must be created to solve problem.
b. *organizes and maintains information* – understands and organizes information from computer, visual, oral, and physical sources in readily accessible formats (e.g., data bases, spreadsheets, video disks, and paper files); can transform data to make it useful (e.g., by sorting, classifying, or more formal methods).
c. *interprets and communicates information* – identifies the information to be communicated; identifies the best methods of presenting information (e.g., overheads, handouts); chooses the best format for display (e.g., line graphs, bar graphs, tables, pie charts, narrative); converts information to desired format; conveys information through a variety of formats (e.g., oral presentation, written communication).

Table 3-1. SCANS Competencies and Foundation Skills.

COMPETENCIES.
Effective workers can productively use:

d. uses computers to process information – entering, modifying, retrieving, storing, and verifying data and other information; choosing the best format for display; ensuring accurate conversion of information into the chosen format.

Systems: Understanding Social, Organizational, and Technological Systems, Monitoring and Correcting Performance, and Designing and Improving Systems;
a. *understands systems* – knows how social, organizational, and technological systems work and operates effectively within them.
b. *monitors and corrects performance* – distinguishes trends, predicts impacts on system operations, diagnoses deviations in systems performance and corrects malfunctions.
c. *improves or designs systems* – suggest modifications to existing systems and develops new or alternative systems to improve performance.

Technology: Selecting Equipment and Tools, Applying Technology to Specific Tasks, and Maintaining and Troubleshooting Technologies.
a. *selects technology* – chooses procedures, tools, or equipment, including computers and related technologies, that are appropriate to specific tasks.
b. *applies technology* – understands overall intent and proper procedures for setup and operation equipment.
c. *maintains and troubleshoots equipment* – prevents, identifies, or solves problems with equipment, including computers and related technologies.

The Foundation. Competence Requires:

Basic Skills: Reading, Writing, Arithmetic and Mathematics, Speaking and Listening.
a. *reading* – locates, understands, interprets written information in prose and in documents such as manuals, graphs, and schedules.
b. *writing* – communicates thoughts, ideas, information, and messages in writing; and creates documents such as letters, directions, manuals, reports, graphs, and flow charts.
c. *arithmetic and mathematics* – performs basic computations and approaches practical problems by choosing appropriately from a variety of mathematical techniques.
d. *speaking* – organizes ideas and communicates orally.
e. *listening* – receives, attends to, interprets and responds to verbal messages and other cues.

Table 3. SCANS Competencies and Foundation Skills.

COMPETENCIES.
Effective workers can productively use:

Thinking Skills: Thinking Creatively, Making Decisions, Solving Problems, Seeing Things in the Mind's Eye, Knowing How to Learn, and Reasoning;

a. *creative thinking* – generates new ideas.
b. *decision making* – specifies goals and constraints, generates alternatives, considers risks and evaluates and chooses best alternative.
c. *problem solving* – recognizes problems and devises and implements plan of action.
d. *seeing things in the mind's eye* – organizes and processes symbols, pictures, graphs, objects, and other information.
e. *knowing how to learn* – uses efficient learning techniques to acquire and apply new knowledge and skills.
f. *reasoning* – discovers a rule or principle underlying the relationship between two or more objects and applies to in solving a problem.

Personal Qualities: Individual Responsibility, Self-Esteem, Sociability, Self-management, and Integrity.

a. *responsibility* – exerts a high level of effort and perseveres toward goal achievement.
b. *self-esteem* – believes in own self-worth and maintains a positive view of self.
c. *sociability* – demonstrates understanding, friendliness, adaptability, empathy, and politeness in group settings.
d. *self-management* – assesses self accurately, sets personal goals, monitors progress and exhibits self-control.
e. *integrity/honesty* – chooses ethical courses of action.

it is seldom in a position to replace them." Thus, while the USA is a market-based economy structured by competition between profit-maximising firms, the government can usefully complement the market by intervening to correct market imperfections and market failures (Office of the U.S. President 1997, 18-20).

The Clinton New Democrats extended this philosophy to international trade policy by recognising "the benefits of free trade, but also the existence of international public goods, not just in the trade arena but in other dimensions of international affairs as well." Hence, as with domestic markets, American neo-liberals argue that unfettered global markets are not, by themselves, sufficient to guarantee the economic welfare of most of the world's citizens. American neo-liberals argue that "markets function best within an institutional environment that makes rules to promote free competition while facilitating the co-operation necessary for a stable world economy." Importantly, Clinton's New Democrats view GATT and the WTO as the appropriate rules-based institutional mechanisms for institutionalising a global trade regime (Ibid., 21-22, 244-46).

Thus, while neo-liberals have often emphasised the "newness" of their economic philosophy, in practice the Clinton Administration largely continued and built upon the bi-partisan policies established during the Bush Administration. These policies include fiscal restraint, trade liberalisation (NAFTA and WTO), and human capital development. Indeed, Clinton's Council of Economic Advisors identified the key elements of his neo-liberal economic agenda as reducing the federal budget deficit, opening markets at home and abroad, and restoring prudence to macroeconomic management (Ibid., 24).

Thus, the Clinton Administration continued the policy of fiscal discipline with the Omnibus Budget Reconciliation Act of 1993 (OBRA93). The Clinton Administration inherited an annual budget deficit of $290 billion in 1992, but by 1996 the annual deficit was reduced to $107 billion. During this same period, the federal budget deficit fell from 4.7 percent of gross domestic product to 1.4 percent. By 1998, the federal budget recorded a surplus for the first time in three decades (Ibid., 80-82). The United States general government deficit (combined federal, state, and local) is now the lowest of any large industrial nation.

The Clinton Administration also continued its predecessors' vigorous efforts to increase exports by completing the NAFTA negotiations in 1993 and the Uruguay Round in 1994. More than 200 other trade agreements were signed between 1993 and 1996, while talks with the Asia-Pacific Economic Co-operation Forum (APEC) and nations in the Western Hemisphere produced commitments to achieve regional free trade in these areas by 2020 and 2005, respectively. From the U.S. perspective, these trading agreements are designed to strengthen the USA's global competitive advantage in services and high technology.[4] Thus, the neo-liberals' objective in promoting free trade is "to raise living standards by ensuring that more Americans are working in areas where the United States is comparatively more productive than its trading partners" (Ibid., 21). Consequently, the Clinton Administration repeatedly emphasised that trade liberalisation "has more impact on the *distribution* of jobs than on the *quantity* of jobs" created by the U.S. economy.

For example, while U.S. exports boomed during the 1990s in areas where trade agreements were reached, the more important fact is that wages in the jobs generated by the export of U.S.-made goods were 13 percent to 16 percent higher than the national average. This relationship between the export sector and high wages has made exports a critical part of the U.S. strategy for creating high-wage, knowledge-based jobs, because exports allow U.S. firms to expand production in high-productivity sectors where they have a competitive advantage. The President's Council of Economic Advisors observes that the USA is especially well positioned to benefit from trade liberalisation in the developing countries of Asia and Latin America, since it is as a major exporter of capital goods, agricultural products, consumer goods, and commercial services in demand in these countries (Ibid., 21-27, 238-39, 242-48). To support this strategy, the Clinton Administration aggressively promoted the human capital development policies of the previous Administration, including the America Goals 2000 initiative and implementation of the SCANS recommendations. These national policies have contributed to a continuing wave of elementary, secondary, and higher education reform at the state and local levels.

However, the "New Democrats" have also been particularly concerned about the role of research and development in the new global economy. A basic premise of neo-liberal economic policy is that private firms will not invest adequate private capital in new science and technology, particularly in basic research, since individual firms do not capture the full benefits of their investment in such areas. Consequently, neo-liberals built on previous policy by identifying the "innovation gap" as a second lacuna in the nation's post-industrial competitiveness strategy.

A recent OECD (1996b, 18) report observes that: "The drive to innovate starts with basic research, moves through applied research and development, and culminates with the successful commercialisation of new products and production and delivery processes." In the USA, the emergence of an innovation gap stems partly from the division of scientific labour between universities, government, and industry (McMahon 1984). During the last 100 years, a division of scientific labour evolved in the USA, where universities conducted basic or pure scientific research for its own sake, federal laboratories and bureaus conducted applied technical research, and private industry engaged in the development of new products and processes (Dupree 1957; MacCordy 1992). These boundaries have never been impermeable, but for the most part, basic research and development have been conducted by different individuals, who are physically separated by location, and who are also divided by the "two cultures" of academia and business.[5] Consequently, basic research, on which technological innovation increasingly depends, has been pursued without regard to its practical applications and, as a result, there is typically a long time delay before basic discoveries work their way through federal laboratories and into industrial laboratories for commercialisation.

Moreover, it became clear in the 1980s that patents are often ineffective in protecting competitive advantage in many leading technology sectors, such as semiconductors, computers, software, telecommunications, and aerospace. In these sectors, companies reap returns, and a competitive advantage, mainly by achieving a head start over rival firms, which they can exploit by seizing the market and moving rapidly down the learning curve. Firms in these sectors fully expect their rivals to appropriate and use their invention, but with a slight time lag. However, the lag between invention, diffusion, and further improvements has become shorter and shorter in recent years as exemplified by rapid improvements in integrated circuit speeds, which double roughly every two years (Ostry 1996, 146-47).

These concerns were addressed during the Clinton Administration in a series of policy recommendations from the U.S. President's Council of Advisors on Science and Technology (PCAST).[6] A major concern expressed by PCAST (1992, xvii) is that:

"The pressure of international competition has introduced a critical time dimension into the system. The issue is not simply how much new knowledge is being generated but also how fast it is being translated into economically and socially beneficial products and processes."

Several widely publicised examples of the gap between basic research and technological development in the United States have highlighted this dilemma. American university scholars pioneered the basic research for such products as high-density television, microchips, magnetic levitation railroads, and satellite launch vehicles, but this research is being commercialised successfully in Europe and Japan. Consequently, PCAST (1992, 30) suggests it is imperative for U.S. industries to "have the benefit of easy and immediate access to the new knowledge and new talent generated by universities." The problem, according to the PCAST (1992, 31) report, "argues for a more deliberate effort to move information and, especially, people between universities and industry." The Clinton Administration repeatedly decried the "false dichotomy" between basic research (universities) and technology (private sector) in the USA and has used the federal budget system to promote stronger and more extensive partnerships between government, universities, and corporations (Office of the U.S. President 1997, 34).

TOWARD A NEW STRATEGIC AGENDA IN HIGHER EDUCATION

Government officials' concerns with workforce quality and technology transfer have moved higher education into the forefront of many national debates about U.S. economic and trade policy (Fairweather 1988). Moreover, as world-wide economic competition increased from the mid-1970's onward, American corporations joined a broad political mobilisation that has given a cohesive voice to its demands since that time (Vogel 1983; Useem 1984; Edsall 1984). During the last twenty-five years, numerous organisations have been created to promote a new strategic alliance between business, government, and higher education. Sheila Slaughter (1990, p. 2) documents how such organisations have argued convincingly that higher education policy should be linked explicitly to the goal of regaining a competitive advantage for American business mainly by promoting "advanced applied technology, technology transfer, and the training of a competitive scientific and professional labour force."[7]

Similarly, James S. Fairweather's (1988, 19-23) survey of scholarly and professional literature affirms that the main "focus of federal policy [on higher education] is to resolve the trade imbalance, increase productivity, ensure that university research activities meet the needs of industry, increase the transition from basic research to product development, and establish a coherent national research and development plan." There is also ample evidence that state government officials and higher education administrators are actively embracing these concerns as part of the strategic mission for higher education at the sub-national and institutional levels (Chmura 1987; SRI International 1986). A survey by the Western Interstate Commission on Higher Education (WICHE), for example, recently examined 48 planning documents related to state-level economic development and higher education planning. The WICHE (1992d, p. 3) study concludes that despite a continuing disjuncture between state level economic planning and higher education planning, by the early 1990s many higher education master plans were beginning to refine the traditional university mission to include:

1. Teaching – the education of a new professional workforce with increasingly symbolic and interdisciplinary skills,
2. Research – to provide research, development, information, and technical assistance to government and industry, rather than for its own sake,
3. Service – defined as participation in public-private partnerships with industry and government agencies.

The WICHE (1992d, pp. 5-6) survey finds that public higher education master plans and institutional vision statements increasingly identify their own role in economic development with meeting the technological challenge of international competition and with providing a workforce that has internationally competitive skills relevant to a post-industrial economy.

Beyond the Multiversity

College and university faculties have often been reluctant to embrace this post-industrial refinement of the traditional university mission, but a fiscal crisis in American higher education has provided the wedge for injecting these concerns into the university community and its internal discussions. For the most part, following World War II, American higher education experienced a phase of robust expansion. Student enrolments increased six-fold from 1946 to 1986 and, to accommodate these enrolments, the number of colleges and universities increased from 1,851 to 3,155 during approximately the same period (U.S. Department of Education 1992). State governments simultaneously increased appropriations to public higher institutions, while new federal programs were adopted to assist students with tuition and to defray the capital costs of constructing new classroom and research facilities. Finally, as part of the Cold War strategy of superpower competition, the federal government increased its funding of university-based basic research in a variety of academic fields (Rudy 1991). The bottom line is that over four decades real revenues per student increased by forty-nine percent at public higher institutions and by seventy-five percent at private higher institutions (Halstead 1992, pp. 14-15).

In this fiscal environment, higher institutions could respond to a plethora of competing political, economic, and cultural demands with administrative strategies that relied on additive solutions or growth by accretion. Colleges and universities merely added new courses, programs, majors, graduate degrees, or non-academic services to satisfy constituencies inside and outside the university. Thus, as Karel Tavernier (1993, p. 84) observes, the availability of funding has encouraged not simply an enlargement of universities' product content (i.e., numbers of students and course offerings), but "a *multiplication of the services* the university can provide." Indeed, the centrifugal forces set in motion by the post-war expansion of American higher education were so dramatic that Clark Kerr (1977), the former president of the University of California, suggested that higher institutions were best described as multiversities, rather than universities, because they had become such diffuse, multi-functional, organisations.

There were two notable exceptions to the post-war pattern of growth by accretion; namely, the recessions of 1974 and 1982 (Scott 1983). Yet, even while these periods resulted in widespread retrenchment, Janice Newson (1993, p. 289) notes that funding shortfalls were often viewed within the academic community as short-term setbacks within a long-term pattern of growth. Consequently, retrenchment strategies were temporary policies designed to "bridge the difficulties of the present moment and a not too distant future when funding would return to the more affluent (or realistic, depending on point of view) levels of the late 1950s and 1960s." Mussey and Hulfactor agree that institutional responses to the recessions of 1974 and 1982 were largely shaped by the view that financial setbacks were temporary disturbances related to the business cycle. As a result, recessionary fiscal strategies were based on the assumption that budgets would return to normal soon after economic recovery (Massy and Hulfactor 1993; Mims 1980; Mortimer and Tierney 1979).

With the onset of the 1990-91 recession, American higher education seemed on the verge of repeating this short-term cycle. However, Massy and Hulfactor (1993) emphasise correctly that the early 1990s were fundamentally different from the recessionary years of 1974 and 1982 because they marked the onset of a *structural fiscal crisis* in American higher education. By definition, a fiscal crisis consists of an identifiable long-term tendency for operational costs to rise faster than operational revenues (O'Connor 1973; Kettinger and Wertz 1993; Barrow 1993). Consequently, the contradictions of a fiscal crisis, unlike a short-term cyclical shortfall, can be resolved only through forms of fundamental institutional restructuring that bring long-term costs into line with operating revenues. For this reason, Sean C. Rush (1992, p. 1) notes that downsizing, retrenchment, and doing more with less became themes, if not necessities, for most institutions in the 1990s. More and more university administrators are adopting reform strategies designed to simultaneously slow expenditure growth in real terms, while reallocating resources into programs and research areas that will make it possible to rebuild business and government support for higher education. The apparently contradictory imperative that higher institutions "do more with less" is catalysing a wave of strategic planning, restructuring, and reallocation in U.S. higher education that is inevitably forcing higher education administrators to move beyond the ideals of the multiversity.

Institutional responses to the continuing fiscal constraints in American higher education, as well as state and federal policy initiatives, are pushing multiversities toward four interrelated structural reforms: (1) a shift from institutional emulation to differentiation, (2) a shift from basic research to applied research, (3) a shift toward multidisciplinary and interdisciplinary studies, and (4) a shift from department-based research activities toward organised research units with external funding such as centres and institutes. Although budget cuts, program reductions, curriculum reform, and other changes have often seemed disjointed and chaotic to the individual faculty member, these actions have not been temporary or confused responses to a short-term crisis. Instead, the business, government, and administrative policy-makers who control system-level decisions about resource allocation in higher education increasingly share an explicit consensus about a strategy of selective excellence. The strategy of selective excellence is designed to rationalise the American system of higher education by further differentiating the missions of individual institutions, eliminating programs that do not support that mission, and by shifting research activities into interdisciplinary applied research centres. The central objective of this strategy is to allow individual institutions to meet the constraints of a fiscal crisis, while enabling the system as a whole to adjust to the needs of the new economy.

The Strategy of Selective Excellence

It is widely acknowledged that various structural characteristics of higher education – most notably, its labour intensity – partly account for why the real costs of higher education tend to increase over time (Verry and Davies 1976; Bowen 1980; Baumol, Blackman, and Wolf 1989; Halstead 1992). Nevertheless, there are also structural problems peculiar to the multiversity that intensify the underlying "productivity problem" in higher education. First, Massy and Hulfactor (1993, p. 27) and Massy and Zemsky (1994) conclude that many colleges and universities have drifted away from their fundamental missions, because the multiversity strategy of response by addition allows divergent goals and objectives to be added incrementally to an institution's mission over time. Thus, a common theme in strategic master plans and restructuring proposals is the idea that individual institutions must sharpen their mission by concentrating on specialised areas of institutional strength or on areas of high market demand. For example, the Western Interstate Commission on Higher Education has proposed a strategic agenda for public higher education that dramatically rejects the ideal of the multiversity with its conclusion that:

> "No single higher institution can meet all of the current and emerging needs of society...Given limited fiscal and human resources the efficient, effective, and quality state system of higher edu-

cation will be one in which different campuses devote their energies to addressing different needs" (WICHE 1992e, pp. 3-4).

Similarly, Daniel S. Cheever, Jr. (1992), Director of the Massachusetts Higher Education Assistance Corporation, observes that the future of most higher institutions in the Northeast will depend on specialisation and differentiation. He predicts that colleges and universities will emphasise their specialised differences, as opposed to their comprehensiveness, by developing a well-focused core business that appeals to a sharply defined niche market (Cf. Townsend, Newell, and Wiese 1992). This theme is echoed by James Martin and James E. Samels (1994), both higher education consultants, who find that private colleges and universities are also reviewing their educational niches to focus on programs that enhance their quality and competitiveness within the higher education marketplace.

Hence, under the pressures of fiscal crisis, numerous institutions are abandoning the multiversity ideal of offering a comprehensive range of undergraduate majors or graduate programs by adopting the strategy of selective excellence (Grassmuck 1990). The strategy of selective excellence depends on a clarification of institutional mission, the identification of mission-oriented programs, and the identification of comparatively weak academic programs, along with areas of low student demand on campus (Academy for Educational Development, Inc., 1979). Once the latter type of programs are identified, they are reduced to a service role through faculty attrition, or even eliminated, so that financial resources can be reallocated to offset rising institutional costs and so that faculty lines can be reallocated to maintain program quality in a fewer number of academic fields.[8]

The American Council on Education estimates that up to two-thirds of U.S. public research universities have made substantial program cuts since 1991 and further reductions are continuing in many states (El-Khawas 1992). Similarly, an internal survey conducted by the Association of American Universities finds that nearly sixty percent of its members are consolidating, eliminating, or reducing academic departments ("Cornell Faculty" 1989, A25). Of greater significance, however, are the criteria being used for implementing these cutbacks in the 1990s. A survey of 101 public colleges and universities in nine North-eastern states by Marvin Druker and Betty Robinson offers considerable insight into the criteria being employed to make program reductions and cutbacks in higher education. Druker and Robinson (1994, 93) find that a majority of institutions are using four interrelated criteria: centrality to mission (77%), quality of programs (74%), student demand (66%), and relevance to a strategic plan (56%). Thus, as Druker and Robinson conclude, the criteria cited by public university officials clearly "exhibit a concern...with the long-term missions of the institutions and the attempt to maintain the quality of the programs." As a strategy for dealing with fiscal crisis, selective excellence entails a policy of narrow but deep cuts, or growth by substitution, as opposed to temporary across-the-board reductions in academic programs as in the past (Cameron and Tschirhart 1992; Langfitt 1989).

A corollary of the emphasis on quality amid fiscal constraint - or growth by substitution – is an organisational shift from comprehensiveness to differentiation. According to a WICHE (1992d, 2) survey, throughout the public sector, especially, official advisory groups, co-ordinating councils, and governing boards have begun recommending that master plans "force institutions to focus on what they do best by mandating that institutions have differentiated roles and missions." The proposed mandates go beyond the traditional sectoral differentiation between research universities, teaching colleges, and community colleges, to create greater distinctions in the roles and areas of expertise assigned to institutions *within* the same sector. Rush (1992, p. 10) argues that this concept of selective excellence will have to prevail throughout the industry if reasonable quality standards are to be maintained" in the midst of a fiscal crisis.

Importantly, the effort to restructure American universities on a principle of selective excellence will probably be met with minimal or ineffective faculty resistance. Faculty and union perceptions of the current fiscal crisis have been shaped primarily by their previous experience with the retrenchments of the mid-1970s and early 1980s. Consequently, faculty organisations have been ill-prepared to deal with the problems of structural readjustment because they continue to act on the assumption that budget constraints are cyclical and that budgets will soon return to "normal" if they can "weather the storm." However, even if affected faculty choose to "batten down the hatches" there are several reasons to believe they will be ineffective at resisting a strategy of selective excellence.

First, most faculty union contracts in the USA provide little protection against retrenchment. Gary Rhoades' (1993, 313) study of retrenchment clauses in faculty union contracts finds they provide faculty with only "a limited and reactive role in retrenchment decisions, whereas administrative discretion is extensive." Second, because faculty retirements are expected to accelerate in the latter half of the 1990s, it may be possible to restructure academic programs over several years simply by eliminating or reallocating *vacant* faculty lines (Bowen and Sosa 1989). Strategic planners and university administrators increasingly understand that the anticipated surge in faculty retirements presents a once-in-a-century window of opportunity to completely recast the structure of academic programs (WICHE 1992e, 48-51).[9] Third, the strategy of selective excellence is already being implemented at many campuses with the co-operation of those selective faculty who identify with the language of meritocracy (e.g., research stars) or who actively embrace a sharpened mission that promises growth in their own programs (Gumport 1993; Slaughter 1993). Finally, proposals for program elimination at many institutions have short-circuited resistance by linking program reductions to future salary increases for the remaining faculty ("Cornell Faculty" 1989, A-25).

Mission-Oriented Research

Federal and state governments are also changing the structure and criteria for government-sponsored research in ways that further induce a strategy of selective excellence, while providing additional incentives for individual faculty to adopt a more entrepreneurial approach to research. The post-war growth of major research universities in the USA was fuelled by federal grants and appropriations for basic research and research facilities linked to national defence and the Cold War. Following passage of the National Defence Education Act, federal funding for university research nearly tripled between 1958 and 1968 (National Science Foundation 1982). By 1970, universities accounted for more than half of all basic research (on a dollar basis) conducted in the USA and the majority of this research was funded by the federal government (WICHE 1992a, 39).

However, the end of the Cold War and a new emphasis on federal deficit reduction led the President's Council of Advisors on Science and Technology (1992, 10) to conclude that "it is unreasonable to expect that the system of research-intensive universities will continue to grow as it did during periods in the 1960s and 1980s." On the contrary, PCAST estimates that there is now excess research capacity in the USA and, therefore, cutbacks in research funding will only pose a risk to national security and economic competitiveness if federal agencies distribute research funding too thinly among too many institutions, scholars, and projects. Significantly, PCAST attributes the development of excess research capacity to the fact that research-intensive universities have all sought to compete with each other by maintaining world class research capabilities in all or most areas of scholarship and education. Meanwhile, "mission creep" has gradually overwhelmed many four-year teaching institutions that have sought to attract increased grant funding by emulating the more prestigious research universities (Massy and Zemsky 1994). The most recent PCAST (1992, 10) policy recommendations note that these institutional aspirations "cannot be fully realised in an era of significantly constrained resources."[10] Therefore, PCAST recommended eliminating excess research capacity by pressuring grant-recipient universities to "adopt more highly selective strategies based on a realistic appraisal of the future availability of resources."

Consistent with this objective, the twenty federal agencies that fund university-based research have been advised to "refrain from developing or implementing research or education programs that would increase the net capacity of the system" (Ibid., xii-xiii). Instead, federal funding agencies are now being directed to allocate research funds selectively and only into areas where the USA has a clear competitive advantage in frontier research. PCAST (1992, 12) has warned university administrators that institutions which "have maintained the highest standards of quality by being selective in their investments in faculty and physical plant are the ones that will be in the best position to compete successfully for...any significant new resources that might become available." PCAST emphasises that maintaining selective excellence in a time of declining resources will require universities to "eliminate or downsize some departments and specialities" and to "collaborate with nearby institutions (academic, industrial, and governmental) in sharing instructional and research facilities and programs, with the aim of conserving limited resources." Not coincidentally, as the federal government targets its reduced funding more selectively, state governments are beginning to channel more of their funding into targeted incentive grants and centres for excellence designed to attract shrinking federal funds. Such efforts are frequently designed to encourage the voluntary reallocation of funds within institutions by enhancing their strengths in areas of selective excellence (Layzell and Lyddon 1990, 72-79).

Selective Excellence and the Interdisciplinary Movement

In the process of restructuring U.S. higher education, it is becoming evident that programs with a high degree of multidisciplinary support within an institution are the programs most likely to be targeted for selective excellence. This is because a relatively small departmental nucleus can better offer high quality programming when it is able to draw on the personnel and resources of cognate disciplines. Furthermore, programs with extensive multidisciplinary linkages are also likely to enjoy the strongest political support among faculty, since they will have a wider on-campus constituency (Gumport 1993, 305-306). Programs or departments that are not targeted for selective excellence, however, will also fare better to the extent that they develop a network of interdepartmental connections that wire individual faculty members into the institution's targeted areas of selective excellence. Indeed, as administrators target and concentrate institutional resources into fewer and fewer areas on particular campuses, entrepreneurial faculty are induced to create intra-campus and inter-campus networks that build on a defined area of selective excellence in order to gain access to the scarce targeted resources. Conversely, departments and individuals which fail to develop high levels of programmatic interface and interdisciplinary connectivity are likely to wither on the vine until they are phased out or terminated through attrition and budget reductions.

Likewise, the organisational impact of federal and state reallocations for research are inducing changes that go beyond the mere concentration of frontier research at fewer facilities on fewer campuses. As early as 1992, for example, an Ad Hoc Working Group (1992, 2) of the Federal Co-ordinating Council for Science, Engineering and Technology (FCCSET) adopted the principle that "federal policies should serve to maximise the benefits resulting from the Nation's investment in universities and provide increasing dividends in the form of improved quality of life and economic growth."[11] As noted earlier, Presidential science and technology advisors are deeply concerned that the USA now faces increasing economic and technological challenges from other countries, particularly Japan and Europe. Consequently, a nascent trade war has replaced the Cold War as the major stimulus for federal research support, because frontier "science and technology are recognised as critical elements in the emergence of a global international economy" (Ibid., 1). Thus, there is now an expectation among federal policy makers that selective excellence will entail a systematic reallocation of research funding to projects and areas that promote economic growth and technology transfer. FCCSET (Ibid., 1) predicts that achieving this aim will also require "far reaching changes in the research environment...including the intellectual organisation of the [research] task."

Similarly, the WICHE research staff conducted a series of interviews in 1992 that capture how these changes are interrelated in the current thinking of federal officials, state higher education executive officers, and state legislators. A central theme emerging from the WICHE interviews was a concern with the structural disjuncture between the concrete problems that confront society and the conceptual paradigms that organise disciplines. The WICHE (1992c, 13) report summarizes a series of complaints from government officials and business leaders with its observation that universities are dominated by disciplines, whereas governments and businesses must solve problems.[12] This same concern is expressed in a 1992 FCCSET analysis, which points out that economic, social, and political problems are typically multi-faceted and, therefore, they are never fully comprehensible with the perspectives and methods of a single discipline. Consequently, federal science and technology policymakers are now calling attention to the notion that "new challenges and opportunities have increased the importance of multidisciplinary research" (Ad Hoc Working Group 1992, 1). As a result, FCCSET (Ibid., 6) is now implementing a policy recommendation to encourage "significant multidisciplinary initiatives that might otherwise not be funded."

However, Fairweather's survey of the literature on such initiatives finds that disciplinary affiliations, the ponderous pace of university research, and a bureaucratic academic culture each pose obstacles that make it difficult to mesh departmental structures with interdisciplinary applied research and technology transfer. Consequently, Fairweather (1988, 50) concludes that any strategic shift in this direction depends on "the ability of a college or university to develop and support non-traditional organisational structures." As a practical matter, it is unlikely that most faculty are prepared to break with their disciplinary affiliations at the present time. Nevertheless, Janice Newson (1993, 293) observes that an important step down this path is that structures which once hovered "around the edges of the traditional university...have begun to have a central place in defining and achieving the (shifting) objectives of the university." These organisations include centres of excellence, spin-off companies, joint-ventures, research parks, offices of intellectual property and technology transfer, and various other applied research units that institutionalise relationships between universities and corporations and between universities and government agencies.

The development of centres and institutes as a locus of faculty activity, particularly multidisciplinary and applied research activity, is becoming the university equivalent of the virtual corporation. Because these virtual organisations rarely involve contractual issues of faculty tenure or disciplinary standing, the product mix of a particular centre can be changed rapidly by bringing in faculty from other departments, from nearby campuses, through the addition of part-time retirees, adjunct faculty practitioners, visiting faculty, etc. Thus, unlike a heavily tenured department, institutes and centres can respond to uncertain funding opportunities by maintaining a small permanent nucleus of flexible specialists supplemented by an ever-changing satellite faculty and research staff. For this reason, Newson (1993, 294) concludes that faculty unions are again not likely to be successful in resisting such changes, since "typically, these structures are not governed by the academic policies of the university," including research guidelines, hiring procedures, and collective bargaining agreements governing the terms and conditions of employment.

In fact, such centres are being organised on U.S. campuses in unprecedented numbers to provide a focus for faculty research and to concentrate declining research support. Between 1982 and 1985, for example, the number of research and development consortia between industry and academic institutions increased by five times (Dimancescu and Botkin 1986). Furthermore, a sixteen state survey by WICHE (1992b, vii, 2) finds that these initiatives are usually cross-disciplinary efforts designed as a response to fiscal constraints and to meet the needs of a dynamic global economy. The institutes and centres being created are usually anchored in business, engineering, or the social sciences, although most of them are designed to bring together flexible specialists from across the traditional boundaries that separate disciplines, schools, and colleges.

The creation of research institutes and interdisciplinary centres in response to fiscal constraints is a major departure from past precedent. During previous times of fiscal difficulty, institutes and centres were usually among the first cost-units eliminated at universities in order to preserve departments. It is now often the case that departments are being merged, reduced, or eliminated to create new centres that concentrate the remaining resources and personnel on a common set of problems. Thus, centres and institutes are rapidly moving from the periphery of institutional culture to the core of the research and teaching enterprise, including the granting of degrees (Ibid., 2-7).

Equally important, as federal grants policy requires, many of the new institutes and centres are designed to change the way research is conducted and to change the kind of research activity being pursued by scholars. The Ad Hoc Working Group (1992, 9) of FCCSET concludes that:

"It is not enough to generate new knowledge, the new knowledge must... translate gains in knowledge into tangible gains in economic activity."

Indeed, PCAST (1992, xvii) now rejects the existing division of scientific labour as "completely at odds with today's world," where "shorter time horizons between concept and application and more iterative relationships between fundamental research and technology have increased the need for collaborative relationships among researchers" (Cf. Ad Hoc Working Group 1992, 1). Thus, business leaders and federal policymakers both agree that "growth in the utility of knowledge" will require "the continued development of knowledge networks and collaborative relationships among academic institutions, industry, and government" (Ibid., 9).

The collaborative research arrangements between academic institutions, industry, and government are also increasingly transnational in scope because many of the research projects (e.g., public health, economic development, environment) cannot effectively study problems within national boundaries. As a result, more and more university research is being conducted through international and multidisciplinary networks that can be very complex and fluid in their organisational structure. This structure typically revolves around a research university or institute that is responsible for organising research, attracting funding, and arranging subcontracts with multiple satellite organisations, i.e., other university research centres, industrial laboratories, government bureaus, and individual faculty. The complex structure of these regional and transnational arrangements requires frequent communications throughout the network, but computer-based storage and retrieval systems have made it possible for groups of individuals (e.g., research teams) to share data and information stored at a "home base" anywhere in the world. The possibility for inter-institutional and international research collaboration has also accelerated with the development of international postal systems, electronic mail, facsimile machines, and teleconferencing, which allow the exchange of ideas and information between widely separated nodal points more frequently and at less cost than previously (Skilbeck and Connell 1996, 73).

To facilitate such arrangements, FCCSET (1992, 6) has recommended that federal agencies fund projects which encourage "new institutional arrangements to increase the dissemination and utilisation of knowledge and increase emphasis on university/industry co-operation." In fact, WICHE (1992a, 41) surveys have found that "decreased state and federal funding are encouraging universities to seek stronger relationships with business and industry, and to capitalise financially on faculty innovations" (for example, see, SRI International 1986; Business-Higher Education Forum 1988).

While universities remain focused primarily on basic research, there are both pressures and incentives to shift that emphasis and to close the gap between the two cultures of academia and industry. The chief mechanisms for closing this gap are research centres and institutes that specialise in applied policy analysis, economic development, small business development, business and technology incubation, advanced technology, technology transfer, entrepreneurship, and even more specialised permutations depending upon the industries central to a state's or region's economic base (Smilor and Gill, Jr. 1986; Smilor, Kozmetsky, and Gibson 1988; Gibson and Smilor 1991; Matkin 1990; Brett, Powers, Powers, Betz, and Alsanian 1988). Moreover, there is mounting evidence that non-traditional academic and research units are not only successful in bridging the cultures of academia, business, and government, but that such units provide incubators for a new type of entrepreneurial faculty with the potential to transform academic cultures (Etzkowitz 1989; Rahm 1994).

Notably, the shift to applied research and development also provides a vehicle for thwarting mission creep by focusing the research capabilities of many four-year comprehensive universities into areas that do not compete directly with the research-intensive universities. The WICHE (1992e, 3) strategic agenda proposes that in an era of scarce resources "few campuses can be fully committed to basic research, but a large number can be engaged in the application of knowledge to the solution of problems." By focusing on applied problem-solving, comprehensive regional universities can build on the discoveries of research-intensive universities in selective areas deemed important to a particular state or region.

CHAPTER 3

GLOBALISATION, NAFTA, AND THE INTERNATIONALISATION OF HIGHER EDUCATION IN THE USA

The various reports calling attention to the skills gap and the innovation gap in the USA rarely address the question of international competencies and multicultural skills even though concern over these gaps is linked to U.S. competitiveness in the new global economy. Thus, the debates about restructuring higher education, and the strategies for linking it more closely to economic development and trade policies, are often strangely dissociated from academic discussions about the need to internationalise higher education. Yet, the concern with developing an internationally competitive workforce has direct implications for how one defines a variety of skills including interpersonal, information management, and communications skills (CIEE, 1988; Lambert 1989; National Task Force 1990; Garavalia 1992).

For example, in a ranking of international management performance across ten countries, the USA occupied the tenth and last position in both its managers' understanding of foreign cultures and languages and the international experience of its senior management (Chartrand 1992). A Rand Corporation study found that despite increased interest in international competencies among corporate representatives, they rarely look toward higher education to meet these demands because they are sceptical about whether traditional foreign language departments and study-abroad programs can supply their need for international competencies (Bikson and Law 1994). Consequently, the study found that transnational firms are more likely to acquire international competencies by recruiting foreign nationals studying in the USA, using international search firms, providing in-house training, contracting to private educational services firms, or outsourcing selected operations to overseas firms with "local knowledge" in accounting or law. Only recently have U.S. corporate executives begun to draw links between the drive for a high performance workforce and international competencies and to view second language proficiency and "multiculturalism" in the curricula as useful preparation for working in a global economy (OECD 1993b).

The internationalisation of higher education encompasses cross-border educational travel, student enrolment at foreign institutions, temporary faculty exchanges, cross-border employment opportunities among faculty, and opportunities to conduct research or present research findings in foreign countries. It also includes studying the history, economics, politics, and culture of other countries, since greater attention to these subjects is likely to stimulate and facilitate greater cross-border educational movement (Weintraub 1994, 75). There has been a great deal of dialogue on U.S. campuses about the importance of "multiculturalism" and "global awareness," but previous studies have documented a failure to internationalise higher education in the USA (Leyton-Brown 1996; Goodwin and Nacht 1991; Altbach and McGill 1998). Our findings are consistent with previous studies and suggest that international higher education linkages between the USA and its NAFTA partners in particular are quite limited, although a variety of new government programs and non-governmental initiatives seem to be increasing the levels of North American activity.

There is some evidence that many higher education institutions in the USA are slowly and selectively increasing their commitment to internationalisation. For example, in its 1995 annual survey of *Campus Trends*, a majority of higher education institutions claim to have increased their level of international activity during the previous five years. The most common form of internationalisation in U.S. higher education has consisted of adding an "international perspective" to existing programs, although many colleges and universities report they are developing institutional agreements and partnerships with foreign higher education institutions, changing core courses to include an international perspective, and more aggressively recruiting foreign students (El-Khawas 1995, 13).

International and Area Studies in the USA

International and Area Studies includes the study of the language, history, culture, politics, and economy of foreign countries. In the USA, these courses are frequently combined into clusters as interdisciplinary "area studies" or "international studies" programs. The most extensive study of international studies in the USA found that U.S. higher education institutions offer "a very large number" of internationally oriented courses, which represent a substantial investment of institutional resources and faculty time. Approximately, two-thirds of these courses focus on a single region or country with 40 percent of the courses devoted to a single country (Lambert 1989, 114-15). At four-year higher education institutions, more than 40 percent of all internationally oriented courses still focus on Western Europe, while approximately 30 percent of such courses are devoted to issues such as international conflict, world hunger, terrorism, etc. Nearly two-thirds of internationally oriented language and literature courses are devoted to Western Europe (Ibid., 117). The intensive study of Canada is usually promoted through Canadian Studies Programs, while the study of Mexico is usually subsumed within a Latin American Studies Program.

Canadian Studies
In academic year 1998, 13 four-year colleges and universities offered a baccalaureate degree in Canadian Studies (Latimer 1998a), while only one university (Johns Hopkins) offered a graduate degree in Canadian Studies (Latimer 1998b). The availability of an undergraduate or graduate major is an imprecise measure of the extent to which individual courses are available to students at higher education institutions in the USA. Consequently, the Association for Canadian Studies in the United States (ACSUS), established in 1971, periodically conducts a more comprehensive survey of Canadian Studies in the USA. The ACSUS defines a Canadian Studies course as one with content that is exclusively or partially (at least 25%) devoted to the study of Canada. The first Canadian Studies survey was conducted in 1983 and it found that approximately 1,100 courses were being offered in Canadian Studies at higher education institutions in 46 states. More than 18,000 students were enrolling annually in these courses (Kenski and Kenski 1991, 1). In 1990, a new survey by ACSUS found

that approximately 700 faculty are now engaged in teaching and research on Canada. The number of courses with exclusive or partial Canadian content had increased to 1,308 and the number of students enrolled in courses with Canadian content had increased to 23,000 (Ibid., 2). Most of the incremental growth in U.S. Canadian Studies was stimulated prior to the Canada-United States Free Trade Agreement by the Canadian government's financial support of U.S. faculty engaged in cultural travel, research, and curriculum development.

However, despite the small the increase in absolute numbers, these figures actually mean that the percentage of total domestic students who annually enrol in a course with Canadian content decreased from 0.20% in 1983 to 0.17% in 1990. Furthermore, these ratios suggest that less than 1 percent of all U.S. college and university students (0.17% annually) have ever taken a course with Canadian content by the time they graduate. This finding is consistent with Lambert's (1989, 116-18) earlier study, which found that only about 1 percent of all internationally oriented courses offered at four-year U.S. higher education institutions were devoted to North America with only 0.5 percent focused exclusively on Canada. About the same proportion of internationally oriented language and literature courses offered in the USA were devoted to Canada and North America (Lambert 1989, 117).

Latin American Studies
In academic year 1998, 199 four-year colleges and universities offered a baccalaureate degree in Latin American Studies (Latimer 1998a), while 35 colleges and universities offered a graduate degree in Latin America Studies (Latimer 1998b). The United States Latin American Studies Association (1996) publishes a select listing of institutions with courses and programs in Latin American Studies offered at 101 U.S. higher education institutions. Forty-one (41) of these programs identify Mexico as a significant strength or special emphasis, including special library collections, faculty specialisation, or exchange agreements with Mexican universities. These programs tend to be focused at the intersection of the humanities and social sciences with course courses in history, political science, sociology, anthropology, and economics. Lambert's (1989, 116-18) study found that depending on the type of higher education institution between 5.2 percent and 6.8 percent of all internationally oriented courses offered at U.S. higher education institutions focused on Latin America. Among four-year higher education institutions, only 1.1 percent of all internationally oriented courses focused exclusively on Mexico. Only 4 percent to 7.9 percent of internationally oriented language and literature courses are devoted to Latin America depending on the type of institution.

Foreign Language Studies
In 1998, there were 949 four-year colleges and universities offering a baccalaureate degree in Spanish language and literature (Latimer 1998a). In the same year, there were 794 four-year colleges and universities offering a baccalaureate in French language and literature (Ibid.). The Modern Language Association (MLA) has been

compiling data on foreign language course registrations since 1958 at two-year and four-year higher education institutions in the USA (Brod and Huber 1997). This data reveals that in 1995, 83 percent of all two-year institutions and 93 percent of all four-year institutions offered foreign language instruction to students. The most dramatic overall increase in foreign language registrations occurred during the peak years of the U.S.-Soviet Cold War (1960-1968) and this increase was supported by federal funding under the National Defence Education Act of 1958. Since that time, however, registrations in foreign language courses have not changed significantly.

In 1968, there were 1,073,097 students registered in foreign language courses and in 1998 there were 1,193,830 students registered in foreign language courses (see Figure 5). However, the ratio of college and university students enrolling in a foreign language each year has decreased from 14.3 percent in 1968 to 7.9 percent in 1998.[13] The most popular languages in the USA are Spanish, French, German, Japanese, and Italian. Notably, Spanish language registrations have more than tripled since 1960 and now constitute 55.0 percent of all foreign language registrations at U.S. colleges and universities (see Table 2). Language study seems to follow trends in global economic relations with recent registrations declining in French, German, and Russian, while enrolments continue to increase in Spanish, Japanese, and Chinese.

Student Mobility to the United States

The USA started promoting student mobility during the 1950s as part of its Cold War foreign policy strategy (Brubacher and Rudy 1997, 233-35). The passage of the National Defence Education Act in 1958 provided the first federal financial support for U.S. students to study in foreign countries, to learn foreign languages, and to support the expansion of area studies programs. In the 1960s, Fulbright scholarships and U.S. Agency for International Development (USAID) grants greatly increased the funding available for faculty and students conducting research in foreign countries and for bringing foreign scholars and students to the USA (Ibid., 440). These programs were designed to enhance U.S. capabilities for diplomacy, foreign policy-making, and intelligence gathering and to showcase American-style democratic capitalism to the future elites of less developed and non-aligned countries (Davis 1996, iii; Rudy 1991). The initiatives of numerous private associations and non-governmental organisations committed to international education exchange, the study of particular countries, or the study of specific languages reinforced these government policies.

These policies were quite successful in the sense that 34,232 foreign students enrolled in U.S. higher institutions in 1954-55 and by 1996-97 foreign student enrolments had increased by 1,200 percent to 457,984. Currently, more than 1.4 million students per year matriculate world-wide at higher education institutions outside their own country and approximately one-third of these students matriculate at U.S. higher education institutions (Davis 1995, 79). However, despite the increase in foreign student enrolments over the last four decades, the ratio of foreign students in the USA increased from only 1.4 percent to 3.2 percent of the nation's total higher education enrolments (Davis 1997, 2; see Table 3). This is a much lower percentage than one

Figure 5. Modern Foreign Language Registrations, 1960 to 1998.

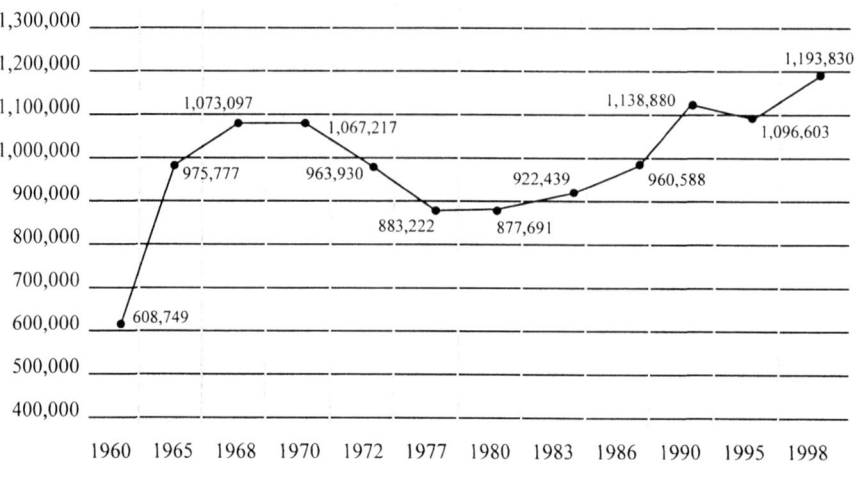

Source: Brod and Huber 1997; Brod and Huber 2000.

Table 2. Registrations in Ten Leading Modern Foreign Languages, 1960-1998.

	1960	1970	1980	1990	1995	1998
Arabic	541	1,333	3,466	3,475	4,444	5,505
Chinese	1,844	6,238	11,366	19,490	26,471	28,456
French	228,813	359,313	248,361	272,472	205,351	199,064
German	146,116	202,569	126,910	133,348	96,263	89,020
Hebrew	3,834	16,567	19,429	12,995	7,479	6,734
Italian	11,142	34,244	34,791	49,699	43,760	49,287
Japanese	1,746	6,620	11,506	45,717	44,723	43,141
Portuguese	1,033	5,065	4,894	6,211	6,531	6,926
Russian	30,570	36,189	23,987	44,626	24,729	23,791
Spanish	178,689	389,150	379,379	533,944	606,286	656,590
Total	604,328	1,057,288	864,089	1,121,977	1,071,685	1,193,830

Source: Brod and Huber 1997; Brod and Huber 2000.

Table 3. Foreign Students and Total U.S. Student Enrollment in Higher Education, 1954/55 to 1996/97.

Year	Foreign Students	Total Enrollment	Percent Foreign
1954/55	34,232	2,499,800	1.4%
1959/60	48,486	3,402,300	1.4%
1964/65	82,045	5,320,000	1.5%
1969/70	134,959	7,978,400	1.7%
1974/75	154,580	10,321,500	1.5%
1979/80	286,343	11,707,000	2.4%
1984/85	342,113	12,467,700	2.7%
1985/86	343,777	12,387,700	2.8%
1986/87	349,609	12,410,500	2.8%
1987/88	356,187	12,808,487	2.8%
1988/89	366,354	13,322,576	2.7%
1989/90	386,581	13,824,592	2.8%
1990/91	407,529	13,975,408	2.9%
1991/92	419,585	14,360,965	2.9%
1992/93	438,618	14,422,975	3.0%
1993/94	449,749	14,473,106	3.1%
1994/95	452,635	14,554,016	3.1%
1995/96	453,787	14,419,252	3.1%
1996/97	457,984	14,286,478	3.2%
1997/98	481,280	14,350,000	3.4%

Source: Davis, 1996-1997, 2.

Figure 6. Share of U.S. Total World Trade with NAFTA Partners, 1983 to 1998.

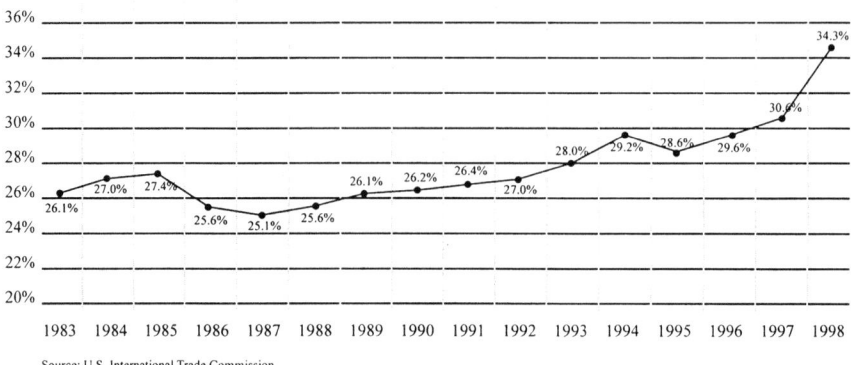

Source: U.S. International Trade Commission

Table 4. Leading Places of Origin for Foreign Students in the United States.

Place of Origin	1972/73	82/83	93/94	94/95	95/96	96/97	97/98
Japan	4,653	13,610	43,770	45,276	45,531	46,292	47,073
China			44,380	39,403	39,613	42,503	46,958
Korea, Rep. Of	3,730	11,360	31,080	33,599	36,231	37,130	42,890
India	10,656	12,890	34,800	33,537	31,743	30,641	33,818
Taiwan	9,633	20,770	37,580	36,407	32,702	30,487	30,85
Canada	9,679	14,020	22,660	22,747	23,005	22,984	22,051
Thailand	5,759	6,800	9,540	10,889	12,165	13,481	15,090
Malaysia		14,070	13,720	13,617	14,015	14,527	14,597
Indonesia			11,740	11,872	12,820	12,461	13,282
Hong Kong	10,298	8,610	13,750	12,935	12,018	10,942	9,665
Mexico	3,054	7,260	8,021	9,003	8,687	8,975	9,559
Germany			8,510	8,592	9,017	8,990	9,309

Source: Davis (1994-1995 through 1997-1998).

finds in many European countries, where foreign students account for 6 percent (Denmark) to 28 percent (Switzerland) of total higher education enrolments (Davis 1995, 81).

Asian students, particularly those from the newly industrialising East Asian "tigers" and "dragons" constitute more than one-half of the U.S. international student population, while the NAFTA countries are a small percentage of foreign student enrolments (Davis 1997, 7). In 1997-98, there were 22,051 Canadian students and 9,559 Mexican students enrolled in U.S. higher education institutions. While Canada and Mexico account for 34.3 percent of U.S. total world trade in goods and services (see Figure 6), Canadian and Mexican students account for only 6.6 percent of all foreign students enrolled in the USA (See Table 4).

Moreover, since NAFTA was ratified in 1993, the number of Canadian students enrolled in U.S. higher education institutions has actually decreased by 609 students and the number of Mexican students attending U.S. higher education institutions has increased by only 1,538.[14] The proportion of foreign students originating in the NAFTA countries decreased from 6.8% in 1993/94 to 6.6% in 1997/98. Thus, there has not been any significant "NAFTA effect" on student mobility from Canada and Mexico to the USA as many international educators anticipated in the early 1990s. In fact, the marginal enrolment increases from NAFTA countries that did occur in the 1990s are much smaller than the increases of the 1970s and 1980s, whether measured in absolute numbers or percentage rates of growth.

Student Mobility from the United States

The number of U.S. students receiving academic credit for study abroad has increased from 48,483 in 1985/86 to 99,448 in 1996/97 (Davis 1998). This remains a very small percentage of the students enrolled in U.S. higher education institutions. The percentage of all U.S. higher education students studying abroad for any length of time has increased only from 0.4 percent to 0.7 percent over the last decade. Moreover, unlike foreign students who come to the USA to pursue full-time studies leading to a baccalaureate or graduate degree, most U.S. students study in foreign countries for brief periods of time ranging from a single semester to one year. Thus, U.S. students study abroad mainly for purposes of "enriching" their higher education by completing limited coursework that will count toward a U.S. degree. For example, 53 percent of U.S. students who study abroad do so for one semester or less and only 12 percent studied in a foreign country for one year or longer and the trend is toward ever shorter stays (Davis 1997, 135).

However, among U.S. students studying abroad, Mexico is now the fifth most popular destination after the United Kingdom, Spain, Italy, and France (See Table 5). In 1996-97, there were 6,865 U.S. students in Mexico, which accounts for 6.9 percent of all U.S. students abroad. A less favourable way of looking at these numbers is that approximately 0.18 percent of all U.S. college and university students will spend some time studying in Mexico during any four year period.[15] In 1996-97, there were only 682 U.S. students in Canada, which accounts for a mere 0.7 percent of all U.S.

Table 5. Host Countries of U.S. Study Abroad Students.

Host Countries	1991/92	93/94	94/95	95/96	96/97	96/97
United Kingdom	16,610	16,812	19,410	20,062	22,787	37.2%
Italy	5,346	6,410	7,062	7,890	9,074	69.7%
Spain	7,125	6,937	7,473	8,135	8,840	24.1%
France	8,160	7,919	7,872	7,749	8,362	2.5%
Mexico	4,600	4,718	4,715	6,220	6,865	49.2%
Germany	3,458	3,512	3,504	3,552	3,815	10.3%
Canada	618	507	573	653	682	10.4%
Total Abroad	71,154	76,302	84,403	89,242	99,448	39.8%

Source: Davis (1994-1995 through 1997-1998).

Table 6. Origins of Foreign Visiting Scholars at U.S. Higher Institutions.

	1993/94	94/95	95/96	96/97	97/98	
China	11,156	9,866	9,228	9,274	10,709	4.0%
Japan	5,458	5,155	5,127	5,365	5,472	0.3%
Korea	3,299	3,163	3,493	4,419	4,520	7.0%
Germany	4,139	4,369	4,251	4,301	4,783	5.6%
India	4,139	3,912	3,623	3,731	4,092	1.1%
United Kingdom	2,759	2,690	2,698	2,794	2,936	6.4%
Canada	2,459	2,498	2,350	2,613	2,882	17.2%
Mexico	600	634	732	787	828	38.0%
TOTAL	59,981	58,074	59,403	62,354	65,494	9.2%

Source: Davis, (1994/1995 through 1997/1998).

students abroad. This means that a mere 0.02 percent of all U.S. college and university students will spend any time studying in Canada during any four year period. However, an interesting trend may be developing, since 14.3 percent of the increase from 1994/95 to 1996/97 in the total number of U.S. students studying abroad was the result of an increase in the number of students going to Mexico. Mexico has become one of the fastest growing destinations for U.S. students and, in this case, there may be a noticeable NAFTA effect underway, albeit one that is starting from a very small numerical base.

Faculty Mobility to the United States

In 1997/98, there were 65,494 foreign visiting scholars at U.S. higher education institutions, although this number does not include non-U.S. citizens who are regular faculty employees. This number has increased by 9.2 percent since 1993/94 (see Table 6). Patterns of foreign scholar mobility to the USA closely parallel those of foreign students studying in the USA. The largest percentage of foreign scholars come from the same East Asian countries as foreign students and they are also concentrated at major research universities. Nearly eighty-two percent (81.9%) of foreign visiting scholars come to the USA primarily for the purpose of conducting research and this ratio has increased slightly during the last few years (Davis 1997, 184).

In 1997/98, there were 2,882 Canadian scholars and 828 Mexican scholars visiting at United States higher education institutions, which accounts for 4.4 percent and 1.3 percent, respectively, of all visiting scholars in the USA. This is only a slight increase since NAFTA's ratification in 1993, but both countries are showing rates of increase that exceed the average rate of increase in the numbers of foreign scholars visiting the USA (see Table 6). On the other hand, visiting Canadian scholars constitute only 0.50 percent of the full-time professoriate at U.S. higher education institutions, while visiting Mexican scholars constitute 0.15 percent of the full-time professoriate at U.S. higher education institutions (*Almanac of Higher Education, 1995,* 3-5), which means their visibility is negligible on most campuses.

Cross-Border Participation in U.S. Scholarly Conferences

The rates of cross-border participation in scholarly conferences held in the USA States is also quite limited even though such participation requires a commitment of only a few days per year. A selective survey of participation in scholarly conferences in the social sciences, chemistry, and engineering in 1998 and 1999 indicates that of the total conference participants in these fields only 2.75 percent were from Canada or Mexico (see Table 7). NAFTA participation rates ranged from a low of 1.70 percent in the American Sociological Association to a high of 5.5 percent in the American Psychological Association. While one would expect low rates of participation based on the relative size of each country's faculty, these numbers suggest that there is still very little regular direct interchange between faculty members in the three countries through the normal channels of disciplinary interaction.

Table 7. Cross-Border Participation in U.S. Academic Conferences by NAFTA Partners, 1998-1999.

Scholarly Association	Total Participants (universities only)	Canada Participants/Percent		Mexico Participants/Percent		NAFTA Participants/Percent	
American Historical Association	1,047	21	2.01%	2	0.19%	23	2.20%
American Political Science Association	4,498	75	1.67%	18	0.40%	93	2.07%
American Sociological Association	5,414	86	1.59%	6	0.11%	92	1.70%
American Economic Association	950	17	1.79%	0	0.00%	17	1.79%
American Psychological Association	9,096	490	5.39%	10	0.11%	500	5.50%
Am. Acad. for the Advncmnt of Science	578	12	2.08%	0	0.00%	12	2.08%
American Chemical Society 3/29 - 4/2/98	10,292	175	1.70%	17	0.17%	192	1.87%
American Chemical Society 8/23 - 8/27/98	13,887	356	6%	17	0.12%	373	2.69%
American Society of Civil Engineers	332	6	1.81%	1	0.30%	7	2.11%
American Society of Mechanical Engineers	4,918	92	1.87%	0	0.00%	92	1.87%
Total	51,012	1,330	2.61%	71	0.14%	1,401	2.75%

Sources: AHA Annual 1998 Meeting Program; APSA 94th Annual Meeting Program; ASA 1998 Program Schedule; AEA Annual Meeting Preliminary Program, 1999; APA 106th Annual Convention Program, 1998; AAAS 1998 Annual Meeting Program; ACS 1998 Annual Meeting Programs; ASCE 1998 Annual Meeting Program; ASME 1998 Annual Meeting Program.

Macroeconomic Determinants of Academic Mobility

Despite declining U.S. federal support for faculty and student exchange programs, academic mobility continues to increase world-wide, rising from 394,492 international students world-wide in 1970 to 1,404,061 in 1995 (Davis 1995, 79). These increases are occurring for several reasons. Many individuals recognise the competitive advantage of international and multicultural competencies in the new global economy (Davis 1995, iv). The governments of Japan, Australia, New Zealand, Canada, and the European Union are pursuing foreign student recruitment strategies as part of an aggressive educational services export policy. In the USA, individual higher education institutions have often absorbed the costs of international educational exchange or actively pursued foreign students to generate additional tuition revenues. Thus, the absolute number of students and scholars coming to the USA continues to increase even though the USA commands a declining share of the world market for international students (see Figure 1).

However, the composition and levels of student mobility appear unrelated to trade agreements and are evidently determined far more by domestic economic and political developments in the sending countries than by the exchange policies of the host country. The USA has maintained a decisive competitive advantage in providing higher education services since the end of World War II, but this advantage is unrelated to trade and investment liberalisation between the USA and the rest of the world. Thus, contrary to more optimistic predictions, there is no reason to anticipate any *spontaneous* increase in rates of academic mobility between Canada, Mexico, and the USA purely as a consequence of NAFTA.

Rather, Lambert (1995, 20) observes that "foreign student flows operate in a complex, highly differentiated market in which most of the decisions are made overseas and on grounds not readily affected by institutional behaviour in the United States." For example, there was a large influx of Middle Eastern students into the USA during the 1970s when the OPEC cartel was able to command high prices for oil. The number of students originating in the Middle East increased from 13,278 in 1969/70 to 83,700 in 1979/80. Middle Eastern students increased from 9.9 percent to 29.2 percent of foreign students in the USA during this time, but that number and percentage has fallen dramatically since the end of the OPEC oil price boom (Davis 1997, 8). Similarly, in the early 1980s, the number of Asian students in the USA increased from 81,730 in 1979/80 to 143,680 in 1984/85. Asian students increased from 28.6 percent to 42.0 percent of foreign students in the USA during this time. Asian student enrolments reached a peak of 264,690 or 58.9 percent of foreign student enrolments in 1993/94. The increase was stimulated largely by the economic success of the Asian "tigers" and "dragons" such as China, Korea, Taiwan, Malaysia, Thailand, Indonesia, and Hong Kong (Davis 1995, 67-69, 77-79; Davis 1997, 8). As economic conditions have improved in Mexico, there is some indication of increased student mobility to the USA, but there is no indication that NAFTA is stimulating large-scale academic migration to the USA or Canada.

International Competition and Academic Mobility

The U.S. position in the world market for international students is already being affected by increased global competition and regional economic integration elsewhere in the world. The effect of increased competition is evident in the fact that the USA's share of the international student market has been decreasing since the mid-1980s (Davis 1995, 79; Lambert 1995, 22; see Figure 1). The European Union has adopted a policy to promote academic mobility among member countries with the explicit goal of improving the Union's economic competitiveness in comparison to the USA, Japan, and the emerging economies of the Far East (Davis 1995, 29). Under the European Community Action Scheme for Mobility of University Students (ERASMUS) Program, European universities have established inter-university agreements for credit and credential equivalency, program articulation, and tuition and fee payments that far exceed anything currently contemplated under NAFTA. The ERASMUS initiative is designed to insure that higher education integration keeps pace with economic integration given its central importance to the development of knowledge-based economies (OECD 1996b; Baumgratz-Gangl 1996). If ERASMUS is fully implemented by the EU, 10 percent of the college and university students in each European country will obtain at least part of their higher education in another European country (Lambert 1995, 35).

Within the Asia-Pacific Economic Co-operation (APEC) Forum, Japan has established the goal of increasing foreign student enrolment in its universities from 45,000 in 1991 to 100,000 by the year 2000. With 53,847 foreign students in 2000, Japan fell far short of this goal, but it is drawing more students from China, Korea, and Taiwan, which have been among the largest U.S. markets for foreign students and scholars. Similarly, Australia is actively recruiting Asian students into its universities and successfully increased foreign student enrolments from 16,075 in 1985 to 47,834 in 1995 (Davis 1995, 78, 182; Lambert 1995, 22-23). Thus, Japanese and Australian programs are drawing significant numbers of Asian students into those countries, while the number of Asian students coming to the USA is declining for the first time in two decades.

If the USA expects to retain its dominance in the world higher education export market, it will need to capitalise on the potential advantages of regional economic integration with North and South America. However, Mexico and the European Union ratified a free trade agreement in 2000 and given the EU's aggressive policy of higher education integration and education services exports, such an agreement may divert international students from Mexico to EU countries (e.g., Spain). Other free trade agreements between Mexico and Chile (1991), the G-3 (Columbia and Venezuela, 1995), Bolivia (1995), and Costa Rica (1995) may also aid Mexico in becoming a regional provider of higher education services, because the native language is Spanish (Banco de Mexico 1998, 222).

NORTH AMERICAN HIGHER EDUCATION COOPERATION: U.S. GOVERNMENT INITIATIVES

The U.S. higher education system is a complex and diffuse power structure, where policy is formed and implemented by a combination of fifty state governments, major public and private universities, higher education associations (administrators), disciplinary and professional associations (faculty), labour unions (faculty and staff), accreditation agencies, non-profit foundations, and a plethora of federal grants programs, among others. Thus, the federal government that negotiated the North American Free Trade Agreement (NAFTA) has little direct capacity to control policies in the field of higher education or professional services. The federal role in U.S. higher education has been aptly described as one of "government by influence" (Brown 1909). The U.S. federal government has the capacity to influence higher education policy, but not control it, mainly by acting as an information clearinghouse, by providing narrowly targeted financial inducements (i.e., seed money), and by providing political leadership in forging partnerships among the numerous subnational governments, non-governmental organisations, and higher education institutions that actually make decisions about higher education policy in the USA. These activities allow the federal government to promote a national agenda through co-operation with non-governmental organisations, rather than by direct federal intervention in higher education. The U.S. Government's effort to promote stronger higher education linkages between the USA, Mexico, and Canada in response to NAFTA is continuing to follow this well-established strategy.

The Vancouver Communiqué foresaw a network of trilateral arrangements linking U.S., Mexican, and Canadian higher education institutions, but it also proposes an overlapping web of trilateral partnerships between national governments, higher education institutions, and private businesses. The U.S. Government's most important trilateral initiatives in higher education are explicitly designed to implement both meanings of trilateral co-operation. Many of the U.S. Government's programs in international higher education are funded through the U.S. State Department and the U.S. Agency for International Development, since these programs are viewed primarily as instruments of U.S. foreign policy (USAID 1999c, 1).

There have been three phases of international student mobility in the USA since the end of World War II. The first phase (1946-1964) was defined by the preoccupation of the world's two superpowers with preventing the recurrence of Nazism and Fascism in Europe. Thus, the major student flows were from Eastern Europe to the Soviet Union and from Western Europe to the USA. The United States Government actively promoted academic mobility during this phase of its foreign policy with the establishment of the Fulbright Program in 1946 (Brubacher and Rudy 1997, 233-35). The Fulbright Program was established to facilitate academic exchange and research by graduate students and scholars. However, the passage of the National Defence Education Act in 1958 provided the first federal financial support for U.S. students to study in foreign countries, to learn foreign languages, and to support the expansion of area studies programs, particularly those that supported the USA's Cold War foreign policy. In the 1960s, Fulbright scholarships and U.S. Agency for International Development (USAID) grants substantially increased the funding available for U.S. faculty and students conducting research in foreign countries and for bringing foreign scholars and students to the USA (Brubacher and Rudy 1997, 440).

These programs were carried forward into a second phase of international student and faculty mobility, when the programs were expanded and realigned to focus on the problems of de-colonisation and the growing political competition between the USA and the Soviet Union for allies among the non-aligned and developing nations (1964-1981). This phase of international academic mobility resulted in a significant flow of students and faculty from the developing to the advanced industrial countries and direct government funding was important to financing this flow of students and faculty (Skilbeck and Connell 1996, 75-76). During the Cold War, it was in the direct political interests of the United States Government to fund international exchange programs. These programs were designed to enhance U.S. capabilities for diplomacy, foreign policy-making, and intelligence gathering and to showcase American-style democratic capitalism to the future elites of less developed and non-aligned countries (Davis 1996, iii; Rudy 1991).

Since the early 1980s, however, the U.S. Government's interest in international higher education has shifted from the problems of superpower diplomatic and political competition to the challenges of global economic competition (Barrow 1996, 1999). In particular, the U.S. Government has declared interests in developing potential export markets for U.S. companies and developing a professional and technical workforce with the multi-cultural skills necessary for U.S. companies to compete in a global economy (SCANS 1991, 1992; Office of the U.S. President 1997, 21). At the same time, however, the instability of public sector higher education budgets, when coupled to the deficit reduction strategies of federal and state governments, has resulted in an explicit policy to shift the costs of academic mobility from government agencies to private businesses, individuals, and higher education institutions.

The United States Agency for International Development

The U.S. Agency for International Development was created in 1961 under President John F. Kennedy to assist developing countries with economic and social development. The Agency's mission is:

> "...to contribute to U.S. national interests by supporting the people of developing and transitional countries in their efforts to achieve enduring economic and social progress and to participate more fully in resolving the problems of their countries and the world" (USAID 1999, iii).

In FY 1999, USAID's total annual budget was approximately $7.2 billion – less than 0.5 percent of the total federal budget – and only $10.4 million of this amount is allocated to development assistance, economic support, and public health in Mexico (USAID 1999d, 1; 1999e, 1). USAID currently administers programs in more than 100 countries world-wide with an emphasis on bi-lateral actions between the USA and developing countries (USAID 1999a, iv). USAID deploys its program resources toward achieving six strategic objectives:

1. Economic Growth and Agricultural Development,[16]
2. Strengthening Democracy and Good Governance,
3. Human Capacity Development through education and job training,
4. Stabilisation of world Population and the improvement of Public Health and Nutrition,
5. Protecting the world Environment for long-term Sustainability.
6. Saving Lives, Reducing Suffering, and Re-establishing Conditions for Political and Economic Development (USAID 1999e for a discussion of these goals).

These goals are explicitly linked to U.S. national interests to the extent that "economic growth around the world also benefits the U.S. economy directly" (USAID 1999a, 1). U.S. exports to developing countries increased at a rate of 13 percent per year from 1987 to 1997, which exceeded the 9 percent rate of growth in U.S. exports to other industrialised nations. Thus, USAID's programs are guided by the principle that "economic performance in developing countries has a large and growing impact on the U.S. economy. Promoting it is in the U.S. national interest" (USAID 1999a, 1).

In 1997, USAID had 145 programs supporting broad-based economic growth and agricultural development in 76 operating units (countries, regional offices, and central bureaus), which accounted for 29 percent of all USAID programming (approximately $2.3 billion). Of these programs, 67 were in developing countries, 68 were in countries making the transition from communism, and another 10 programs were globally oriented. The most common objective of the programs is to promote economic growth by strengthening critical private markets. This was an objective for 78 percent of USAID's economic growth programs. Agricultural development is a second major objective being pursued in 60 percent of USAID's operating units. In Latin America, including Mexico, the main focus of USAID programming is also to strengthen critical private markets with agricultural development a secondary objective. The common focus of economic growth and agricultural development programs in Latin America is to facilitate the integration of Latin American economies, including their agricultural sectors, into the global economy (USAID 1999a, 3-4).

In pursuing these objectives, USAID has increasingly recognised that:

"The skills and capabilities of a nation's people are key factors in maintaining economic, social and political development. Higher education is essential to build human capital and to sustain all aspects of technological, scientific, social, cultural and economic development. A mutually responsive and supportive partnership between USAID and the U.S. higher education community is vital to broad global development objectives" (USAID 1999b).

Consequently, in 1992, USAID negotiated the Higher Education Community Partnership agreement with the American Council on Education, the American

Association of Community Colleges, the American Association of State Colleges and Universities, the Association of American Universities, the National Association of Independent Colleges and Universities, and the National Association of State Universities and Land-Grant Colleges. The purpose of the agreement was to co-ordinate the international development activities of U.S. colleges and universities with development initiatives sponsored by USAID. The six agencies established the Association Liaison Office for University Co-operation in Development (ALO) as a joint interface with USAID.

In addition to establishing the framework for greater co-operation between USAID and higher education institutions in the USA, the agreement catalysed several "Regional Roundtables" between officials from the two sectors. Partly as a result of these Roundtables, USAID's strategic plan was modified to enhance the role of higher education in its economic growth programs. In July of 1997, for example, "Human Capacity Development" was added to the list of Agency goals. Other actions were taken to increase higher education's involvement in USAID strategic planning at the operating unit level, to facilitate staff exchanges, identify common agendas, and improve communications (ALO and USAID 1997a, 2).

In 1997, the initial co-operative agreement between USAID and the ALO was continued through 2002. The current HEPC agreement seeks to broaden the involvement of U.S. higher education institutions in global development by mobilising and reallocating institutional resources for this purpose. Federal seed money is provided as an incentive for higher education institutions to participate in new initiatives and pilot projects. The Higher Education Community Partnership seeks greater co-ordination of existing higher education programs in global development, the mobilisation and reallocation of institutional resources, involvement of higher education in USAID program development, and the strengthening of higher education institutions in developing countries to support sustainable development. A key component in achieving the latter goal is USAID's active promotion of linkages between U.S. higher education institutions and foreign higher institutions. This facilitates a targeted linking of resources from USAID, foreign governments, and higher education institutions in bi-lateral partnerships. The main types of linkage are academic exchange (faculty and students), collaborative research, instruction and training, seminars and conferences, curriculum development, and technical assistance.

A central element of USAID's Higher Education Community Partnership is its emphasis on cost-sharing. USAID encourages cost-sharing and requires financial participation from partner institutions as a mechanism for mobilising and reallocating existing higher education resources toward its global development objectives. USAID typically provides 75 percent of program cost, while the partner institutions share 25 percent of the cost. The government's financial contribution is considered "seed money" and, consequently, higher education institutions are expected to institutionalise collaborative projects by "keeping in mind the immediate needs of the private sector" so that private partners will be interested in supporting the initiatives over the long-term (ALO and USAID 1997, 9).

The ALO currently administers four initiatives under the USAID Higher Education Community Partnership (AASCU 1999b). These initiatives are the:

1. Institutional Partnerships in Higher Education for International Development (IPHE). The IPHE program is aimed at linking the technical and human capacity-building strengths of U.S. and foreign higher institutions with USAID's strategic objectives.
2. Workforce Training Program (WTP). The WTP is a partnership with the American Association of Community Colleges, which supports pilot partnerships to build workforce capacity in developing countries in areas such as environmental management, wastewater treatment, etc.
3. Policy Roundtables. The Policy Roundtable Series on Higher Education and Global Development brings USAID staff together with representatives from higher education to discuss areas of mutual co-operation.
4. Co-operative Partnerships. The ALO is promoting "development co-operation networks" among U.S. states and cities, higher education institutions, business and industry partners to create regional development networks in various parts of the world.

The USAID Higher Education Community Partnership is a world-wide, globally oriented program, but beginning in 1995 USAID funded six pilot projects that specifically paired U.S. and Mexican higher education institutions.[17] The six partnerships each received seed grants of less than $15,400. The objective of the pilot projects was "to further the goal of economic integration through regional higher education co-operation" (ALO and USAID 1997, 1, 6). The pilot projects were designed to "enhance the institutions' contribution to economic and social development through collaboration with business and industry on sector-specific topics" (ALO and USAID 1997, 1-2) and to thereby leverage modest governmental support to attract additional resources from foundations and corporations (De la Garza et al. 1997). After two years, USAID declared several of the pilot projects "success stories in human capital development, institution building, and technology generation" (ALO and USAID 1997, 3).

The successful pilot projects led to an expansion of the USAID/ALO Institutional Partnerships in Higher Education for International Development program. The IPHE program objective is to mobilise higher education resources in the USA and developing countries to:

1. Strengthen higher institutional capacities for teaching, research, and service that address global development priorities and that address development problems collaboratively;
2. To contribute to the preparation of a responsible citizenry and a proficient work force engaged in a global marketplace; and,
3. To increase the attention to and understanding of international education and development issues on campuses and among the institutions' constituencies (AASCU 1999d).

USAID's mission is oriented mainly towards projects in less developed and transitional countries so it is no surprise that the Agency's North American linkage programs are concentrated more in Mexico than in Canada. The USAID/ALO partnership has resulted in U.S. higher education institutions establishing approximately 140 linkages with Mexican higher education institutions since 1995 and 23 linkages with Canadian higher education institutions.[18] About 50 percent of the linkages to Mexico, and 65 percent of the linkages to Canada, involve faculty and student educational exchange programs. The establishment of collaborative research projects accounts for another quarter (24%) of the linkages to Mexican higher education institutions and less than a fifth (17%) of the linkages to Canadian higher education institutions. In both countries, the main purpose of the linkage projects is human capacity development – 50 percent in Mexico and 81 percent in Canada – although economic growth (18%) and agricultural development (17%) projects are also being implemented in Mexico. Most of the linkage arrangements established through USAID programs emphasise academic exchange and collaborative research in the fields of engineering, business, agriculture, public health, and nutrition (see Table 8).

USAID's higher education partnership network has linked 46 U.S. colleges and universities, 70 Mexican universities and research institutes, and 17 Canadian higher institutions into an overlapping web of bi-lateral partnerships. The depth, penetration, and impact of these partnerships is certainly much greater in Mexico, where a large percentage of colleges and universities are participating in the programs as compared to the USA, which has more than 4,100 higher education institutions. The most active Mexican higher education institutions are the Monterrey Institute for Higher Technological Studies (ITESM), the University of Guadalajara, the Autonomous National University (UNAM), and the Autonomous Universities of Nuevo Leon, Guadalajara, and Sonora. The most active U.S. higher education institutions are New Mexico State University, Texas A&M University, the University of California at Davis, the University of Missouri – St. Louis, the University of Illinois – Urbana/Champaign, the University of Idaho, the University of Nebraska – Lincoln, the University of Southern Florida, and Michigan State University; nearly all of them located in states with a large Mexican-American and Mexican immigrant population (see Appendix D).

United States Bureau for Educational and Cultural Affairs

The Fulbright Program is still the USA's flagship educational exchange program. Until recently, the Fulbright Program was administered by the United States Information Agency (located within the U.S. State Department), with assistance from the Council for International Exchange of Scholars (CIES), a private non-profit organisation (CIES 1999a) and an affiliate of the Institute of International Education.[19] The Fulbright Program has a global focus and operates in 135 countries world-wide. It is funded with an annual appropriation from the U.S. Congress, although foreign governments and private organisations contribute to the program through direct support and indirect cost sharing. Non-government and foreign government contributions account for approximately one-quarter of the program's total annual expenditures.

Table 8. Summary of USAID Institutional Higher Education Linkage Project.

Type of Linkage	Mexico	Percent	Canada	Percent
Academic Exchange	70	50%	15	65%
Instruct/Training	10	7%	2	9%
Curriculum Development	2	1%	0	0%
Collaborative Research	33	24%	4	17%
Seminars/Conferences	3	2%	0	0%
Technical Assistance	1	1%	0	0%
GCA/MOU	21	15%	2	9%
Total	140	100%	23	100%
Purpose of Project				
Agricultural Development	20	15%	0	0%
Economic Growth	23	18%	2	13%
Environment	13	10%	1	6%
Human Capacity Development	65	50%	13	81%
Pop./Health/Nutrition	8	6%	0	0%
Democracy	1	1%	0	0%
Total	130	100%	16	100%

Source: Tabulated from data in American Association of State Colleges and Universities (1999c, 1999d), accessed on October 15, 1999.

Since 1946, approximately 220,000 Fulbright awards have been funded by the program with 82,000 awards to U.S. students and scholars travelling abroad and 138,000 awards to students and scholars coming to the USA from abroad. The program currently awards about 4,200 new grants each year (U.S. Department of State 1999a).

The Fulbright Program actually consists of seven different programs:

1. The American Scholar Program sends nearly 700 scholars and professionals each year to more than 100 countries world-wide where they lecture or conduct original research in those countries.
2. The Visiting Scholar Program awards grants to foreign scholars to come to the United States to lecture or conduct postdoctoral research.
3. The Pre-Doctoral Fellowships provides full or partial support to nearly 800 U.S. undergraduate seniors and pre-doctoral graduate students to study abroad

each year, while approximately 1,400 awards annually are made to foreign students for study in the United States. The Fulbright Teacher Exchange Program facilitates one-on-one exchanges between elementary, secondary, and post-secondary teachers involving about 200 persons each year.
4. The Hubert Humphrey Fellowship Program was established in 1979 to bring successful mid-career professionals from developing countries to the United States for a year of study and professional experience.
5. The College and University Affiliations Program facilitates linkages between U.S. and foreign universities through the exchange of faculty and staff. The Program funds approximately 17 institutional grants each year (350 over the lifetime of the program to date) to initiate linkages, particularly in the social sciences, humanities, arts, and business administration. In the first year of funding, four affiliations were funded to link four U.S. higher education institutions with 14 Canadian and Mexican higher education institutions through a network of faculty exchanges (WICHE 1994, 11).
6. The Fulbright-Hays Foreign Area and Language Training Program, funded at $6.3 million annually (FY 1999), is administered by the U.S. Department of Education's Centre for International Education to conduct doctoral research in foreign languages and area studies, faculty research in foreign languages and area studies, curriculum development, and seminars abroad. The program funds approximately 114 fellowships per year world-wide and supports nearly 600 persons who participate in seminars abroad. Since 1990, one seminar has been held in Mexico each summer, although DOE is planning a trilateral seminar with participants spending time in both Canada and Mexico (WICHE 1994, 10-11).
7. The Bi-national Business Grants are "designed to enhance the knowledge, expertise and understanding of post-NAFTA Mexico for U.S. graduates of business, law and engineering programs." The new BBG program funded 15 grants for AY 2000-2001.

A bi-national Fulbright Commission oversees the administration of the program in each country. Many of the commissions were reorganised by the Bush Administration in 1991 as public-private partnerships. The purpose of this change was to involve private business directly in defining the program's new economic mission and to shift some of the funding from government to private sector beneficiaries of the program. While the restructuring of the Fulbright Commissions represents a general shift in government philosophy, NAFTA was certainly a key stimulus to creating the Mexico-U.S. Commission for Educational and Cultural Exchange, which now serves as the Mexico-US Fulbright Commission. When it was established in early 1991, the Mexico-U.S. Commission was charged with promoting a rapid increase in the level of scholarly exchange between the two countries. However, Stanley Katz, President of the American Council of Learned Societies, has expressed doubts about "whether this goal is realistic" given the limited financial resources allocated to the Mexico-U.S. Commission (Katz 1996, 233). The Mexico-U.S. Commission received an initial annual budget of $3.3 million ($2.3 million from the

United States and $1 million from Mexico).[20] In contrast, the budget for the European Union's ERASMUS program for 1990-1992 was approximately $192 million (Lambert 1995, 35).

The Foundation for Educational Exchange for the United States and Canada was also established in 1991 to operate the Fulbright exchange programs and to attract new private funding for Canadian-U.S. educational exchange programs. At present, about 50 percent of the Foundation's funding comes from the U.S. and Canadian governments, 17 percent from private foundations, and 33 percent from corporate donations (Katz 1996, 233). The public-private partnership arrangement has not increased exchange funding substantially, but has been used to shift the cost from public to private sector beneficiaries. Thus, the new partnerships have made it possible to sustain programs and to refocus their mission, but it has not led to their expansion in any significant way.

In Academic Year 2000-2001, for instance, the Fulbright Visiting Scholar Program offered 6 awards for U.S. scholars to teach or conduct research in Canada and 23 awards for travel to Mexico.[21] This is a marginal increase from pre-NAFTA levels when 5 to 6 U.S. citizens were funded each year for teaching and research in Canada and approximately 20 awards were funded annually for teaching and research in Mexico (CONAHEC 1999b). In AY 2000-2001, the Fulbright Program also funded 25 Fulbright/Garcia Robles Grants for American graduate students to study at Mexican universities and 22 grants for graduate student research and study in Canada (IIE 1999c).[22] However, the Fulbright Program receives from 100 to 165 applications per year for study in Mexico and from 65 to 85 applications for study in Canada (IIE 1999d). These numbers may reflect that many applications are not worthy of funding or it may represent an unfunded interest in trilateral educational exchange opportunities among U.S. students and scholars.

At the present time, the U.S.-Mexico Commission and the Mexican Council for Science and Technology (CONACYT) are collaborating to increase the number of Mexican graduate students in the USA by providing up to 300 new scholarships each year for five years (Salazar 1996, 239). The United States government provided direct support to only 13 percent of Mexican graduate students in the USA with the rest being dependent for funding on the Mexican Council for Science and Technology (CONACYT). Similarly, about half of the Mexican undergraduates attending U.S. higher education institutions receive no financial support and depend mainly on family and personal income. Host institutions provide financial assistance to about 25 percent of the Mexican undergraduates studying in the USA, while the Mexican and U.S. governments provide financial assistance to the remaining 25 percent of Mexican undergraduates in the USA (Ibid., 239). The vast majority of U.S. students studying in Canada and Mexico depend on personal financial resources or limited institutional support for educational exchange activities.

The USIA facilitates this private academic mobility through a support network of more than 450 educational advising centres world-wide. These centres provide information to foreign nationals about opportunities for study in the USA (IIE 1999b). The USIA has one Educational Advising Centre in Mexico City, which was established in 1974 and is administered by the Institute of International Education (IIE 1999a). USIA also facilitates the exchange of information about educational exchange opportunities through financial support for NACHE-Net (North American Co-operation in Higher Education). NACHE-Net is a list-serve that announces North American academic conferences, exchange opportunities, and fellowships. It is administered by the IIE and had 250 subscribers in 1996 (CONAHEC 1999b).

North American Higher Education Mobility Program

The Program for North American Higher Education Mobility (NAHEM) was an initiative of the USIA, the Canadian Department of Human Resource Development, and Mexico's Director General of Higher Education. The NAHEM program was launched in 1993 as a direct response to the Wingspread Statement. From 1993 to 1995, the program funded six trilateral activities in the areas of North American curriculum development and environmental protection (Craven 1996). Beginning in 1995, the program funded 11 consortiums for a three-year period ($120,000 each) and committed $1.3 million for the entire program. The program initially emphasised academic and work exchanges in architecture, engineering, health, law, and technology, although the program has included additional fields in the second round of proposals. It currently involves 24 U.S. higher education institutions in tri-lateral collaboratives with 13 Mexican higher education institutions and 18 Canadian universities. By and large, the institutions participating in the 11 tri-lateral partnerships are the same institutions involved in many of the USAID projects. Consequently, these activities often facilitate a deepening (rather than an expansion) of North American collaboration at U.S. colleges and universities, where such initiatives have already been identified as an institutional priority.

United States Department of Education

The U.S. Department of Education also sponsors several globally oriented initiatives through the Office of Post-secondary Education. The role of the Department of Education is mainly to assure equal educational opportunity for U.S. citizens by providing financial aid to individuals and to supplement the efforts of the 50 states, the private sector, and non-profit foundations. The USDOE funds improvements to the international education curriculum of U.S. colleges and universities, particularly in foreign languages, area studies, and international studies. The USDOE's programs support comprehensive language and area study centres within the United States, research and curriculum development, and opportunities for American scholars and students to study abroad. In addition to promoting the general understanding of other countries and cultures, the Department's international programs also serve the economic, diplomatic, defence, and security interests of the USA (USDOE 1999a).

The U.S. DOE's strategic policy objectives now include enhanced student mobility and preparing students for work in new international contexts. The DOE funds projects that promote mutual recognition and portability of credits, tuition reciprocity, and the development of joint curricula between the USA and EU countries and between the USA and its NAFTA partners.[23] The U.S. DOE currently spends $65.5 million annually to support programs in international higher education, which provide grants to more than 400 institutions of higher education and supports more than 900 individuals though fellowships and projects. The USDOE, mainly through the Fund for the Improvement of Post-secondary Education (FIPSE), supports eight programs with NAFTA-relevant components (USDOE 1999a, 1999b).

NON-GOVERNMENTAL INITIATIVES

Institute of International Education

The Institute of International Education (IIE) is a private non-profit organisation based in New York City. IIE administers over 250 programs under co-operative agreements with the U.S. Information Agency, the U.S. Agency for International Development, private foundations, corporations, international organisations, and foreign development assistance agencies (IIE 1999e). It operates the USIA's Educational Advising Centre in Mexico City and it administers a number of programs to facilitate trilateral and bilateral education exchange with the USA's NAFTA partners.[24]

IIE's most significant trilateral initiative has been the North American Regional Academic Mobility Program (RAMP). RAMP is an academic exchange program between Canada, Mexico, and the USA designed to foster academic and professional mobility in the fields of engineering, business, and environmental studies (Salazar 1996, 240). RAMP was an informal consortium of Canadian, Mexican, and U.S. universities administered and co-ordinated by the IIE that currently includes 47 North American universities (18 in Canada, 16 in Mexico, and 13 in the United States). Although the program is focused on promoting academic mobility in engineering and business, students are required to take language and cultural coursework "as an essential part of their preparation for career opportunities in the North American Free Trade Zone" (IIE 1999e). For the most part, a different cluster of U.S. campuses participate in RAMP than in the USAID funded partnerships.

RAMP was implemented in 1992 under a grant from the U.S. Department of Education's Fund for the Improvement of Post-secondary Education (FIPSE) with cost-sharing by the IIE and participating universities. Cost-sharing is funded through "tuition swaps" where students pay tuition to their home campuses, rather than the host university and receive credit at their home institution for courses taken abroad. Students must pay all personal, transportation, and living expenses unless they receive financial assistance from their home campus. Beginning in 1993, the Mexican Ministry of Education set aside $100,000 annually for the participation of needy Mexican students seeking to study in the USA and Canada. By 1996, approximately 200 students had participated in RAMP, but only 11 percent of the participants were from the USA. There has been very little interest in the program among U.S. students, which resulted in many of the original U.S. partners withdrawing from the program. The program is now defunct after giving way to the North American Higher Education Mobility Program.

Direct Exchange Relationships

There is an apparent tendency for more and more institutions to negotiate general cooperative or exchange agreements directly with each other as part of their efforts to internationalise curriculum (National Task Force 1990). These exchange agreements sometimes include provisions for tuition swaps, which allow students to pay tuition to their home institution and to receive credit for coursework completed at the host institution. For faculty exchanges, the arrangements frequently require the home institution to pay a faculty members' salary while teaching abroad. However, this means that most of the cost of these exchanges are borne by the individuals or institutions involved in the exchange arrangements.

Most exchange agreements negotiated by U.S. higher education institutions are bi-lateral in structure, although a few universities are moving toward trilateral approaches to collaboration since NAFTA. Western Kentucky University provides an instructive example of how a web of bi-lateral agreements can evolve into a trilateral agreement. Western Kentucky University had established a bilateral exchange agreement with Trent University in Canada, while Trent University had also established a bilateral exchange agreement with the Autonomous University of Chapingo. Consequently, as the nexus in a trilateral web, Trent University initiated the request to negotiate an expanded and explicit trilateral agreement between the three institutions to include collaborative research, curriculum development, faculty and student exchange. The trilateral agreement is negotiated on a three-year cycle as it continues to evolve over time (Sanchez et al 1996, 267-69).

A larger consortium – the North American Studies Exchange Program – was established recently among 2 institutions in Canada, 2 in the USA, and 2 in Mexico. The participating institutions include York University, the University of Montreal, Duke University, Northwestern University, Universidad de las Americas – Puebla, and the Centro de Investigacion y Docencia Economicas (CIDE) (York University 1999). Not coincidentally, Duke University is the first U.S. higher education institution to establish a North American Studies Program (Center for North American Studies 2000).

Another innovative development in international higher education exchange is the emergence of "work abroad" programs to supplement internships and study abroad programs. Texas A&M University has established a trilateral Corporate Alliance composed of Canadian, U.S., and Mexican companies. Each company in the Alliance sets aside a paid summer internship for a university student from one of the other NAFTA partner countries. U.S. students, for example, are placed in paid summer internships in Canada or Mexico, while Canadian and Mexican students are given opportunities for internships in the United States (Sanchez et al 1996, 263-64). On a wider front, the Council on International Education Exchange (CIEE) now administers an increasing number of work abroad programs with one of the most recent additions being a "Work in Canada" program. The CIEE work abroad program is sponsored by the Canadian Federation of Student Services, which provides support services and an arrival orientation for foreign students coming to Canada (CIEE 1999).

TOWARD AN INTERNATIONAL HIGHER EDUCATION POLICY

The National Association of Foreign Student Advisors (NAFSA) has recently emerged as the leading higher education association promoting the expansion of international higher education policy at the federal level. The basic premise of NAFSA's policy position is that the USA mistakenly scaled back its commitment to international higher education with the end of Cold War. Despite recent initiatives by the Agency for International Development, the U.S. State Department, and the U.S. Department of Education, NAFSA argues that "the United States effectively lacks a coherent, co-ordinated, operational policy for educating its citizens internationally" (NAFSA 2000a). To rectify this situation, NAFSA proposed an international higher education policy for the USA that includes the promotion of foreign-language learning, the study of other nations' cultures, increased study abroad by U.S. students, recapturing the USA's declining share of the international higher education market, facilitating more exchanges between scholars, and financial support for the educational infrastructure required to produce international competencies and research.

As a first step toward closing the gap between the rhetoric and reality of international higher education, the National Association of Foreign Student Advisers entered into a strategic planning process in 1999 that included the Alliance for International Educational and Cultural Exchange, the Academy for Educational Development, and the Institute of International Education. A major consensus that emerged from this process was that NAFSA should become a strong public advocate for international higher education by mobilising a political coalition behind an international higher education policy in the USA.

NAFSA's proposal for a U.S. international higher education policy includes four major initiatives with quantifiable outcomes to be achieved between 2010 and 2040 (NAFSA 2000a):

1. International, Foreign Language, and Area Expertise:
   a. Set an objective that international education become an integral component of U.S. undergraduate education, with every college graduate achieving proficiency in a foreign language and attaining a basic understanding of at least one world area by 2015.
   b. Promote cultural and foreign language study in primary and secondary education so that entering college students will have increased proficiency in these areas.
   c. Through graduate and professional training and research, enhance the nation's capacity to produce the international, regional, international business, and foreign language expertise necessary for U.S. global leadership and security.

d. Encourage international institutional partnerships that will facilitate internationalised curricula, collaborative research, and faculty and student mobility.
2. International Student Recruitment
   a. Set an objective to arrest the decline in the proportion of internationally mobile students who select the United States for study at the post-secondary level and to recapture 40 percent of this market for the USA.
   b. Promote the study of English by international students in the United States, and promote the USA as the best global provider of English training services and materials.
   c. Streamline visas, taxation, and employment policies and regulations to facilitate entry into the USA for bona fide short-term and degree students and to enable these students to maximise their exposure to American society and culture through internships and employment (work abroad).
3. Study Abroad
   a. Set an objective that 20 percent of American students receiving college degrees will have studied abroad for credit by 2010 and 50 percent by 2040.
   b. Promote ethnic, socio-economic, and gender diversity in study abroad.
   c. Promote the diversification of the study abroad experience, including increased study in non-traditional locations outside the United Kingdom and Western Europe; increased study of major world languages – such as Arabic, Chinese, Japanese, Portuguese, and Russian – that are less commonly learned by Americans; and increased study of under-represented subjects such as mathematical and physical sciences and business.
   d. Promote the integration of study abroad into the higher education curriculum and increase opportunities for international internships and service learning.
4. Exchanges of Citizens and Scholars
   a. Invigorate federal programs and reform regulations governing private efforts in order to promote citizen, professional, and other exchanges that bring future leaders from around the world to the United States for substantive exposure to our society and that give future American leaders opportunities for similar experiences overseas.
   b. Promote the international exchange of scholars in order to enhance the global literacy of U.S. scholars , ensure that the USA builds relationships with the best scholarly talent from abroad, and strengthen the international content of American curricula.

The proposed policy is not a radical departure from current practice, although it sets very ambitious goals given the current rates of study abroad, foreign language registrations, and growing competition for international students in the global higher education market. A further paradox, of course, is that the implementation of most of NAFSA's recommendations depend on thousands of separate decisions by boards of trustees (funding), higher education administrators (programs), individual faculty members (curriculum), business executives (internships and work abroad), and various government agencies. The federal government has little capacity to force program development or the expansion of international higher education except through limited financial inducements. Hence, NAFSA's proposed policy recognises that "the federal government cannot do it all. Colleges and universities, state governments, and the business community (which will be the primary beneficiary of a globally literate workforce) all need to accept their responsibilities and increase their support for international education" (NAFSA 2000a). In this respect, NAFSA's proposal accepts the neo-liberal framework established during the last decade and seeks to strengthen or expand programs within that framework, while recognising that a significant portion of the funding for international higher education initiatives will have to come from non-federal sources.

However, Marlene M. Johnson, NAFSA's president observes that:

> "Without a comprehensive national policy on international education it is difficult for university presidents, governors, business leaders, and other well-meaning leaders to situate within a coherent plan, the international initiatives they may be contemplating. The lack of an overarching policy framework also makes it unnecessarily difficult for those same leaders to justify or defend – sometimes even to their own organisations – actions they know *instinctively* to be important" (NAFSA 1999).

In this respect, NAFSA's proposal considers a federal role to be "crucial in setting a policy direction, creating a conceptual understanding within which members of the public can define their roles, and using federal resources to leverage action at other levels" (NAFSA 2000a). Consequently, NAFSA's proposal calls on the federal government to:

1. Clearly articulate the national interest in international higher education and set a strong policy direction to which citizens can relate their own efforts,
2. Dedicate federal resources that are appropriate for the national interests served, and
3. Stimulate involvement by, and leverage funding from, the states and the higher education, business, and charitable communities.

Shortly after its completion in November of 1999, the proposed policy was circulated to various federal departments, such as State, Commerce, and Education, and to the various Presidential campaign organisations. In a statement on the proposed policy before the Council for International Educational Exchange, Ms. Johnson announced that "our ultimate goal is not a federal appropriation, but rather a framework within which leaders at the national, state, municipal, and community level, as well as educational institutions and companies, can situate, justify, and defend their efforts" (NAFSA 2000f). After a successful lobbying campaign, President Clinton embraced NAFSA's proposal in an "Executive Memorandum on International Education" issued to the heads of executive departments and agencies on April 19, 2000 (NAFSA 2000b). The Executive Memorandum declares that:

"To continue to compete successfully in the global economy and to maintain our role as a world leader, the United States needs to ensure that its citizens develop a broad understanding of the world, proficiency in other languages, and knowledge of other cultures....A coherent and co-ordinated international education strategy will help us meet the twin challenges of preparing our citizens for a global environment while continuing to attract and educate future leaders from abroad....It is the policy of the Federal Government to support international education" (NAFSA 2000c).

President Clinton directed the heads of executive departments and agencies, working in partnership with the private sector, to take the following actions:

1. The Secretaries of State and Education shall support the efforts of schools and colleges to improve access to high- quality international educational experiences by increasing the number and diversity of students who study and intern abroad, encouraging students and institutions to choose non-traditional study-abroad locations, and helping under-represented U.S. institutions offer and promote study-abroad opportunities for their students.
2. The Secretaries of State and Education, in partnership with other governmental and non-governmental organisations, shall identify steps to attract qualified post-secondary students from overseas to the United States, including improving the availability of accurate information overseas about U.S. educational opportunities.
3. The heads of agencies, including the Secretaries of State and Education, and others as appropriate, shall review the effect of U.S. Government actions on the international flow of students and scholars as well as on citizen and professional exchanges, and take steps to address unnecessary obstacles, including those involving visa and tax regulations, procedures, and policies.
4. The Secretaries of State and Education shall support the efforts of State and local governments and educational institutions to promote international awareness and skills in the classroom and on campuses. Such efforts include strengthening foreign language learning at all levels, including efforts to achieve bi-literacy, helping teachers acquire the skills needed to understand and interpret other countries and cultures for their students, increasing opportunities for the exchange of faculty, administrators, and students, and assisting educational institutions in other countries to strengthen their teaching of English.
5. The Secretaries of State and Education and the heads of other agencies shall take steps to ensure that international educational exchange programs, including the Fulbright program, are co-ordinated through the Interagency Working Group on United States Government-Sponsored International Exchange and Training, to maximise existing resources in a non-duplicative way, and to ensure that the exchange programs receive the support they need to fulfil their mission of increased mutual understanding.
6. The Secretary of Education, in co-operation with other agencies, shall continue to support efforts to improve U.S. education by developing comparative informa-

tion, including benchmarks, on educational performance and practices. The Secretary of Education shall also share U.S. educational expertise with other countries.
7. The Secretaries of State and Education shall strengthen and expand models of international exchange that build lasting cross-national partnerships among educational institutions with common interests and complementary objectives.
8. The Secretary of Education and the heads of other agencies, in partnership with State governments, academic institutions, and the business community, shall strengthen programs that build international expertise in U.S. institutions, with the goal of making international education an integral component of U.S. under graduate education and, through graduate and professional training and research, enhancing the Nation's capacity to produce the international and foreign-language expertise necessary for U.S. global leadership and security.
9. The Secretaries of State and Education, in co-operation with other agencies, the academic community, and the private sector, shall promote wise use of technology internationally, examining the implications of borderless education. The heads of agencies shall take steps to ensure that the opportunities for using technology to expand international education do not result in a widening of the digital divide.
10. The Secretaries of State and Education, in conjunction with other agencies, shall ensure that actions taken in response to this memorandum are fully integrated into the Government Performance and Results Act (GPRA) framework by means of specific goals, milestones, and measurable results, which shall be included in all GPRA reporting activities, including strategic plans, performance plans, and program performance reports (NAFSA 2000c).

Despite the significance of Clinton's memorandum as a statement of national policy, it also cautions that action items contained in the memorandum "shall be conducted subject to the availability of appropriations." The memorandum does not promise any additional funding for international higher education, but in fact warns proponents that: "the Federal Government cannot accomplish these goals alone. Educational institutions, State and local governments, non-governmental organisations, and the business community all must contribute to this effort" (NAFSA 2000c).

In response, Johnson notes that since the International Education Act was passed by Congress (but never funded) in 1966, the "proponents of international education programs have never succeeded in moving our concerns high enough up on the list of national priorities to obtain significant funding." Thus, in a major departure from past practice, NAFSA urged Congress to increase appropriations for international educational and cultural exchanges to $250 million in the Fiscal Year 2001 budget. This amount would have restored the exchange programs to their funding levels before the deep budget cuts of the mid-1990s and allowed the government to implement the commitments made in Clinton's memorandum, including the maintenance of overseas advising centres, an expansion of the Fulbright-Hays Program, and rebuilding cultural, professional, and citizen exchange programs (NAFSA 2000d).

Despite the bold rhetoric on international higher education, and the flurry of activities involving North American higher education co-operation, the fundamental reality of U.S. higher education is that it still faces an era of fiscal constraint, which will likely continue for the foreseeable future. The continuing emphasis in strategic plans on program reductions and selective excellence makes it virtually impossible to add or expand international programs unless such programs are woven into the very fabric of existing curricula and identified in campus missions as a core area of selective excellence. It is unlikely that most institutions will make significant funds available to faculty for professional development, international exchange, or trilateral research. Indeed, NAFTA's impact on U.S. higher education outside the borderlands has been so minimal that most faculty and administrators are still unaware that NAFTA contains any provisions on higher education or that the U.S. Government was a major participant in the Wingspread Statement and the Vancouver Communiqué. Thus, it is likely that the internationalisation strategies of U.S. higher education institutions will continue to be narrowly focused market-based initiatives designed to generate revenue, rather than organised by a national policy with any deep commitment to the ideals of North American regionalism or global community.

CHAPTER 4

GLOBALISATION, NAFTA, AND HIGHER EDUCATION IN CANADA

INTRODUCTION

The purpose of this chapter is to examine issues of globalisation and trade liberalisation and to analyse their effects on higher education policy and practice in Canada. Both issues are subjects of highly contentious debate in Canada and the same can be said of their impact on higher education. Canada is a highly decentralised federation composed of ten provinces and three territories. Constitutionally, higher education is the responsibility of the provinces. However, because of its importance in developing highly-educated individuals, there is also pressure for the federal government to be involved (Watts 1992). There are two main systems of higher education in Canada: the community college system and the university system. All universities, with the exception of one or two denominational universities, are publicly-funded institutions, but enjoy institutional autonomy (Cameron 1992). Community colleges, on the other hand, fall directly under the control of provincial governments.

There are 150 community colleges and 90 universities in Canada. The community colleges offer three-year technical programs and two-year pre-university and university transfer programs, while bachelor and first degree professional programs in the universities are usually three years in length. Masters degrees frequently call for one or two years of study and doctoral degrees a further two or three years. Teaching is a graduate profession and teacher education programs are offered by Faculties of Education in the universities.

The approach adopted in the following pages consists of a general review of related literature, governmental documents, briefs prepared by higher education associations, institutional surveys, press reports,s and commentaries. Published research on the impact of globalisation and trade liberalisation on Canadian higher education is thin on the ground. The same is true of efforts to internationalise the colleges and universities. Case studies do not exist and, as a consequence, the chapter tends to emphasise debates over policy rather than detailed accounts of current practice.

The organisation of the chapter is straightforward. First, there is a brief introduction. Attention is then drawn to the highly contentious nature of the political-economic debates over globalisation and trade liberalisation in Canada. This is followed by reference to the influence of the paradigm that dominated policy discussions of higher education and led to major reductions to its core funding. Next, consideration is given to the various approaches adopted towards the internationalisation of Canadian higher education—major institutional responses to globalisation and trade liberalisation—followed by a detailed examination of stakeholder views and activities. A section on trade liberalisation and international trade in education services comes next, followed by an examination of the significance of the North American Free Trade Agreement (NAFTA) for the professions and higher education. The penultimate section deals with six major challenges that need to be faced and overcome. The final section is devoted to some brief concluding remarks.

GLOBALISATION, TRADE LIBERALISATION, AND HIGHER EDUCATION

Together and independently, globalisation and trade liberalisation have fuelled highly contentious debates, both inside and outside the academic community. At the most general level, the globalisation debates focus on what constitutes its essential nature and effects. Among the more important effects are the development of a global economy, an accelerating rate of technological change, the growth of cross-border strategic research, the increasing influence of transnational corporations, and the intensifying competition for highly skilled and educated personnel (Mallea 1999).

The debate over the emerging global economy has attracted the greatest public attention and controversy. A whole array of academics, journalists, politicians and former politicians have had much to say on the topic. Indeed, the titles and sub-titles of recently published books are themselves illustrative of the range and tone of the debate: *In Search of a New Left: Canadian Politics after the Neo-Conservative Assault* (Laxer 1997); *The Cult of Impotence: Selling the Myth of Powerlessness in the Global Economy* (McQuaig 1998); *MAI: The Multilateral Agreement on Investment and the Threat to Canadian Sovereignty* (Clarke and Barlow 1997); The *Evil Empire: Globalisation's Darker Side* (Hellyer, 1997); *Whose Brave New World? The Information Highway and The New Economy* (Menzies 1996); *Universities for Sale: Resisting Corporate Control over Canadian Higher Education* (Tudiver 1999); and *A New World of Knowledge: Canadian Universities and Globalisation* (Bond and Lemasson 1999).

Trade liberalisation, and more particularly the Canadian-U.S. Free Trade Agreement (CUFTA) and the North American Free Trade Agreement (NAFTA), has also elicited passionate avowals of support and criticism. The debate over CUFTA, for example, constituted the central and most volatile issue in the fiercely contested federal election won by the Progressive Conservatives in 1988. And NAFTA, CUFTA's subsequent extension, via the inclusion of Mexico, was the defining issue in the 1993 federal election campaign.[1]

These trade agreements, their potential expansion southwards, and trade liberalisation in general, continue to spark controversy. For example, supporters of NAFTA argue that in the long run it will improve the country's standard of living and quality of life. Opponents, on the other hand, believe it is having a generally negative effect, particularly on the lives of workers and the poor, and that it threatens Canada's cultural sovereignty. Within the higher education community, supporters argue that the agreement is resulting in more collaborative activities, that students are becoming more mobile, and that trilateral co-operation in research is being fostered and enhanced. Critics, on the other hand, believe it is responsible for the competitive restructuring of institutions and the redirection of funding towards commercially-oriented programs and research. They also believe that priority is being given to programs that foster greater economic integration and provide for the needs of the business sector for an internationally mobile labour force (Calvert and Keuhn 1993). Advocates argue that these changes are necessary responses to increased international competition, the search for greater productivity, the changing nature of work, and the restructuring of the labour market. Opponents, on the other hand, argue that they are eroding core academic values, undermining the importance of basic research, creating overcrowded classrooms, limiting student access to higher education, and creating student debt loads of unprecedented proportions.

Notwithstanding the contentious nature of these debates, the dominant line of argument in Canada has rested on six major premises. First, that geo-political power and influence are increasingly to be found in three major regions of the world: North America, Europe, and Asia. Second, as these regions pursue the search for competitive advantage, a nation's future prosperity will depend upon its ability to compete in the global marketplace. Third, a nation's ability to compete in the global economy depends on its ability to add value to the market. Fourth, accelerated technological change is promoting the growth of more integrated and interdependent economies. Fifth, the world's leading economies are increasingly dependent on knowledge and its applications for their productivity. Sixth, the education of a nation's citizens is its best hope for continued successful economic development.

It is a central paradox therefore that this line of argument did not lead to increased investment in higher education. Instead, it led to a decade or more of disinvestment, which in turn destabilised higher education institutions in Canada to such an extent that more energies were spent on survival than on responsive change and reform. Despite the pervasive rhetoric on the need for more supportive infrastructures in human resource development, science and technology, the fundamental base on which they rest was seriously eroded. This erosion occurred at a time when it was commonplace for Canadian business and political leaders to trumpet the importance of developing an increasingly knowledge-based economy.

In effect, over a decade of federal and provincial disinvestment in higher education has provided the defining context in which Canadian colleges and universities have attempted to come to terms with the twin challenges of globalisation and trade liberalisation. The plain and unvarnished facts are startling. While student enrolments increased, cash transfers decreased. Over the five years between 1987 and 1991, per-student transfers fell by almost 25 per cent. Overall, the Progressive Conservative federal government unilaterally cut Established Programs Financing (EPF)[2] for post-secondary education from $2,199B[3] in 1987-1988 to $1,873B in 1991-1992. The successor federal Liberal government followed up with an additional cut of $1.5B in EPF for post-secondary education in 1994.

Table 9. Federal Contributions for Post-Secondary Education in Canada

Year	Cash Transfers (millions of $)	Full-time Enrolments	Per student Transfer
1987/88	2,199	528,610	4,159
1988/89	2,223	541,930	4,102
1989/90	2,259	555,727	4,064
1990/91	2,126	577,931	3,682
1991/92	1,873	600,908	3,116

Source: Canada, Department of Finance; Canadian Federation of Students

Reductions in provincial funding for higher education, and thus the core budgets of institutions, have tracked these cuts and have resulted in a cumulative impact that has led experienced observers to express deep fears about declines in the quality of higher education (Lewington 1995). Direct support for university research also declined over the same period to a point less than one-third of its counterpart in the USA (Brown 1999). Even more important, as one university president has pointed out, these cuts when coupled to student fee increases "advance the unsavoury possibility of Canada returning to a caste system, in which rich kids take the expensive professional degrees which generate higher incomes, middle-income people take the rest which generate middle incomes, and the low-income are kept out of universities altogether, generally to earn the lowest incomes" (Strong 1999, 29).

GLOBALISATION AND THE INTERNATIONALISATION OF HIGHER EDUCATION

Systematic analysis of the impact of globalisation on the internationalisation of higher education is meagre. One reason for this is that research on higher education in general is somewhat limited and research on international higher education even more so. Discussions of globalisation and the internationalisation of higher education, moreover, are rarely placed within a larger political and economic context. An initial contribution by Warner (1991), for example, which called for a much more explicit exploration of the assumptions underlying internationalisation elicited little response.

Warner identified three different models of internationalisation: the *competitive market model*, the liberal model and the social transformation model. In the competitive market model, countries compete globally for economic markets, cultural ideas, and political influence. The emphasis in higher education is placed on strengthening international contacts and activities—mainly in the area of sponsored research. Research is tailored to meet perceived national and corporate needs in the international competition for knowledge, and international students are seen as a lucrative source of revenue. Under the *liberal model,* emphasis is given—without denying the element of national or institutional self-interest—to global co-operation rather than to global competition. Priority is placed on the development of those competencies that promote effective communication and dialogue with people from other cultures. Higher education institutions stress the importance of international exchanges and collaboration with a broad range of countries in an effort to enhance global consciousness (both within the university and the local community) and correspondingly expand the cultural elements of the curriculum. A third model – the *social transformational model* – underlines the importance of critical social analysis so that internationalisation is seen as contributing to the reduction of global economic inequality and the inequities of gender, race and ethnicity.

Tillett and Lesser (1992) also identify three models of internationalisation. Their benign market model assumes that if Canada's higher education institutions were attractive enough they would attract international students. Their social model assumes that Canadian higher education institutions have a moral obligation to help educate students in developing countries. In the competitive model, on the other hand, higher education is seen mainly as a product or commodity to be sold on the international market. It is this model, they argue, that was clearly gaining in favour among key stakeholders in Canada.

Over the years a number of attempts have been made to define the term "internationalisation". Harari has argued that the internationalisation of higher education consists of three strands: the international content of the curricula, the international movement of scholars and students, and technical assistance and education co-operation programs. Later he enlarged his definition to include a commitment to the creation of an attitude of global awareness that permeates a whole institution and shapes its ethos. Harari (1992b) now insists that internationalisation is not a policy, program, or event, but a *process* (see Chapter 2).

According to the OECD's Centre for Educational Research and Innovation (CERI), the main aim of internationalisation is "to put in place programs and activities which enable higher education—its institutions, students and staff—to take part effectively in a world characterised by increasing international co-operation, exchange and interdependence" (OECD 1993a, 7). These programs and activities include: foreign language study; international elements in the curriculum; work/study abroad opportunities; the presence of international students; faculty/staff exchange or mobility programs; international development assistance programs; institutional co-operation agreements; transnational research projects; area studies; cross-cultural training; and extra-curricular activities and institutional services (Knight 1993).

More recently, the work of the OECD on internationalisation has developed along two different tracks: international trade in professional and educational services and the development of models of quality assurance. Canadian academics have played a leading role in the development and publication of materials in these two areas (Knight and De Wit 1997; Mallea, 1994b, 1996, 1998a). They have participated actively in efforts to document the views of major stakeholders in the internationalisation of higher education, and have contributed to two international reviews commissioned by the OECD to determine the views of multilateral organisations, governments, non-governmental agencies, higher education associations, institutions, and the private sector (Mallea 1996).

Stakeholder views and motivations, it was found, varied both within and across sectoral boundaries. Thus while multilateral organisations emphasise the values of international co-operation, national governments more frequently stress the need to be internationally competitive and place less importance on international education as an extended form of cultural diplomacy (that is, as a means of reducing political and cultural isolation, a way of providing overseas aid to developing countries, or a vehicle to promote the value of international citizenship). Non-governmental organisations, on the other hand, were more likely to advocate multilateral student exchanges, increased support for visa students, the strengthening of linkages between institutions, the expansion of transnational opportunities for young scientists, and increased participation in multilateral research programs (Mallea 1998a).

CANADIAN STAKEHOLDERS AND THE INTERNATIONALISATION OF HIGHER EDUCATION

Shute (1999) points out that the internationalisation of Canadian higher education was initially much more focused on development, co-operation and international students than on globalisation or trade liberalisation. By the end of the 1960s, a significant number of university-based twinning projects had been established in the field of development co-operation with the support of the Canadian International Development Agency (CIDA). Some 2,326 development co-operation projects were put in place after the mid-1970s, and an additional 2,781 linkage agreements created with universities and research institutions. Thereafter, however, development aid as a percentage of Canada's gross national product (GNP) dropped steadily. During the 1980s and 1990s, both the Conservative and Liberal federal governments cut Overseas Development Assistance (ODA). It fell from roughly 0.5 per cent of GNP in 1979 to 0.27 per cent in 1998—its lowest proportion in thirty years. As national priorities changed, Knight (1996) observes that the higher education community, governments, and the private sector all came to agree that the most important rationale for internationalisation was the achievement of competitive standards of quality and the preparation of internationally knowledgeable and inter-culturally competent graduates.

Institutional Development

Much work on the strengthening of the international dimensions of Canada's community colleges and universities has occurred over the last decade (Knight 2000). Inhouse institutional reviews, inter-institutional linkages, program development, and structural reorganisation measures are indicators of increased activity on this front, as is the broadening and deepening of the International Office's mandate. Aggregate information on the community colleges, regrettably, is lacking. The Association of Universities and Colleges of Canada (AUCC) conducted and published surveys of internationalisation in 1993 and again in 1999.

The 1999 AUCC survey (Knight 2000) was distributed to 89 member institutions, with 77 institutions completing and returning at least one of the six questionnaires circulated. Responses revealed that senior leaders ranked internationalisation as either a high priority (50%) or a medium priority (35%). In terms of objectives, preparing internationally and inter-culturally sensitive graduates ranked first in importance (73%). The importance of universities addressing the interdependent nature of the world ranked second (23%). The need to maintain Canada's economic, scientific and technological competence ranked third (21%). In fourth place (21%) was the desire to generate additional income by recruiting more international students. Improved student mobility and the redesign of academic programs and curricula were among the most frequently cited outcomes of internationalisation.

Faculty and Students

Early leadership in the internationalisation of Canadian universities was provided by faculty members and students who brought "a sense of mission, commitment and energy to the proposition that the universities have a central role to play in making a better world" (Bond and Lemasson 1999, ix). Thus, beginning in the period 1950-1968 and accelerating in the period up to 1980, faculty and students played an important role in Canada's international assistance efforts (Lemasson 1999). As Shute reminds us, it was those with international experience who brought their experiences back to their institutions, laboratories and classrooms (Shute 1999). In brief, faculty members were the "invisible champions" of internationalisation (Bond and Scott 1999, 54).

Students have also been champions of internationalisation. They have participated in development co-operation projects as members of organisations such as Canadian University Service Overseas (CUSO) or World University Service Canada (WUSC). They have travelled abroad to further their studies. And today this tradition is broadening as students pursue student work exchanges with the help of bodies such as the Association for International Exchanges of Students in Economics and Commerce (AIESEC).

An insight into how current students think about the internationalisation of higher education can be gleaned from a report of a student forum on the subject. The forum was part of an initiative by York University's Academic and Policy Planning Committee Task Force to prepare an international strategy for the institution. The students were very clear as to what internationalisation of higher education meant: "They determined that the fundamental reason for institutional internationalisation was that knowledge systems are and should be more international. They also reported that the curriculum design/program content and co-curricular components were deemed central to all internationalisation efforts and that current curriculum needed to be 'revolutionised'" (CBIE 2000a, 12).

University Researchers

A recent review, entitled "The Internationalisation of University Research in Canada" (Gingras et al. 1999), notes that while internationalisation was supported by the National Research Councils in the early 1990s, budget cutbacks in 1996 at the Social Sciences and Humanities Research Council of Canada (SSHRC) and the Natural Sciences and Engineering Council of Canada (NSERC) led to the termination of international programs. On the other hand, an increasingly important place is being given to articles written in collaboration with international colleagues (Gingras et al.1999). An analysis of co-authorship of publications with foreign colleagues showed that the growth of international collaboration rose from 17 per cent of total publications in the sciences and engineering in 1981 to 30.7 per cent in 1995, and from 11 per cent to 17.7 per cent in the social sciences and humanities during the same period. The greatest degree of international collaboration took place with colleagues from the USA and, in descending order of importance, in mathematics, physics, earth sciences, and biomedical research. Variations between disciplines were more pronounced in the humanities and social sciences, and a less systematic growth trend was observed than in natural sciences and engineering. Gingras et al. (1999) also point out the important role of the International Development Research Centre (IDRC) in internationalising university research. Founded in 1970 and funded by an annual grant from the Parliament of Canada, the IDRC is dedicated to the sustained development of the research capacity in developing regions. Its funding is of the order of $60 million a year, with funding for Canadian co-operative research projects rising from $96.1 million in the 1980s to $101.7 million in the 1990s.

Federal Government

The Canadian federal government's views on the internationalisation of higher education are best illustrated by discussions that took place within the context of an overall foreign policy review involving Canada's ten provinces and two (now three) territories (Canada 1994a). Regret was expressed over the longstanding lack of co-ordination among key stakeholders and a wide array of weaknesses were identified, including the following:

- Poor integration, co-ordination, and coherence in government policies and programs, both among federal bodies and between federal and provincial governments;
- Virtually no investment in international activities and work that supports them including marketing, when compared to other G-7 countries;
- A disproportionately low level of public funding for initiatives between Canadian institutions and their counterparts in the industrialised world where Canadian interests are most engaged, relative to the funding available for similar initiatives with the developing world;
- No coherent strategy for building on existing strengths and achievements;

- Vague international policies within institutions;
- No coherent approach to tuition fees for foreign students;
- Limited offerings and low enrolments in foreign language classes;
- Low level of Canadian student and faculty mobility;
- Ad hoc treatment of networking and partnerships;
- Limited appreciation of the influence of cultural factors on teaching, learning, and research;
- Diminishing funding for higher education, which threatens its quality;
- No approved general, integrated and appropriate marketing strategy for educational services;
- No sense of urgency about the need to co-ordinate policies and activities in support of a national global competitive strategy.

Given the nature, scope, and extent of these weaknesses, the Department of Foreign Affairs and International Trade (DFAIT) concluded that a coherent national policy on the internationalisation of higher education could only be achieved by the promotion of closer relations with higher education institutions, industry, and different levels of government, both within and across national boundaries. It also spelled out the specific policy *objectives* and *mechanisms* that would be needed if these strategic partnerships were to be established and strengthened:

Objectives:
- Inform and co-ordinate all actors concerning international higher education, research and training policies, and programs;
- Develop national consensus on key issues and ensure a coherent national approach to them;
- Increase awareness in Canada of international higher education, research and training issues, and of the experience of other countries;
- Reinforce the role of the CMEC (Council of Ministers of Education Canada) as co-ordinator for the provincial governments working in partnership with FAITC as the co-ordinator for the federal government in international education-related activities;
- Provide guidance on federal priorities to Canada's delegates (e.g., the provinces) to meetings organised on international education by the OECD, the continuing North American policy dialogue, The European Union Task Force on Human Resources, APEC, the Council of Europe, the OAS, UNESCO, the Commonwealth, and La Francophonie;

Mechanisms:
- Interdepartmental committee on international higher education, research, and training, composed of the main federal departments and agencies concerned (e.g., CIDA, the granting councils, IDRC, Industry, Canadian Heritage, Human Resources Development, Citizenship and Immigration, Health) to meet quarterly;
- Federal-Provincial Consultative Committee on Education-Related International

Affairs, which normally meets twice yearly;
- Roundtable of main actors from governments and institutions (e.g., the CMEC, ACCC, CBIE, CAUT, ARUCC, Corporate-Higher Education Forum), to meet twice yearly.

DFAIT declared that a new policy framework should:

- Strengthen the policy dialogue by encouraging the exchange of information on issues and experiences of common concern and on existing effective international collaborative ventures, and by pursuing areas of co-operation;
- Increase networking by encouraging focused and mutually reinforcing collaborative ventures among higher education institutions in priority regions (North America, Asia-Pacific, Europe) and in priority areas of research;
- Increase the visibility and role of Canadian delegations to such multilateral meetings;
- Increase awareness internationally of Canadian strengths and initiatives;
- Facilitate student and faculty mobility including mutual recognition of credits, degrees, and diplomas; increasing awareness and mutually satisfactory removal of impediments to mobility; enhanced use of people-to-people exchange programs;
- Develop stronger partnerships among higher education institutions, professional associations, public authorities, and business and other organisations that have a stake in the quality of higher education and research; and
- Promote Canadian higher education in selected markets.

DFAIT's report and its findings were subsequently forwarded to a Special Joint Parliamentary Committee Reviewing Canadian Foreign Policy, where submissions tended to focus on *economic issues and concerns*. During the Committee's hearings, witnesses emphasised the importance of internationalising higher education if Canada were to compete successfully in the new and more competitive global economy. They stressed the key role of knowledge as an important source of job creation and innovation (technological, organisation, distributional and managerial). They underlined the economic value of Canada's approximately 60,000 visa students, pointed out the trade implications of their future role as leading members of their home communities, and drew unflattering comparisons with other countries regarding the marketing of Canada's educational services abroad. In addition, they emphasised the role of international partnerships and alliances in helping build Canadian competitiveness, and recommended that a Commission on the Internationalisation of Canadian Education for Global Competitiveness be established (Ibid.).

For their part, Committee members were impressed by the strong consensus (in higher education) on the need for Canada's foreign policy to address the strategic importance of the internationalisation of higher education. They endorsed the view that Canada's capacity to compete in the global economy depended "in part on the next generation of the best and the brightest developing the knowledge and skills necessary to deal with other cultures and to participate in foreign environments". They recommended that Canada's cultural, scientific, and educational policies be formulated in such a way as to make Canada a major participant in a global, knowledge-based economy (Ibid., 64-65).

The Committee concluded that high priority should be given to the establishment of joint ventures between higher education and the private sector, and that the latter should also be centrally involved in the creation of international scholarship and exchange programs. The federal government, it stated, should seek the co-operation of interested provincial governments to increase support for the internationalisation of higher education (academic and student mobility, institutional exchanges, and the development of international research and development networks). And in conclusion, it reaffirmed the lead role of DFAIT in developing federal policy on international education, while calling for greater transparency and the clarification of the roles and responsibilities of its various units (Ibid.).

The federal government's response was positive. Priority was to be given to cultural, scientific, and educational relations in Canada's foreign policy. Knowledge, in the form of technology, organisation and innovation, it stated, was a key ingredient of Canada's future international competitiveness, and higher education's role was critical. It confirmed its intention to participate actively in the development of a global information highway, declared that Canadian educational products, services and expertise should form an integral part of its International Business Development Program, and expressed its support for more transnational exchanges in research and development. It agreed that more scholarly exchanges were needed and that academic mobility with Europe, North America, and the Asia-Pacific should be improved. The vitality of Canada's academic community, it concluded, was "largely dependent upon its access to, and success on, the international stage" (Ibid., 87). In early 1995, to an expectant and supportive higher education community, the federal government announced that culture and education would form the "third pillar" (alongside trade and diplomacy) of Canada's new foreign policy. A new "Global Issues and Culture" unit was created within DFAIT composed of three divisions: Academic Relations, Arts and Letters, and the Promotion of Educational Goods and Services (Canada 1994c).

Provincial Governments

In Canada, as noted earlier, the provinces possess jurisdiction over education. Provincial Ministers of Education come together to form a body known as the Council of Ministers of Education of Canada (CMEC) and it is this body that represents Canada at the governmental level internationally. While a federal government representative is invited to attend CMEC meetings, he or she is not a full member of the Council and does not possess voting powers.

Provincial governments have taken steps to strengthen their international linkages and trilateral ties over the last decade. The Ontario Ministry of Colleges and Universities announced that it is seeking to promote "the advancement of scholarship and research and the strengthening of people-to-people and trade links in an interdependent global community" (CBIE 1992, 11). The Quebec provincial government increased funds for research and the training of researchers in order to enhance the province's competitiveness in strategic areas such as biotechnology, space research, information technology and the environment. The provincial government of Saskatchewan expressed an interest in expanding the province's consultancy services as a means of internationalising their system. Manitoba involved its colleges and universities in the implementation of a trade agreement with the state of Jalisco in Mexico.

Quebec and Alberta, in particular, are approaching the internationalisation of their higher education institutions in a more systematic manner. The former has allocated a $10 million fund per year (1999-2002) for two-way student exchange; the latter is contemplating taking a leadership role in marketing educational services overseas. The government of Nova Scotia is also showing a keen interest in marketing and trading educational services.[9] New Brunswick has created a Universities International Centre which is an arm of the provincial government. Manitoba has established a Manitoba Council for International Education made up of educational institutions and the provincial Department of Education which works in tandem with other departments of government (Farquhar 2001).

Probably the most systematic approach has been taken by the province of British Columbia which established and funded the British Columbia Centre for International Education (BCCIE). Observing that the province's future prosperity depends on a work force that could compete effectively in the global economy, and that Canada was moving from a resource-based to a knowledge- and information-based economy, the BCCIE concluded that the internationalisation of higher education was not only desirable but essential. Its position is that colleges and universities have a responsibility to ensure that their students are given the opportunity to acquire an international outlook and perspective. To help them fulfil this responsibility, the BCCIE publishes materials and offers a practice-oriented workshop on internationalisation.

Higher Education Associations

The primary response of higher education associations to globalisation and trade liberalisation has been to direct more time, energy and ideas to strengthening the international dimensions of their work and that of their member institutions. Two national associations, the Association of Universities and Colleges of Canada (AUCC) and the Association of Community Colleges of Canada (ACCC), have played key roles in this process. As the voice of Canada's universities, AUCC has identified the increased internationalisation of its member institutions as one of its three main priorities. In addition to its work in the area of development aid, it has adopted a formal statement on internationalisation with two goals in mind: first, to "attest to the growth of interest, the effort and the extent of change that have contributed to internationalising Canadian universities"; and second, to encourage "further advancement of this process by proposing a framework for action which should be considered and discussed in the context of each institution's mission, resources and priorities". Furthermore, it proposes identifying the nature and objectives of internationalisation, developing human potential for living and working in a context of global interdependence, providing a forum for the discussion of global issues, fostering international co-operation, enhancing student mobility, and contributing to international development assistance (AUCC 1995b).

AUCC's framework of action speaks to the ways and means of internationalisation. Internationalisation, in its view, is a multifaceted phenomenon involving a deliberate and pro-active transformation of existing mandates. It is a bottom-up and a top-down process involving changes in institutional, academic and administrative policy, research opportunities, and community service and extracurricular activities. It also calls for changes in provincial and federal government policies, including the removal of administrative barriers to greater student mobility (provincial governments) and ensuring that ministerial policies reflect the needs and opportunities for universities brought about by globalisation (federal government).

At the college level, ACCC (1994) outlined three major reasons why its member institutions should internationalise:

- Our colleges have a duty to prepare Canadians for the future, to enable them to live co-operatively and productively in a changing world. ACCC wishes to support our members' efforts to open themselves to the international community, to prepare students to enhance Canada's competitiveness and to prepare their students to be true citizens of the world. The new world economic order leaves us no choice.
- ACCC believes that each college and institution has a duty to help its students prepare both for a future technological workplace and for world citizenship. In many colleges we already have a significant student clientele of new Canadians and visiting nationals from other countries. Our colleges have already noted growing competition with foreign firms and institutions, while others are opening up new educational markets in other countries. Some Canadian colleges are only beginning to grapple with the economic, cultural and social consequences of this inevitable internationalisation.
- ACCC believes that our institutions must prepare our students to compete internationally and to live and work in the global village. Colleges must also be ready to receive foreign students, to export and import skills and to educate all college personnel to the realities of international life and to the ensuing responsibilities that they must bear.

ACCC's mandate, like that of AUCC, embraces the marketing of member institutions' capabilities and capacities to meet the educational and training needs of other countries as well as Canada. Its goals include the development of mutually beneficial activities for addressing international issues. And its strategic priorities emphasise the development of partnerships with institutions in other countries. As a former President of ACCC has observed, the association considers that working overseas in competitive environments ensures that member colleges and their personnel are exposed to other cultures and economies, as well as state-of-the-art developments in various domains of knowledge and practice. These experiences give them more and diverse information to pass on to their students, and encourage them to foster business contacts around the world (*The Globe and Mail*, 1994). Aggregate data on the colleges, as noted earlier, is lacking. Regrettably, surveys of institutions such as those conducted on the universities by the AUCC in 1993 and 1999 do not exist. International activity, though, is widespread and is probably more contract-oriented than in the universities

Non-Governmental Organisations

There are a number of non-governmental organisations that have made significant contributions to internationalising the higher education system over the last several decades. The Canadian University Service Overseas (CUSO) and the World University Service of Canada (WUSC) have done sterling work in the area of international exchange. The Inter-America Organisation of Higher Education (IOHE) has led the way in developing international co-operation in the Americas. The Canadian Bureau of International Education (CBIE) has been active in the area of public advocacy.

CBIE's stance can best be summarised as follows: education and training not only help improve international understanding, enhance sustainable development and protect human rights, but they are also an important investment in the future. CBIE's position is that Canada can only trade effectively with countries it understands and which in turn understand it. Canadian students, therefore, must be encouraged to cross national borders if they are to learn first-hand how to be effective internationally (CBIE 1994).

Over the past few years, the CBIE has developed a number of specific recommendations directed at a variety of major stakeholders in internationalisation–higher education institutions, governments, and the private sector. Those aimed at higher education institutions can be summarised as follows: (1) the inclusion of internationalisation as a goal in all institutional mission statements, (2) the establishment of a program review process aimed at ensuring programs are internationalised, (3) the establishment of policies on both the percentages of foreign students enrolled and their national composition, (4) the review of available learning resources to ensure participation in international research, (5) the recruitment of faculty with international experience and the establishment of reward structures that value international work, (6) the review of programs to enable international students to become more active cross-cultural educators on campus, (7) the establishment of mechanisms to increase the number of Canadian students having educational experiences abroad, and (8) the review of institutional capacities for international research.

Recommendations aimed specifically at the federal and provincial governments include: (1) the further development of scholarship programs for international students, (2) support for a national co-ordinating office on exchange agreements, (3) the funding of research and study for faculty members seeking to develop their international expertise, (4) improved information services in Canadian diplomatic posts relating to opportunities for study in Canada, (5) a streamlined process for granting international student authorisations, and (6) adoption of internationalisation as a fundamental objective of Canadian higher education.

The CBIE has articulated two key recommendations for the private sector: the need for private lending institutions to forego international indebtedness in exchange for a debtor country's support of educational exchange programs and the need for private corporations to share the financial burdens (as well as the benefits) of the exchange of students, researchers and faculty in those fields that are most closely associated with their short- and long-term trading interests.

The CBIE's (1995) views on international higher education as an investment are spelled out in a document entitled, *International Education is a Bottom Line Position: A Strategy for Building an Internationally Competent Workforce.* It proposes the establishment of "The Canadian Program for International Learning" (CPIL) that focuses on foreign markets and economies of major strategic importance to Canada. The initiative is conceived as a joint venture between Canada's post-secondary education and business communities, in co-operation with government and non-governmental organisations representing students and members of the workforce. Funding, which to date has not been forthcoming, would consist of the establishment of several new funds directed by a national advisory council whose membership would be drawn primarily from business and post-secondary education.

CBIE's energies have also focused on co-operative work with the ACCC and AUCC in the publication of the report *Internationalising Higher Education: A Shared Vision?* It has developed an advocacy plan urging the federal government to adopt an international education strategy aimed at having 10 percent of Canadian post-secondary students studying abroad. And it has adopted a new strategic plan that stresses three major objectives: (1) the definition of ethical and quality standards for the provision of international education, (2) the establishment of standards and codes of conduct for international education professionals, and (3) the piloting of new and innovative programming in international education (CBIE 1999).

Private Sector

Canada's Corporate-Higher Education Forum[4] initiated discussions as early as 1985 on the importance of higher education in developing the international business skills necessary for the nation to be competitive. It subsequently established a task force, made up of members drawn from business and academe, whose final report, *Going Global: Meeting the Need for International Business Expertise in Canada* (Corporate-Higher Education Forum 1988), was based on the results of surveys and interviews with a broad selection of corporate, academic, and government respondents complemented by a review of published international research.

Members of the task force minced no words in reporting their findings. They concluded that despite Canada's dependence on world trade few corporate enterprises considered education to be an important factor in developing international expertise.

On the contrary, human resource managers (unlike CEOs) sought immediate and specific functional skills among job applicants rather than giving priority, for example, to graduates with foreign language competence. Moreover, many international business education programs in Canadian universities did not meet world-class standards.

Only 4 of 37 Canadian universities responding to the Forum's survey in 1998 had an undergraduate international business speciality. Only one university awarded a bachelor's degree in international business. Six of 29 MBA or equivalent business programs offered IB majors, but none offered an international MBA. Foreign language requirements were almost unknown at all degree levels. Half of Canada's business undergraduates and 40 percent of MBAs graduated without a significant exposure to international business education. Nineteen business schools reported active support for foreign study exchange programs. Only six offered overseas company internship opportunities. No comprehensive degree program incorporating business-management functions, foreign languages and geographic or cultural area specialisation was available from any of the 87 educational institutions recognised by the Association of Universities and Colleges of Canada (AUCC) (Ibid., 3). Only a few Canadian corporations provided their managers with professional-level international skill development programs. And only non-governmental organisations insisted on the importance of a combination of functional skills and a broad understanding of international issues.

A second illustration of Canadian private sector interest in the international aspects of higher education was the Business Council on National Issues' (BCNI) joint project with the federal government titled "The Prosperity Initiative." Members of this joint project considered the promotion of international learning to be an essential factor in what it describes as the growing global competition among nations to attract and retain highly skilled personnel. If Canada was to be successful in this competition, they argued, it would need to strengthen its international linkages, keep pace with developments outside Canada, participate in international technology projects, and secure access to new knowledge and techniques (Ministry of Supply and Services, Canada 1991a). The goal of improving the economy's competitiveness was the main driving force behind the reform of learning systems internationally. Consequently, they called on Canadian post-secondary institutions to internationalise their curricula, promote interest in and access to training in foreign languages, strengthen programs leading to international accreditation and the international exchange of students, teachers and scholars, and foster co-operative research across international boundaries. They also called for the provision of competency-based credits for skills and knowledge acquired outside of Canada, more intensive marketing of Canadian educational services abroad, and the doubling of the number of international students in Canada (Ministry of Supply and Services, Canada 1991b).

Today the situation is changing. A growing number of MBA programs now include an international mobility component as a requirement. Other degree programs provide for this component, but on a voluntary basis. A handful of major companies now fund international scholarships.[5] Once again, however, data on these developments in aggregate form are hard to come by. Nor is it clear to what extent these specific initiatives foster specifically North American co-operation in higher education.

Trade Liberalisation in Education Services

The Uruguay Round (1987-1994) of the General Agreement on Tariffs and Trade (GATT) has a special relevance for higher education. This is because it established a framework for trade liberalisation in the services sector. The General Agreement on Trade in Services (GATS) includes education and is fully integrated into the WTO. Under GATS, international trade in educational services is classified as follows: (1) cross-border supply in which only the service crosses the border, as in distance learning, (2) consumption abroad wherein the consumer travels abroad to receive the service, (3) commercial presence wherein foreign providers establish a presence within a country so as to deliver education, and (4) the presence of natural persons wherein a professor travels to another country to deliver a service (CHERD 2002).

There can be little doubt that participation in GATS and the WTO strengthened the Canadian federal government's interest in international trade in education services. It has already been noted that in 1995 DFAIT created a new division of Promotion of Educational Goods and Services within its Global Issues and Culture unit to address this issue. Increasingly federal government trade missions abroad have featured groups of college and university presidents intent on promoting the educational services their institutions could supply. Other federal departments and provincial governments have entered the field with enthusiasm.

Both the size of the global market in education and training services and Canada's interest in it are undoubtedly increasing. One estimate suggests that business, professional, and educational services represent 20 percent of world trade and enjoy an average annual growth rate of 8 per cent (Holmes 1996). Global revenues from foreign students, for example, rose considerably as their numbers doubled between 1960 and 1970, almost doubled again from 1970 to 1980, and reached 1,168,075 by 1990 (UNESCO 1992). Canada ranks about sixth globally as a destination of choice for foreign students, with their numbers rising from 42,000 in the mid-1970s to 87,000 in 1993-94. Students came from more than 100 countries, contributed $2.3B in foreign exchange earnings, and helped create 21,000 jobs in Canada (Killian 1997).

Canada has expressed ambitions to become a significant global player in the export of education and training services as illustrated by Industry Canada's (1998) study of this sector, which was completed as part of a competitiveness framework review in 1998.[6] It reported that the Canadian education and training providers fell into one of four categories. The first category encompassed firms specialising in education and training programs and/or courseware, curriculum design, train-the-trainer programs, and training needs assessments. The second was composed of accounting, engineering, management consultant and telecommunications companies that provide education and training services either as a supplement to their main product or service line, or on a stand-alone basis. Private sector schools and training institutions made up the third category. The fourth category was composed of public educational institutions such as colleges and universities (Industry Canada 1998).

Canada's strengths were identified as being distance education and technology-based learning, public sector management training, second language acquisition (in both French and English), and the flexibility demonstrated by its private providers. However, its limitations include the lack of a national accreditation process, international marketing skills, international experience and know-how, and an absence of research on the sector. To help overcome these limitations, Industry Canada suggested that smaller enterprises could benefit from working with larger ones in development and distribution, while larger companies could benefit from the creativity demonstrated by their smaller partners.

Industry Canada also identified three areas it considers important to increasing international trade in education and training services: technological change, trade agreements and the development priorities of multilateral organisations. Of these three, it considers technological change to be the most significant. For instance, with respect to Canada exploiting the potentially huge global market in distance education, it underlined the importance of utilising new media learning materials (which combined text, graphics, pictures, and animations) and their application to various electronic-based training products. In addition, it noted that telecommunications, cable, and satellite companies were becoming more active in the area but that more investment was needed if the market was to be fully exploited.

There are signs that such investment may well be forthcoming. For example, the Canadian Imperial Bank of Commerce and the Export Development Corporation recently launched a $20 million loan program for knowledge-based businesses to finance the costs of supplying goods and services abroad. The Canadian Business Networks Coalition, made up of approximately 100 organisations, has approved several education and training networks that are targeting international markets. The Calgary Centre for International Training, consisting of five companies and institutions, is providing training for major public infrastructure projects. The Canadian Showcase Consortium, made up of a group of educational institutions in four provinces, is seeking to attract interest in its offerings. And hospitality education and training is being exported by Creative Communications International.

Industry Canada recommends that education and training firms develop strong links with the consulting engineering, construction and manufacturing industries, and that they develop expertise in developing formal international marketing plans. It recommended niche marketing in areas of strength, and the idea of government entering into partnerships with private suppliers. It proposed that training services should be added to larger export packages in areas such as telecommunications, health care, transportation, power generation and engineering. It acknowledged finally the importance of co-operation rather than competition, and underlined the need for enhanced and expanded networking and information exchange.

In response, more of a cost-benefit approach is being adopted to the delivery of education and training services. Custom-designed programs, institutional twinning and credit transfer mechanisms are being developed, a strong and sustained local presence is being encouraged, professional networks are being formed to better coordinate responses to fast-moving changes in rapidly expanding international markets, and a number of important partnerships are being established. In April of 1995, DFAIT entered into a partnership with the Department of Citizenship and Immigration, the Canadian International Development Agency, and the Asia-Pacific Foundation of Canada to create a Network of Canadian Education Centres (CECs). These centres' mandate is to gather market intelligence, identify corporate and group training opportunities, and negotiate contracts.

Emphasis is being placed on attracting clients on a fee-for-service basis. To assist in this process, market studies were conducted to identify both the characteristics and the potential of the markets being targeted. The USA, with an estimated market for education and training products of U.S. $52B, is a top priority. Also, while annually over 70,000 U.S. students study abroad, Canada does not rank among their top countries of choice and most seem indifferent to educational opportunities in Canada. Moreover, Canadian diplomatic posts in the USA lack the promotional and reference materials (in both electronic and print formats) that are absolutely essential if one wishes to reach and influence a wider segment of the student population.

DFAIT notes that an increasing number of Latin American students are able to personally finance overseas studies and that inquiries about Canadian educational opportunities are increasing. Canada's potential was seen to be in the following areas: undergraduate and graduate studies, short- and long-term second language courses in English and French, distance education programs, university-private sector joint ventures, and edu-tourism packages. The market in Mexico, which grew 70 per cent from U.S.$ 26.4M to U.S.$ 44.8M between 1991 and 1993, is of major interest.

DFAIT's market focus analysis said the Mexican market demonstrated an increased need for Mexicans to learn English as a Second Language (ESL), and that interest in doing so remained strong. Five other areas were identified as having potential within the Mexican market. These were the provision of graduate and undergraduate programs, FSL/ESL short-term and summer programs for secondary and post-secondary students, continuing education and technical training programs, "train the trainer" packages for the private sector, and distance education programs, packages and technologies.

The analysis also contained information on barriers to future trade such as under-utilised promotional channels, under-developed electronic tools and a lack of co-operative promotional activities among Canadian exporters. The market, moreover, was dominated by the USA, which enjoyed over 60 per cent of the market share of Mexican students studying abroad. And the British were offering more complete aid packages, easier application processes, and shorter master's degree programs. The Canadian advantage, on the other hand, lay in lower tuition costs, a safe study environment, less stringent visa requirements, and the opportunity to enjoy a bicultural and multicultural experience.

Market studies such as those conducted by DFAIT suggest that the recruitment of international students, particularly from the USA and Mexico, is a current priority of the Canadian federal government, but that the ways in which they benefit Canada are now seen in economic rather than academic terms: job creation, economic stimulation, imports/exports, investment, technology/knowledge transfer, and strategic academic, business and political ties. These differences in perceived benefits between government and higher education institutions, moreover, help explain the relative lack of knowledge and enthusiasm among higher education institutions in turning to government agencies for help in exporting their services. As the Canadian Bureau for International Education (CBIE) survey of higher education institutions points out, key decision-makers in colleges and universities were typically unaware of federal export-promoting services. And even when they were aware of them, they had concerns about the orientation, transparency, and relationship of these services to the core mission and values of their institution (CBIE 1999).

NAFTA: THE PROFESSIONS AND HIGHER EDUCATION

The impact of NAFTA on Canadian higher education can best be understood by examining those trilateral initiatives to which it gave rise. The two most important are the efforts of professional associations to achieve Mutual Recognition Agreements (Mars) and the initiative of the three governments to foster trilateral North American co-operation in higher education.

The Professions

As noted in Chapter 2, the passage of NAFTA encouraged professional associations in Canada, Mexico and the USA to establish trilateral working groups in actuarial sciences, accounting, agronomy, architecture, dentistry, engineering, law, medicine, nursing, pharmacy, psychology and veterinary sciences. The primary goal in each case was to develop a Mutual Recognition Agreement (MRA). Canadian professional associations have participated enthusiastically in the trilateral working groups, but progress to date has been mixed.

In architecture, considerable advances have been made toward an MRA. In accounting, the Canadian Chartered Accountants have an agreement with the U.S. Chartered Public Accountants and the Certified General Accountants Association of Canada and U.S. International Qualifications Board are carrying out a credentialing review. In agronomy, agreement on mutually agreeable standards (but not an MRA) was reached in 1996. In dentistry, reciprocal agreement exists between professional bodies in Canada and the USA, and discussions with their Mexican counterparts are under way. In law, joint recommendations have been drafted, but not signed off. Although there is a joint accreditation program for undergraduate programs in medicine between the Committee on Accreditation of Canadian Medical Schools and their U.S. counterpart, reciprocity does not yet exist. The same is also true in nursing where four working groups dealing with education, licensure/registration/practice, speciality certification, and approval/accreditation have published a monograph on these and related subjects. Several trilateral conferences have been held in pharmacy and informal talks on an MRA have been initiated. In psychology, neither recognition of equivalency nor reciprocity of accreditation is imminent. And in veterinary medicine, while reciprocity exists between Canada and the USA, progress toward concluding an agreement to co-operate and exchange information is slow.

The engineering profession is the first and only profession to have developed and approved an MRA. The agreement has been ratified by all except one of the licensing authorities in Canada. It sets out criteria for mutual recognition that are based on objective and transparent criteria, such as competence and the ability to provide a service; that are not more burdensome than necessary to ensure the quality of a service; and that do not constitute a disguised restriction on the international provision of a service (OECD 1997, 179-286). It also details the educational experience and examination requirements to obtain a temporary license to practice in these countries.

Representatives from the professions and higher education in Canada first came together to share ideas on internationalisation in November of 1996. This was at the AUCC's conference titled *Internationalisation: Moving from Rhetoric to Reality*. Included on the program was a workshop on "Internationalising the Professions," where members of the accounting, engineering, nursing and occupational therapy professions participated. Discussion focused mainly on the process of successful professional accreditation and the factors critical to its achievement. These included core support from the professions, emphasis on outcomes, adoption of a service orientation, and the building of external partnerships. The negotiation process under NAFTA's chapter 12 on cross-border trade in services was addressed and representatives from the engineering profession stressed the importance of three underlying premises: (1) the competency of professional engineers in each country, (2) a credible system to validate that competency exists, (3) restrictions to mobility only on the basis of competence, public health, and safety.

Canadian professional associations are experiencing difficulties as they try to come to grips with differences in licensing systems, legal requirements for licensure, control of the profession, education requirements, experience requirements, examination requirements, and languages. Despite these differences, however, a mutual recognition agreement (MRA) on the engineering profession was signed on June 5, 1995. In commenting on the lessons learned from this experience, the Director of Educational Affairs, Canadian Council of Professional Engineers, had seven recommendations to offer for other professions wishing to follow suit. These were to (1) establish support from national constituencies and affiliations, (2) develop an appropriate feedback mechanism, (3) establish relations with government officials responsible for trade issues, (4) identify acceptable compromises to reach an agreement, (5) explore the desirability of independent legal advice early in the process, (6) select an appropriate negotiating team, (7) and allocate sufficient resources to the activity (Ryan-Bacon 1996). It is doubtful whether any of this advice is being heeded by the other professions. Information on the progress other professions are making is hard to obtain, while the view of most knowledgeable observers is that the pace of progress towards MRAs is painfully slow.

North American Co-operation in Higher Education

Opinion is divided regarding the impact of NAFTA on higher education in Canada. Opponents believe it will lead to a competitive restructuring of higher education along primarily economic lines. Funding will be targeted towards commercially-oriented programs and research and priority will be given to student and faculty mobility programs that lead to greater economic integration. In addition, it is thought that educational harmonisation efforts will be shaped by the growing need of the business sector for an internationally mobile labour force. Advocates, on the other hand, believe that the agreement will lead to an expansion of trilateral activities, that North American students will become more mobile, that the professional development of faculty will be strengthened, and that it will encourage trilateral co-operation in research and development.

The primary motivation of the signatories to NAFTA – Canada, Mexico and the USA – was economic, but the three governments also saw international trade in education and training services, the promotion of academic excellence, and the strengthening of cross-cultural understanding as important by-products of co-operation. However, in a survey published recently by the AAUC, it was found that internationalisation strategies emphasising North America remain a low priority for most Canadian colleges and universities. The geographic priority areas for international co-operation are Central and South America, followed closely by Asia and the Pacific Rim (Knight 1996). Western Europe ranked third in the survey, while North America ranked fourth. Moreover, Canadian development projects in Mexico actually decreased in the 1990s, although the USA easily occupied first place in the list of countries engaged in collaborative research projects with Canadian colleges and universities. In terms of inter-institutional agreements by geographic region, the USA occupied sixth place (5%) and Mexico and Central America occupied fifth (6%). Of all full-time undergraduate and graduate students in the 99 institutions surveyed, only 0.9 percent had studied abroad.

North American Mobility in Higher Education Program

Perhaps the most successful Canadian outcome of North American Co-operation in Higher Education has been the North American Mobility in Higher Education program. Launched in June of 1995, it is designed to enhance co-operation and academic exchange among Canadian, Mexican and U.S. institutions. In 1995-96, the Canadian federal government budgeted $1.3 million over three years to fund projects involving more than 200 Canadian students in academic and work/study exchanges from fifteen universities and four colleges. Projects covered a wide range of fields including architecture, business, engineering, health, law and technology. The following year (1996-1997), nine new projects were approved with a federal budget of $1.1 million over three years. The projects in business, engineering, political science, geology, and computer science involved thirteen Canadian universities and four colleges and more than 180 students. Ten additional projects were approved in 1997-98 at a cost of $1.3 million over three years.

In summarising Canadian participation in the program, Human Resources Development Canada (HRDC) reports that over the three year period from 1995 to 1998, a total of thirty projects were approved, with departments from 40 universities and colleges, and some 600 students participating in the program.[7] Quotas were over-filled for Canada-Mexico exchanges and under-filled for exchanges between Canada and the USA.

It appears that credit transfer was not a problem and in the vast majority of cases the institutions involved had signed formal institutional agreements. In almost three-quarters of the projects, it was expected that some contact would continue, mainly in the form of faculty linkages. Also, funding permitting student exchanges would continue. Significantly, over half of the institutions reported that some form of curriculum evolution or tailored development had occurred as a result of participation in the projects, and over a quarter had applied or developed learning technologies to aid in the internationalisation of course instruction (HRDC 1999).

The mobility program has also had an impact beyond its own boundaries. It has contributed to the raising of the general consciousness within higher education institutions of the USA and Mexico as sources of students, and led to overall increases in enrolments from these two countries (see Table 4). Between 1992-1993 and 1996-1997, student enrolments from Mexico went from 623 to 1,098, while those from the USA rose from 3,644 to 4,500. These increases undoubtedly contributed to the Trilateral Steering Committee on North American collaboration in Higher Education deciding to continue the program in early 2001. Nevertheless, the number of Canadian students in these trilateral programs is very small given that the nation's colleges and universities enrolled 1,321,376 full- and part-time students in academic year 1998-1999 (Statistics Canada 2001).

The Trilateral Steering Committee on North American Collaboration in Higher Education discussed five other initiatives at its meeting in early 2000. Work on the Alliance for Higher Education and Enterprise in North America, for example, is still being pursued on several fronts. In Canada, the Alliance has proposed to the federal government's Department of Human Resources and Development that a project be carried out to explore ways in which private sector and community college participation in international education and student mobility could be increased. The AUCC, along with its Mexican and U.S. counterparts, is pursuing research on models of international academic co-operation, working on the development of a design for a "virtual marketplace" (using the existing EL Net), and exploring work-study issues in North America.

Perhaps the most interesting initiative is the one concerning quality assurance geared toward promoting mutual understanding of and exchange of information on existing quality assurance mechanisms. It is an initiative that is not expected to lead to a new and integrated system of North American higher education accreditation. Rather, it is one that would help advance academic and professional mobility through recognition of each country's quality assurance practices (Gagnon 2000).

Table 10. Students in Canada from Mexico and USA

Mexico	1992-1993	391/72	160/632
	1993-1994	447/N/A	N/A /N/A
	1994-1995	531/286	151/968
	1995-1996	408/247	184/839
	1996-1997	555/307	236/1,098
USA	1992-1993	840/1,496	1,308/3,644
	1993-1994	1,039/N/A	N/A/N/A
	1994-1995	952/1,497	1,154/3,603
	1995-1996	1,122/1,786	1,295/4,203
	1996-1997	1,280/1,912	1,308/4,500

Source: Canadian Bureau for International Education (1999)

Canada remains supportive of North American studies, although it is a given that any assistance it provides should reinforce its Canadian Studies program and not be seen as a substitute for this program. It is supportive of the initiative to upgrade the EL Net website and electronic information exchange services, especially with regard to the development of a "matchmaking capacity" that will enhance faculty mobility across the region. Canada is also interested in El Net's capacity to promote Canadian education throughout North America.

Key Issues and Challenges

It is clear that the major response of Canada's colleges and universities to the forces of globalisation and trade liberalisation consist primarily of efforts to strengthen the international and inter-cultural dimensions of their role and function. However, it is difficult to assess these initiatives in Canada due to the lack of aggregate or comparative information and data on the policy and practice of internationalisation at both the system and institutional level. There is also not much evidence on efforts to develop core international competencies or to internationalise the curricula. There is also the challenge of internationalising the initial and continuing education of professionals, while priority must also be given to the reversal of negative trends in international student mobility. Most important, there is a need to create a national strategy that will bring greater coherence to Canada's continental and global initiatives in this field of endeavour.

Information, Assessment and Research Needs

Within the higher education community there is an urgent need to document and consolidate existing data and information on internationalisation. Basic research on policy and practice needs to be encouraged and carried out. Systematic efforts to analyse international activities are rare. Where they do exist, they often take the form of in-house unpublished documentary reports. External assessments are virtually non-existent and comparative studies are only now being considered and proposed (CHERD 2002). In addition, major new phenomena need to be recognised, studied and monitored such as the growing commercialisation of research and educational services, and the ambitious use of multi-media communications technology for delivering them across borders. The latter in particular pose interesting new challenges of quality assessment, consumer protection, and regulatory processes. The growing internationalisation of the professions also needs to be documented and analysed by scholars. The international dialogue emerging between higher education and the professions needs to be examined in greater depth, accreditation and recognition procedures clarified, measurement and benchmarking issues addressed, and case studies of individual professions conducted.

Development of Core International Competencies

Canada is one of the most trade-dependent countries in the world. One-third of its jobs are trade-related and it is therefore ironic that the qualifications of its international managers have been placed in question and deep concern expressed over their lack of international skills. At this point in time, Canada needs more globally-oriented business leaders than ever, but very few companies seems to have a system in place to develop them (Church 1999).

However, this is not for want of advice or information on the subject. Tug (1998) has identified six factors contributing to what she describes as the growing convergence of forces that demand new skills and competencies of international and domestic managers in Canada. They are (1) the globalisation of industry, (2) the formation of co-operative agreements between entities from two or more nations, (3) quantitative advances in telecommunications and data processing, (4) organisational downsizing, (5) growing diversity in the domestic workforce, (6) and a workforce that is becoming more global. These forces in turn give rise to the need for managers to balance the conflicting demands of global integration versus local responsiveness, to work in and lead teams composed of people of diverse backgrounds.

Wilson (1998) has similar points to make. After reviewing the most recent Canadian literature on the subject, he concludes that it is imperative for educational policy-makers, planners and employers to examine what international competencies are needed, where and by whom they can be taught, and how best they might be measured–all questions that have significant implications for the internationalisation of curricula in higher education.

Internationalising the Curriculum

Two recent publications provide insight into the extent to which efforts to internationalise curricula in Canadian higher education are progressing. In 1996, the BCCIE and the Centre for Curriculum and Professional Development organised an exploratory regional conference on "Internationalising the Curriculum" (BCCIE 1996a, 1996b). Individual presenters at the conference represented a wide variety of institutions, fields and viewpoints. They addressed goals, expectations, case studies, models, projects, strategies, processes, content, competencies, skills, standards, resources, barriers, constraints, challenges and benefits. While the rich diversity of these presentations is in itself encouraging, it also suggests that systematic discussion of the internationalisation of undergraduate curricula is at a very early stage of development.

The title of the second publication *From Reluctant Acceptance to Modest Embrace: Internationalisation of Undergraduate Education* confirms this claim (Bond and Scott, 1999). Its authors point to the paucity of academic thought and action in the area. They observe that what has been done to date is rarely the result of orderly planning, but rather the work of academics and student volunteers who have a sustained commitment to aid and development projects. Moreover, they report that administrators commonly evaluated such efforts "in terms of their economic potential for their universities, rather than on intellectual or cultural merit" (Ibid., 54).

Reversing Negative Trends in International Student Mobility

A key indicator of a nation's performance in international higher education is its ability to support its students studying abroad and to attract students from other countries. Recent evidence suggests that Canada's performance on both counts is seriously lacking. According to the CBIE, international enrolments in Canada's colleges and universities have declined by 3 percent since 1993, graduate enrolments by 13 percent, and doctoral enrolments by 25 percent. Canada's ranking as a host nation for international students has fallen from fourth to seventh over the past ten years (CBIE 2000c), while only 3 per cent of Canadian students are studying abroad.[9]

CBIE gives six reasons for this disheartening state of affairs: (1) aggressive competition from abroad (especially other English-speaking countries), (2) fluctuating fee schedules, (3) a federally-financed marketing strategy that is more supply- than demand-driven, (4) a lack of commitment to reciprocal scholarship schemes, (5) a lack of brand recognition for Canadian higher education institutions, (6) and negative impressions of Canadian visa processing (CBIE 2000b).

Meanwhile, Canada is far more preoccupied with fears about a brain drain to the United States than it is about the decline in its ability to attract international students. While much of the evidential material advanced in support of these fears is anecdotal (Lindgren 1997; Laver 1999), data from Statistics Canada suggest that any loss is more than offset by the arrival of large numbers of highly-educated immigrants. Immigrant engineers, computer scientists and natural scientists, for example, vastly outnumber those in these fields who emigrate to the USA. Similarly, the number of managerial workers emigrating to the USA is small relative to the new supply in the Canadian labour force. Overall, Canada gains at least four times as many university graduates from abroad, and a disproportionate share of these possess graduate degrees (Statistics Canada 1998).

Internationalisation of the Professions[10]

Advances are being made in internationalising the professions by applying the principles of transparency, comparability and convertibility to both voluntary and mandatory systems of regulation. They are taking place, moreover, in the context of fundamental and far-reaching changes in the ways in which higher education and continuing professional education are being conceived and understood. The question of whether continuing education should be mandatory or voluntary is a source of extended discussion in professions like nursing. Professional re-certification is being considered in others, and efforts are being made to translate the principle of lifelong learning into action at the level of both policy and practice. Despite these advances, however, a number of issues need to be addressed. There is an urgent need to co-ordinate and consolidate existing data bases and information systems. Accreditation and recognition procedures need to be clarified and models of disciplinary action for professionals practising in another country developed. Competency-based testing, the assessment of prior learning and the measurement of work experience are also challenges to be met and overcome.

Creation of a National Vision and Strategy for International Education

The most important challenge, however, is the creation of a national vision and strategy for international higher education within which co-operation with Mexico and the USA can find its place. Put simply, no national agenda for international higher education exists. Nor, it seems, is this weakness likely to be remedied soon. This is clearly not the case elsewhere. Australia has led the way in recent years with federal government financing and the active co-operation of higher education institutions and the professions. France has launched a campaign to dramatically increase the size of its international student body. The United Kingdom has committed millions in order to strengthen linkages with leading international institutions. And in the USA, President Clinton signed an executive memorandum outlining a ten-point plan to enhance international education. In Canada, on the other hand, the country's much-ballyhooed foreign policy—in which education and culture were to form the so-called "third pillar"—has all but disappeared from view.

CONCLUSION

The forces of globalisation have resulted in Canadian higher education policy being seen over the last fifteen years almost exclusively in terms of international competitiveness and the global economy. In practice this has meant reductions in core funding, increased student fees, the introduction of targeted funds, the promotion of inter-sectoral partnerships (governments, academe and the private sector), the creation of centres of excellence and the increasing commercialisation of research.

Participation in a series of trade liberalisation initiatives has had a similar and reinforcing effect. This is especially the case in international higher education. Here trade in education services has occupied centre stage. Funding for co-operative development work has been reduced. Visa students are seen largely as sources of increased revenue and differential fees have been introduced.

It is within this context, shaped as it is by the forces of globalisation and trade liberalisation, that higher education institutions are struggling to become more international and to prepare graduates possessing globally-oriented values, hemispheric perspectives, continental experiences, and inter-cultural skills and competencies.

It is within this context, shaped as it is by the forces of globalisation and trade liberalisation, that higher education institutions are struggling to become more international and to prepare graduates possessing globally-oriented values, hemispheric perspectives, continental experiences, and a range of inter-cultural skills and competencies. Results are at best mixed. Canada may well be one of the world's most internationally-minded and trade-dependent nations. It may well stress the imperative of achieving international standards of quality in the creation, dissemination and application of knowledge. In the final analysis, the gap between rhetoric and reality remains large and is yet to be bridged.

CHAPTER 5

GLOBALISATION, NAFTA, AND HIGHER EDUCATION IN MEXICO

GLOBALISATION, NAFTA, AND TRANSITION IN MEXICO

On the Mexican national scene, the North American Free Trade Agreement (NAFTA) has symbolised the country's entry into the process of globalisation. No matter how widespread the perception, however, NAFTA was only a landmark in a continuous process of economic liberalisation, which began in 1986 with the country's entry into the General Agreement on Tariffs and Trade (GATT).[1] NAFTA formalised as well the old process of silent integration between the economies of Mexico and the United States. Although that Agreement only had a trade component, the discussion around its suitability as an integral part of a national plan of long term development soon overtook the original framework and became part of a larger socio-political debate. This explains, first, the importance of NAFTA to the strategy of President Carlos Salinas de Gortari's cabinet. It also clarifies the struggle that occurred among political parties in a country that was initiating the slow process of alternation in power after seven decades of near hegemony by the Institutional Revolutionary Party (PRI), and finally, the difficult but very important relationship between Mexico and its Northern neighbour.

Controversy surrounded the inclusion of particular products in the spheres of jurisdiction of NAFTA, as well as the mechanisms for the resolution of disputes. Paradoxically, NAFTA also dealt with some areas that had been excluded from the negotiating agenda. Although themes such as migration and drug trafficking were not strictly trade-related – in spite of their economic impact– they constituted recurring foci of tension in the bilateral relations between Mexico and the United States. They were, therefore, matters of interest and mobilisation for several national sectors. Beyond praise or criticism, the discussions on NAFTA and its implications soon went beyond the circle of thematic specialists. These discussions provoked generalised thinking about globalisation as a project of socio-economic organisation. They soon gave way to an examination of how to place Mexico in an advantageous position as a developing country in the world scene as well as in a large region. There was recognition that the region was not internally balanced, given the relative weight of the respective national economies, and of their different social, political and cultural structures. Close scrutiny generated an analysis about the indirect impact of NAFTA on political, cultural and educational matters. NAFTA revived the familiar school of thought that was concerned with the maintenance of a strong national identity and the relationship with its own history and with that of other nations. It served as an excuse to return to a discussion about relations with a North American neighbour that had been historically defined as antagonistic as well as one with which there was a tradition of mutual need. Ultimately, discussion had a bilateral rather than trilateral reference point, with greater emphasis placed on the United States than on Canada.

Despite the continuing opposition on the part of intellectual groups located in the centre-left of the political continuum, as well as certain business sectors, NAFTA brought about the restructuring of the Mexican economy. Together with the accompanying phenomenon of the intellectualisation of production, it raised the importance of the service industry, thereby modifying the previously prevalent sectoral industrial schemes. New efficiencies in the productive processes affected small and medium-sized enterprises negatively, focused as they were on the satisfaction of local demands, and lacking the resources to undertake a process of reorganisation. On the other hand, efficiencies opened up new vistas to export-oriented firms in their distribution of products. They also contributed to the deepening of the crisis in which the primary sector had been immersed for years, especially the sectors organised around small farms, that existed simply to ensure the subsistence of their inhabitants. For that reason, the areas of the Mexican countryside that were already in great difficulty continued to witness the exodus of their people. These areas continued to survive only thanks to the financial support of the migrant workers. In some regions –particularly in the north and the centre of the country – NAFTA caused the rapid transition of regional economies toward the maquiladora system of North American and Asian origin. It transformed some local cities into attractive meccas and modified the normal pathways to national migration. By bringing about a "new geography of production," [2] it affected the fragile equilibrium in the cities, especially the twin border towns. Finally, it affected adversely the customary relations in the organisation of families and the generation of income.

In turn, adjustments in the labour sector caused the lessening of a competitive advantage– based on low wages– of a workforce that was cheap but also poorly educated. They explained the emergence of new demands for a workforce with high or medium training, combined with demands for a workforce—then scarce—in all levels of education. These adjustments also renewed the latent struggle for wide access to the system of education for all social groups. They justified a strategy of public policy centred on the establishment of a certification system for labour proficiency, designed to set the foundations for a more flexible scheme for the validation of knowledge.

In December 1994, twelve months after the signing of NAFTA, an economic and financial crisis hit Mexico. As on previous occasions,[3] the so-called "tequila effect" witnessed the arrival of inflationary spirals,[4] national currency devaluation, the loss of a number of jobs,[5] and the deterioration of living conditions for the great majority of people. Despite the recovery achieved by some macro-economic indicators, old structural problems also gained in importance, the most worrisome being the unequal distribution of income. Six years after the crisis, according to some sources, it is estimated that between 40 and 60 percent of the population is either in poverty or in abject poverty. The Department of Social Development (SUDESOL) was created in 1987 and it established outreach assistance programs such as the National Program of Solidarity (PRONASOL), later replaced by PROGRESA, but these only alleviated some of the more severe strains caused by the new state of affairs.

During the last decade, poverty has become a fundamental source of instability, placing in jeopardy the viability of sustainable development projects. At the same time, other factors worsened the divisions in public opinion and caused a climate of social and political uncertainty. There have been partial advances in some areas such as respect for the results of elections – thanks to the creation of a civic organisation for the operation and supervision of electoral processes, the Instituto Federal Electoral. The crisis of legitimacy and of representation that affects all political parties, the recurring scandals related to corruption, drug trafficking and the administration of justice, crimes that go unpunished, and general civic insecurity have, however, undermined the confidence of both foreign investors (OECD 1995) and the general population. The political scene has also become strained. The on-going armed conflict in Chiapas, which started –might one say symbolically – the day of the implementation of NAFTA, continues to complicate party relations, collectively and individually. Although Mexican society possesses new mechanisms to place limits on the arbitrariness of power practices, it lacks the ability to create a new consensus and paths for participation. It finds itself in a situation of increasing polarisation, not only in economic and social terms but also in terms of political mobilisation, planning for development, life opportunities and expectations.

The birth of NAFTA and its reception by Mexican society explain the ideological nature of posturing on globalisation and the resurgence of nationalistic perspectives, anchored in the political culture and the history of Mexico. Therefore, many interpretations around NAFTA deal with the themes of dependency and sovereignty, identity and alienation. If Blade Runner or Titanic are the symbols of a world culture dear to the U.S. mass culture, the blue tlacayos are part of a passionate attachment to tradition and idiosyncratic behaviour. NAFTA, however, did not provide just a pretext to renew old controversies. It contributed as well to firing up the societal debate about democratisation and the proper role of government, fundamental to Mexico during the 1990s. Its opponents presented trade integration with the United States as an autocratic decision that had not been the subject of consultation. After the errors made in December 1994, which brought forth the 1995 crisis, the perception of NAFTA as well as the establishment of forces for and against, changed. Its opponents became stronger. They established alliances with groups that were formed after the economic collapse, such as the Barzon[6] (bank debtors), which brought together middle class sectors unable to pay the high new rates of interest. However, despite the criticism, NAFTA moved forward while negotiations with its North American neighbours brought to a standstill other processes of trade integration, where Mexico had been involved in negotiations with geographically distant partners such as the European Union.

The relationship of Mexican society and, mainly of intellectual and university groups, to the questions of globalisation, NAFTA, and higher education was determined by the existing national situation as well as by an intellectual history that always saw relations with the United States as inevitable but fraught with danger. The two explain the questions posed by specialists and by diverse leaders of public opinion representing many social sectors. In the educational context, these questions related to the capability of the national higher education system to compete advantageously with the more developed U.S and Canadian counterparts. A school of thought became organised around that discussion. It warned of the negative consequences of NAFTA (Aboites 1997). Conflicts began to occur around public policies designed to harmonise the national educational system with those of the trading partners. This explains why the policy of internationalising the higher education institutions in Mexico (IESM) has not had the importance and the consistency that it has had in the other two countries. It provides us with analytical elements because, at the end of the 1990s, a school of thought became consolidated around questions related to the policy of reform of higher education, a school that was based on strong criticism of neo-liberalism and globalisation (Acosta 2000)

NORTH AMERICAN INTEGRATION: ITS IMPACT ON HIGHER EDUCATION IN MEXICO

NAFTA and the Educational Actors

Unlike the situation in the United States and Canada, in Mexico the question of the full reform of the national education system vis-à-vis the trilateral economic integration has not been broached in a comprehensive manner nor become the target of a long-term plan. In the educational programs corresponding to the past two presidential periods (1988-1994 and 1994-2000), there have been numerous references to the conditions which guarantee global competitiveness in human resources and business enterprise, including the role of research in improving production processes and the need to promote internationalisation and cross-border co-operation policies in higher education. However, these references have been superficial. Although topics related to these issues receive the obligatory mention in sectoral documents, it is evident from rectors' reports that the declarations of federal administrations and elected officials have not been translated into strategic proposals by most higher education institutions or by the relevant governmental bodies. The public discussion has not directly engaged the question of labour productivity, except through vague references to the notion that the higher the level of education attainment, the higher the level of labour efficiency. By and large, globalisation in general, and NAFTA in particular, have been components of higher education's development scenario that are still seen as remote and ill-defined. These issues have not been perceived as features of a new and problematic sphere of interest, which require immediate attention through the design of goal-oriented programs, or through treatment of their terms and the allocation of financial resources. The lack of a common frame of reference that might serve to identify challenges and articulate responses in the cultural, the curricular, and professional areas is one of the most striking differences between Mexico and its partners, especially in the public high education sector.

By contrast, some prestigious private institutions have sought to respond in a more articulate manner to the challenges of globalisation and internationalisation. They have done this by reviewing the profile of skills and abilities of graduates and by promoting an institutional policy of co-operation and academic mobility. By coincidence, the National Council of Science and Technology (CONACYT), the chief organ for scientific research in Mexico, has defined strategic areas in which intervention may be warranted. These include the development of resources for production at high levels and links between the private sector and the universities. CONACYT has created co-operative programs between academia and industry. It has provided technological support to the IESMs and for research into areas of shared interest.[7] In chapter 6 of its Program for Science and Technology 1995-2000, CONACYT also included a plan for exchanges and international linkages.

The Program had the following objectives:

- Defining in a more active way Mexico's interests in joint programs with foreign counterparts,
- Intensifying the level of co-operation with the countries included in NAFTA and opening new channels of co-operation, particularly with the European Union and the Asia-Pacific region,
- Establishing programs to bring highly recognised foreign researchers to Mexico, as well as Mexican scientists residing abroad,
- Analysing international experiences in matters of university-industry co-operation with a view to adapting them to the national situation, whenever possible,
- Encouraging international co-operation projects involving members of academia and the industrial sector,
- Promoting two-way flows of scientific and technological information and putting these at the disposal of potential users at the appropriate time.

In order to accomplish these objectives, CONACYT designed activities that would support them. These included:

- Establishing shared international financing schemes for joint activities to encourage scientific research, technological development, and human resource training,
- Promoting greater participation by Mexico in multinational programs of advanced science and technology and facilitating access for Mexican scientist and technologists in top level laboratories abroad,
- Organising international meetings to encourage linkages between the academic and industrial sectors.

The appropriate strategies for achieving these goals were consist of:

- Analysing the patterns of interaction among national institutions of higher education and research so that programs of co-operation can respond to the needs of international linkages,
- Establishing strategies for the development of new scientific areas through alliances with foreign centres that have experience in them,
- Carrying out studies to better define a program of support by CONACYT for research projects that have an international co-operation component,
- Exploring on-going program offerings by international foundations and establishing joint programs with shared funds,
- Systematically collecting information on offers of international collaboration through the preparation of catalogues.

CONACYT recognised the urgency of integrating a system of information and inducements, by setting out the following objectives:

- Publicising international programs of scientific and technological co-operation,
- Carrying out campaigns of national consultation in order to set clear cut requirements for scientific and technological information from abroad,
- Facilitating the gathering of electronic information available in other countries to members of the scientific and academic communities,
- Encouraging the publication of periodicals on international scientific and technological themes,
- Providing incentives to enterprises involved in the distribution of periodicals and scientific books produced in Mexico so that they can increase their sales in international markets,
- Providing incentives for the creation of firms and organisations that will convey information to the entrepreneurial class in Mexico about technological innovations,
- Putting together basic packages of information regarding events in the international sphere of science and technology and to put them at the disposal of researchers and institutions in all regions of the country,
- Elaborating and publishing information bulletins on advances in science and technology in Mexico,
- Integrating and keeping updated data bases about linkages between universities and firms arising from international programs of technological co-operation,
- Supporting entrepreneurial organisations in the selection of technologies available abroad,
- Registering in a systematic fashion the results of international programs of co-operation.

Therefore, CONACYT proposed:

- To establish adequate co-ordination between the Department of External Relations, CONACYT, and the offices of international liaison of the various branches of the federal executive, as well as of the research and development institutions in the country,
- To sign international agreements on science and technology in more precise language in terms of collaboration, objectives, outreach and methodologies,
- To select highly significant international political forums that support the interests of Mexican science and technology.

In addition to the programs specifically devoted to the support of international activities, both globally and in the North American area,[8] CONACYT strengthened the domestic process of internationalisation. It acquired an appropriate infrastructure for distance telecommunications and laboratory equipment and supported national linkage projects with the private sector, one of the areas where greatest asymmetry was believed to exist between Canada, Mexico, and the United States. Together with the Department of Higher Education and Scientific Research (SESIC), CONACYT became the organisation that supported most investment in the international arena. Its investments focused on priority areas in Science and Technology, as well as on enhanced international competitiveness in these fields. It defined internationalisation as a vehicle for sustained application of research and technological development that contributed to the establishment of strong, highly innovative enterprises, ready to compete in the international context (CONACYT 1994, 13). In order to accomplish this goal, CONACYT has sought to transform academic behaviour by providing the necessary support to Mexican researchers to become active participants in forums, publications, and research projects sponsored by international organisations. In Article 13 of a draft law that the Congress of the Union discussed in 1999, CONACYT reaffirmed its position by stating that the formulation of the National Program of Science and Technology should contain "at the very least," the following components:

I. A general policy of support for science and technology
II. Policies, strategies, and priority actions in matters of:
  a) Scientific research
  b) Innovation and technological development
  c) Formation of top-level researchers and professionals
  d) Diffusion of scientific and technological knowledge
  e) National and international collaboration in the activities mentioned above
  f) Strengthening of national scientific and technological culture (CONACYT–Draft Legislation, March 1999, http://www.conacyt.main)

For their part, the associations that group together institutions in the higher education sector have sought to sensitise their members to the challenges in the current situation. They have done this whether they represent them in general terms –for example the National Association of Universities and Institutions of Higher Education

(ANUIES) or by segments –such as the National High Council of Teaching (COSNET) – for Technological Institutes. They have also taken the lead in seeking basic consensus for action in the process of globalisation. ANUIES has put together positions in support of evaluation, accreditation and certification among both administrative leaders and staff. It has taken part in conceptualising international education cooperation through its own contributions and through the diffusion of specialised articles[10] on co-operation in international bilateral or trilateral education. In the high technology education sector, the Department of Education and Technology Research (SEIT) and COSNET began reflecting on the challenges that economic liberalisation posed for the sector that had begun in the early 1990s.[11] They responded by initiating a curriculum revision process throughout Mexico. Their most important aims consisted of restructuring programs and decreasing –from 52 to 19– the number of careers that existed in order to form competitive professionals with the knowledge, ability, and skills to compete successfully at the national and international levels. However, despite their key role in the diffusion of concepts and their espousal of new policies at the national level, those organisations have not articulated in a consistent way a proper discourse among their members about the changes required to achieve macroregional integration. They have not considered either the organisational and knowledge-based challenges brought about by this integration or the appropriate modifications required in the organisations required to promote internationalisation.

Consequently, it is the education researchers themselves, along with those officers involved in trilateral organisations – such as the Trilateral Task Force in Higher Education (TTFHE) – and in the promotion of international relations in central administration who have made proposals or who have provided the most relevant analysis on higher education and globalisation. The topic that most interests these individuals is the perceived asymmetrical development of the three systems of higher education.[12] Starting from different perspectives, they identified the same problems. Mexicans had a small number of young people entering the system, a small number of scientists in relation to the economically active population (PEA), an insufficient graduation record for students, and deficient equipment and infrastructure. Consequently, the rate of education received by the general population and the PEA was lower than in other countries.[13] There were differences in the distribution of per capita expenditures associated with education in general and higher education in particular as a percentage of the Gross National Product.[14] There were also differences in the two organisational models of higher education with respect to the degree of centralisation. The lack of consolidation of the academic staff, the weak role of research groups, the poor interaction of the IES with the social and productive environments, as well as the difficulty experienced by the organisations in responding to the emerging demands for human resources required by the private sector, and to the specific requirements of the sectors involved in globalisation, all became matters of great concern.[15] Perceived problems included the degree of institutional and disciplinary diversity, the few opportunities available to obtain degrees of short duration, and the lack of formulas for the retraining and modernisation of professional qualifications. These problems lessened the possibility that the educational system would develop properly in order to fit well with those of the more developed northern neighbours. Therefore, in order to better fit into the regional bloc, Mexico would have to increase the quality of university education, strengthen teaching and research, and reinforce the evaluation system.

As a consequence of these asymmetries, analysis of the situation in the higher education has adopted a macro-regional perspective, whether in relation to North America or Latin America. While specialists of various disciplines and other educators tackled questions related to NAFTA, specialists on higher education rarely did the same on issues such as the transformations taking place in national identity, ethics, and formation of the citizenry. These were of course questions traditionally treated by anthropologists and political scientists, as well as in the primary schools. With some exceptions, the specialists' treatment of these themes was excessively restricted. The idea that asymmetrical realities largely explained relations between Mexico and its North American neighbours was used as the rationale for differences in their respective treatment of fundamental issues. On a tri-national scale, this notion made it difficult to define shared strategies that would establish common educational paths for Canada, the United States, and Mexico.[16]

Nevertheless, the growing importance of globalisation and macro-regional integration to the development of Mexican higher education is beyond doubt. In recent years, the number of documents, articles, and papers that deal with these subjects and their consequences has increased dramatically. Both concepts, however, remained ill defined in these discussions. In particular, biases for or against globalisation and NAFTA predominate in most discussions of these topics. In Mexico, globalisation is not a problem requiring resolution; it is seen as a political question, and therefore, a permanent justification for heated argument.

Globalisation and Strategic Decision-Making in Higher Education

What has been said above is the more worrisome when one realises that essential information is lacking for evaluating the progress made in the elaboration of policies on higher education, globalisation, and macro-regional integration. This is the case in spite of the fact that the problem as such was identified in the middle of the 1990s. Although there is a consensus on the importance of obtaining updated and trustworthy data on the result of public policies, data available– either in the central administration or in the academic institutions themselves–on issues such as international collaboration, scholarships, international funds for research, study abroad by Mexican students, and in Mexico by foreign students, is either inadequate or contains gaps. The data is not appropriate for measuring with certainty the impact of NAFTA on the strengthening of relations between academic partners. At the same time, knowledge gathered by research works is scattered and qualitative in nature. Both in decision-making and subsequent follow-up, the delay in producing this information, the untrustworthiness and poor handling of the data, especially of a financial nature, make it difficult to produce a balance sheet, comparing the national situation with that of other countries or analysing its historical evolution.

This situation has not been resolved due to the absence of an organisation with sufficient legitimacy and adequate resources to organise and spread the information with any degree of continuity. The lack of discussion about the need to have congruent and comparable international data available demonstrates that despite a great deal of research on matters of globalisation, integration, and education since 1992, the whole issue has not been given priority, either by the institutional decision-makers or by the federal or regional authorities. In fact, the Mexican higher education system has been undergoing a profound process of reform since 1988. In essence, policies designed to improve its efficiency and operations, to make the use and handling of financial resources transparent, to build mechanisms of evaluation that will give a full account of results, are themselves a response to the obvious malfunctioning of the system. Although the adopted solutions and the actual values of reform – based on quality, rationality and equity – are similar to those chosen by many other countries, and are supported by international organisations, the reach of the educational actions continues to be national in scope, and in the case of institutions, often regional or local. While the pending questions are of great magnitude and resources are limited, the eradication of immediate problems appears more urgent than the development of preventive actions. Consequently, the policies are oriented more toward the short- than the long term, and proactive action is always subordinate to corrective or reactive considerations.

The fact that boards of directors or representative bodies of national higher education have not produced a framework on education for both learned societies and knowledge-based economic bodies is not so much the result of a decision not to politicise the issue – although globalisation and internationalisation are both delicate topics in the political and intellectual spheres – but of the establishment of a hierarchy of urgent needs that gives precedence to the present over the future. There appear to be in Mexico educational policies and responses to these issues that have become a legitimate part of the new international and macro-regional order, but they lack the visibility and internal coherence that they have in other countries, particularly given the fact that they are regarded as being of secondary importance.

THE POLITICAL RESPONSES AND THE SPHERES OF ACTION

Taking Action on Asymmetries

Some of the public policies that were supposed to tackle recent social changes, as well as changes in the productive structures, had a slim connection with those changes. Others, however, were direct responses to them. As an illustration of the former, the transition from a model of financial grants to public higher education institutions which is based on size – first on fees, later on allocations for full-time personnel – to one that is semi-competitive and contractual and has access to its own sources of funds, was a decision in part inspired by the recommendations of international organisations. However, it was not a specific response to the formal situation of macro-regional integration. The replacement of a financing model justified by a populist vision of education by another more in tune with international considerations opened up a new point of convergence between the Mexican government, and other national governments and international organisations, which saw the scheme as having good practical value. Yet, it was done in an indirect form and not as a result of an effort to harmonise or to come up with a list of solutions on education that was shared by a number of countries tightly linked economically. It was a response to a series of questions about the quality of the national education system and to a situation of fiscal crisis, where the federal government had less and less resources available to maintain the commitments it had assumed in matters of higher education since the 1970s.

By contrast, documentation of the asymmetries with respect to the United States and Canada had clear consequences for Mexico. It introduced new educational problems into the public and specialist debate. It helped bring up old topics under a different focus. For instance, the high increase in fees in the 1970s and 1980s had been analysed traditionally as a factor in the deterioration in the quality of teaching and research processes. By comparison with the United States and Canada, as well as with other Latin American countries, this concept was given a higher value, given that the national rate of young people of university age that actually attended was less than that in many countries in the region. Expansion became an objective of public policy and was regulated in accordance with sectoral and regional patterns of growth. In a similar fashion, the lower level of education of Mexican academics in relation to their American and Canadian colleagues made it possible to stress the need, detected fifteen years earlier, of improving their levels of education. At the same time, these questions justified the replacement of the old perspective that relied on improving the ability to teach with another that stressed the acquisition of degrees at the masters and doctoral level.[17] Starting as it did from an asymmetrical position, defining useful reforms in the context of integration modified the direction of the national debate on higher education and the selection of policies related to that area. It granted full legitimacy as well to new actions on educational matters as long as they were congruent with the reorganisation policies previously chosen by the Mexican government.

Continuity in higher education policies since the late 1980s is, therefore, more evident than any change that might have taken place after the introduction of NAFTA. The reforms undergone in the 1990s were the result of the demise of the historical model of consolidation of the higher education system and of a will to tackle critical areas. Many national policies – evaluation, financial autonomy, the beginning of a contractual relationship between the state and the institution – are in agreement with the policies recommended by international organisations and by experts as the most appropriate in view of the rise of the higher education systems in practically all countries. They have been appropriate also because they responded to a situation in which problems and orientations in public policy were becoming increasingly tied to higher education concerns. Paradoxically, however, educational and sociological analysis on globalisation was related to the neighbours of the North and more precisely to the bilateral dimension with the United States. There has been confusion, rather than differentiation, between the concepts of globalisation and macro-regional integration. Although a reaction has been evident to the opportunities available by the existence of tri-lateralisation, intellectual thought veered permanently between thinking along global, macro-regional, bilateral, and international lines.

Evaluation, Accreditation, and Certification

Although education was not specifically included in NAFTA, Chapters 12 and 16 relating to Border Trading of Services and Temporary Entry of People had an indirect impact on it. These chapters affected national regulations in matters of professional certification and indirectly in accreditation of degrees. The first tri-lateral meetings on these aspects demonstrated in fact that there were enormous differences between the situation in Mexico and in the partner countries. In the United States and Canada, accreditation was a regular—though voluntary—exercise carried out by non-governmental agencies at the regional and/or specialised level. Similarly, certification was a process led by professional bodies that alone determined the possibility of practising a profession. In Mexico, however, everything was in the hands of educational institutions. The features of the system were as follows:

- Neither specialisation nor institutional accreditation was a common practice. Only a few prestigious private institutions utilised the American agencies to obtain institutional or degree accreditation, for instance through the Southern Association of Colleges and Schools.
- Recognition of degrees for professional practice and the granting of the appropriate certificate in the professions were dependent on the General Branch of Professions (DGP) in the Department of Public Education (SEP). This body verified the legality of the documents in order to grant the professional certificate required for practising. It was, however, each higher education institution that itself guaranteed the quality of the education acquired by the applicant in accordance with its own criteria of evaluation, apprenticeship, and the granting of a degree. There was no intervention from any other labour or professional organisation external to the institution itself (Mendez Lugo 1995). Although dating back to 1945, the Law on the Professions in the Federal District which guides the process continues without any modifications up to the present time.[19]
- Except in some states (Baja California Sur, Chihuahua, Jalisco, San Luis Potosi and Zacatecas) and in a very few professions, such as medicine, most state laws regulating the professions do not make it compulsory for professionals to maintain certification.
- The formation of colleges within professional associations is voluntary. Traditionally, the political affiliation of any association is with the PRI in accordance with the realities of a corporatist system. As political pluralism grew, this tight relationship lost some of its elasticity and each professional association become more autonomous and representative. Whenever this did not occur, other associations were born. Despite those changes, the percentage of members is

low, varying between 3 and 33 per cent, depending on the profession (Ortega 1999).

The reduced role played by professional colleges, the nearly complete absence of intermediary bodies watching over the minimum norms of quality in the granting of professional services, and the incompatibility of national legislation on this matter with that of the partner countries, led to a recognition that the national processes of accreditation of degrees and certification of professional competence were structurally different from those of the trading partners. Solving these differences depended on the ability of all three countries to reach an agreement on these points of discussion. Creating a basis for negotiation on this matter, however, implied a greater effort for Mexico than for any of its partners. It became a matter of reviewing the mechanisms of professional certification and making ad hoc arrangements that would guarantee to users and/or employers that the academic knowledge transmitted by the IESMs to their graduates would have a degree of professional applicability sufficient so that the service provided would be of good quality. By playing that role, these associations were potentially exercising an autonomous role that was crucial for the stability of the public university system. The third article of the constitution determined the right of each institution to decide the contents of its programs and plans. Throughout the last century, the battles around this concept and its interpretations by the authoritarian regime had caused a lot of protests within universities.

Facing the crossroads of a change that was inevitable and the beginnings of a conflict that was becoming evident, the government opted for setting up parallel agencies of evaluation, accreditation, and certification, that would exercise their control function only upon the request of the interested parties. The civil associations created for this purpose generated conditions likely to facilitate the mobility of professionals in the North American context in the medium-term. They contributed to a lessening of the national problem of supervision and they provided a guarantee to the institutions or individuals, supplementing, but not substituting those given by the institutions of higher education or by the governmental agencies. The federal agencies expected that these solutions would lessen the risks caused by tension at the same time as they closed the gap between Mexican and American and Canadian counterparts. In order to accomplish this, they brought in both civil associations and professional bodies as relevant players in the educational arena.

Notwithstanding the progress, the political imperative of accrediting quality produced gaps, especially considering that the mechanisms for accreditation and certification are still being set up. For the public universities, the Padron de Posgrados en Excelencia supervised by CONACYT, serves as a national mechanism for accreditation. Thus, its initial objective was changed. It normalised the distribution of additional financing after evaluating the extent to which the institutions met predetermined conditions of quality. In a similar vein, the National Centre for Evaluation (CENEVAL), a civil association created in 1994, had as its principal aim promoting the homogenisation of the basic contents of the plans and programs through entry examinations for high school and undergraduate education (EGEL),[20] but it succeeded in providing an indirect indicator for the performance of the institutions themselves through that of their students.

The effort to establish mechanisms that would allow quality controls for institutional and individual performance was complemented by the creation or revitalisation of professional bodies on a national and particularly macro-regional scale. Since November of 1996, the Legal National Committee of General Medicine is charged with the role of professional certification and re-certification. In May of 1998, the Council for Professional Certification of Public Accountants was created. In the trinational arena, since 1992, the DGP established professional bodies as the leaders of negotiations with their Canadian and American counterparts, regarding the conditions for labour relations of the Mexican professionals in North America. It organised twelve working groups to search for ways to facilitate procedures for mutual recognition of degrees, licenses, and certificates. In order to formalise its structure, the DGP turned these working groups into Mexican Committees for the International Practice of the Profession (COMPIs) in 1994. These function in areas such as actuarial science, agronomy, architecture, accounting, law, nursing, pharmacy, engineering, veterinary medicine, dentistry, and psychology. Their advances with respect to harmonisation of criteria such as education, examinations, experience, behaviour and ethics, professional development, renewal of certification, field of activity, local knowledge, consumer protection, differ according to the profession concerned. In September of 1999, the Committee on Actuarial Science succeeded in becoming incorporated into chapter 16 of NAFTA. That same month, the appropriate COMPI presented a document on the Mutual recognition of Architects. In 1995, engineering representatives signed a mutual recognition agreement in July of 1999, with authorities of the three countries giving it their support in principle, although to date only Texas has signed with Mexico. The delegation of lawyers of the three countries signed recommendations that were submitted to the Free Trade Commission in July of 1998, allowing the latter to signify its agreement with NAFTA's own dispositions and with the national regulations. Should such an agreement come about, the Commission would recommend its implementation. The Committee on Veterinary Science and Zoology is preparing a similar document. By contrast, the Committee on Accounting has thus far only held meetings with its American and Canadian counterparts. The committees of Agronomy, Medicine, Psychology, Nursing, and Pharmacy have worked solely at the national level (DGP 1999).

Progress in accreditation matters has been irregular and different according to the subject areas. As in the previous case, this has been in addition and parallel to the system of higher education owing to the establishment of new agencies. In July of 1994, the Council for Accreditation for the Teachers of Engineering was created as a civil association with the assistance of the committees corresponding to the areas of the Inter-institutional committees of Evaluation of Higher Education (CIEES), which were originally designed to assume functions of evaluation and accreditation. In March of 1995, the National Council of Education of Veterinary Medicine and Zoology (CONEVET) was established. This was followed by the Committee of Accreditation of the Mexican Association of Faculties and Schools of Medicine AC

(AMFEM) in November of 1995, and the Council for Accreditation of Teaching of Accounting and Administration (CACACA) in June of 1996. The functions of the latter were complementary to those carried out by the Council of Professional Certification of Public Accountants. In August of 1998, the Program of Quality for Nursing Education was established followed by the National Council of Computer Science in July of 1999.

The following emerged as civil associations under the same legal conditions: the Association of Teaching Institutions for Architecture in the Mexican Republic (ASINEA), the Mexican Council for Accreditation in Computer Science (CONAIC), the Mexican Association of Members of the Faculties and Schools of Nutrition, the National Association of Faculties and Schools of Law and the Institute of Research in Jurisprudence. A National Commission for Regulations of the Practice of Nursing and the subcommittee for Accreditation, part of the Mexican Committee for the International Practice of Pharmacy was also set up. The Mexican Council of Social Sciences put together groups on accreditation in its area (ANUIES 1998). Although the greatest tendency has been to separate the bodies charged with accreditation from those specialising in certification, in some professions both functions have been combined in a single body (Ortega Amieva 1999). For instance, the National Council of Education of Veterinary Medicine and Zoology AC (CONEVET) and the Council of Dental Education (CONAEDO), established in April of 1998, assumed both responsibilities.[21]

The accreditation and certification initiatives demonstrate that national policy was intended to create conditions that would gradually harmonise the national system with those of Canada and the United States, at the same time, they were supposed to avoid structural changes, which are a politically delicate matter in the country. Regardless of progress, the accreditation of degrees is still far from being the norm in higher education institutions. The CACEI, between July of 1994 and November of 1999, only accredited seventeen plans and study programs, the CONEVET two, the ANFEM sixteen, the CACECA four (with eight more in process), and the nursing system three.[22] Certification is still uncommon. The CONEVET is the body that has certified the most specialists via examinations or curricula (http://168.255.115.5/dgp/index.html). Membership in professional colleges continues to be low and unequal depending on regions – important in Mexico City, Jalisco, and Guanajuato – and the professions – high in accounting, medicine, and law (DGP 1999, 46-7). Although differences between the three countries have lessened in the past five years, they are still significant. In Mexico, colleges and universities have still only a limited ability to act alone and to exercise autonomy.[23] Despite their increase in numbers,[24] the fact is that their power to make their own decisions, and to act as managing mechanisms in the regulation and updating of the professions is still relatively low, which is a reflection of their very recent involvement in that arena of activity.

Despite some resistance and inertia, the organs responsible for the accreditation and certification procedures have become consolidated in the past six years. Two factors stand out as important in this regard. First, there is a need to regulate the liberalisation of professional services and to protect Mexican professionals in the face of possible unequal competition on the part of Canadians and Americans interested in practising in Mexico. Second, there is a duty to insure that the outcomes of higher education institutions are more transparent to those inside and outside academia.[25] Despite some resistance and inertia, both national and international evaluation and accreditation are currently matters permanently included in the rectors' discussions held by ANUIES.[26]

Altogether, the accreditation and certification mechanisms contributed to improving the knowledge of educational processes even though works on the system and information about the quality of the educational process continue to be scarce. Available public data is still insufficient for specialists and users of higher education to evaluate the institutional capacity that will guarantee satisfactory learning conditions for the students. Internally, however, because there is systematic collection and use of data prior to evaluation and external scrutiny, institutional authorities are provided with important elements for the detection of potentially sensitive aspects of the university system. Externally, they help legitimise Mexico's negotiations with their counterparts in advancing the definition of common requirements for professional practices in North America.

Without deterring from the power of innovation or their growing adoption by the institutions themselves,[27] the fact is that accreditation and certification policies have generated problems. The use of different performance indicators has become the norm in the various sectors of the higher education system. This has been particularly important in public universities. Despite discussion on the topic, the large majority of private or technological institutions, however, have made less progress in that direction. Another internal and external problem is that despite the fact that certification and accreditation practices have intensified in recent years[28] this has not led either to a minimum quality standard or to a greater integration and flexibility of the educational system. Both at the national and international levels, two questions that were considered problematic since the coming to power by the present administration are still pending. These relate to students' transfers between universities of the national educational system throughout their studies, and the recognition of credits acquired in academic mobility during both short and long periods of study abroad. There is still a great deal of variation regarding existing conditions for class delivery as well as the contents of undergraduate and graduate programs. This is particularly the case in places that have developed graduate degrees quickly – such as private institutions – or in those that are in a fragile state as far as the educational level of teachers is concerned (e.g., technological institutes). Although entry and exit examinations for the CENEVAL have contributed to the institutions' acceptance of the idea that there must be a basic standard of knowledge, it is not clear how much the process of homogenisation has helped.

In the national context, problems confronting students to have the credits they have acquired during their stay abroad recognised are becoming more acute. Mexico has no tradition of proposing flexible mechanisms for recognising periods of study abroad and has not resolved two important issues in this area. First, many students turn from disciplinary studies to linguistic studies once they are abroad. Second, bureaucratisation of the procedures for granting equivalencies persists in Mexico. Equivalencies are usually granted by administrative departments, such as registrars' offices, which usually work outside the realm of qualified academicians and sometimes in opposition to them. Although several of the agreements that have been signed by the three NAFTA partners, both bilateral and trilateral, have included clauses for the recognition of credits obtained elsewhere, the fact is that obtaining equivalencies is never guaranteed to all participants in exchanges. Thus, the national context has made it very difficult to quickly create a trilateral mechanism that will ensure the recognition of courses taken abroad, largely because of the heterogeneous nature of the institutions, but also owing to the vagueness of the curriculum processes and the mutual mistrust between the parties.

The introduction of evaluation and accreditation mechanisms has had an impact on our knowledge of the realities and the problems of the national system, both in its own behaviour and in institutional practices. Despite resistance and criticism, it has contributed to normalise the operations of a properly conducted external evaluation, to which neither the institutions or the individuals concerned are accustomed. It has assisted in the opening of academic life and in eliminating arbitrariness. At the same time, organisational guidelines have revealed the strategies required for conflict management and avoidance, strategies that Mexico has utilised in order to advance in a complicated process of multinational harmonisation. This is a particularly significant achievement in a country that has entered macro-regional integration from a position of inequality.

Mexican Higher Education Institutions in Context

The comparison of Mexico's national situation with that of its North American partners has renewed traditional arguments around the questions that need to be discussed on the education front. The development of opportunities for international co-operation has served to add new dynamism to certain traditional activities. This is the case with linkages in the social and private sectors. In recent years, exchanges between Canada and the United States on the one hand, and Mexico on the other, have encouraged the relationship between the IESMs with social and economic players under less conventional methods than had previously been the case. Through an accord with the Mexico-United States Foundation, the SEP organised a program to publicise successful linkages between U.S. and Mexican higher education institutions. In co-operation with the U.S. National Science Foundation, CONACYT organised workshops to identify new strategies for establishing additional linkages. As far as services to the social sector are concerned, the network for Bi-national development between Mexican and American schools and industry, affiliated with the Association Liaison Office for University Co-operation and Development (ALO) disseminated information about models of co-operative development. Other agreements, such as the one signed between ANUIES and the ALO, have allowed documentation of state of the art of linkages in North America (Sanchez, Castaneda and McCaffley 1996). Finally, tri-national meetings among educational representatives of the countries concerned helped interested parties in Mexico to become acquainted with new formulas of association between universities and their environment.

Starting from an exposition of the asymmetries caused by national public policy priorities, the search for sound mechanisms to propel the national educational project closer to macro-regional integration has had both positive and negative consequences. It has contributed to the emergence of serious problems in the Mexican higher educational system, including the lack of monitoring, a loss of credibility in the type of education provided in the public universities, and insufficient regulation of professional services. On the other hand, it has helped develop new approaches to certain questions, including the inefficiency of Mexican higher education institutions. However, the search for solutions to these problems has also had a negative impact in other areas. It has prevented the elaboration of a reform proposal for higher education, one based not so much on harmonising it with Canada and the United States, but on making it adequate to face the general challenges of globalisation. This proposal would make globalisation the primary basis for assessing national research policies, the provision of higher education services, and human resource training.

GOVERNMENTAL POLICIES FOR CO-OPERATION AND INTERNATIONALISATION

The Political Use of Co-operation and Internationalisation in Mexico

A "Program for the Modernisation of Education (PME)" was produced by the same Presidential cabinet that negotiated NAFTA (1988-1994), but this early program conceived internationalisation in a limited fashion, while targeting its modernisation efforts only at Mexico's research capabilities.[29] In a subsequent plan known as "The Program for Educational Development" (PDE), the relations between globalisation, internationalisation, and higher education were broached in a more complex and systematic manner.[30] This sectoral plan addressed concerns about academic mobility, accreditation,[31] and curriculum reform.[32] At the same time, during the five years (1995-2000) when the plan was being implemented, there was an increase in the number of research articles on related topics: first, on the existing asymmetries among the three higher education systems; second, on comparative higher education policies; third, on the expectations tied to international co-operation; and fourth, on the advances made in these areas throughout North America (Mungaray and Green 1997). The effects of globalisation in border regions have been well documented, particularly with reference to the organisation of the SES (Ganster 1994) and to professional employment (Ruiz 1996), as well as to the challenges and opportunities for the SES and IES (Marmolejo and Garcia 1997).

In accordance with the emerging interest in internationalisation, the implementation of international activities has become a criterion for evaluating research capabilities, postgraduate education, and even undergraduate education in Mexico. The process of internationalisation has gained increasing importance in perceptions of institutional performance. Indeed, regulations have been created to stimulate improved teaching performance in this area and these regulations assign a high number of points to international activities, although these regulations failed to take into account the fact that these activities had hardly begun and had little more than a modicum of institutional support.

Official documents produced by SEP project a rich vision of internationalisation and they identify the paths for a new policy that will integrate this vision into the country's development. However, there has been no framework document setting out desirable objectives or outlining priority areas of state intervention either on a national or a sectoral level. This is unlike the situation in the U.S. and Canada. In Mexico, there was little reflection on the problems of information or education networks or on the repercussions these would have on educational projects. Neither the SEP, the private sector, or representative organs are seeking consensus in the various areas of the educational system around strategic plans for internationalisation and co-operation. They have not proposed either a definition of priorities and timelines or identified resources to support internationalisation. They have not lead collective discussions on the challenges of macro-regional education, nor on the demands facing higher education as a result of globalisation in spite of the fact that in the early 1990s there were high hopes that North America would become the preferred partner in educational co-operation, with such co-operation eventually replacing Mexico's Latin American counterparts as its traditional partners. This also implied an in-depth review of the usual patterns of educational co-operation.

University institutions felt compelled to internationalise as soon as NAFTA was implemented even though there was no clear understanding of the desirable direction for the process, its benefits, risks and content. Consequently, in order to accomplish this task, they turned to federal programs that were precise in the definition of their objectives and spheres, albeit heterogeneous in nature, given that they had no common frame of reference. These had either an international component – that is to say, they mobilised resources for a goal different from internationalisation but actually helped to reinforce it nevertheless – or they dealt with a very specific line of internationalisation such as sabbatical stays abroad or reducing the brain drain. For this reason, supports to internationalisation, although numerous, were essentially atomised in Mexico. The dispersal of existing opportunities made it difficult for institutions lacking previous experience to be able to develop their exchanges in a manner that would have a positive feedback on institutional development objectives.

Moreover, in the 1990s, Mexico designed general programs to support internationalisation activities beyond those for North American integration.[33] These were utilised by the institutions of higher education to come up with proposals for exchanges and co-operation with the U.S. and Canada. They were not, however, specifically designed to consolidate the tri-national relationship. Despite the signing of agreements oriented to create an educational component for North America, policy of support for macro-regional integration was gradually replaced by a policy designed to strengthen internationalisation generally. Paradoxically, publicising the theme of internationalisation depended to a great extent on the developments occurring elsewhere within NAFTA. The federal authorities had just begun to concern themselves with identifying the features of international co-operation in the IESMs, when during one of the first meetings, the FDTES requested from the ANUIES a diagnostic survey on the tri-national effort. This survey, carried out in 1992, shed the first significant light on the situation. But although it helped to identify the degree of, and the guidelines for consolidating inter-institutional co-operation between Mexico and its North American counterparts, it did not provide a framework for Mexico to define a precise profile of its efforts of co-operation toward the North American region. It merely described the general features of a situation that continues to exist ten years later. It indicated that the few institutional leaders were those that had developed their international exchanges before NAFTA. They were either prestigious private universities or large public universities. Geographically, the more dynamic institutions were located in Mexico City, on the northern border (Universidad Autonoma de Baja California), or in the large cities (Guadalajara, Puebla, Monterrey). A large part of the advances were concentrated in the big public universities and in some private higher education institutions (ANUIES 1994).[34] Even after NAFTA was signed, the preferences in choosing partners remained variable, depending on institutional history and the moment at which the institutions developed their international activities. In the Northern Mexican higher education institutions, in private ones, and in the technological institutes – which all consolidated their internationalising process in the middle of the 1990s – the tendency was to select public North American universities, particularly in the United States. In contrast, the large public universities maintained their previous tendency to diversify co-operative arrangements and select a large number of partners. This was particularly the case with the Universidad Nacional Autonoma de Mexico (UNAM) and with the Universidad de Guadalajara. Although the number of international co-operation agreements registered by the ANUIES in subsequent research updates has tripled,[35] institutional action plans continue to be similar. There has been an intensification of co-operation rather than a change in its objectives (Didou 2000).

The Axes of International Co-operation: The Mexican Perspective

Among the national public policies that had an international component or were devoted to the promotion of specific internationalisation activities during the second half of the 1990s, three sets are of particular importance. The first set grouped together policies for training teaching and research staff; the second related to strategies for encouraging academic and research staff mobility; and the third concerned co-operation among higher education institutions. In the 1990s, one of the central strategies for the transformation of higher education consisted of teacher training and the strengthening of academic bodies – groups organised around a research leader and a line of activity and composed of academics with various degrees of maturity and scholarship.[35] Two programs were designed with this objective.

The Program for the Improvement of Academic Staff (SUPERA) has operated since 1994 with government funds and under the supervision of ANUIES. In 1996, a program with similar objectives was created – the Program for the Improvement of

Teachers (PROMEP) – although this program soon became part of SUPERA. Under the aegis of the Under-secretary of Higher Education and Scientific Research (SESIC), PROMEP required higher education institutions to involve their departments in the planning process. Unlike SUPERA, PROMEP systematically channelled part of its resources into scholarships for teacher training abroad. Twenty percent of those who benefited from PROMEP and who took postgraduate courses between January 1997 and April 1999 did so outside the country, including, in descending order of preference, the United States, Spain, Great Britain, and France. Canada was not an important destination. After 1998, PROMEP earmarked a special fund for linking academic bodies with similar organisations abroad. It financed interinstitutional linkages with various institutions in Great Britain, with Carnegie-Mellon University, and with Cuban universities (Poder Ejecutivo Federal 1998, 1999). Some institutions, such as the Universidad Autonoma de Chihuahua and the Universidad Autonoma Metropolitana,s utilised PROMEP as a way to absorb much of the cost of teacher training. However, the majority of higher education institutions in Mexico continued to employ the traditional format for teacher training despite the offer of international support from the federal government. This was probably due to the demographic profile and the living conditions of the applicants, to the criteria of access to funding of PROMEP, and to the previous state of international co-operation at different institutions.[36]

PROMEP's results have reinforced the decision to link public higher education policies to the resolution of important domestic problems through the strategic use of international co-operation. The results also suggest that Canadian and American institutions have not succeeded in structuring proposals that are tightly articulated with Mexico's own needs. For instance, although the U.S. receives a high number of scholarship recipients, it only receives those who meet its criteria for selection, regardless of demand in Mexico. This is illustrated by the fact that out of twenty-five post-graduate degree programs initiated by SESIC for teacher training under this program, none of the five that are based on international co-operation have been carried out with a North American partner.[37] This suggests that it is difficult for Canada and the U.S. to identify or respond to the specific needs of Mexico, particularly where these needs are in conflict with their own programmatic standards. There have been interesting offers of co-operation on the part of Canadian and American institutions concerning student mobility, which is a common agenda item between the three countries. However, there has been no adaptation to Mexico's specific requirements or to its problems with teacher education.

Other national programs were more directly oriented toward internationalising academic life. The Program for the Support of Science in Mexico (PACIME) is administered by CONACYT and between 1991 and 1997, it was co-financed by the Mexican federal government and the World Bank.[38] PACIME facilitated the repatriation of Mexican scholars who had been educated abroad. This program also included the so-called heritage chairs for foreign academics as well as support for Mexican academics taking sabbatical leaves abroad. Although these sub-programs have consistently received low funding as a percentage of PACIME's total budget,[39] they have had a positive impact in articulating a policy of "cosmopolitisation" of the staff within the framework of teacher education. They have contributed to a reduction in the endogamy of teaching personnel and to a diversification of the profile of the players in university life. These results are particularly noticeable in the SEP-CONACYT centres and in public state universities, which were not generally accustomed to receiving foreign academics. The greatest number of repatriated researchers came from the United States, which was consistent with the geographic distribution of CONACYT scholarship recipients. The destinations of Mexican academics in the sabbatical leaves abroad program also show a strong bias for the U.S. and, more recently, for Canada. These schemes are consistent with the existing guidelines for the acquisition of post-graduate degrees, guidelines that determine the way in which academic linkages are established and subsequently maintained.[40] On the other hand, programs devoted to encouraging foreign scholars to come to Mexico have not been attractive to its North American partners. This is perhaps due to the low income received by even better paid teachers. These programs have attracted university staff from Europe and in particular from Eastern Europe, which has considerably modified previous patterns of intellectual migration. The fact is that countries that are linguistically and culturally close to Mexico, such as Spain, have learned how to utilise the potential of European co-operation with Latin America.[41] It is clear that while national policies on internationalisation designed by Mexico have not been attractive to its North American partners, neither have the partners adjusted their own policies to suit the needs of Mexico.

By contrast with PACIME's immediate successes regarding repatriation, diversification of the paths for academic education, and attracting foreign academics to Mexico, its medium-term objectives have only been partially fulfilled. The repatriation program has been qualitatively attractive, especially for young researchers or those at the end of their careers, rather than for other types of researchers. Quantitatively speaking, the chances for those visiting professors to stay in the institutions that received them, once PACIME's support is finished, are very low given the lack of positions available in those universities. For that reason, the internationalisation movement that was initiated was for the most part ad hoc and dependent on the federal government. The institutions' dependence on public resources suggests that in the universities at least, internationalisation has depended more on new funding than on real institutional commitments. It is a very fragile process for Mexican institutions, which are not competitive in salaries and working conditions and which are poorly placed within the international higher education market.

The examination of national policies for internationalisation demonstrates that these have not been appropriate for the development of a special North American space for higher education. Six years after the signing of NAFTA, the axes of the type of co-operation that is likely to benefit all partners equally, and to overcome the restrictive realities of academic and student mobility, are yet to be defined. To do that, it will be necessary to make resources available to permit discussions and to finance the proposals that may serve as the basis for creating a special North American space for education co-operation. Should these aspects not be addressed, bilateral co-operation projects, or perhaps even a type of internationalisation that does not favour the regionalisation of the North American system, might prevail. For Mexico, the challenges concern the ability of the country to negotiate a statute of "asymmetrical partner" within any scheme of co-operation. Its possibilities in structuring an adequate strategy for co-operation, designed to end its inferiority within the North American space and to equalise its position, will be dependent on the type of policies designed as both a receiver and producer of co-operation. Mexico's capacity to stop and turn back the grave problem of the brain drain to the United States is also a major challenge (Finn 1997). Transforming "the brain waste" into a "brain circulation" is one of the main challenges facing Mexican society even though Mexicans still have a lower rate of intellectual migration than Asians.[42] If co-operation develops without improving the conditions of re-incorporation to the national academic market, if there is an increase in opportunities of mobility without guaranteeing better working conditions back home, it is very likely that the country will lose highly qualified human capital and that the internationalisation of Mexican academic institutions via repatriation and invitation to foreign professors will be of little consequence.

Academic Mobility in Mexico

Mexico exports more human resources through its academic mobility programs than it currently imports. According to ANUIES, between 1995 and 1997, the number of Mexican students who went abroad was 40 per cent higher than the number of foreign students who came to Mexico (ANUIES 1998b). In that traditional framework, NAFTA has been important as a causal factor in the quantity of demand for both short- and long- term stays abroad. It has not been so with respect to the design of schemes of trilateral mobility allowing students to acquire a greater knowledge about macro-regional problems. The great demand for mobility opportunities in Mexico, on the one hand, and the U.S. and Canada, on the other, has been met through the establishment of new bilateral exchange programs within North America, rather than through the search for innovative solutions in trilateral matters.[43] In essence, this is a continuation of the historical situation, characterised since the 1970s by Mexicans' desire to pursue their postgraduate education abroad. In contrast to the increased opportunities for outward mobility, there has not been any notable change in the numbers or types of foreign students coming to Mexico. The sale of educational services has been left to chance or to the decisions made by each higher education institution. Although private institutions such as the Universidad de las Americas or Universidad Autonoma de Guadalajara, as well as a few public universities (Universidad de Guadalajara), have achieved good results there has not been a public policy on educational exchange.

Following the weakening of Mexico's European connection after World War II, the United States has been the main destination of CONACYT scholarship recipients. Canada is selected less frequently, although the number of Mexican students selecting Canada has increased significantly since 1999. In 1999, there were 82 CONACYT scholarship recipients studying in Canada and another 433 of these students studying in the United States. Thus, 16 percent of the CONACYT scholarship recipients who study in North America are now attending Canadian higher education institutions compared to only 8 percent in 1994. Although NAFTA has not greatly transformed the traditional bilateral relationship between Mexico and the United States in educational matters, it has facilitated an increase in linkages between Mexico and Canada.

CONACYT's scholarships are for long periods of time. The objective of these scholarships is to support in the academic disciplines and especially the acquisition of a doctoral degree. The scholarships for technical training are few in number, and are granted essentially in co-operation with the Japanese and German governments. Their financing rests fundamentally on national investment and international co-operation. Their volume has varied depending on the resources available to the organisations and to the proposals for co-operation. They have been handled by bodies such as the Department of External Relations, ANUIES, and even by the institutions themselves. Although there has been a steady flow of scholarships granted for the purpose of study abroad, their numbers have fluctuated, particularly during periods of economic crisis (e.g., the 1994 peso crisis) when their availability has been severely curtailed.[44] The nature of these grants, their duration, and the rate of waste are factors that make the Mexican policy of grants abroad an expensive and inefficient proposition. The relative maintenance cost is high vis-à-vis the national grants, although less so in recent years.[45] The legal system that supports the recovery of investment in scholarships does not function well. Consequently, an important percentage of those who benefit either do not obtain the degree or do not return the cost of their training to the financing body, even if they do not work in academia.[46]

Although it is known that undergraduate mobility occurs in Mexico, there is simply no data to measure it with certainty. In many cases, undergraduate mobility tends to be instrumental – essentially, English language instruction – rather than tied to a degree in a foreign country. Therefore, it is shorter than mobility at the postgraduate level. This type of mobility rarely receives official program or institutional support and is more the result of personal or family investment. It is therefore less egalitarian, both socially and academically, than postgraduate academic mobility.

Nevertheless, in recent years, Mexican student mobility reveals some important changes:

- The growing emphasis in Mexico on the importance of academic stays abroad, and the prestige accorded to foreign postgraduate degrees vis-à-vis domestic degrees, has generated a veritable explosion in demand for mobility opportunities and this demand is now far higher than the current system of scholarships can meet. This gap is evident in both short duration stays and what, for Mexico, are the more traditional long-duration stays abroad. Consequently, higher education and government institutions are now compelled to select applicants with greater care, particularly those wishing to go to North America, which is the area of greatest demand. There has been a marked gap between supply and demand due to the fact that the demand has grown parallel to the

advent of globalisation, as well as to the national pressure for the acquisition of higher degrees. On the other hand, policies to bridge this gulf have not only failed to keep up, they have rarely attempted to recover the ground lost during the 1993-94 peso crisis.
- By comparison to the relative inertia in support for long-stay mobility programs, there have been some major changes in short-stay mobility programs. In both undergraduate and graduate education, there are now more slots available for students seeks stays abroad in North America and Europe. Although the supply is still lagging the demand for mobility opportunities, the new policies have provided a significant impulse to both the concept of mobility and the types of students who benefit from it.
- In addition to the creation of more short-term mobility opportunities for Mexican students, many issues have arisen out of the design of bilateral and trilateral programs need attention. For instance, Mexican, as well as Canadian and American students, generally use short-term stays to receive language instruction, rather than disciplinary training. How can recognition in the form of credits given for such stays be regulated and how can students take advantage of these short stays in order to improve their professional education? These are questions that require national responses and trilateral decisions.
- The national context for traditional long-stay mobility existed has changed in Mexico during the last decade. The number of Mexican higher education institutions that offer graduate degrees, including doctorates, has increased and this has led to a decrease in the number of scholarships available to study abroad for masters degrees. Mexico's need for foreign degrees to fill internal demand – particularly masters degrees, but in the medium-term also doctorates– is continually decreasing. This fact demonstrates the need to review and change the current policies of student exchange, not so much to replace them, but to ensure that stays abroad are qualitatively different and provide a decided advantage to the students' educational training.
- The diversity of co-operation agreements has allowed us to contrast the classic type of mobility with one that is shorter and more beneficial. It is possible that Mexico's expectations will change in the very near future by focusing more on the latter alternative in light of the national environment and the type of student that wishes to go abroad. It is likely that more systematic changes in undergraduate education will permit a blend of domestic and international education that benefits more and more students.
- As far as policies for long-term stays are concerned, the emphasis on quality suggests that there will be closer control of the commitments of the sending and receiving universities, as well as the duties and rights of the students with scholarships. This will make it necessary to come up with new norms and monitoring systems for mobility programs.

By contrast, mobility from abroad has changed little in recent years. The inertia that has characterised national institutions represents a clear difference from their counterparts. Several institutions have sought to adapt themselves in the area of language training to the demands of interested parties – for example, the Universidad of Guadalajara or the Universidad Veracruzana – thereby increasing their number of foreign students in recent years. On a national scale, however, there is a tendency to undervalue the importance of that clientele as a source of income or as group that enriches Mexican students through cultural interaction. There has been no thinking about the meaning of this type of service, either in terms of the financial costs-benefits to the institution or in relation to marketing strategies for these programs. In general, departments that are charged with providing foreign students with language training operate separately from the others with *de facto* autonomy, but they are also marginalised in relation to participation in the institutional decisions that are important to their future.

Even after NAFTA's implementation, the foreign demand for undergraduate and postgraduate education in Mexican higher education institutions has not changed significantly. Foreign demand for access to Mexican higher education institutions is very small and is only equals 0.5 percent of total registrations in undergraduate education and 1.4 percent of the total registrations in postgraduate education. Foreign students are also concentrated in a few disciplines – anthropology and medicine – and in a few institutions such as UNAM and the Universidad Autonoma de Guadalajara. In most cases, this mobility occurs without official or institutional support, while the mobility in medicine is largely limited to U.S. students who find it easier to obtain a medical degree at UAG than in their own country. This pattern is a long-standing historical phenomenon that has not changed much in the past decade.

Academic mobility includes both student and professorial mobility, but in Mexico it is difficult to differentiate between the two types of mobility, because such a large percentage of higher education faculty do not have a graduate degree. Although data to assess the breadth of the problem is lacking, many holders of CONACYT scholarships are professors without graduate education recruited by the IESMs. Once they complete the age requirements, they utilise the CONACYT as a financing body to obtain the degree that guarantees their stability and promotion in the academic marketplace. This situation is complicated by the ambiguity of differentiating between young students and young academics, which was not solved by the creation of PROMEP and its scholarship programs. An examination of the opportunities available for teachers and researchers reveals the following features:

- In the 1990s, there was an effort to improve mobility opportunities for both short and long stays abroad, mainly through CONACYT's new programs, which include sabbatical and postdoctoral stays. There has been an increased effort on the part of American and Mexican higher education institutions to collaborate along the border area, whether through co-operative graduate studies or through the establishment of cross-border research programs. Studies by Mexican students and academics in the United States have usually led to extended academic relations and to an overall strengthening of the bi-lateral relations with the United States. The potential for similar types of co-operation with Canada,

either between universities or through tri-level agreements, will depend on the extent to which the increase in postgraduate opportunities currently in place is maintained and increased.
- Governmental policies have sought to differentiate between students and academics among those applying for scholarships, in order to homogenise the categories conventionally accepted on the international scene. The demand from the academic sector is such that this type of rationalisation has been abandoned. This indicates that academic training at the BI-national, tri-national, or international level, is one of the more urgent areas requiring attention in Mexico.
- The national criteria utilised both by the CONACYT and by other bodies in relation to all types of mobility – both long and short, and in particular mobility for the acquisition of postgraduate degrees – are clearly discriminatory with respect to age and gender, especially for women seeking to return to an academic career after long periods of absence due to maternity or other reasons. Countries such as the United States and Canada, which have experience in the area of affirmative action, could help solve this problem by paying special attention to social groups that have not been adequately supported by Mexican national policies.

Toward Bilateral, Trilateral, or International Relations?

In Mexico, there is definitely greater interest in the issues of internationalisation and cross-border co-operation in higher education. Moreover, the growing interest in internationalisation and cross-border co-operation has catalysed the creation of new organisations and programs that specialise in the North American region or the promotion of international higher education. It has also led many public and private higher education institutions to diversify their educational offerings into new areas related to internationalisation and regional integration.

In a national context where university associations such as ANUIES have traditionally had an international section, but where there was no specialised body to manage and promote these relations, the 1990s became a period of adjustment and transition. The university bureaucracy and those charged with international affairs in the institutions of higher education began to widen their participation in larger regional or international bodies. The rectors and senior university administrators, as well as ANUIES representatives, became actively involved in trilateral organisations such as the Consortium for North American Higher Education (CONAHEC). The SEP authorities co-signed the trilateral agreement launching the Program for North American Mobility in Higher Education, which was established in 1995 in Cupertino with Canada and the USA, to promote increased academic mobility on a trilateral basis. Mexico also participated in the Regional Academic Mobility Program (RAMP), which funds mobility between university partners in the areas of engineering, business, and environmental science. From 1993 to 1998, RAMP supported 347 participants, including 131 from Canada, 188 from Mexico and 28 from the USA (Adelman 1999).

These initiatives led to the emergence and strengthening of non-governmental organisations specialising in the development of international collaboration. The Mexican Association for International Education (AMPEI) was created in July of 1992 and is now the main professional association for international education administrators in Mexico. The Mexico-United States Foundation for Science and Collaboration in North America, in collaboration with the National Academy of Science, supported the implementation of research projects in the areas of health, environment, and the socio-economic impact of regional economic integration. It promotes cross-border programs in human resource development and job training that are linked directly to the private sectors in Mexico and the USA (Bueno Zirion 1996). In 1994, several private and public institutions[47] created the Fideicomiso para Estudios de la Region Norteamericana for the purpose of financing tri-lateral research projects in the social sciences. At the same time, higher education institutions that had research centres or programs of specialised research on the North American region enhanced their operation. For example, UNAM transformed its Centre for Research on the United States into a Centre for Research on North America (CISAN).

Higher education institutions have also increased their educational offerings with degrees that contain an international dimension in areas such as business, public administration, the social sciences, and languages. Between 1994 and 1997, the proportion of students registered in those areas increased from 0.56 percent to 2.27 percent of total undergraduate registrations, and from 1.28 percent to 1.38 percent of total graduate registrations. In contrast with what occurred in the European Union, where new career offerings were primarily at the graduate level and in macro-regional studies, in Mexico larger enrolment increases occurred at the undergraduate level in these areas. Most of the undergraduate degrees awarded in these areas were in international trade and customs (119 degrees) and international relations (46).[48] The number of postgraduate degrees with an international component reached 34 at the masters level and three at the doctoral. Higher education institutions close to the Mexico-U.S. border, as well as those in central Mexico, have also designed programs with a specialised emphasis on cross-border affairs. However, their offerings are still limited in scope. For example, there is a masters degree program in Mexico-United States Studies at the ENEP Acatlan, a program in regional U.S. Studies at the Autonoma de Puebla (BUAP), and a program on border enterprises in Tamaulipas (ANUIES 1998a). Unlike the situation in undergraduate education, graduate degrees tend to emphasise regional and territorial issues rather than those of a broad international nature.

In addition to increased registrations in professional degree programs, the demand for language study has also increased in Mexico. This demand has been met primarily through informal studies, such as more intensive use of existing language laboratories to learning a language with some immediate practical aim in mind. At the same time, however, the number of students registered in language degrees for teaching purposes, has also increased in Mexico. These undergraduate degree programs are offered under many names, such as education science for the English language, teaching English, foreign languages, or simply languages, but there are at least 18 degree programs where undergraduates can pursue professional training in English, which is the language most demanded in Mexico at the current time.

Finally, in a very few cases, higher education institutions met the challenges of globalisation by introducing specific new subjects of study. On the recommendation of J. Coombs, BUAP introduced the subjects of globalisation, human rights, and the environment, as well as English and computer use, into the basic framework of all undergraduate degrees. Although unique within the Mexican context, this BUAP experience has not had the desired impact due to organisational and teacher-related problems. It is an initiative that has been much criticised within the institution. This far-reaching curriculum initiative was retained after a review in 2002, but in a way that is consistent with the availability of textbooks and the proper re-training of the academic staff that teaches these courses.

The IESMs have also attempted to respond to the new realities of globalisation and regional economic integration. This adaptation is demonstrated by the introduction of centres specialising in the North American region, programs devoted to research on trilateral affairs, new curriculum, and increased participation in co-operation and educational exchange agreements. It is undoubtedly in research where the will to adapt to the trilateral context is strongest, particularly through the creation of specialised centres and with tri-lateral research projects. Beyond formal structures, the ARIES database at UNAM, which registers research projects in the country, indicates that since 1994 there has been a growing number of projects devoted to the themes of globalisation, internationalisation, and NAFTA. This is particularly the case in the area of social sciences, especially in the disciplines of international relations and trade (www.unam.ariesmx). Despite the fact that international relations has become a research subject of choice for Mexican specialists and a popular and growing area in universities, trilateral relations are still not an important topic in Mexico. Official and individual activities refer more to the international dimension, to the global or even to the bilateral than to the tri-lateral dimension of Mexico's international relations. Co-operative programs that link Mexico with either the United States or Canada are greater in number than trilateral ones. This is explained by several factors, including the absence of a tradition of international work in the academic sphere and a higher degree of specialisation on individual countries in international affairs. Also important are political questions and matters of support: trilateral projects are always more difficult to establish than bilateral ones, they are not attractive financially, it is more difficult to obtain resources for tri-lateral projects, and they are more complicated to administer.

Given these comments, initiatives to encourage tri-lateralisation in higher education co-operation are characterised by the following organisational features:

- Their progress is difficult to define, because they are subsumed under general efforts in the internationalisation of higher education. A part of the reason that explains their relative stagnation is that despite initial interest there are few programs geared to tri-lateral Cupertino that have proven unequivocally successful.

- The previous statement places limitations on Mexico's efforts to develop a critical mass of national specialists on trilateral affairs, both in relation to the education of young researchers and in the retraining of specialists in international affairs. The existence of numerous projects on issues related to NAFTA does not imply that there are sufficient institutional possibilities to guarantee a long term change in specialisation for academic groups, even of those that were initially curious about the issue of macro-regional integration.
- The possibilities of obtaining financial support for research on the problems of tri-lateral relations in North America are limited in comparison to the support available for research on bilateral relations.
- The range of opportunities for trilateral co-operation was greatest in the years immediately preceding and following the signing of NAFTA. Since that time, the research topic has remained comparatively stagnant without any significant increase in research proposals or financial support for North American research projects.
- The programs and organisations that support the involvement of public servants, administrators, and researchers in international or trilateral affairs are working in parallel. An umbrella organisation needs to be created that will establish and ensure continuity in the dialogue among interested parties, while consolidating a multi-disciplinary trilateral dimension in North America higher education.
- Although academic and student communities have an interest in participating in trilateral projects, their situation hardly permits it. The participating institutions currently involved in this type of program are few by comparison with the many that would need to become involved in the future. Participation by professors and students is also limited at present. In the absence of specific actions for particular groups, the access to opportunities is sporadic, random, and profoundly unequal. As a consequence, the institutional efforts are far below the potential that exists for tri-lateral activities in higher education.

Given this situation, the challenges to increased tri-lateral co-operation in higher education are varied and numerous. A significant expansion of trilateral co-operation clearly entails directing more funds into these activities to provide a new dynamic start to tri-lateral co-operation. Above all, it requires a review of the existing tri-lateral programs with a view to removing the bureaucratic obstacles that make many of these program unattractive to faculty, students, and higher education administrators. Another challenge is to institutionalise these programs for the long-term to ensure the formation of national experts specialising in the different dimensions of cross-border and trilateral relations in North America.

Some internationalisation activities have become significant since the mid-1990s. The leading organisations in this field have increased their activities, particularly in negotiating co-operation agreements, offering careers tied to the international arena, and designing support systems that allow academics to obtain graduate degrees abroad. By contrast, other areas have been neglected due to current economic conditions as well as entrenched ways of thinking about higher education. As a nation, Mexico has certainly not been at the forefront of career- or language-training services, nor has it made much progress in internationalising the higher education curriculum.[49] Activities have multiplied in areas traditionally considered important in international co-operation. On the other hand, there has been no evolution in the meanings associated with a policy of internationalisation, either in a world that is globalised or in a society that is integrated on a macro-regional basis.

This situation has precluded widespread participation by Mexico's higher education institutions in the internationalisation process beyond adjustments that respond to short-term pressures or opportunities. The window of opportunity created just before NAFTA was signed has been used by a small number of higher education institutions that had already positioned themselves earlier in the North American field because of geographical location or academic interest. Certainly, there have been changes in the way that certain internationalising activities are carried out as demonstrated by the fact that the sole mobility scheme previously in existence – namely long- term stays and training in specific subject areas – has been replaced by more diverse opportunities for academic mobility. However, changes of this type have not led to much new thinking about the challenges of macro-regional integration or the implications of an international higher education policy for Mexican higher education. In short, NAFTA has not brought about significant new participation in cross-border co-operation by higher education institutions that previously lacked experience in the area. It has not transformed the idiosyncrasies of the national or the individual culture around a vision of international higher education.

Moreover, some asymmetries have arisen as a result of the peculiarities of the NAFTA countries and their location on the North American continent. In contrast to Canada and the United States, Mexico's higher education community has not viewed the controversial issues raised by NAFTA as a possible source of new opportunities. This is particularly the case in Mexicans' resistance to the idea that higher education should be treated as a marketable service or product. In Mexico, the major issues in higher education continue to be approached from an explicitly political or ideological viewpoint. This approach is most evident in domestic national politics, but it also surfaces in venues convened for tri-lateral discussions of North American higher education. Consequently, Mexico has paid almost no attention to the issue of selling its higher education services to foreigners either within or outside its borders. However, since 1994, several Canadian and U.S. higher education institutions have begun operations in Mexico by offering undergraduate degrees that are now a source of market competition, especially for Mexico's prestigious private higher education institutions. In the meantime, UNAM is the only Mexican higher education institution to open foreign branches in North America, including Extension Centres in Hull (Canada) and San Antonio, Texas (Libertas 1998). Although regionalisation has created new opportunities for the three higher education systems, the results are very uneven across the three NAFTA countries. Regionalisation has actually produced some additional structural biases that could accentuate Mexico's problems as a dependent country in matters such as educating its own domestic elite and its relative position within co-operative arrangements.

With respect to internationalisation, the response of Mexico's higher education institutions is largely characterised by inertia, reactions to short-term pressures or opportunities, and their focus on urgent national problems. In fact, efforts to internationalise higher education in Mexico remain concentrated at a few private and public universities. The effort is strong in some disciplines that have an established intellectual tradition of exchanges with foreign countries – for example, physics — and in some activities promoted by public funds (e.g., academic mobility). It has also been the focus of some institutional efforts – for example, conventional graduate studies based on international co-operation, such as those on professorial training at ITESM. However, internationalisation activities have not been the result of a coherent public policy covering all areas requiring attention by government. NAFTA created high expectations among many academics, but ten years after its adoption, these expectations have not been met to any great degree.

GLOBALISATION, NORTH AMERICAN INTEGRATION, AND HIGHER EDUCATION IN MEXICO

The interest in analysing the internationalisation of higher education at the institutional level in Mexico is of recent origin. Institutional case studies and comparative national studies are still rare among higher education scholars in Mexico. This is unlike the situation in Canada and the United States, where there are a number of research studies on these topics.[50] For purposes of this chapter, a preliminary study was conducted to help fill this gap. It examined how different institutional players in Mexico's public universities and technological institutes, including rectors, academic secretaries, international education administrators, academics, and students conceive of and perceive internationalisation policies at their institutions. Interviews were conducted with a cross-section of individuals at public universities involved in teaching and research and at institutions focused on graduate education and research.[51]

The Institutional Actors

The interviews indicate that a process of internationalisation is just beginning in Mexico's higher education institutions, despite the fact that references to globalisation and education exchange have become commonplace in official discourse and in discussions among academic specialists. Internationalisation is not a central element in the planning efforts of most Mexican higher education institutions, although these institutions typically have several plans for internationalisation that coexist alongside each other within the same institution. The institutional authorities, and the middle management in charge of international activities, normally have interests and perspectives that differ from those of the researchers who participate in educational exchange.

A recurring theme in the interviews is that internationalisation programs tend to be exclusionary. Even though recent efforts have opened new windows of opportunity for

Mexican researchers, the existing programs have discriminated against most members of the academic community, rather than included them. The fact that a small group of researchers tends to promote internationalisation on university campuses tends to skew participation toward those individuals and institutions. Moreover, higher education institutions that focus on research and postgraduate education are better placed to benefit from this situation than persons at institutions dedicated to undergraduate education or technological development. This inequality tends to be reinforced or softened by the researcher's field or subject matter. For example, in both technological institutes and public universities, agronomists insist that the type of research they carry out gives them little opportunity to apply for CONACYT programs, since its selection criteria tends to exclude them and their special research is seldom approved for support. Consequently, many players in the academic community become marginalised by the internationalisation process, especially to the extent that they self-admittedly lack the linguistic skills which are a precondition for membership in a foreign peer group and that is necessary to their participation in Mexico's federal and/or institutional internationalisation programs. These academics are angry about the poor distribution of benefits and insufficient attention paid to policies designed to equalise opportunities. They claim that access is restricted generally to Mexico's research elites. In recent years, post-secondary teachers in particular have showed signs of frustration even though their knowledge about the opportunities and institutional commitments to internationalisation was superficial. Their opinions were characterised by a blend of ignorance and strong concerns about how globalisation in general, and internationalisation programs in particular could affect the traditional ways of university teaching and internal relations within the university community, especially those between teachers, researchers, and students. Excluded from any position of strength, and without any possibility of participating in the internationalisation programs, they perceive the phenomenon as a threat to their professional position. In addition, they complained of losing a feeling of community with those who benefit from the new state of affairs. Many interviewees observe that these new academic elites in Mexico were becoming separated from their local peers and integrated into an international peer community, especially at the regional level, which made them different from other academics in Mexico. Thus, internationalisation was perceived as weakening the idea of an academic community with shared ideals, while reinforcing the tendency to atomise individual interests and academic society. These interviews also highlighted a new reality where the newly internationalised academic elites also pointed to this lack of academic community, since they were gradually losing their dependence on the institutions where they worked and were now solely interested in accessing resources and in broadening or renewing their new-found legitimacy abroad.

Thus, even though internationalisation policies are not a central feature of Mexico's higher education institutions, these policies have caused battles of disproportionate magnitude among institutional players. The movement away from mutual accommodation and the emergence of deep differences around the institution's mission – international excellence or a local commitment – are even more serious because progress in the internationalisation of higher education has happened only in traditionally sought after areas, namely research and the training of highly qualified personnel. For the great majority of students and academics, particularly teachers, the opportunities offered by internationalisation are currently beyond their reach. This situation constitutes a source of deep internal dispute at some higher education institutions. It makes careful and constructive thinking about the internationalisation of higher education a very difficult process in Mexico. In fact, for most academics, the internationalisation of higher education is associated mainly with opportunities for cross-border mobility and professional interaction outside the local institution. Unlike the situation in Canada and the United States, the thinking about internationalisation continues to be quantitative; it is concerned most with how to increase opportunities for academic mobility, continue financial support for internationalisation programs, and diffuse these programs to more institutions. In contrast, other topics such as internationalising the curriculum, improved teaching practices, curriculum review, and the internationalisation of the professional cadres have hardly been analysed in Mexico.

The insertion of Mexico's higher education system into a macro-regional system is already problematic due to the lack of symmetry between Mexico's higher education system and those of Canada and the United States. This problem is heightened because this process has reinforced, rather than minimised, the initial inequalities in the Mexican system of higher education, both within and without the North American context. In particular, it has emphasised Mexico's place as a partner that is at the receiving rather than the giving end of co-operation.

Organisational Problems in Managing International Activities

The interviews with the various institutional players demonstrate that interpretations of the proper role of internationalisation policies vary depending on the players. The difficulty in putting together internationalisation activities, which are perceived as necessary but not essential by many key players, is related to a series of unfavourable institutional conditions, including:

- the fact that internationalisation projects are not well co-ordinated within higher education institutions,
- the fact that the majority of professors do not have sufficient command of the languages required for exchanges with the U.S. and Canada (i.e., English and French),
- the fact that neither the users nor those responsible for administering internation alisation programs have a clear view of the institutional or individual commitments required for their success,
- the fact that there is no permanent public information about the costs and bene fits of internationalisation.

There is a general consensus about the insufficiency of the existing support systems for internationalisation programs, especially in relation to academic mobility, but there are also organisational obstacles to maximising the results of the existing programs. Internationalisation programs are not considered strategically important to institutional development and, consequently, internationalisation activities continue to be handled in an manner with little co-ordination among the various efforts. It would be useful to have some degree of regulation to provide an account of existing financial support, to avoid misunderstandings about the purpose of such programs, and to guarantee greater continuity of effort in this area. At present, the success of internationalisation programs in Mexico is highly dependent on a variety of different government offices, while many activities are carried out directly by individual university departments. Thus, internationalisation activities are often highly creative initiatives, but they are scattered and uncoordinated even within the same campus.

Another problem that stems from the same situation is the inability to measure the actual amount of resources devoted to internationalisation activities in Mexico, which makes it almost impossible to evaluate either the individual or social costs and benefits of internationalisation programs. The only data available on the cost of internationalisation, if it exists, is the budget of the office of international activities at the individual campuses. However, this is not the type of information that is useful in estimating institutional efforts and it is even less useful in helping analyse the extent to which these activities actually result in real efforts to become more involved in the North American region.

The signing of NAFTA, as well as the larger interest becoming a part of globalisation process, has led to the widespread incorporation of terms such as "globalisation" and "internationalisation" into even the vernacular language of higher education. This discussion has at least provoked a governmental response to the current situation through the design of general programs. These programs are oriented toward sustaining internationalisation activities such as research, student exchange, and professorial mobility and on occasion these programs have focused on various aspects of North America.[52] In a direct or indirect form, international support by PROMEP, the repatriation funds, and the invitations to foreign academics were each intended to improve the educational level of the teaching staff at post-secondary institutions and to eliminate their current tendency toward faculty inbreeding. In contrast to these new public policies, a general inertia and a lack of financial support for internationalisation efforts still predominates at the institutional level and this makes it difficult for even the earlier programs to have the expected results. For instance, the lack of opportunities in the technological area is probably the most problematic in organisational and political terms.

In fact, none of the public higher education institutions have made organisational reforms that would facilitate the implementation of the new government programs or to derive the greatest benefit possible from existing co-operative agreements. The institutional emphasis on international activities is, in many cases, dependent on the rector's own personal interest and this leads to uncertainty about the continuation of such activities after his/her departure. Where offices of international activities exist on a campus, they do not usually have much autonomy in making decisions, but instead tend to function as middle managers of these programs with the real decisions left to higher levels of the administration. According to a recent survey by AMPEI, this situation is compounded by the high rate of turnover among the persons who manage international activities on the campuses. Moreover, the heterogeneous background and lack of training among the middle managers responsible for administering internationalisation activities in Mexico creates further difficulty in achieving the intended results (AMPEI 1999).

Therefore, there are several delicate problems that need to addressed within the higher education institutions. Information is one problem, since many academics and students complain that information does not circulate appropriately, while program managers complain that most academics show little interest in their activities. Other problems include the need to:

- establish clear criteria for the distribution of financial support and explicit rules for applying to internationalisation programs and for selecting recipients or beneficiaries,
- provide advice and technical assistance to institutions and individuals who are new to the process of internationalisation,
- make decision-making mechanisms transparent, including the criteria for inclusion in the programs, expectations of matching efforts by the higher education institutions, and discussion of the purpose of these efforts in the appropriate campus bodies,
- link internationalisation strategies to the institutions' larger development plans.

However, field work indicates that Mexico's higher education institutions will also have to modify their internal processes for monitoring and evaluating international activities, including their impact on individuals and the institution. The ability to improve the assessment of these impacts will depend on the extent to which internationalisation policies are institutionalised at the federal and institutional levels. Thus, their success is tied to several strategic decisions, including:

- Formalising and defining the role of departments, or other units, charged with designing and operating a campus internationalisation policy,
- Integrating this policy into the fundamental plan for institutional development,
- Mobilising the required financial resources for a guaranteed period of time to ensure that the institution can play an active role in co-operative agreements with its foreign counterparts,
- Facilitating campus discussions about internationalisation and its impact on the institution to achieve a clearer understanding of its role and impact among key players on campus.

Needs and Responses

Despite the significant gap between public policies and the institutional realities of internationalisation, higher education institutions have made some important strides in the right direction. At least with the senior management of Mexico's higher education institutions, it is becoming evident that internationalisation is a good investment in the future of their institutions. The normative commitment to internationalisation at least has placed new value on the international activities of some campuses (e.g., Autonoma del Estado de Morelos). In other cases, there has been a hard search for an integrated policy on internationalisation even in decentralised institutions that have numerous campuses dispersed over a large territory (e.g., Universidad Veracruzana). In smaller institutions, offices of international education have been established and charged with seeking out funding sources and providing advice on the development of academic projects by specialised personnel (e.g., El Colegio Mexiquense AC). However, the need to institutionalise and regulate international activities is particularly acute in the technological institutes, where central administrations are in a position to respond to demands for internationalisation, but does so only in a bureaucratic and highly centralised fashion. Finally, in recent years some higher education institutions have begun to guarantee their students the opportunity to complete part of their disciplinary studies through stays abroad (e.g., undergraduate students of International Relations and doctoral students in Asian studies at El Colegio de Mexico). The Department of Computer Science at the Universidad de Colima utilises international co-operation to broaden mobility opportunities for especially gifted students who are completing graduate theses in this area.

In addition to the particular actions or specialised activities implemented by individual higher education institutions, more general responses are now emerging in the university sector. These responses include offering a greater number of opportunities to learn foreign languages, particularly through the establishment of special laboratories and centres that permit individualised learning by students (Gilbons and de Mas 1996). This pattern is reflected in the increasing number of higher education institutions now seeking support from the Fund for the Modernisation of Higher Education (FOMES) to acquire equipment for language laboratories. In the technological sector, language centres have been established belatedly, but with greater frequency. Other institutional responses are more innovative and more appropriate to the demands of highly efficient language training such as the appointment of native teachers and the opening of the Casa de Ingles in the Benemerita Universidad Autonoma de Puebla, which help advanced students enhance their oral language skills so they can become competitive players in North American co-operation.

Finally, many of the most pressing institutional problems involving the consolidation of an internationalisation policy have been tackled in specific and direct ways by the Universidad Autonoma de Mexico and the Universidad de Guadalajara. Both of these institutions have commissioned an external review of their internationalisation policies by recognised international experts in the field.[53] In both cases, their purpose was to diagnose the current situation and develop initiatives that will increase the occurrence of international activities in the future. Currently, these activities remain scattered on both campuses and have had little impact on the larger university.

The combination of self-evaluation with external evaluation has helped define the situation that exists in each institution, although such a process is still novel in the Mexican university system. In the case of the UdeG, the evaluations found that the intensity of internationalisation had actually decreased since the adoption of NAFTA. The evaluations also revealed the rectors' interest in defining internationalisation strategies that were more efficient, less exclusive, and more likely to support other institutional development projects. Finally, the evaluations incorporated the concerns and proposals voiced in various institutional circles and, hence, provoked a campus debate about the goals of the university's internationalisation plan. In fact, if the evaluation documents been more openly discussed on campus, the evaluation process could have renewed a campus discussion on the relation between globalisation and higher education at a higher level of discourse. This process could well have contributed to change in policy that would make broader efforts a possibility on these campuses.

The institutional conditions for internationalisation in Mexico are not ideal. Their improvement depends on the resolution of several problems:

- A significant proportion of the Mexican higher education institutions that initiated international activities in the mid-1990s have sought partners within North America. However, the ways in which they have sought partnerships, particularly with their lack of previous experience, specialised staff, earmarked funds, and clear direction, have made the process of identifying potential academic partners very difficult. These problems could be gradually solved if higher education institutions emphasised greater professionalisation of the academic and administrative personnel involved in international activities, placed international offices in more prominent positions within the institutions, and diffused mobility opportunities throughout the academic community.
- In the few instances where macro-projects in North American co-operation have been carried out by Mexican higher education institutions, they have not succeeded in responding to the real demands and opportunities created by NAFTA.
- As a result, trilateral co-operation in higher education has not produced the expected results in Mexico and this has often resulted in a renewed search for different academic partners. Cross-border co-operation based on linguistic identity with Latin America and Spain is now on the upswing in Mexico. Instead of the growth expected due to NAFTA in the area of educational exchange and co-operation, the result has been a blend of bi-lateral exchanges, especially with Canada and a "hispanisation" of internationalisation activities due to the greater accessibility of study programs in Spain and Latin America.
- These recent changes in the pattern of higher education co-operation suggests that Mexico has yet to define a consistent internationalisation policy even while choosing new counterparts for co-operation projects. Thus, given the controversial nature of the idea of "North American" higher education, Mexico must also analyse whether it is convenient to focus its internationalisation processes in that geographical context.
- The problem of institutionalising the process of internationalisation instead of making it dependent on individual personal relationships has not been dealt with

at most higher education institutions. There is as much creativity and commitment in individual projects of co-operation as there is uncertainty about their future at the institutional and financial levels. Reforms in the laws, regulations, and organisations that are essential to ensure their long-term continuity have been rarely accomplished to date.
- Institutional visions regarding the institutionalisation of international activities are very hierarchical and typically involve the rector and his/her immediate staff. A change in the institutional venue where internationalisation policies are developed and implemented requires an agreement on these policies, a more transparent accounting by the decision-makers, and similar accountability by those involved in implementing and benefiting from these policies.
- Particularly within the North American context, internationalisation measures have had a positive impact only on small circles of key researchers, where this impact has been registered in strengthened cross-border disciplinary networks. However, these measures have not promoted the participation of new institutional players, including both administrators and teachers, who have been marginalised by the processes of liberalisation and internationalisation. This situation is quite different from what occurred in the European Union's internationalisation programs.
- Given its developmental profile, Mexico has specific needs that are different from those of its NAFTA counterparts. Thus, beyond identifying areas of shared interest, such as those defined during the Wingspread Conference, Mexico needs to negotiate macro-regional co-operation programs that will help solve the problems inherent in being a less developed country. Mexico must confront two challenges vis-à-vis North America. First, Mexico must identify how it can contribute to the creation of a trilateral space in higher education. Second, Mexico needs to make it clear to its NAFTA partners that it is different, rather than trying to adapt to co-operative offers that do not always respond to its own needs. This implies that internationalisation efforts at the national and institutional levels must define how such efforts are consistent with Mexico's peculiar situation and the identity of its higher education institutions.

In this context, it would be necessary to go from a quantitative evaluation of the progress toward internationalising Mexico's higher education institutions to a qualitative evaluation. However, meeting this objective would require a series of consultations around questions that have not been really answered at this point. These questions include: (1) why internationalise higher education, (2) how and with what resources can Mexico internationalise its higher education institutions, and (3) which institutional actors and which foreign counterparts should be involved in internationalisation programs?

CONCLUSIONS

The Mexican higher education system changed rapidly and profoundly during the 1990s. First, it has continued and renewed a policy of decentralisation based on a territorial redistribution of the higher education system. Today, even in a more centralised system such as the higher technological institutes, the autonomy of certain sectors has increased in matters related to the definition of each institution's development priorities. Some universities, such as the Universidad de Guadalajara, have restructured relations between academic units and the central administration by granting the former new decision-making powers. Second, the Mexican higher education system has also strengthened the national process for evaluation and accreditation with the goal of improving the internal cohesion of the system. There have been efforts to establish trilateral mechanisms for the mutual recognition of credits and degrees to facilitate academic and professional mobility. Both actions have improved control quality in higher education. The strategic use of tri-lateral co-operation has promoted a certain level of academic harmonisation with Mexico's system of higher education and in relation to its NAFTA partners.

Finally, Mexico has attempted to rationalise its budget allocation model for higher education. The federal government has awarded higher education institutions significant amounts of money when they meet the requirements of competitive programs. Institutional access to financial support for internationalisation efforts has been structured according to the same competitive logic, which has mainly reinforced the advantages held by the pioneer institutions in this area.

Internationalisation policies and co-operative programs have promoted the selection of specific actions in higher education designed to address national problems. Paradoxically, however, there are some pending questions regarding the challenges posed by internationalisation and especially North American integration. It is evident that Mexico's national policies have peculiar characteristics when compared to the Canadian and U.S. situations. These include:

- the lack of a regulatory framework that will make efforts toward co-operation internally coherent, while giving greater precision to an institution's orientation, goals and objectives.
- the absence of umbrella structures that will organise, articulate, and facilitate internationalisation policies, which until now have been carried out by parallel organisations with different areas of coverage and competing interests.
- the failure of most higher education institutions to define strategic priorities for internationalisation projects beyond the original points agreed upon at Wingspread,
- The failure to articulate topics in the national context that are at the centre of the higher education discussions in other countries,
- the dependence of internationalisation policies on federal funds, rather than on institutional investment.

At the beginning of our analysis of the relation between globalisation, NAFTA, and higher education, we underscored the strong ideological and political baggage inherent in all three concepts. Several years after NAFTA's signing, many questions remain unanswered about the benefits and risks of internationalisation and harmonisation policies. However, apart from the specific difficulties inherent to these concepts, there are additional problems with respect to the more generalised challenges posed by globalisation. The consolidation of graduate education in Mexico has been one of the more significant responses to the demand for a highly skilled labour force. The strengthening of regional systems of research, institutional specialisation, and the new system of flexibility for acquiring proficiency are other significant leaps forward for higher education. It is very likely that in the years ahead other issues of this type will be added to the list and most likely these too will centre on the need to develop new human resources for both the educational and economic systems. It is anticipated that the new instructional methodologies will emerge in higher education that involve less direct forms of classroom learning, the outsourcing of early undergraduate education to non-university level institutions, and the gradual allocation of scarce resources to the new certification system. These changes will allow Mexico to confront some of the challenges facing a knowledge-based society.

Nevertheless, the very idea of a "knowledge-based society" continues to generate concern in Mexico. This is due to the enormous lack of educational opportunities for a large number of social groups and the fact that eradicating this education gap would require a massive financial investment that has not yet taken place. Given these concerns, conflicts about the aims higher education reform continue to emerge throughout Mexico. The 2000 strike at UNAM attests to the presence of this conflict as do the lasting problems in rural pedagogical schools. In this situation, new and strong criticism is being directed at a national education plan that is characterised as "neo-liberal" by its critics who question its very assumptions. Schools of thought that clamour for new thinking around the identity of Mexico's higher education institutions have been gaining ground and these ideological perspectives will have great bearing on the implementation of national policies and on the relationship between Mexico and North America.

CHAPTER 6

THE TRIUMPH OF THE MARKET MODEL IN NORTH AMERICAN HIGHER EDUCATION

The future of international higher education (IHE) in North America is now inextricably bound up with the future of NAFTA and there are three major reasons why this will continue to be the case. First, Articles 1201-1210 of NAFTA make professional services subject to cross-border competition and within this framework higher education is "just another industry" subject to the general provisions on free trade established by the Agreement. The Agreement institutionalises the expectation that higher education services will be increasingly traded across national boundaries through a variety of delivery mechanisms: distance learning, joint programs, student and faculty exchange programs, and branch campuses, to name a few. Second, Annex 1210 of the Agreement certainly anticipates that increased international trade in professional services will indirectly affect higher education by requiring negotiations on cross-national accreditation and mutual recognition agreements on testing, credentials, degrees, and professional licensing.

Finally, direct government action and official rhetoric have made higher education an important component of NAFTA's implementation. The Trilateral Steering Committee (TSC)[1] was created in 1992 to both stimulate and facilitate new initiatives in higher education cooperation under the aegis of NAFTA. The Trilateral Steering Committee stimulated educators' interest in NAFTA through the Wingspread Conference (1992), the Vancouver Conference (1993), and the Guadalajara Conference (1994), which each generated important official statements about North American higher education and indirectly stimulated the creation of new trilateral associations such as the Consortium on North American Higher Education Collaboration (CONAHEC), the Alliance for Higher Education and Enterprise in North America, and the North American Partnership.

THE RHETORIC OF INTERNATIONAL HIGHER EDUCATION

The government-sponsored initiatives at Winspread, Vancouver, and Guadalajara generated enthusiasm among educators and a flurry of official rhetoric about the importance of higher education collaboration to the success of NAFTA. These initiatives have stimulated additional conferences, new academic mobility and trilateral research programs, and even new organisations aimed at stimulating cooperative ventures in international and North American higher education. Yet, many of North

America's leading educators are dissatisfied with the pace of development in North American higher education and have become increasingly critical of government and business for their unwillingness to provide significant financial support to these initiatives, particularly when compared to the Eurpean Union's IHE initiatives such as ERASMUS and SOCRATES (Mallea et al. 1997). These European initiatives have been successful partly because the European Commission has provided substantial, stable, and long-term funding for such programs. In contrast, the initial excitement among North American educators has slowly given way to disappointment and in some cases resignation to the fact that the governments of Canada, Mexico, and the USA are unwilling to provide long-term funding for IHE initiatives at a level comparable to Europe (Katz 1996, 233).

Thus, Marlene M. Johnson, the Executive Director and CEO of the National Association of Foreign Student Advisors (NAFSA) points to "a huge gap" between the official rhetoric and the actions taken by governments, higher education institutions, and transnational corporations to support the development of IHE generally (NAFSA 1999). Sylvia B. Ortega Salazar, the former Rector at UAM – Azacapotzalco, echoes this sentiment by suggesting that regional academic collaboration in North America is "rather unimpressive" despite the favorable context created by NAFTA (Salazar 1996, 240). Stanley Katz (1996, 221), president of the American Council of Learned Societies, observes that despite the rhetoric generated by NAFTA "the current level of North American educational exchange is not very high."

More recently, these concerns were voiced officially in a comprehensive report on North American higher education collaboration submitted to the Trilateral Steering Committee in March of 2000 by the American Council on Education (ACE), the National Association of Universities and Higher Education Institutions (ANUIS), and the Association of Universities and Colleges of Canada (AUCC). The TSC's comprehensive report finds that trilateral exchange activity "fell short" of the hopes generated by the official rhetoric around NAFTA, while "most (non-governmental) programs are confined to student mobility, rather than the range of possible collaborations" identified by educators at the Wingspread Conference in 1992 (ACE, ANUIS, and AUCC 2000, 1-2).

Our own research findings reaffirm that conclusion, but with two caveats. First, a number of new initiatives have been launched in recent years which promise to increase the levels of educational exchange, cross-border research collaboration, and trilateral institutional partnerships. These include the many programs sponsored by the Consortium for North American Higher Education Collaboration (CONAHEC), the North American Institute (NAMI), the North American Higher Education Mobility Program (NAHEM), BORDER PACT, the Fulbright Program, and the Higher Education Community Partnership (HECP), to name a few. These initiatives may not satisfy the original expectations generated by the Trilateral Steering Committee and they are certainly not comparable to the programs sponsored by the European Commission, but they are nonetheless a significant and new foray into the heretofore explored idea of North American higher education collaboration.

Second, the internationalisation of higher education can be defended with any number of arguments, but it is economic and trade considerations that have acquired the greatest salience, particularly among government officials and business leaders (Skilbeck and Connell 1996, 66). The sovereignty, cultural, and national civic issues raised by many academics occasionally intrude on this neo-liberal paradigm, but among most political, corporate, and educational elites the commitment to internationalize higher education is now directly linked to concerns about workforce development, technology transfer, and international competitiveness and, for the foreseeable future, these concerns will continue to shape the content and delivery of international higher education in North America.

These two developments are still moving on parallel tracks and they tend to be institutionalised in different organisations (e.g., CONAHEC and NAMI), but as North American educators continue to interact with business and government leaders a new concept of international higher education is emerging around the dual meanings of trilateralism. International educators have advanced the intuitive notion that trilateralism requires greater cooperation among the higher education institutions of the three North American countries. Business and government leaders have promoted a view of trilateralism based on greater cooperation between business, government, and higher education to solve specific problems related to North American economic integration. International education was previously justified by reference to its role in personal development, cultural enrichment, and international understanding, but the new concept of international higher education links its content and purpose to the objectives of North American economic integration and regional competitiveness in the global economy. From this perspective, IHE is not a public good to be provided by government at prices affordable to all who can benefit from it, but a private good that should be financed by those individuals (students) and institutions (transnational corporations and post-secondary institutions) that ostensibly receive its major, if not exclusive, direct economic benefits. This leads to the conclusion that trilateral collaborations which cannot attract long-term financial support from private individuals and institutions do not serve any tangible purpose and therefore should not receive long-term public subsidies.

Thus, the discussion about North American higher education collaboration is now clearly structured around two competing conceptions of international higher education. There is no question that the dominant concept of IHE in North America derives from the market model ensconced in NAFTA, while a more liberal model derived from the European experience has found little support outside the ranks of a few academics. Yet, paradoxically, both visions of North American IHE are expressed and defended in the Wingspread Statement (1992) and Vancouver Communique (1993), which catalyzed much of the activity and research in this field. Both documents refer to NAFTA as a rationale for North American higher education collaboration, but at the same time they envision a level and type of higher education cooperation that goes well beyond NAFTA and its narrowly defined economic rationale.

TOWARDS A NORTH AMERICAN HIGHER EDUCATION MARKET?

There are three aspects to the economic argument for internationalizing higher education. First, the direct economic impacts of higher education exports are potentially significant, since there is a $30 billion world market for international higher education defined exclusively in terms of consumption abroad (i.e., student mobility). The direct economic impacts of international higher education include the creation of professional and technical jobs at traditional HEIs, which are supported by the presence of foreign students, as well as the jobs supported by their expenditures on living expenses in the host country. In 1998, for example, the USA officially exported nearly $9 billion in higher education services and recorded a trade surplus in higher education services of about $7.4 billion (U.S. Department of Commerce 2000, D-56). Higher education is the USA's fifth largest service export.[2]

While the USA is the world's leading exporter of higher education services, with approximately 30 percent of the world market, the OECD countries receive more than 80 percent of the 1.5 million international students who study abroad each year (Skilbeck and Connell 1996, 73). Higher education receives much greater attention and investment in the OECD countries than elsewhere in the world and in many of these countries (e.g., Canada and the USA) there is "surplus" capacity in the higher education system. Consequently, as the global demand for higher education continues to increase faster than the supply, the liberalization of trade in education services will facilitate the global market's tendency to shift the delivery of higher education to the developed countries (World Bank 1995, 2-32) and, hence, secure their competitive advantage in this knowledge-intensive sector of the world economy.

A second aspect of the economic argument for IHE is its indirect contribution to the competitive advantage of nations (Porter 1990; Reich 1992; Thurow 1991, 1992). The OECD countries have produced a vast literature on the importance of a highly skilled workforce and rapid technology transfer to the post-industrial economy (Becker 1993; Hornbeck and Salamon 1991; Bartel and Lichtenberg 1987). The growing importance of these factors to post-industrial economic development has put higher education at the center of many national strategies for international competitiveness and domestic economic renewal. However, the importance of higher education to the expansion of knowledge-intensive industries does not by itself point to any need for international higher education.

The need for an international dimension to higher education is related to the fact that the new economy is not only a post-industrial economy, but a global economy, where transnational enterprises and cross-border transactions are an increasingly important element of economic activity. Thus, individual students and businesses are beginning to recognise the economic value of employees with multicultural competencies and international skills (Davis 1997, 4). These skills can include fluency in a foreign language and knowledge of the government, economy, and culture of foreign countries (area studies). Study abroad and international education exchange are certainly an important part of learning these competencies (Opper, Teichler and Carlson 1990). Furthermore, applied research and technology transfer are central to the competitiveness strategies of countries like Canada and the United States, which want to achieve or secure a global market advantage in the export of high technology and professional services.

Finally, a third aspect of the economic argument for IHE is the intangible impact of threshold externalities. The foreign graduates of colleges and universities often become leaders in business, the professions, government, education, and the media when they return to their home countries, but they are likely to maintain professional contacts in the country where they received their higher education (Davis 1997, 81). These individuals are also more likely to develop an appreciation for the culture, values, and products of the host country and to become a reservoir of goodwill toward the host country that facilitates future transactions and exchanges.

However, to the extent that one embraces these arguments as a rationale for IHE policy, they not only define the purpose of IHE, but frame the issue in such a way that policy makers are inclined to pursue a market-based policy, particularly since North American higher education initiatives are being developed in response to NAFTA. On this point, government officials and international educators are often talking past each other, rather than engaging in direct dialogue. What appears as little activity to international educators is significant activity from the perspective of government and business. Each of the three governments, as well as the Trilateral Steering Committee, have consistently defined their role since Wingspread as one of market development and market facilitation, rather than one of permanently funding large new programs of the type sought by international educators.

In their March 2000 report to the Trilateral Steering, ACE, ANUIS, and the AUCC again reaffirmed Wingspread's basic premise that the North American Free Trade Agreement provides the main "rationale for government involvement not only in enhancing opportunity, but also in removing barriers that limit the flow of students, scholars, and academic projects across North American borders" (ACE et al. 2000, 1). Consequently, the Trilateral Steering Committee's new plan for *Increasing North American Higher Education Cooperation, Collaboration, and Exchange* (2000) also reaffirms that any government involvement in cross-border North American higher education programs must be "consistent with the economic cooperation and trade goals underlying NAFTA" (ACE et al 2000, 2). One of the 2000 report's key conclusions is that "sustainable support for a complex new structure would be difficult to ensure and a new structure may not be the best way to address current obstacles" to trilateral cooperation in higher education (Ibid., 2). Instead, the Trilateral Steering Committee is proposing a new "market initiative," where the three government's main role will be to facilitate the creation of "a marketplace for higher education cooperation and exchange" consistent with the NAFTA framework (Ibid., 1). The objective of the new market initiative is not just to strengthen the economic role of higher education within the three NAFTA countries, but to fully integrate higher education as *a service industry* into NAFTA under the provisions covering trade in services (Barrow 2002).

There are both advantages and disadvantages for higher education in this line of reasoning. A wholesale and uncritical adoption of the economic argument for IHE may accelerate an already overwhelming colonization of higher education by narrowly defined corporate and political interests that erode its broader egalitarian democratic, and humanitarian goals. This is certainly one of the critics' main lines of argument against a policy of internationalisation linked to trade liberalization and the human resource demands of transnational corporations exclusively. On the other hand, the economic role of higher education so dominates high level policy making that it is virtually impossible to engage the policy making process without acknowledging higher education's importance to technological innovation, human resource development, and international competitiveness.

Moreover, while compelling on their face value, these arguments may have been oversold by educators, private organisations, and higher education institutions seeking to attract additional public funding to support these activites. The economic argument for international education certainly does not provide a compelling reason for why *government* should subsidise marginal macro-economic benefits that are realised mainly by private beneficiaries; namely, individuals, transnational corporations, and selected higher institutions. For instance, the claim that foreign students generate $7.2 billion in total U.S. economic impacts (1997) is an impressive number until one puts it in the context of a $7.6 trillion U.S. Gross Domestic Product. This means that higher education exports actually account for only 0.1 percent of total GDP and this would still be a minuscule number even if more generous economic estimates are accepted as accurate or even if the USA commanded a 100 percent share of the world international student market.

Similarly, the estimate that foreign student expenditures generate 80,000 to 100,000 jobs in the USA each year seems significant until one juxtaposes that number to total U.S. employment of 123.4 million persons (1997). This means that higher education exports account for only 0.06 percent to 0.08 percent of total U.S. employment, albeit a disproportionate number of the jobs generated are probably in high wage professions. The export of higher education services to the NAFTA countries probably generates no more than $504 million annually (1997) in net economic impacts. This figure is quite small in comparison to the $223.2 billion in total exports to Canada and Mexico, since higher education exports amount to only 0.22 percent of total U.S. exports to Canada and Mexico or 0.005 percent of U.S. gross domestic product (1997).

When viewed from a macro-economic perspective, neither a more liberal calculation of economic impacts, nor significant growth in higher education services is likely to make higher education services a significant U.S. export cluster in comparison to other industries and services such as electronics, automobiles, textiles and apparel. Even accounting for the fact that foreign students in the USA are concentrated in a few metropolitan states, a recalculation of the total economic impacts generated by these students on a state by state basis does not alter the macro-economic picture (see Table 9). There are only two states – Massachusetts and Hawaii – where higher education exports account for more than 0.2% of total state employment so it is also not likely that any state government will regard higher education service exports as a significant industry cluster. Given their shares of the international higher education market, these facts are likely to be even more striking in Canada and Mexico.

Table 11. Estimated Academic Year Foreign Student Expenditures and Job Creation by State, 1994.

State	Foreign Students	Jobs Created	Total Employment	Percent of Total Employment
Massachusetts	24,327	6,350	2,981,814	0.21%
Hawaii	5,625	1,074	544,996	0.20%
Utah	5,708	1,565	938,050	0.17%
Iowa	8,155	2,468	1,508,666	0.16%
North Dakota	1,842	529	323,508	0.16%
Kansas	7,668	1,785	1,259,474	0.14%
Oregon	6,617	1,881	1,556,948	0.12%
Rhode Island	2,275	561	465,399	0.12%
Washington	10,164	2,838	2,542,821	0.11%
District of Columbia	9,067	282	275,034	0.10%
California	56,673	14,381	14,122,088	0.10%
Oklahoma	7,600	1,466	1,454,355	0.10%
Vermont	923	298	300,056	0.10%
New York	47,278	8,419	8,605,102	0.10%
Michigan	16,074	4,156	4,538,629	0.09%
Pennsylvania	18,848	4,898	5,468,822	0.09%
Arizona	7,741	1,608	1,885,059	0.09%
South Dakota	1,066	308	365,194	0.08%
Montana	1,290	349	417,225	0.08%
Colorado	6,087	1,545	1,917,043	0.08%
Missouri	8,576	2,059	2,566,903	0.08%
Wisconsin	7,522	2,102	2,668,025	0.08%
New Hampshire	1,793	449	595,102	0.08%
West Virginia	2,012	528	717,410	0.07%
Connecticut	5,839	1,187	1,640,558	0.07%
Ohio	16,170	3,812	5,318,880	0.07%
Florida	18,555	4,508	6,363,390	0.07%
Illinois	19,368	3,997	5,651,393	0.07%
Minnesota	6,517	1,717	2,473,515	0.07%
Louisiana	6,246	1,237	1,785,01	0.07%
Delaware	1,439	247	363,680	0.07%
Idaho	1,598	378	558,589	0.07%
Texas	27,619	5,787	8,802,65	0.07%
Indiana	8,755	1,886	2,898,395	0.07%
Virginia	8,308	2,009	3,250,202	0.06%
New Jersey	10,005	2,289	3,742,505	0.06%
Maine	1,360	321	569,027	0.06%
Wyoming	646	124	238,307	0.05%
Maryland	8,520	1,316	2,558,208	0.05%
Arkansas	2,633	583	1,142,941	0.05%
Nebraska	2,832	424	854,975	0.05%
Alabama	5,212	926	1,906,756	0.05%
New Mexico	1,800	345	729,322	0.05%
South Carolina	3,228	08	1,709,446	0.05%
Tennessee	4,726	1,154	2,537,123	0.05%
Kentucky	3,535	767	1,725,887	0.04%
Georgia	7,520	1,466	3,391,782	0.04%
Nevada	1,674	310	733,469	0.04%
Mississippi	2,153	493	1,169,750	0.04%
North Carolina	6,444	1,426	3,439,864	0.04%
Alaska	582	40	281,417	0.01%

Source: Davis, Open Doors, 1995, p. 111 and Bureau of Labor Statistics.

Consequently, the macro-economic impacts of academic mobility will not be a significant incentive for federal or sub-national governments to become deeply involved in subsidising the movement of academic personnel, while the major growth sectors for trade in higher education services are more likely to occur in areas such as commercial presence, cross-border delivery, and presence of individuals, which are direct revenue generators for public and private HEIs that cannot justify public subsidies. In other words, for both political and economic reasons, the three governments in North America are not likely to pursue a vigorous policy aimed at deepening North American integration beyond the more significant industries specified in the treaty: transportation, investment, financial services, government procurement, automobiles, textiles and apparel, and agriculture. Consequently, IHE initiatives in North America will be hard pressed to justify increased government funding on the basis of economic arguments alone, since there is only a marginal public interest that is largely confined to providing equal opportunity, foreign policy capacity, and export development.

TOWARDS A NORTH AMERICAN COMMUNITY?

The conception of higher education as a service industry and a service export has largely captured thinking about international higher education in North America, particularly among the political and business leaders who control the resources available for higher education. There is no question that the Wingspread Statement and the Vancouver Communiqué contain very clear declarations about the importance of university-industry partnerships and cross-border collaboration to promote technological "innovation and human resource development." However, these documents also articulate an alternative conception of North American higher education and it is this vision beyond NAFTA that has captured the imagination of many academics and international educators.

The Wingspread Statement calls for enhanced cross-border collaboration in higher education to promote an "understanding of our respective distinctive cultures and identities," while declaring that "enhanced trilateral cooperation has merit in its own right." The Vancouver Communiqué also articulates this alternative conception of North American higher education:

> "We recognize that our countries cannot fully prosper in all the ways that matter if they remain no more than trading partners. A new sense of a North American community, made up of our 360 million people, should be forged, one which will provide impetus to greater cooperation among and within our countries, support our relations with countries outside the region, enhance our distinct cultural identities and acknowledge our asymmetries."

To achieve this vision of North America, Stanley Katz (1996, 221) of the ACLS proposes that the basic goal of North American educational exchange "ought to be nothing less than the creation of a common regional commitment." Katz argues that North America is little more than a geographical term and that NAFTA has linked the economic fortunes of three countries that have almost no sense of a common regional purpose or identity. However, Katz (1996, 221) suggests that if the underlying purpose of NAFTA is to create "a regional power, fit to compete socially and intellectually, as well as economically, with European and Asian regional groupings, it seems essential than an entity that is recognizably North American should come into existence" (Cf. Wirth and Earle 1995; Wirth 1996).

This social and cultural argument for North American higher education cooperation is supported by the broader cultural agglomeration already underway on the continent, but which is most pronounced in the "border cultures" between the USA, Canada, and Mexico. Much of the growth in Mexico's economy has been stimulated by the maquiladoras along the U.S.-Mexico border, while the vast majority of Canada's population lives within 100 miles of the U.S. border. The U.S. dollar is readily accepted by merchants and businesses on both sides of the border, where it *de facto* functions as a second currency in both countries. Canadian and Mexican government officials have both tentatively floated the idea of adopting the dollar as the single North American currency. While NAFTA has raised anxieties about sovereignty, nationality, and culture in Canada and Mexico, especially, the impact of Mexico and Canada on the USA receives much less attention. While NAFTA's purpose is to facilitate regional trade within North America, trade has also been accompanied by the legal and illegal movement of people and with them their cultures and national identities.

In 1990, 9 percent of the U.S. population was Hispanic and this proportion increased to 12.5 percent in 2000, which for the first time makes Hispanics the largest minority in the USA. Persons of Mexican ancestry account for 62.5 percent of the USA's Hispanic population. The proportion of the total U.S. population that has a Mexican ancestry (or citizenship) has increased from 5.4 percent in 1990 to 7.9 percent in 2000. In 1990, there were nearly 19.8 million foreign-born residents in the USA with Mexico and Canada accounting for the 1st and 3rd largest numbers of foreign-born residents, respectively. Mexico (21.7%) and Canada (3.8%) combined account for 25.5 percent of all foreign-born residents in the USA. Mexico and Canada also account, respectively, for the 1st and 5th largest number of resident aliens (30.7% of total) and naturalized citizens (17.2% of total) in the USA (U.S. Census 1990, 2000).

There is also an increasing movement of non-immigrants between the three countries. The USA admitted 31.4 million non-immigrants in 1999 for business, pleasure, and temporary work compared to 22.6 million in 1995 (+38.9%). During the same period, the total number of non-immigrants admitted to the USA from Canada increased by 45.6 percent (to 367,000), while the number of non-immigrants admitted from Mexico increased by nearly 212 percent (to 3.8 million). The proportion of non-immigrant admissions to the USA from Canada and Mexico has increased from 13.7 percent of total admissions in 1995 to 22.6 percent in 1999 (U.S. Department of Justice 1999, 11-12). Since NAFTA's passage, there has also been a significant increase in the intra-regional movement of tourists, temporary workers, intra-company transferees, and citizenship. The populations and cultures of North America are increasingly interacting if not integrating on a daily basis.

WHY NORTH AMERICA?

In addition to the conflict between the "economic" and "cultural" missions of international higher education, NAFTA has also stimulated a second debate between proponents of a global mission for IHE (i.e., multilateralism) as opposed to a regional (i.e., North American) mission for IHE. The Wingspread Statement contains potentially contradictory commitments in taking "note of the North American Free Trade Agreement," while suggesting that enhanced trilateral collaboration should not be pursued in lieu of "bilateral relations with third countries and relevant multilateral organizations." These two positions – regionalism and multilateralism – are not necessarily in conflict, but they do raise questions about priorities and they force proponents of North American collaboration in all three counties to compete for resources directed toward multilateral or global objectives. There are many economic and cultural reasons to argue that IHE in Canada, Mexico, and the USA should place a special, if not exclusive, emphasis on collaborations and exchanges among the three countries' post-secondary institutions.

The first reason is that NAFTA exists and the agreement explicitly incorporates provisions aimed at encouraging closer collaboration among the three country's post-secondary institutions. This intention was conveyed to the three countries' higher education and business leaders in the Wingspread Conference, the Vancouver Communiqué, and the Guadalajara Conference. These conferences accelerated the growth of the Consortium on North American Higher Education Collaboration, which now has 60 institutional affiliates, including many of the three countries' leading higher education institutions and associations. It has become a major focal point for college and university administrators, researchers, and international educators seeking to promote educational exchange and research collaboration within North America. The Guadalajara Conference catalyzed the North American Institute's Alliance for Higher Education and Enterprise in North America (AHEENA). NAMI has emerged as the nation's leading independent think thank on questions of North American identity, while actively promoting trilateral collaboration among business and political leaders.

However, as noted previously, NAFTA is not a finished project. The U.S. Congress and the Canadian Parliament approved NAFTA by narrow margins and the treaty is still controversial among important segments of all three societies. The North American Free Trade Agreement was the culmination of a trilateral movement among the three countries' political and business elites who enthusiastically embrace the neo-liberal or "Washington consensus." The elite consensus forged by the new Democrats in the USA, the Progressive Conservatives in Canada, and the Institutional Revolutionary Party in Mexico is not shared by most intellectuals, labor leaders, and political activists on the far left or the far right in any of the three countries (Pastor 1992; Aboites 1997). There is a strong and tenacious opposition to NAFTA among "progressive" social forces in all three countries, including organized labor, consumer advocates, environmental groups, and leftist intellectuals (Grayson 1993; Lee 1995). These constituencies argue that NAFTA has resulted in the loss of U.S. and Canadian jobs to Mexican workers who are exploited by multinational corporations that also degrade environmental standards on the U.S.-Mexican border (AFL-CIO 1991; Scott, Lee, and Schmitt 1997; Rothstein and Scott 1997; Scott 1996; Levinson 1993). Ironically, many on the North American political left have found common cause with conservative and nationalist social forces, which are concerned about a range of "sovereignty" issues that involve the preservation of national cultures, languages, and religion.

The depth of these concerns cannot be underestimated following the "Battle of Seattle," particularly since that confrontation was shortly followed by large demonstrations against the IMF and World Bank in Washington, D.C. and violent confrontations in Genoa, Italy. The opposition to globalisation ranges from groups and individuals who oppose the process outright as a threat to national sovereignty and a step toward "world government" to those who are seeking to humanise globalization by making labour and environmental standards part of the trade liberalisation process (Steger 2002). Therefore, it is important to note yet again that globalization and regionalization are not only an economic process, but a policy – a set of agreements and decisions about how citizens and businesses will interact with each other across national boundaries. The question for educators is whether higher education will play its traditional role as outside critic or play a pro-active role in NAFTA's development by participating in the construction and implementation of NAFTA's provisions on higher education. Thus far, most academics have remained outside the process – not critical of it, but in fact completely unaware that major trade agreements such as NAFTA and WTO have any implications for higher education.

A second reason for focusing on the development of North American higher education cooperation is that even from a narrow economic perspective, international trade in higher education is already concentrating on a regional basis, particularly in Europe and Asia. The aggressive IHE strategies by the E.U., Japan, and Australia suggest that the regionalization of IHE is likely to intensify in those areas in the next decade. Okamoto's (1990) analysis of international student flows finds "a broad pattern of movement both to and within the industrial countries, but with evident regard to language, history, and geographic proximity." Leyton-Brown (1996, 12) also finds that international student flows are "more pronounced along networks defined and reinforced in terms of culturally attractive emulation models" related to levels of economic development, language, historical links (e.g., colonial ties), and geography. For example, the most popular foreign destination for U.S. students is the United Kingdom. Hayward (1995, 121) observes that the United Kingdom's continuing popularity as a study abroad destination for USA students "is no doubt partly a reflection of the limited foreign language proficiency of most American students." In fact, Hayward (1995, 121) argues that there is a direct relationship between foreign language enrollments in U.S. colleges and universities and the rank order of students' choices of non-English-speaking countries for study abroad (e.g., U.K, Spain, France, and Germany).

The importance of a common language to educational exchange is equally evident among Central and South American students, who account for about one-quarter of Spain's foreign student enrollments, while Francophone Africans constitute more than one-half of France's foreign student enrollments. The significance of economic relationships and geographic proximity is evident in the fact that Asians account for 76 percent of Australia's foreign student enrollments and 92 percent of Japan's foreign enrollments (Davis 1995, 82; Anderson 1996; Skilbeck and Connell 1996, 75). Likewise, about 40 percent of foreign students in 11 European countries are from other European countries" (Skilbeck and Connell, p. 75). These patterns of student mobility suggest that geographic proximity and the economic relationships established by NAFTA should induce greater student mobility and other forms of collaboration among the three countries, but this mobility is obstructed by a number of physical, technical, fiscal, and cultural barriers (Barrow 1999).

A DECADE AFTER WINGSPREAD

Nevertheless, the idea of trilateral cooperation in North American higher education has steadily gained currency in the last decade mainly due to the efforts of the Trilateral Steering Committee, CONAHEC, and NAMI. The Wingspread Conference in 1992 provided new impetus for collaborative activities, while the Vancouver Symposium in 1993 charted an ambitious, forward-looking agenda for trilateral cooperation in North American higher education. However, the implementation of the Vancouver Communiqué has been uneven in the sense that some of the proposed initiatives have advanced significantly in the last decade, while others have lagged or been discarded entirely.

The Vancouver Symposium convened leaders in education, government, and business from across North America and reached an agreement on six action initiatives to stimulate North American co-operation in higher education. The Vancouver Communiqué, which announced these initiatives, embraced the immense possibilities of NAFTA, but it was issued against the backdrop of a major U.S. recession (1990-91), fiscal crises in state government, declining government support for higher education institutions, and the first serious efforts to balance the U.S. and Canadian federal budget (Barrow 1993). Thus, the Vancouver Communiqué was premised on the fact that additional governmental resources would not be available to support new initiatives and that advancing the proposed initiatives would require the reallocation of existing higher education resources toward international education priorities.

These six action initiatives proposed in the Vancouver Communique include:

1. The establishment of a North American Distance Education and Research Network (NADERN),
2. The formation of a trilateral mechanism (through the existing professional associations) to examine issues related to mobility, portability, and certification of skills across national borders,
3. The establishment of programs to enable faculty and administrators from the three countries to meet and develop trilateral higher education collaborative activities,

4. The establishment of an electronic information base with co-ordinated sharing of information on initiatives and resources relevant to trilateral co-operation,
5. The strengthening and expansion of North American studies programs,
6. The establishment of a program to support trilateral exchange, research, and training for students.

The establishment of a North American Distance Education and Research Network (NADERN) has not fared well, but this "failure" is largely because rapid growth in use of the Internet for cross-border communication and information-sharing rendered the idea obsolete almost from its conception. Although some higher education institutions, particularly in Mexico, were not technologically equipped for such networking in 1993, distance learning capabilities in that country have been expanded through Mexico's Fund for the Modernization of Higher Education (FOMES). There is clearly an increasing amount of distance education taking place within and among the three countries of North America through the initiative of individual higher education institutions (HEIs). However, there are no reliable statistics available for measuring the growth of distance education within North America.

The proposal for a mechanism to facilitate trilateral certification and career learning has advanced slowly if at all. A major obstacle to meeting this goal is that Canada, Mexico, and the USA have different mechanisms for certifying professional and vocational credentials. In Mexico, the professions are certified by the individual higher education institution, while in the USA and Canada, the states and provinces license many occupations based on tests administered by professional or occupational associations. An obstacle to the development of a North American accreditation agency is the fact that the accreditation and evaluation agencies in Mexico were either recently created or they are undergoing rapid development, which has resulted in many questions about their role and authority in relation to post-secondary institutions in Mexico. The Canadian and U.S. accreditation and evaluation systems are long-established and well developed in comparison to the Mexican system, which has led a small number of private higher education institutions in Mexico to seek accreditation from the Southern Association of Colleges and Schools (SACS 2001).[3] Despite resistance from the higher education sector, the Mexican government has launched a number of significant new actions, including the creation of a Labor Competencies, Normalization, and Certification Council.

The development of North American Studies is also far from being fully realized as an academic field of study. For nearly 40 years, efforts have been made to foster American (i.e., USA) Studies in Canada and more recently the task has been begun in Mexico. Canadian Studies are still rare in the USA despite considerable support from the Canadian government, while Canadian Studies is even weaker in Mexico notwithstanding the creation of a few new programs (Katz 1996, 228-29). There is a large number of Latin American Studies programs in the USA, but most of these are not specifically focused, or even significantly focused, on Mexico.

North American Studies programs have been created at Duke University in the USA, the Autonomous National University (Mexico City), and the University of the Americas (Cholula, Mexico). In Canada, Simon Fraser University sponsors the Council for North American Business Studies, while UCLA's School of Public Policy and Social Research hosts the North American Integration and Development Center. The North American Institute has supported the publication of some excellent books on the concept of North American community and identity, but otherwise there has been comparatively little activity in this area. In addition, the Western Interstate Commission on Higher Education (WICHE) has sponsored the publication of a small comparative series, entitled *Understanding the Differences,* which explores the three systems of higher education. The El Colegio de Mexico's Inter-Institutional Program for Comparative Studies of North America has also advanced the creation of a multi-disciplinary research network on North America, particularly in the social sciences.

However, with few exceptions, college and university administrators in the three countries have not responded to the North American initiative with much commitment or enthusiasm. Part of the problem has been the intractable difficulty of launching new interdisciplinary programs in a balkanized academic culture controlled by traditional disciplines, while at the same time these programs must compete for resources with existing area studies programs. North American Studies does not yet command the visibility or the resources of Asian, African, Latin American, Middle East, and other high-profile area studies programs. Meanwhile, institutional leaders in all three countries have been absorbed with the broader financial problems of declining public funding and soaring costs in higher education. Higher education administrators have been reluctant to spend political or financial capital to support something as experimental and uncertain as North American Studies.

On a more positive note, the proposal to create programs for the trilateral exchange of ideas among faculty and administrators has been fulfilled to a small but increasing degree during the last decade. The Program for North American Mobility in Higher Education (NAMHE) and the University Affiliations programs have generated several faculty/administrator partnerships. The CONAHEC conferences, the EL-NET, BORDER PACT, and other institutional networks have yielded considerable North American faculty contact and cross-border collaboration. Similarly, the establishment of an electronic information base with data relevant to trilateral cooperation has been largely fulfilled by the creation of EL-NET, which is also administered by CONAHEC. The proposal to establish a program to support trilateral exchange for higher education students in North America has also made some limited progress. The three countries allocate modest sums to the North American Mobility in Higher Education program, which supports some trilateral mobility among students, but this program has been difficult to sustain.

Consequently, progress toward genuinely trilateral cooperation in North American higher education has been inconsistent since Wingspread and Vancouver, while the objectives articulated at those meetings have failed to generate much enthusiasm or attention within the academic community. The trilateral conferences themselves may well have established a negative perception among faculty by linking cross-border collaboration in North American higher education directly to NAFTA, which was widely opposed by academics in Canada and Mexico, especially. As these perceptions have widened to include the WTO, the IMF, and the World Bank, U.S. academics have also grown increasingly skeptical about cross-border collaboration that is defined in the terms of free trade in higher education services. The inability to establish any "depth" to North American higher education cooperation is also made difficult by the fact that most initiatives have been top down projects organized by the Trilateral Steering Committee or emanating from conferences attended by leading higher education administrators, top corporate executives, and high level government officials, but with little to no input from college and university faculty, faculty unions, or scientific, professional, and disciplinary associations. Thus, the entire process of building North American higher education cooperation has failed to enlist widespread support from the constituencies most able to insure its success or failure in the long-term.

At the same time, Wingspread and Vancouver both envision a model of ever-increasing cooperation among North American higher education institutions, but the dominant cultural model in North America emphasizes competition between institutions and the pursuit of competitive advantage. This underlying orientation is likely to grow stronger under NAFTA since HEIs in all three countries are now looking for ways to export their own services to other countries over those of their domestic and international competitors. North American initiatives in higher education have also run up against broader interpretations of internationalism in foreign policy, where they compete for funds with programs aimed at other forms of transnationalism linked to Europe, Latin America, Asia, and Africa.

The availability of government resources to support international higher education initiatives has generally declined in all three countries and, despite explicit warnings from government officials that funding would be limited there has been substantially less government funding for North American initiatives than was expected by educators. Indeed, regardless of the country, the three governments have been willing to fund North American higher education collaboration only to the degree that it is directly aligned with national economic development and regional trade policies. Traditional objectives related to cultural exchange and international assistance have increasingly fallen by the wayside since the Wingspread Statement and Vancouver Communiqué. These traditional objectives are likely to remain on the sideline for the foreseeable future due to the continuing emphasis on fiscal restraint among the national governments of all three countries. The unrelenting budget pressures on sub-national governments (i.e., states and provinces) have further limited the public funding available for trilateral programs.

In Canada, for example, policy discussions about North American cooperation in higher education first occurred during a major review of the country's foreign policy. The review identified education and culture as important pillars of Canadian foreign policy, but in implementing the policy, Canada's Department of Foreign Affairs and International Trade (DFAIT) has placed most of its emphasis on the development of international trade in education services, including a number of concrete measures to promote the export of higher education services. Canadian Education Centres (CECs), representing over 250 institutions have been established, along with high level "Team Canada" regional trade missions to Asia and Latin America. As a result, provincial systems and institutions of higher education have viewed the internationalisation of higher education mainly as a business enterprise for generating revenues from student fees, consulting, and international research projects.

Mexico and the USA also have their own national priorities and funding constraints in higher education. Mexico's key national initiatives include the National Program for Faculty Development (PROMEP) and a strong push to create a nationwide system of technological universities that are considered crucial to the country's future economic development. In the USA, the agency previously responsible for overseas educational programs, the United States Information Agency (USIA) absorbed a 25 percent reduction in its student and faculty exchange budget from 1993 to 1997, while being assigned additional policy-driven priorities in the Middle East, Africa, Vietnam, and China, where the country has substantial economic and political interests.

Furthermore, trilateral cooperation in higher education has been slowed by conflicting views over how collaboration should be implemented, who should lead it, and who should be the responsible agents in trilateral programs. Canada and the USA both have highly decentralized higher education systems, where leadership and institutional development is largely the responsibility of individual campuses or state systems. On the other hand, Mexico has a highly centralized higher education system, where most funding is controlled by the federal government and where institutional leaders naturally look to the federal government for signals about appropriate actions and policies. Thus, it has often proven difficult to establish a coordinated policy on North American higher education, since higher education officials (e.g., Trilateral Steering Committee) in Mexico have a much greater capacity to steer the national system of higher education than federal officials in Canada and the USA.

Furthermore, the decentralised character of Canadian and U.S. higher education makes it exceptionally difficult to achieve a national consensus on the role of higher education under NAFTA, which remains contested by many academics, students, union officials, environmentalists, and legislative representatives. While there is general agreement that trilateral collaboration is useful in furthering the traditional goals of international understanding, cultural tolerance, and political rapprochement, there is no commonly shared view of the best process for achieving this collaboration. In general, Canadian officials tend to view the development of North American collaboration as an integrated, extensive, and orderly process, not unlike that taking place in the European Union, where the different national models of higher education will remain intact, while being held to reasonably high standards of accountability. In the USA, trilateral cooperation has received much less national attention, and given the size and variety of its system, trilateral collaboration has been strongest in the border area with Mexico, where cooperation has emerged largely due to the initiatives of individual higher education institutions. Mexico's public officials tend to view collaboration as a process leading to a convergence of higher education in the three countries and, for this reason, its potential impact in Mexico has been far more controversial and immediate for those seeking to preserve the distinctive features of Mexican higher education.

These controversies and obstacles are overlaid with the practical difficulties of establishing working partnerships on a trilateral basis. Higher education institutions, like governments, have found it more comfortable to work in a conventional one-to-one institutional relationship. Higher education institutions working with a single foreign partner can more easily identify shared goals, while the administration of bilateral programs is less cumbersome. In addition, many higher education leaders who favor international collaboration, but who do not believe that continental integration is an important goal argue that trilateralism often hinders cooperation and that it is more important for higher institutions to establish mutually beneficial partnerships than to pursue lofty long-term foreign policy goals. On the other hand, proponents of a genuinely trilateral cooperation argue that bilateral projects simply represent more of the same and merely repeat what has been done for years in higher education. The call for trilateral programs is typically linked to NAFTA and the goal of creating a regional identity for higher education in North America. Although some trilateral programs have been developed in the last decade, higher education institutions in North America generally continue to pursue bilateral programs (i.e., Canada-Mexico, USA-Mexico, Canada-USA).

North American higher education cooperation has also proven more difficult than anticipated in the Wingspread Statement due to deep differences of culture, education, history, fiscal resources, and government that distinguish the three North American countries. These asymmetries were acknowledged at Wingspread and Vancouver, but the effect of asymmetry was underestimated in how it shapes the way educators and government officials in the three countries interpret the objectives and possibilities of collaboration. The higher education system and academic culture in each country are unique and they are not easily blended with those of the other countries. The largest North American partner, the USA, has a vast, diverse and often unwieldy universe of 4,070 colleges and universities compared to 740 in Mexico and 240 in Canada (Canales et al. 1995).

In the trilateral initiative's formative stages, NAFTA/higher education linkages were promoted with the seductive allure that North American transnational corporations would be active partners with post-secondary institutions and governments. This expectation has not been fulfilled in many cases. With few exceptions, corporations have not assumed a leadership role in promoting or funding trilateral initiatives in higher education. When faced with their own financial and competitive pressures, the region's corporations have made limited commitments to higher education and these are typically linked to very narrow company objectives. Individual firms may fund programs that are closely associated with their economic interests (e.g., workforce training), but the corporate sector has been largely unwilling to participate in broader based North American projects in higher education. Even the Alliance for Higher Education and Enterprise in North America (AHEENA) quickly backtracked on its bold objectives. Similarly, corporations have failed to back up the rhetoric of globalisation with visible efforts to recruit graduates that have international experience and multi-cultural skills. Despite the increased importance of overseas markets, the available studies do not show that major companies are consciously recruiting individuals who study and live outside their home country. The failure to hire graduates with foreign study and internship experience undercuts the incentive to pursue such studies for any but purely "cultural" reasons.

At the same time, our research documents that some progress has been made in promoting collaboration among higher education institutions in North America. There are many more higher education institutions involved in cooperative enterprises than a decade ago and many different types of collaborative projects are being implemented beyond student exchange (Institute of International Education 1997). However, the forms of collaboration, as well as the number of faculty and students participating in these programs, will need to greatly increase before trilateral collaboration in higher education can be declared a successful policy.

The Wingspread/Vancouver process was mainly directed by governments but, as noted earlier, in the future there will have to be more forceful and visible leadership by higher education administrators and wider participation by faculty in all three countries. CONAHEC is an important step in this direction, but its efforts have remained largely confined to work with higher education administrators and the directors of international education programs. Yet, long-term strategies that involve curriculum change, degree and credit recognition, faculty and student mobility, and increased interdisciplinary cooperation will require widespread support and understanding from rank and file faculty. Governments may continue to facilitate the Wingspread process and they can reiterate foreign policy priorities, but the ultimate success of North American cooperation in higher education will depend on broad-based support within the higher education institutions that participate in these programs.

At the same time, any further development of cooperation in North American higher education needs to be based on well-grounded analyses of current developments in international higher education within and between the three countries. The planning and implementation of future trilateral initiatives by higher education leaders will prove unsuccessful if it fails to take into account existing trends in political, economic, and foreign policy. It is also quite clear that the three countries' public officials are willing to participate in the trilateral process only so far as it contributes to national priorities as they understand them. For example, the continued expansion of international trade in professional services will have important implications for trilateral initiatives in higher education as officials in all three countries seek to expand this trade to the benefit of their own countries.

Thus, however apparent the manifold benefits of collaboration in North American higher education may be to those individuals who are already active in the process, it is necessary to realize that most people inside and outside academia still do not see any particular purpose or advantage to trilateralism. NAFTA certainly provides an obvious rationale and the Agreement is not likely to be rescinded by any of the countries. Consequently, educators also need to take a more active role in shaping its impact on their institutions. It is also necessary to document the results of successful linkages, effective organizations, and model projects to transfer these successes and to convince more people, institutions, organizations, and businesses of the value of North American cooperation in higher education. This body of knowledge can support an advocacy strategy for representative organizations in higher education, including those in each country involved in international education.

THE MARKET MODEL OF COLLABORATION

Government's participation in North American higher education collaboration is for the present specifically oriented toward advancing regional economic integration under the North American Free Trade Agreement (Mallea et al 1997, 10-11). Government participation in higher education collaboration is not viewed as a humanitarian or cultural exchange program and this is evident in the academic fields where mobility is being supported (i.e., business, engineering, health) and the types of collaborative research projects that receive funding (i.e., economic growth and agricultural development).

The identified opportunities for collaboration assume that financial resources will remain limited and scarce in higher education. Government is a partner in collaborative arrangements to the extent that it provides seed money for new projects, but it will not be a primary or a permanent source of funds for collaborative ventures. The three governments have clearly defined their current role as a facilitator of trilateral higher education co-operation that will only deploy resources into areas where it is likely to stimulate the mobilization and reallocation of existing institutional resources toward foreign policy and economic policy goals. These two goals are linked together in the three governments' emphasis on developing trilateral partnerships with local business and industry, which mobilize higher education resources to serve the immediate needs and interests of business firms operating within the NAFTA framework. The governments' expectation is that higher education resources can be reallocated toward these objectives to leverage private financing from business, industry, and foundations for the long-term maintenance of projects with tangible benefits to private industry and international trade.

Consequently, these governments have not been willing to provide significant long-term financial commitments to support higher education collaboration in North America. Although higher education is heavily dependent on government funding in every NAFTA country, the 1990s were an era of widespread fiscal restraint and structural adjustment for post-secondary education. Educators still face the challenge of how to maintain quality in higher education and expand its range of activities despite higher education budgets and real expenditures per student that are being strained across the continent (World Bank, 1994, 1-2). These fiscal constraints have become the major systemic and institutional factor in the development and implementation of higher education policy by individual higher institutions and by systems of higher education in these countries. The proliferating demands on governments, higher education institutions, foundations, and corporations is likely to preclude any large-scale government funded initiative in North American higher education co-operation in the current decade as well.

As a result, most of the collaboration taking place in North America is occurring at the institutional level, rather than at a state or national level (Katz 1996, 233-34). This pattern of micro-collaboration at the institutional level is not an accident, but the result of conscious decisions by government officials to implement a market model of higher education collaboration. The market model is distinctly different from the more liberal model adopted in the European Union, where continent-wide programs of academic mobility, research collaboration, and the development of mutually recognised credentials are heavily subsidized by the European Commission. While international educators often lament the "failure" of government to provide similar subsidies in North America, the market model derives from the limited mandate contained in NAFTA, which creates a narrowly defined "free trade area" for commodities and capital, rather than a continental "union" (Hufbauer and Schott 1992, 1993a). This mandate structures what government officials consider legitimate within the NAFTA framework. While fiscal constraints are the stick that pressures HEIs to seek new sources of revenue in the form of international students, service exports, and university-industry collaboration, federal seed money is the carrot that attracts individual HEIs willing to redeploy institutional resources toward regional goals, while largely limiting those goals to economic ones.

The Trilateral Steering Committee has recently formalized this long-standing policy by proposing a "marketplace for higher education co-operation and exchange" as its alternative to a new and complex transnational structure similar to the European Commission's ERASMUS or SOCRATES programs (ACE et al. 2000, 1). NAFTA establishes a free trade area, rather than a continental union and, hence, top higher education and government officials in the three countries prefer a strategy of removing barriers to market development on the one hand, while using limited seed money to catalyse market formation instead of creating or expanding new government programs. The Trilateral Commission's latest statement on the subject indicates that top officials in government and higher education are well aware of the remaining physical, technical, fiscal, and cultural barriers that "dampen enthusiasm, limit collaboration, and restrict ease of mobility" for participants in trilateral programs (Ibid., 2).

The Trilateral Steering Committee has identified the difficulty of obtaining visas as the major physical barrier to increased educational exchange. However, even if this barrier is eased or removed in the near future, which is unlikely given the events of September 11, 2001, the technical barriers involving credit transfer, program recognition, and accreditation will remain intact because of structural and cultural differences among higher education institutions in the three countries. Moreover, the lack of success in addressing these technical barriers over the last ten years has convinced leading officials in government and higher education that comprehensive systems for eliminating the barriers to mutual course and credit recognition, accreditation, and quality assurance will simply not work at this point because of institutional autonomy and differences in the three country's higher education systems (Ibid., 3). This problem is compounded by the lack of central government authority over higher education in Canada and the USA, while efforts to decentralize higher education have been initiated since the National Action Party's presidential victory in Mexico.

Thus, rather than attempting to launch new initiatives or programs, the Trilateral Steering Committee proposes to deepen and expand the current activities of existing institutions, since "new formal systems to equalize asymmetries and differing priorities may be less practical (and cost-effective) than individual case-by-case agreements based on best practices, without formal structures and systems" (Ibid., 2). It is these case-by-case, institution-by-institution arrangements that will incrementally lay the foundation for a multi-tiered market in North American higher education. In lieu of any new programs, the Trilateral Steering Committee is also now convinced that an extensive network of bi-lateral, as opposed to trilateral programs, criss-crossing North America are the preferred strategy for market development. Finally, the Trilateral Steering Committee recognizes that even if the physical and technical barriers to free trade are minimized or eliminated in higher education, the major fiscal barrier to North American higher education co-operation remains the overall lack of resources and funds to support collaborative endeavors (Ibid., 2). The NAFTA countries are clearly not prepared to fund any major new initiatives in North American higher education collaboration and this reluctance stems from both fiscal and ideological considerations, which mandate a preference for market-based strategies instead of government solutions.

The Trilateral Steering Committee's new plan for *Increasing North American Higher Education Cooperation, Collaboration, and Exchange* (2000) has an explicit expectation that students, faculty, and higher education institutions will continue to shoulder the bulk of the costs for any trilateral initiatives since it is these actors who are the primary economic beneficiaries of the programs. The TSC remains unwavering in its position that programs which cannot sustain themselves financially by attracting private sector partners cannot be justified on the basis of market (cost-benefits) criteria. Similarly, the TSC expects that most funding for student exchanges will come from students, who theoretically benefit financially from international exchange after graduation. To reinforce this link, the TSC has recommended that North American student exchange programs establish more work-based opportunities in the host country that will help generate additional funds for students, while linking student exchange directly to future career opportunities. It is expected that such initiatives will bolster student interest in international exchange, while transforming student mobility from traditional language- and culture-based "junior year abroad" programs into career and workforce development programs. If carried through over the next decade, this transformation has the potential to draw students from a wider range of fields than humanities and area studies. Importantly, the TSC also recommends that any resource asymmetries between the three countries be addressed by using existing resources for need-based exchange awards.

Thus, the current trajectory of North American higher education collaboration will remain an incremental market-based strategy pursued within the limiting framework of NAFTA's rules and objectives. Higher education's role within NAFTA will be to provide inputs (i.e., labor and technology) for the continental economy, while traditional exchange programs will become exercises in the development of new markets for higher education service exports. Those who are seeking major new government expenditures on the European model failed to achieve this breakthrough in the 1990s under governments (Liberals, PRI, Democrats) that were ideologically more receptive to the idea, but which rejected these proposals in favor of strategic trilateral partnerships between government, higher education, and business. Similarly, those who are seeking to promote more humanitarian goals, the creation of a North American identity, or merely greater cultural and political good will among the NAFTA partners are apt to be disappointed in the near future. Yet, in the 21st century, trade, commerce, and people will flow across North American borders on a scale impossible to envision today. There is no greater international education priority than to make North America not just a marketplace for commodities and capital, but a harmonious neighbourhood of mutual understanding, respect, and support in coping with our shared destiny.

APPENDIX A

WINGSPREAD STATEMENT

STATEMENT OF THE CONFERENCE ON NORTH AMERICAN HIGHER EDUCATION COOPERATION: IDENTIFYING THE AGENDA

Racine, Wisconsin, USA
September 12–15, 1992

PARTICIPANTS FROM CANADA, MEXICO AND THE UNITED STATES OF AMERICA AT THE WINGSPREAD CONFERENCE AGREE THAT:

Internationalisation of higher education is the key to the quality of education and research, the standard of living of the citizens and the overall quality of life of our countries, as well as to a better understanding of our respective distinctive cultures and identities.

Better understanding and acceptance of our distinctive realities are essential components of stronger partnerships, greater access to the vast North American potential and effective development of our countriesí growing relationships.

Enhanced trilateral collaboration in higher education builds upon existing relationships and benefits our three countries. This statement is made with full recognition of and respect for the national sovereignty of our respective countries, the responsibilities of our different jurisdictions, and the autonomy of our higher education institutions.

Enhanced collaboration provides additional impetus to greater cooperation within our respective countries and supports bilateral relations with third countries and relevant multilateral organizations. In stating the aforementioned agreements, we take note of the North American Free Trade Agreement negotiated by our respective governments and we affirm that enhanced trilateral cooperation has merit in its own right.

We commend this conference statement, at this defining moment in our history, to the urgent consideration of our respective authorities as a constructive trilateral contribution to the development and implementation of appropriate public policies that support and promote the internationalisation of higher education.

Enhanced trilateral collaboration aims at the following set of related and mutually reinforcing objectives. We commit ourselves to the following objectives and their promotion in our respective countries, and to pursuing, where appropriate, the agreed upon set of recommendations and steps to be undertaken:

OBJECTIVES
1. Development of a North American dimension in higher education;

2. Promotion of exchange of information on common issues of concern and on experiences of common interest;
3. Promotion of collaboration among higher education institutions;
4. Facilitation of student and faculty mobility;
5. Increasing awareness of and mutually satisfactory removal of impediments to mobility;
6. Promotion of strong stronger collaboration among our respective institutions/organizations and public authorities, business, and other organizations that have a stake in the quality of higher education;
7. Exploration and exploitation of the full potential of current and emerging information management and transmission technologies in support of our statement of objectives.

With These Agreed Objectives in mind, the participants at the Wingspread Conference make the following recommendations to our relevant public and private authorities and organizations, and higher education institutions:

RECOMMENDATIONS
That priority consideration for trilateral collaborative actions in higher education be given to:

Inventorying existing programs and relationships;

Increasing the capacity and enhancing the capabilities of institutions and organization with special emphasis on faculty development in our three countries;

Eliminating obstacles and reducing barriers to enhanced trilateral collaboration in the field of higher education;

Developing collaborative pilot projects where there exists already strong mutual interest, such as disciplines directly related to the management of our evolving trade relations; sustainable development; public health; North American area studies and training in languages;

That we take advantage of the use of modern information management and dissemination technologies such as distance learning, computer communications, interactive video conferences, etc., where appropriate, in support of the foregoing initiatives;

That enhanced use be made of people-to-people exchange programs;

That Faculty members, university administrators, and students be included in the interpretation of the special treatment in the issuing of visas to business people, technicians and consultants in the chapter on trade in services in the final draft of NAFTA;

That measures be taken in particular, to disseminate successful collaborative experiences throughout the North American higher education community.

That action be taken to increase and expand student access to international education opportunities.

In addition, we undertake to accomplish the agreed upon initiatives that follow:

ACTION INITIATIVES
A Wingspread Conference report incorporating this statement, a summary of the discussion papers, highlights of the conference proceedings and the list of participants will be produced and widely disseminated to the appropriate decision-makers and organizations in our three countries.

An inventory of existing resources and priority needs will be created within 9 months and distributed within 12 months.

A trilateral Task Force (Canada, Mexico, and the United States of America) on North American Higher Education Collaboration, will be established immediately, with membership to be appointed no later than November 10, 1992. This action-oriented task force will be expected to undertake, among other things, the following:

Developing a proposed strategic plan;
Supporting and monitoring progress on the above initiatives;
Initiating research papers and recommend specific action plans;
Organizing and implementing a trilateral conference with the next 12 months,
in Vancouver, if the Task Force reports sufficient progress within 9 months.

ENDNOTES
This conference on trilateral education issues was supported in part by The Johnson Foundation.
Higher education and higher education institutions encompass universities engaged in research-based teaching, post-secondary establishments of education and training which offer courses of varying duration, regardless of the dissemination vehicles, and of a general or specialized nature leading to qualifications at the post-secondary level. We acknowledge the substantial contribution made to the successful outcome of this conference by the authors of the four discussion papers as well as the overview and context provided on Sept. 12 during the first conference session. The four papers dealt with mutual understanding and cultural identity; exchange of information/data base; mobility; optimizing complementarities. Each of the papers, along with the overview and context, were the subject of extensive discussions by the participants and was instrumental in achieving the broad consensus, reflected in this conference statement. Summary reports on the discussion of each of these agenda items and papers are appended to this conference statement.

APPENDIX B

VANCOUVER COMMUNIQUÉ

Vancouver, British Columbia
September 10 - 13, 1993

In reaffirming the spirit of Wingspread, the participants in the Vancouver Symposium call on our colleagues in teaching, research and training institutions, as well as those in business, government and other concerned organizations, to join us in forging new partnerships for sharing knowledge across traditional boundaries. We view Canada, Mexico and the United States, along with the other regions of the world, as poised on the threshold of the new century, a century in which higher education, research and training cooperation will be central to innovation and human resource development, essential to achieving our goals for social, economic and cultural development.

We recognize that our countries cannot fully prosper in all the ways that matter if they remain no more than trading partners. A new sense of a North American community, made up of our 360 million people, should be forged, one which will provide impetus to greater cooperation among and within our countries, support our relations with countries outside the region, enhance our distinct cultural identities and acknowledge our asymmetries. The compelling vision of Wingspread has motivated the participants in this Vancouver Symposium to take concerted actions to enhance the mutual-well being of the countries of North America and beyond. Current economic, social and cultural forces reshaping our three societies and the rich diversity of our cultures - from the native peoples to the most recent immigrants - have created a climate in which the North American community can flourish.

The expansion and strengthening of intellectual links and academic collaboration across the continent are fundamental to North America's vitality. They underpin the stability, civility and respect for human rights and freedoms necessary to democratic societies. They are fundamental to genuine sustainable development. Wingspread and Vancouver have revealed the vast opportunities which trilateral collaboration offers to build on existing programs and activities and to stimulate new thinking about the directions of education, research and training.

We accept the challenge now to go beyond the defining of shared conceptual goals and broad objectives. We have developed concrete strategies to implement the Wingspread objectives through increased contact and collaboration among students, researchers, administrators and partners in business and government, and other institutions. The variety of trilateral partnership projects announced at the Symposium, those currently being designed, as well as those envisioned during the meeting, are evidence of significant momentum. The conclusions summarized below point the direction we should take together to expand the higher education, research and training components of the deepening North American relationship.

We have concluded that the following initiatives should be undertaken immediately:

1. The establishment of a North American Distance Education and Research Network (NADERN), a consortium to facilitate access to information and to support education, research and training among participating institutions. This symposium gratefully acknowledges the work of three members of the Task Force subgroup on distance learning and requests that they carry forward this proposal through broad consultation with all interested institutions and organizations.

2. The formation of an Enterprise/Education trilateral mechanism to examine issues relating to mobility, portability and certification of skills, and consider common interests and approaches in technical, applied and lifelong career education. Responsibility for carrying forward this proposal should be undertaken by the appropriate national associations and relevant authorities.

3. The establishment of programs to enable faculty and administrators from all three countries to meet with colleagues to explore and develop trilateral higher education collaborative activities in priority areas of concern.

4. The establishment of an electronic information base in each of the three countries, with coordinated sharing of information on initiatives and resources relevant to trilateral cooperation. This electronic information base is to be developed in such a way as to be easily accessible by the academic community, business, governments, foundations and other concerned organizations. It should contain the most relevant, timely and concise information.

5. The strengthening and expansion of North American studies programs to promote trilateral linkages in support of research and curriculum development.

6. The establishment of a program to support intensive trilateral exchange, research and training for students.

For further consideration and action in 1994:

1. The establishment of a North American Corporate Higher Education Council comprised of senior representatives of the corporate and higher education communities from the three countries to act as advocates, within the two communities and across North America, for further partnering in the realization of mutually agreed objectives. It would engage a broad dialogue with all concerned institutions and organizations in support of trilateral cooperation.

The creation, by this council, of a consortium of North American Business for Trilateral Research, Development and Training to operate for an initial period of, say, seven years. The consortium's objective would be to secure private sector funding, through the membership of individual corporate citizens of the three countries, to be used to implement research and training initiatives of value to both the corporate and higher education communities.

2. As part of the long-term operations of NADERN, the development and implementation of a plan for a consortium to broker access to recognized graduate distance education courses and to develop a mechanism for awarding degrees for such composite programs.

3. Continuing and enhanced support by research granting agencies, foundations and

other partners for trilateral collaborative research programs and research networks. We, the participants at the Vancouver Symposium, commend these conclusions and proposals as a constructive contribution to the development and implementation of appropriate policies that support and promote the internationalisation of higher education, research and training.

APPENDIX C

CONSORTIUM ON NORTH AMERICAN HIGHER EDUCATION (CONAHEC)

1999-2000 Members

Canada
Association of Universities and Colleges of Canada (AUCC)
Ecole des Hautes Etudes Commerciales
Mount Royal College
Universite du Quebec a Montreal
University of Alberta
University of British Columbia
University of Manitoba
University of Regina
University of Victoria

Mexico
Asociacion Mexicana para la Educacion
  Internacional (AMPEI)
Asociacion Nacional de Universidades e
  Instituciones de Educacion Superior
  (ANUIES)
Benemerita Universidad Autonoma de
  Puebla
CETYS Universidad (Sistema)
El Colegio de la Frontera Norte
Instituto Tecnologico de Ciudad Juarez
Instituto Tecnologico de Estudios Superior
  de Monterrey (ITESM, Sistema)
Universidad Autonoma de Baja California
Universidad Autonoma de Ciudad Juarez
Universidad Autonoma de Coahuila
Universidad Autonoma de Guadalajara
Universidad Autonoma de Nuevo Leon
Universidad Autonoma de San Luis Potosi
Universidad Autonoma de Tamaulipas
Universidad de Guanajuato
Universidad de las Americas-Puebla
Universidad de Monterrey
Universidad de Sonora
Universidad Iberoamericana
Universidad La Salle, A.C.

Universdad Autonoma de Mexico
Universidad Veracruzana
Unversidades Tecnologicas de Mexcio/Universidad Tecnologica de Coahuila
United States of America
American Council on Education
Arizona State University
Austin Community College
California State University System
Dallas County Community College District
Eastern Oregon University
Kent State University
Maricopa Community College
National University
New Mexico State University
Northern State University
Pima Community College District
San Diego Community College District
Santa Monica College
South Dakota Board of Regents
Texas A&M International University
University of Arizona
University of La Verne
University of Massachusetts at Amherst
Unversity of Missouri System
University of Montana
University of New Mexico
University of Texas at El Paso
Western Governors University
Western Interstate Commission on Higher Education (WICHE)
Yosemite Community College District

APPENDIX D

USAID/ALO HIGHER EDUCATION LINKAGE PROJECT

U.S. Higher Institution	Mexican Partner Institution	Linkage Type	Emphasis Area	Funding Source
Auburn University	Colegio de Post Graduados en Ciencias Agricolas Academic	Exchange	Human Capacity Development	Own Institution
		Collaborative Research		
California State University, Fresno	Several universities in Mexico	Academic Exchange		
Clemson University	Universidad Noroeste (UNO)	Academic Exchange	Human Capacity Development	
	University of the Americas - Puebla	Academic Exchange	Human Capacity Development	Personal
Cleveland State University	Cuernavaca (Summer Program)	Academic Exchange	Human Capacity Development	Own Institution
Georgia Institute of Technology	Autonomous Technological Institute of Mexico			
	Instituto Technologico y de Estudios Sup. de Monterrey			
Indiana University	Cuernavaca (Summer Program)	Academic Exchange	Human Capacity Development	Personal
Indiana University of Pennsylvania	Universidad de las Americas, Puebla	Academic Exchange	Economic Growth	Human Capacity Development
Kansas State University	Universidad de Sonora	Technical Assistance	Human Capacity Development	Own Institution
Michigan State University	El Colegio de Mexico			
	Ibero-American University			
	Technological Institute of Merida			
	Instituto Technologico y de Estudios Sup. de Monterrey			
	Autonomous University of Yucatan			
	Autonomous University of Queretaro			
Michigan Technological University	Instituto Technologico y de Estudios Sup. de Monterrey	Academic Exchange	Human Capacity Development	
	Universidad de Sonora	Academic Exchange	Environment	
			Collaborative Research	
New Mexico State University	Autonomas University of Chichuahua		Human Capacity Development	Own Institution
	Autonomas University of Chapingo	Collaborative Research	Agricultural Development	Own Institution
	Autonomas University of Ciudad Juarez	Academic Exchange	Human Capacity Development	Own Institution
	Instituto la Salle de Sureste (ISTMO)	Academic Exchange	Human Capacity Development	Own Institution
			Economic Growth	
	Centro de Asistencia y Servicios Tecnologicos (CAST)	Instruction/Training	Human Capacity Development	Own Institution

198 APPENDIX D

	Centro do Bachillerato Technologico Industrial y de Servicios (CBTIS #4)	Academic Exchange	Human Capacity Development	Own Institution
	CONALEP	Collaborative Research	Human Capacity Development	Own Institution
	Instituto Technologico y de Estudios Sup. de Monterrey	Academic Exchange	Economic Growth	Own Institution
			Human Capacity Development	
	United States-Mexico Commission for Educatl & Cultl Exch			
	Universidad Anahuac	Academic Exchange	Human Capacity Development	Own Institution
			Economic Growth	
	Autonomous University of Sinaloa	Collaborative Research	Agricultural Development	Own Institution
	Autonomous University of Sonora	Academic Exchange	Agricultural Development	USDOE & Sandia Laboratories
			Human Capacity Development	
	Universidad de Quintana Roo	Academic Exchange	Human Capacity Development	USDOE&N.A.Cn on Envr.Coo
		Collaborative Research		
	Autonomous National University	Collaborative Research	Economic Growth	Own Institution
			Human Capacity Development	
	Autonomous University of Guadalajara	Collaborative Research	Human Capacity Development	Own Institution
North Dakota State University	Centro Internacional de Mejoramiento de Maiz y e Trigo	Collaborative Research	Agricultural Development	Mexican Institution
	Universidad de Sonora	Academic Exchange	Agricultural Development	Own Institution
		Collaborative Research	Agricultural Development	Own Institution
Ohio State University	Colegio de Post Graduados en Ciencias Agricolas, Texcoco	Academic Exchange	Agribusiness	USAID
Oklahoma State University	Centro Internacional de Mejoramiento de Maiz ye Trigo	Academic Exchange	Agricultural Development	Mexican Center
Pennsylvania State University	Instituto Technologico y de Estudios Sup. de Monterrey	Academic Exchange	Economic Growth	Own Institution
	University of Monterrey	Academic Exchange	Agricultural Development	Own Institution
		Collaborative Research	Public Health/Nutrition	Kellog Foundation
Purdue University	Instituto Technologico y de Estudios Sup. de Monterrey			
	Red Interuniversitaria de Educacion Veterinaria de Mexico			USDA
	Autonomous University of Chichuahua			
Rutgers University	Autonomous University of Yucatan	Academic Exchange	Human Capacity Development	Own Institution
	University of Veracruz	Academic Exchange	Human Capacity Development	Both Institutions
		Collaborative Research		
		Instruction/Training		
	Autonomous National University	Collaborative Research	Agricultural Development	Both Institutions
San Francisco State University	Whirlwind Wheelchair Network	Instruction/Training	Human Capacity Development	Own Institution
	Universidad de ECOSUD, Chiapas	Instruction/Training	Human Capacity Development	
South Dakota State University			Economic Growth	
	Autonomas University of Morelos	Academic Exchange	Human Capacity Development	Both Institutions
Southern Illinois University	Centrode Ensenanza Tecnica, Superior Universidad-Mexico	Academic Exchange	Human Capacity Development	
SUNY, Morrisville	Universidad Technologica de Leon	Curriculum Development	Environment	USAID
	Universidad Technologica de Tula-Tepeje	Curriculum Development	Environment	USAID

APPENDIX D

Texas A&M University College Station	Center for Regional Cooperation for Adult Education in Latin America & Caribe		Human Capacity Development	
	Centro de Investigacion y de Estudios Avanzados	Collaborative Research	Biotechnology/Engineering Academic Exchange	
	Colegio Nacional de Educacion Professional Tecnica	Academic Exchange	Human Capacity Development	
	Fundacion Universidad de las Americas	Academic Exchange	Economic Growth	Collaborative Research
	Autonomous Technological Institute of Mexico	Academic Exchange Collaborative Research	Economic Growth	
	Instituto Nacional de Astrofisica de Optica ye de Electronica	Academic Exchange	Human Capacity Development Collaborative Research	
	InstitutoPolitecnico Nacional	Academic Exchange Collaborative Research	Human Capacity Development	
	Instituto Technologico y de Estudios Sup. de Monterrey	Academic Exchange Collaborative Research	Agricultural Development Environment Human Capacity Development	
	Union Ganadera Regional de Jalisco	Academic Exchange	Agricultural Development Collaborative Research	
	Autonomous University of Nuevo Leon	Academic Exchange Collaborative Research	Public Health/Nutrition Human Capacity Development	
	Autonomous University of Tamaulipas	Academic Exchange Collaborative Research	Environment Human Capacity Development	
	Autonomous University of Ciudad Juarez	Academic Exchange	Human Capacity Development Collaborative Research	
	Universidad de Guanajuato	Academic Exchange Collaborative Research	Agricultural Development Public Health/Nutrition	
	Universidad Iberoamericana	Academic Exchange Collaborative Research	Human Capacity Development	
	Universidad LaSalle	Academic Exchange Collaborative Research	Human Capacity Development	
	Universidad Michoacana de San Nicolas de Hidalgo	Academic Exchange Collaborative Research	Human Capacity Development	
	Autonomous National University	Academic Exchange Collaborative Research Instruction/Training	Human Capacity Development Agricultural Development Environment	USAID
Texas A&M University, Prairie View	Universidad Autonoma Agraria Antonio Narro	Academic Exchange Collaborative Research	Agricultural Development	Own Institution
University of Alaska - Fairbanks	Autonomous University of Guadalajara	Instruction/Training	Human Capacity Development	Personal

APPENDIX D

University of Akron	Autonomas University of Guadalajara	Academic Exchange	Agricultural Development Human Capacity Development Democracy/Governance Economic Growth Environment	Own Institution
University of Arizona Internatl Campus	Universidad del Noroeste	Academic Exchange	Economic Growth	
University of Arkansas Coll. Of Agric.	Autonomous University of San Luis Patosi		Agricultural Development	
University of California, Davis	Autonomas University of Queretaro	Gen. Cooperative Agree.		
	CICESE (Research Institute)	Gen. Cooperative Agree.		
	CONIFUT (Research Institute)	Gen. Cooperative Agree.		
	Instituto Nacional de Investigaciones Forestales y Agropecuraies (INIFAP)	Gen. Cooperative Agree.		
	Instituto Politecnia Nacional	Gen. Cooperative Agree.		
	Instituto Technologico y de Estudios Sup. de Monterrey	Gen. Cooperative Agree.		
	Technological Institute of Culiacan	Gen. Cooperative Agree.		
	Mexican Institute of Water Technology	Gen. Cooperative Agree.		
	University of Sonora	Gen. Cooperative Agree.		
	Autonomous University of Baja California Sur	Gen. Cooperative Agree.		
	Autonomous University of Baja California, Mexicali	Gen. Cooperative Agree.		
	Autonomous Metropolitan University	Gen. Cooperative Agree.		
	University of Chapingo	Gen. Cooperative Agree.		
	Universidad de Ensenada	Gen. Cooperative Agree.		
	Universidad de Guanajuato	Gen. Cooperative Agree.		
	Universidad de Sinaloa	Gen. Cooperative Agree.		
	Autonomous National University	Gen. Cooperative Agree.		
	University of Colima	Gen. Cooperative Agree.		
University of Cincinnati	Instituto Technologico y de Estudios Sup. de Queretaro	Academic Exchange	Human Capacity Development	Own Institution
	Autonomous University of Nuevo Leon	Academic Exchange	Public Health/Nutrition	Own Institution
University of Florida	Autonomous University of Yucatan	Instruction/Training	Human Capacity Development	
	Universidad Iberoamericana	Academic Exchange	Human Capacity Development	
University of Georgia	University of Chihuahua	Academic Exchange	Agricultural Development	
	University of Veracruz	Collaborative Research	Human Capacity Development	
		Instruction/Training	Economic Growth Curriculum Development	USDA

APPENDIX D

US Institution	Mexican Institution	Type of Interaction	Subject Area	Funding Source
University of Idaho	Instituto Mexicano del Transporte		Economic Growth	
	Instituto Technologico y de Estudios Sup. de Monterrey		Environment	USDA
	Autonomous University of Nuevo Leon	Instruction/Training	Agricultural Development	
	Autonomous University of Guadalajara	Academic Exchange	Environment	Both Institutions
		Collaborative Research	Environment	
	University of Zacatecas	Memo of Understanding		
University of Illinois Urbana/Champaign	Instituto Panamerican de Alta Empresa (IPADE)	Academic Exchange	Economic Growth	Own Institution
			Human Capacity Development	
	Instituto Technologico y de Estudios Sup. de Monterrey	Academic Exchange	Human Capacity Development	Own Institution
			Economic Growth	
	Autonomous University of Guadalajara	Academic Exchange	Human Capacity Development	Own Institution
	Universidad Panamericana	Academic Exchange	Human Capacity Development	Own Institution
University of Maryland	National Polytechnic Institute		Nutrition	
	El Instituto Tenologico Autonomo de Mexico (ITAM)	Gen. Cooperative Agree.	Human Capacity Development	Foundations
	Instituto Technologico y de Estudios Sup. de Monterrey		Human Capacity Development	Both Institutions
	Autonomous National University	Gen. Cooperative Agree.	Human Capacity Development	Foundations
University of Minnesota	Juarez University of the State of Durango	Academic Exchange	Environment	PEW Foundation
			Human Capacity Development	
			National Agricultural Research	
	Technological Institute of Oaxaca			
University of Missouri, St. Louis	El Colegio de Jalisco	Academic Exchange	Economic Growth	
	Autonomous University of Guadalajara	Academic Exchange	Economic Growth	
	National Autonomas University of Mexico	Academic Exchange	Economic Growth	
	ITESM - Guaymas Campus	Academic Exchange	Economic Growth	
	Autonomas University of Baja California	Academic Exchange	Economic Growth	
	University of San Luis Potosi	Academic Exchange	Economic Growth	
	Instituto de Estudios Superiores de Tamaulipas	Academic Exchange	Economic Growth	
University of Montana	Autonomous University of Baja California	Workshops/Seminars		Own Institution
University of Nebraska, Lincoln	Instituto Technologico y de Estudios Sup. de Monterrey	Academic Exchange	Human Capacity Development	
	Autonomous University of Nuevo Leon		Human Capacity Development	
	Universidad Autonoma Agraria Antonio Narro		Human Capacity Development	
	Autonomous University of Guadalajara		Human Capacity Development	
	Universidad de Sonora		Human Capacity Development	
University of North Carolina Chapel Hill	Fundacion Mexicana para la Salud		Public Health	
	International Institute for Applied Systems Analysis, Merida Campus, CINVESTAV	Collaborative Research	Public Health/Nutrition	
University of Rhode Island	Autonomous National University		Human Capacity Development	CONYCIT, NSF
	University of Quintana Roo		Environment	USAID

University of South Florida	Centro de Investigacion y de Estudios Avanzados	Academic Exchange	Human Capacity Development	Both Institutions
	Autonomous University of Guadalajara	Academic Exchange	Public Health/Nutrition	Both Institutions
	Universidad de las Americas (Puebla)	Academic Exchange	Human Capacity Development	Both Institutions
	Universidad LaSalle, Mexico City	Academic Exchange	Human Capacity Development	Both Institutions
University of Wisconsin, Stout	Instituto Technologico y de Estudios Sup. de Monterrey	Academic Exchange	Human Capacity Development Instruction/Training	Own Institution
Virginia Polytechnic Institute & St. Univ.	Instituto Technologico y de Estudios Superiores		Human Capacity Development	
	Secretariat of Agriculture & Water Resources	Academic Exchange Collaborative Research	Agricultural Development	
	Autonomous University of Nuevo Leon	Academic Exchange	Human Capacity Development	
West Virginia University	Mexican Transport Research Institute		Human Capacity Development	
	University of Guanajuato Agricultural Development		Environment	

Note: Most agreements emphasize academic exchange and collaborative research in the fields of engineering, business, agriculture, public health and nutrition. Predominant activity is faculty and student exchange agreements designed to promote human capacity development, economic growth, environmental and resource management. in business, engineering, agriculture, forestry, and technical fields. This is followed by collaborative research activities for the same purpose

Source: American Association of State Colleges and Universities (1999c, 1999d). Accessed on October 15, 1999.

NOTES

CHAPTER 1

[1] Figures are for USA in 1990 U.S. dollars.

[2] Carnevale (1991, 2) observes that in the new economy: "...competitiveness is based not only on productivity but also on quality, variety, customisation, convenience, and timeliness. People are demanding high-quality goods and services that are competitively priced, available in a variety of forms, customised to specific needs, and conveniently accessible."

[3] The OECD (1996a, 11-12, 59-63) defines non-tariff barriers to trade as "border measures other than tariffs that may be used by countries, usually on a selective basis, to restrict imports." Approximately 20 percent of world trade encounters non-tariff barriers and the trade coverage of these measures had tended to grow as tariff barriers were lowered. The United Nations Trade and Development Administration identifies 72 different types of NTBs in its classification scheme. NTBs include volume restraining measures (e.g., prohibitions and quotas), import authorisations (e.g., licensing, health and safety standards, technical standards, censorship), price controls (e.g., minimum prices, anti-dumping actions), and other barriers such as subsidies, favourable tax treatment of import sensitive industries (Laird and Yeats 1990, 4, 17-19), and anti-competitive practices by private firms (Hay 1996; Janow 1996; Warner 1996).

[4] The members of Mercosur are Brazil, Argentina, Paraguay, and Uruguay.

[5] The members of Caricom consist of the Caribbean island-nations and coastal nations, including Belize, St. Kitts, St. Lucia, Antigua, Monserrat, Bahamas, Guyana, Barbados, and Trinidad and Tobago.

[6] The members of the Andean Group are Columbia, Venezuela, Bolivia, Ecuador, and Peru.

[7] The principles are most-favoured-nation treatment, transparency without requiring the disclosure of confidential information, increasing participation of developing countries, economic integration so as not to prevent entrance into labour market integration agreements, domestic regulation, recognition, monopolies and exclusive service suppliers, business practices, emergency safeguard measures, payments and transfers, restrictions to safeguard the balance of payments, government procurement, general exceptions, security exceptions, and subsidies.

[8] Commercial presence includes corporations, join ventures, partnerships, representative offices, branches, and other legal entities constituting foreign direct investment. Consumption abroad, often referred to as "movement of the consumer" occurs when a service is delivered outside the territory of the member making the commitment (e.g., tourism, ship repair, study abroad). Cross-border supply occurs when a service supplier is not present within the territory of the member where the service is delivered (e.g., services delivered through telecommunications, mail, international transport, e-commerce or internet sales, distance learning). The presence of individuals refers to natural persons who are service suppliers or employees of a service supplier who travels to another country to provide a service in that country (e.g., engineering consultant).

[9] Australia, Austria, Belgium, Canada, Czech Republic, Denmark, Finland, Germany, Greece, Iceland, Ireland, Italy, Japan, Korea, Mexico, New Zealand, Norway, Portugal, Spain, Switzerland, Turkey, United Kingdom, United States (WTO 1998b, 21).

[10] There are no fully satisfactory criteria and definitions for distinguishing high technology and knowledge-intensive industries from traditional industries and services, but the list usually includes pharmaceuticals, computers and information technology, electrical machinery, electronic components, aircraft and aerospace, scientific equipment and services such as telecommunications, engineering, architecture and surveying.

[11] By 1999, exports had grown to account for 38 percent of Canada's Gross Domestic Product. In 1999, resource-based industries such as metals, forest products, energy, chemicals, and food and beverages still accounted for nearly 38 percent of Canada's exports (calculated from Statistics Canada data).

[12] Porter (1991b, 68) observes that like the United States, "Canada's biggest problem is the likely emergence of lower cost competitors. Basic factor advantages are increasingly replicated by countries such as Venezuela in aluminum, or Brazil in pulp and paper."

[13] It is not surprising that business and government officials drew conclusions so similar to their U.S. counterparts, since the national debates over economic and trade policy were directly and explicitly influenced by the very same "competitiveness school" that emerged at Harvard University and the Massachusetts Institute of Technology at this time, see, Reich (1991), Carnevale (1991), Kennedy (1993), Porter (1990), Thurow (1991, 1992), Piore and Sabel (1984).

[14] Other important reforms include the Automotive Decree of 1983, which was a first step toward the more important 1989 Automotive Decree that radically liberalised the automobile industry in Mexico, and the Pharmaceutical Decree of 1984. In 1987, Mexico strengthened intellectual property rights by revising the 1976 Invention and Trademark Law to increase patent protection from 10 to 14 years and increase penalties for patent infringements.

[15] In 1995, the ratio of intra-firm trade of United States foreign affiliates to total Mexican trade with the United States levelled out at 29 percent (UNCTAD 1998, 258).

CHAPTER 2

[1] NAFTA provides for the immediate elimination of tariffs on a number of goods and the elimination of tariffs and non-tariff barriers (NTBs) on substantially all trade over ten years. There are numerous exceptions and nuances to this general rule that are mostly phased out over the ten year transition period. However, for a lucid and detailed treatment of NAFTA's provisions, see Hufbauer and Schott (1993a).

[2] The MFN investment provisions are also included in NAFTA. According to Gestrin and Rugman (1996, 68): "One of the main reasons for having both MFN and national treatment coverage is to ensure that when one of the signatories holds a reservation against the national treatment provisions (in other words, the signatory in question reserves the right to discriminate in favour of domestic over foreign investors), investors from the other signatory parties are at least still guaranteed that they will receive the best possible treatment with the group of other foreign investors."

[3] Mexico's principal trading partner is the United States, which accounted for 85 percent of Mexico's exports and 69 percent of its imports in 1994. Canada, by contrast, received only 2.4 percent of Mexico's exports and supplied 2 percent of all imports to Mexico (OECD 1996e, 27).

[4] The term "deepening" comes from the European Economic Community debates of the 1980s which led eventually to the Maastricht Treaty and the Europe 1992 Project.

[5] The status of higher education as "just another industry" is perhaps best captured by the industrial classification systems developed by countries to collect data on employment, wages, new business formation, and international trade. The USA's Standard Industrial Classification (SIC) System (Executive Office of the U.S. President 1987) assigns every business establishment in – both public and private – one or more SIC Codes based on Division (e.g., manufacturing), Major Group (e.g., textile mill products), and Industry Group (e.g., spinning mills). An establishment's Division is identified by a single letter code (A-J). Its Major Group is identified by a 2-digit numeric code (01-99) and its Industry Group is identified by a 3- or 4-digit numeric code (001-9999). Educational Services are classified in Division I (Services) as Major Group 82, which includes Colleges, Universities, and Professional Schools (SIC 8221), Junior Colleges and Technical Institutes (SIC 8222), Libraries (SIC 8231), Data Processing Schools (SIC 8243), Business and Secretarial Schools (SIC 8244), Vocational Schools (SIC 8249), Schools and Educational Services, Not Elsewhere Classified (SIC 8299).

[6] The United States Information Agency (USIA) is located within the Department of State. It is responsible for overseeing the Fulbright exchange programs that promote academic mobility between U.S. students and scholars and those of foreign countries.

[7] The conference was sponsored and underwritten by the Johnson Foundation, which owns the Wingspread Conference Centre, and the USIA's Office of Academic Programs.

[8] CONAHEC originated as the U.S.-Mexico Educational Interchange Project, which was a partnership between WICHE, AMPEI, the Universidad Autonoma de Baja California and the University of Arizona.

[9] CONAHEC has 27 members in the United States, 24 in Mexico, and 9 in Canada (CONAHEC 1999d).

[10] Participation in the listserv is reserved primarily for individuals invited to attend the Educational

NOTES

Leadership Seminars, but is open to scholars and others interested in the problems of North American higher education.

CHAPTER 3

[1] The CPC was created by the Omnibus Trade and Competitiveness Act of 1988 (P.L. 100-418) as amended by the Customs and Trade Act of 1990 (P.L. 101-382).

[2] Even critics of the projected labour shortage in the United States agree that skill levels are probably increasing too slowly given the pressures of international competition, see, Mishel and Teixeira (1991).

[3] The term neo-liberal is employed in its contemporary "American" usage, rather than its classical "European" meaning. See Dolbeare and Medcalf (1993, 72-83) who define neo-liberalism in its American usage as an ideological orientation that seeks to promote social justice and equity through state action while accepting the principle that such policies depend on the expansion and profitability of the private sector. Unlike neo-conservatives who advocate a laissez-faire economic policy or socialists who advocate public and social ownership of the means of production, neo-liberals advocate a state "industrial policy" organised through government-business partnerships.

[4] The USA has consistently recorded a trade deficit in goods since 1971, but it has recorded a trade surplus in services during the same period. For example, in 2000, the USA had a $449.5 billion trade deficit in goods, but a $79.8 trade surplus in services (U.S. Department of Commerce 2001). Despite the overall trade deficit in goods, the USA has recorded an average trade surplus of approximately $30 billion annually in "high technology" since 1989 (U.S. Department of Commerce 2000).

[5] For example, Parker (1993, pp. 101-103) elaborates a typology contrasting the major points at which academic and corporate research cultures clash with one another. Also, see, Bird and Allen (1989).

[6] The President's Council of Advisors on Science and Technology provides private sector advice to the President of the United States on national science and technology policy. The Council currently includes 13 members from industry, private foundations, academia, and research institutes.

[7] For example, see, Business-Higher Education Forum (1984, 1986).

[8] For example, see Office of the Commissioner of Higher Education (1986); Colorado Commission on Higher Education (1987).

[9] For example, the California Post-secondary Education Commission (1991), p. 7, expects that "as senior faculty members retire, there will be an opportunity for new appointments to be made in areas of current enrolment demand, which will result in a net reallocation of positions away from some fields and toward others."

[10] The PCAST (1992, p. 10) report concludes argues that "if institutions are selective in allocating their resources, the net output of leading-edge research by our nation-wide array of research-intensive universities need not decrease" despite limited and declining financial resources.

[11] The Federal Coordinating Council for Science, Engineering and Technology was established in 1976 to address science and technology policy issues affecting multiple Federal agencies. The Council is chaired by the Director of the Office of Science and Technology Policy and includes Cabinet members or their deputies from the major Federal Departments and the heads of Federal science agencies. The Council's mission is to provide the planning, budgeting, and co-ordination necessary to set government-wide priorities on cross-cutting R&D initiatives. The Council seeks to develop integrated strategies, programs, and budgets for Federal research and develop in high priority cross-cutting areas of science and technology.

[12] Cf. Tavernier (1993, pp. 84-85), who suggests that when knowledge is considered as a factor of production, "the really important questions are becoming university questions insofar as they require a long-term perspective and a multi-disciplinary and even an ethical approach....This shift in methodological approach "also implies more emphasis on competitive funding and centers of excellence."

[13] This probably overestimates the percentage of U.S. college and university students enrolled in a foreign language, since the Modern Language Association measures course registrations and not students. Thus, when dividing foreign language registrations by total higher education enrolments it is not possible to eliminate double counting (i.e., a single student registered for more than one course).

[14] More than two-thirds of Mexican students in the USA are concentrated in the Southwestern states, including California, while only six higher education institutions account for more than half of total Mexican enrolments at U.S. higher education institutions; namely, the University of Texas at El Paso, Pima Community College in Arizona, California Polytechnic University, the University of Texas at Austin, and Texas A&M University at Galveston.

[15] The number of U.S. exchange students in Canada greatly underestimates the cross-border mobility of students between the two countries. In Academic Year 2002, approximately 5,000 U.S. citizens enrolled in Canadian colleges and universities as regular full-time degree-seeking students, which is an increase of nearly 90 percent since 1999. U.S. students report that Canadian universities are increasingly attractive because favourable exchange rates provide access to world quality institutions at only one-third the cost to U.S. students residing in New England and other northern industrial states, while Canadian cities offer comparable cultural attractions and greater personal safety (Nissman 2002). This trend represents a real "NAFTA effect" in higher education.

[16] USAID's Economic Growth objective has been focused mainly on neo-liberal policies that strengthen private markets in foreign countries by (a) improving the policies, laws, and regulations that govern markets, (b) strengthening the private financial institutions that reinforce and support competitive markets, (c) supporting public and private investments in infrastructure, including telecommunications, (d) privatising state-owned enterprises, and (e) promoting the training and technology transfer required for the private and regulatory sectors to maintain a competitive market environment. The Agricultural Development objective has focused on (a) improving agricultural policies (e.g., elimination of state food monopolies), (b) strengthening support institutions (e.g., agricultural research and technological experimentation through mobilising the resources of U.S. land-grant colleges and specialised international agricultural research centres), (c) promoting development transfer of appropriate technology, and (d) generating labour and product market linkages that maximise the outputs of each (USAID 1999a, 2).

[17] The six partnerships established under the U.S./Mexico Partners in Development Program were: (1) Purdue University/Instituto Tecnologico y de Estudios Superiores de Monterrey, (2) Maricopa Community College/Universidad Autonoma de Baja California Sur, (3) Ohio State University/Colegio Postgraduado en Ciencias Agricolas, (4) California Polytechnic State University, San Luis Obispo/Instituto Tecnologico de Culiacan, (5) West Virginia University/Universidad de Guanajuato, and (6) Montana State University/Universidad Autonoma de Baja California. See (ALO and USAID 1997a) for description and analysis of the pilot projects).

[18] These estimates are imprecise, but fairly accurate measures of the level and range of North American activities sponsored by USAID. The estimates are based on data in the IHELP online data base (AASCU 1999c). The estimates include linkages established under the Institutional Partnerships in Higher Education, Workforce Development Partnerships, the Network for Mexico/US Higher Education/Industry Outreach for Co-operation in Development, and other USAID programs.

[19] The Fulbright Program was operated as a largely autonomous branch of the U.S. State Department from 1946 to 1978, when it was incorporated into the United States Information Agency. The Foreign Affairs Reform and Restructuring Act of 1998 abolished the USIA, effective October 1, 1999. However, the international exchange community, and key members of Congress, advocated successfully for the creation of a separate Bureau for Educational and Cultural Affairs within the State Department, which is now responsible for administering federally-funded international exchange programs (Smith 2000, 72; NAFSA 2000d).

[20] The Commission also received funding support from the Rockefeller Foundation, Mexican Council for Culture and the Arts, and the Bancomer Cultural Foundation (Santillanez 1995, ii).

[21] The awards to U.S. citizens travelling to Mexico give preference "to U.S. citizens with limited previous exposure to, and without recent experience in, Mexico" (CIES 1999b).

[22] Of the 22 awards administered by the Canadian Fulbright Commission, 10 to 12 are funded entirely by private sources.

[23] Among the international projects that are currently funded by the Office of Post-secondary Education, 43 percent have developed credit portability, 38 percent have tuition reciprocity, 19 percent

have developed joint curricula, while 40 percent of the funded projects have developed new curricular–not necessarily joint curricular—programs (USDOE 1999a).

[24] The IIE co-operates with the Educational Testing Service (ETS) in foreign countries to administer the Test of English of a Foreign Language (TOEFL), the Graduate Record Examination (GRE), and the Graduate Management Admissions Test (GMAT), which are required for admission to most U.S. graduate programs. IIE administers two graduate fellowship programs in the social sciences for Mexican citizens who want to pursue graduate studies in the social sciences in the United States. The two programs are funded by the John D. and Catherine T. MacCarthur Foundation, the Ford Foundation, and the William and Flora Hewlett Foundation (IIE 1999a).

CHAPTER 4

[1] In the end, however, despite having vigorously opposed the agreement in its election campaign, the new Liberal government signed it into law a month after assuming power.

[2] Under the Established Programs Financing legislation, the federal government transfers a block of funds to the provincial governments to support universities and colleges.

[3] Except where otherwise stated, all amounts in this chapter are in Canadian dollars.

[4] The Corporate Higher Education Forum, as its title suggests, is a forum established to bring chief executive officers of major Canadian corporations together with the Presidents and Vice-Chancellors of Canadian Universities. Membership is limited and by invitation only.

[5] Three examples are the Scotiabanks' Awards for Excellence in Internationalisation, Celanese Canada's Internationalist Fellowships, and Nortel's Globalisation Challenge Program, which offers 15 scholarships of $30,000 each for international study and work assignments in one of six countries, including Mexico.

[6] Sector competitiveness frameworks are produced by Industry Canada's key industry stakeholders. The objective is to seek ways in which government and private industry can strengthen Canada's competitiveness and, in so doing, generate jobs and growth.

[7] The number is not very large when it is recognised that in 1997-1998 alone some 5,058 Canadian undergraduate and graduate students were studying abroad.

[8] An exception, they note, is the University of Guelph, which is reported to have adopted an integrative approach to internationalising all aspects of curriculum in the 1970s.

[9] It should be noted that these trends differ between provinces, individual institutions, and areas of study. For instance, they do not apply to Quebec, where tuition waivers are offered to students from France and some African nations. Engineering enrolments, for example, have doubled of late in L'Université de Québec in Montreal and a similar pattern can be observed in other universities in that province (Lemasson 1999).

[10] A longer paper on the same subject was presented at the OECD/DAFFE workshop in Paris in February, 1997, and was published by the OECD in the proceedings of the workshop (Mallea 1998a).

CHAPTER 5

[1] For Mexico, membership in GATT required the removal of customs barriers, the lowering of tariffs, and the removal of numerous products from its System of Previous Permits to Exports. Mexico also signed free trade agreements with Chile in 1992 and with Costa Rica and Bolivia in 1995. Mexico also joined the Asia-Pacific Economic Co-operation (APEC) mechanism in 1993, the Organisation for Economic Co-operation and Development(OECD) in 1994, and the Economic Council of the Pacific Basin (PBEC) in 1995. In 2000, negotiations for trade liberalisation with the European Union were being completed by Mexico.

[2] "The market conditions regarding sales, consumption, and work, together with the influx of foreign investment (IED) are undoubtedly at the root of the new geography of production in Mexico....Because of the new economic liberalisation, urban regions and cities in the service sector are thriving, while the less competitive sectors are located in cities in economic decline" (Olivera Lozano1997).

[3] Since the 1970s, economic crises have been frequent and have negatively affected the public's expectations about national development. In the past thirty years, cycles of financial boom and bust have been the norm in the Mexican economy. On most occasions, however, the breaking point came at the end of a presidential regime, rather than at the beginning as in 1994.

[4] Between November 1994 and July 1996, the national consumer price index reported cumulative inflation of nearly 80 percent.

[5] Private sector restructuring and numerous company closing, together with the national economic crises and debt repayment, had very important labour costs: unemployment and underemployment increased, especially among young people and women, although the way in which the government calculates this figure tends to underestimate its true magnitude. However, graduates in many fields of higher education are still relatively protected mainly due to their relative scarcity (i.e., about 6 percent of the labour force). In addition, unemployment and underemployment are socially controlled due to the massive movement of workers with the lowest levels of education into the informal sector of the economy, which generates non-remunerated income. The informal sector functions as an escape valve, in situations where there is significant job loss and where unemployment insurance is not available.

[6] At almost the same time in 1992, two organisations were established; namely, the Trilateral Task Force of Discussion on Higher Education and the Trilateral Coalition for the Defence of Public Education in North America. Both organisations were created to promote awareness of the main challenges posed to national higher education systems by North American economic integration.

[7] These programs are Academic-Industrial Linkages (PREAM), Incubators of Enterprises with a Technological Base (PIEBT), the Research and Development Fund for Technological Modernisation (FIDETEC), the Fund for the Strengthening of Scientific and Technological Capabilities (FORCCYTEC), and the Program for Linking Academe and Industry (PROVINC). PROVINC is endorsed by the World Bank.

[8] In North America, CONACYT signed agreements such as the Agreement of Co-operation on Higher Education and Research with the Board of regents of the University of California in July of 1997 with the aim of supporting joint programs of common interest in one or more of the following areas: postgraduate education, academic and research exchange, training periods for postgraduate students that do not lead to a degree, collaboration on research programs, and promotion of joint academic programs.

[10] See for example the document entitled "Concepto y Practica del Papel de la ANUIES en la Colaboracion Interinstitucional en el Ambito Superior en America del Norte" (Mungaray1996), where the author recommends that co-operation serve as a basis for solving national problems mainly by concentrating efforts in priority areas such as linkages with the social and private sectors, training professors at the post-graduate level, student mobility, and curricular innovation.

[11] "The isolationist model of import tariffs and protection is supplanted by the liberalisation of the economy which is allowing the country to show its true competitive advantages and to generate a process which tends to favour the expansion of the export sector. The acceleration of this process since the late 1980s has turned our country into one of the most liberalised economies in the world....The acquisition of a new technological capacity is now a key element in the process of economic modernisation" (SEP/SEIT 1992, 4).

[12] From the Mexican standpoint, the differences between the national situation and those of the other two NAFTA countries is clear: "Canada and the United States have experienced a similar development of their educational systems: the former has a higher overall rate of schooling at the university level, as well as in several other indicators. Mexico, however, is considerably behind those countries in most indicators" (Latapi 1994, 197).

[13] "It is obvious that the level of schooling of Mexican workers is much lower than that of other countries. The percentage of people in Mexico who have completed primary school or less is 52.4 per cent, while in the U.S. it is 9.9 per cent, and in Canada, 13.3 per cent. On the other hand, only 26.4 per cent of Mexicans have completed middle or high school, while it is 71.4 in the U.S. and 59.8 per cent in Canada. (Latapi 1994, 201).

[14]"Mexico spends 5 percent of the GNP as compared to 6.8 percent and 11.7 percent in the United States and Canada respectively....There were, however, marked variations in Mexico during the period of

crisis between 1982 and 1990 (5.2 percent in 1980, 2.4 percent in 1984, 4 percent in 1990 and 5 percent in 1993). The other two countries have assigned proportions that have been fairly constant, between 6 and 7 per cent of the GNP during the past twenty years" (Latapi 1994, 201).

15 "Given the current push toward globalisation and the implementation of NAFTA, it is imperative that linkages be finely attuned to the new demands of qualified personnel, scientific knowledge, development, adaptation to the new technologies...(In Western Mexico) there are no bachelors or graduate programs designed to meet the demands of social groups who have encountered difficulties in becoming part of the push for globalisation, such as producers with low yield crops or the small enterprises" (Ojeda Delgado 1994, 256-57).

16 For instance, Ganster disagrees with his Mexican colleagues in listing the most relevant bi-lateral differences between Mexico and the United States. He indicates that the following are the most significant: (1) the working conditions of academics, (2) their linguistic abilities, (3) differences in physical infrastructures, laboratories, and libraries, (4) the number of academics involved in the study of the privileged classes, and (5) the importance of politics in the administration of Mexico's higher education institutions (Ganster 1994).

17 In the final version of the SUPERA program, its purpose is: "To strengthen academic, cultural, humanist and technological capabilities of the higher education institutions facing the challenges and consequences of NAFTA" (ANUIES 1993a, 66). PROMEP's documentation envisions the possibility of supporting the acquisition of degrees abroad by teachers and linking of national academic bodies with research groups in other countries.

19 The following professions are regulated in Mexico: actuarial science, agronomy, architecture, accounting, law, nursing, pharmacy, engineering, veterinary medicine, dentistry and psychology

20 In 1999, the EGELs were applied in 16 areas: namely accounting, administration, tourism, administration of tourist enterprises, general medicine, dentistry, nursing at the level of undergraduate and technical education, pharmacy, veterinary medicine, civil engineering, electrical engineering, electronic engineering, psychology, agricultural engineering, computer science, and chemical engineering. Other examinations are now being developed for education, law, mechanical and industrial engineering, and architecture (CENEVAL 1998).

21 According to data provided by Lic. Eliseo Diaz of the General Office of Professions, in February of 2000 other councils with accreditation purposes were in the process of being formed such as the Mexican Council for the Teaching of Architecture (COMAEA), the Academic Commission for Quality Standards for the Faculties and Schools of Physical Education, Sports and Recreation, the National Council of Professional Curriculum Certification for Architects, the Council for Accreditation and Certification of Higher Agricultural Education, and the Council for Accreditation of Chemistry and Certification of Chemical Engineering and Chemists.

22 In 1998, there were 6,188 bachelor programs registered at public universities and 1,946 in postgraduate education (714 specialised, 1,016 masters programs, and 216 doctoral programs).

23 The General Office of Professions signed agreements with higher education institutions in 1999 to promote, modernise, and simplify professional registrations with the goal of increasing the registration of professional titles and diplomas in Mexico. Among the public higher education institutions, the signatories include the Autonoma Universidad de Baja California, Chiapas, Mexico State, Morelos, Nuevo Leon, San Luis Potosi, Tamaulipas, and the Universities of Colima, Guadalajara, Sonora, Veracruzana. The private higher education institutions to sign agreements are the Autonoma de Guadalajara, the Instituto de Estudios Superiores de Occidente, and the Escuela Bancaria y Comercial. Ten other public universities and one private school are close signing agreements (DGP, Colegios y Profesiones 1999, 7).

24 The DGP registered 219 professional colleges between 1945 and 1994. Between 1995 and 1999, it registered 70 more professional colleges (DGP, Colegios y Profesiones 1999, 27).

25 The first mention of accreditation was made by the international expert P. Coombs in his report entitled "Strategy for Increasing the Quality of Higher Education in Mexico," which was published in 1992. The justification for accreditation was more national than international: "This suggested evaluation and accreditation system can make at least two important contributions in this direction. First, it can make more visible the true diversity that exists within the system...Second, as time goes on, the basic effects of

this evaluation and accreditation system should be to progressively elevate the quality and effectiveness" (Coombs 1992, 51-2).

[26] In 1996, ANUIES proposed creating a system of Evaluation and Accreditation of Higher Education to organise, co-ordinate, and improve the development of institutional capacities. In November of 1997, at the 28th ordinary session of its General Assembly, ANUIES proposed establishing an umbrella civil association that would become self-financing in the medium-term. In September 1998, at the 11th ordinary session, the rectors supported the reactivation of the National Commission of Evaluation (CONAEVA), the adoption of standardised examinations for evaluating student learning, the generalisation of the EGELs, the consolidation of the bodies, and the articulation of accreditation procedures for programs leading to professional certification.

[27] According to data provided by technical office of CENEVAL, in December of 1999 nine institutions (eight public universities and one private university) had incorporated in their internal regulations the obligatory use of the EGEL as a prerequisite to graduation in all or some of the applicable areas.

[28] The number of individual or institutional users of the CENEVAL and of peer committees has increased constantly over the past seven years. In 1994, CENEVAL administered 234 examinations, but by 1999 this number had grown to 17,085. The number of evaluations carried out by the CIESS went from 13 in 1992 to 82 in 1994 and 1,110 in 1999 (ANUIES 1999b)

[29] "We are seeking to strengthen development of postgraduate degrees in close liaison with research in to create highly qualified cadres on the basis of quality standards and international competitiveness....to broaden co-operation in matters of science and technology and to bring about agreements that will co-ordinate national and foreign institutions, that will bring researchers up to date in priority areas" (PME 1989-94, 156).

[30] In the presentation of the chapter devoted to higher education and to high school, it is observed that "middle and higher education has today great strategic value to bring about the transformations that the country's development demand in a ever more interdependent world, characterised by a rapid technological and scientific transformation" (PDE 1995-2000, 127).

[31] "We will strengthen collaborative programs with educational institutions from other countries, with the objective of facilitating mobility of students and academic staff, the transfer and recognition of credits, the work in research programs and the establishment of mutual support networks." (PDE 1995-2000, 158).

[32] "We will support actions that will enhance students' abilities in computer science and languages, among other areas" (PDE 1995-2000, 146).

[33] The SEP, CONACYT and ANUIES signed agreements for bi-lateral or tri-lateral co-operation with the U.S. and Canada. This notwithstanding, the theme of constructing a North American space for higher education did not show the same neatness as, for example, the European Union, where internationalisation had a europeanisation component for mobility and co-operation. The lack of resources and permanent structures on a tri-lateral scale, and at the national level, the permanent swing of the pendulum between Latin America and North America, probably explain the poor advances made in exchanges within North America.

[34] For example, six years after the first report, the ALO registered similar occurrences of geographic and institutional concentration: in 1998, 24 of the 122 co-operation agreements with Mexican higher education institutions had been signed with institutions in the capital city, while 41 agreements were signed with universities near the U.S. border. The ITESM alone, in Nuevo Leon, signed 15 agreements (http://www.alo).

[35] The three ANUIES censuses of the IES program on international co-operation were conducted in 1992,1995, and 1996-98, respectively. These censuses show a growing interest among institutions in signing international agreements and providing information on them. In 1992, the response rate among affiliated institutions was 44 percent; in 1995, after NAFTA was signed, it increased to 74 percent. The number of agreements went from 193 to 1,368 during this time (ANUIES 1994, 1998b).

[36] According to PROMEP's latest report, academics who receive scholarships to obtain a post-graduate degree abroad have an academic and demographic profile different from those scholarship-holders who stay at home. They are younger and better trained and they usually leave to obtain a doctorate. On average, they are 38.5 years old (with a majority between 31 and 45 years of age), while the average age

NOTES

for those who benefit from the PROMEP in general is 44. Opportunities abroad are dependent on age and previous academic experience (Poder Ejecutivo Federal 1999).

[37] The post-graduate degrees that may be considered unconventional, based on international co-operation, were the doctorate in Architecture and Urbanisation, offered by the Universidad Veracruzana and the Universidad Politecnica de Madrid, the masters in financial economy by UAM Azcapotzalco as a joint collaboration with the University of London, the masters of art offered by the Universidad de Chihuahua and Cuba, the masters in community cultural development offered by the Universidad Autonoma de Sinaloa and the Universidad de Occidente in Cuba (http://www.sesic.sep.gob.mx/promep/convoca.htm).

[38] The sabbatical leaves abroad program, the post-doctoral stays abroad, the special chairs for visiting academics, and the special chairs for the repatriation and retention of Mexican researchers are still in place after PACIME's termination.

[39] They received about 4.2 percent of the total resources from 1991 to 1997. During this period, the repatriation program helped 1,364 Mexican researchers return home on a more or less permanent basis. By contrast, the program of Heritage Chairs II reached its peak in 1994, when conditions in the Mexican academic market were more attractive (Didou 2000).

[40] By 2000, the postdoctoral stays authorised by CONACYT were distributed in the following way: 22 of 32 awardees went to the United States and among those who renewed, the pattern was similar (11 of 22 went to the U.S.). Sabbatical leaves abroad follow a similar pattern with 9 of 23 authorised in 2000 going to the United States (http://www.nodo51.adm.conacyt.mx8890).

[41] Spain has offered co-operation programs of mutual interest such as the "young Spanish medical doctors" program, which permits the sending country to generate work for people who are highly qualified and allows the receiving countries to benefit from their services at a relatively low cost.

[42] The OECD (1997) reports that the movement of highly skilled people can be understand with two main basic concepts: brain exchange and brain waste. Brain exchange implies a two-way flow of expertise between a sending country and a receiving country. Yet, when the net flow is heavily biased in one direction, the terms brain gain or brain drain are often used. Another term – brain waste – describes the waste that occurs when highly skilled workers migrate into forms of employment not requiring the application of their experience and skills (OECD 1997). Recently, Johnson and Regets (1998) have introduced a new concept into the debate; namely "brain circulation." This refers to the cycle of moving abroad to study, then taking a job abroad, and later returning home to take advantage of a good opportunity" (Mahroum 1998).

[43] The majority of foreign students originate in North America. Their stays, which range from weeks to months, are cultural in character and have language learning as their main objective (AMPEI 1999).

[44] "The financial crisis that took place after December 1994 produced a strong drop in the volume of national and particularly of international grants. Between 1996 and 1998, the total number of national grants fell from 6,669 to 5,524; international grants dropped from 1,123 to 851 during the same period, with the largest drop being for studies in the U.S. and Canada (Didou 2000, 113).

[45] In recent years, there has been a cost rationalisation for both foreign and national grants, with the difference in 1997 being 21.5 percent higher for study abroad than at home (Didou, 2000, 114).

[46] According to existing regulations, the grantee must or should work in an educational institution upon returning home, for as long a period as they had a scholarship; otherwise they must reimburse the whole or part of the grant, depending on the place where they end up working.

[47] Co-ordinated by El Colegio de Mexico AC, participants include the Centre for Economic and Education Research (CIDE), the Colegio de la Frontera Norte, the Instituto Tecnologico de Estudios Superiores de Monterrey (ITESM), and the Fundacion Universidad de las Americas.

[48] In 1998, many public and private higher education institutions offered degrees with an international component. These degrees are in administration (5), political science and public administration (2), international commerce (119), law (10), economics and development (3), trade relations and international relations (50). Some other areas, such as accounting (1), tourism (2), sales and marketing (10) also had international components (ANUIES 1998a, 1998b).

[49] Internationalising the curriculum is a process that includes the following activities:
•"Internationalisation of the curriculum is a process of educational change aimed at improving the quality of higher education;

•Internationalising the curriculum, together with student mobility and staff mobility constitute the three central effects and interrelated elements in the implementation phase of the process of internationalisation
•Effects and outcomes of internationalising the curriculum can be distinguished between short term effects on students, staff and educational content and long term effects on profiles of graduates, labour market positions and the quality of education
•Internationalised curricula can be developed both in a single national context or in collaboration with foreign partner institutions (joint curriculum development) and can be aimed at either professional training or social and intercultural integration" (Van der Wende in OECD 1996).

[50] For example, among recent works are the 1996 doctoral thesis by B. Ellingboe on the process of internationalisation at the University of Minnesota, as well as comparative works by the OECD's CERI, which examine the institutional processes of internationalisation.

[51] For reasons of accessibility, field study was conducted in three institutions in the northern region of Mexico; namely Universidad de Colima, Universidad de Guadalajara, and Universidad Autonoma de Nuevo Leon. The rest were located in the central region of the country and included Universidad Autonoma del Estado de Mexico, Universidad Autonoma de Puebla, Universidad Autonoma Metropolitana, Universidad Nacional Autonoma de Mexico, El Colegio de Mexico AC, and El Colegio Mexiquense AC. The study also included interviews with administrators at ANUIES, SESIC, CONACYT, and SEIT for the Technological Institutes. Finally, the researchers also attended several meetings dealing with sectoral policies and research in the technological institutes of the central-northern region of the country in Vallarta, Tepic and Saltillo. The aim of these meetings was to obtain data on the process of internationalisation in that sector, especially information on academic mobility and research.

[52] For example, the U.S.-Mexico CONACYT program encourages relations between Mexican higher education institutions and the University of California.

[53] The evaluation of internationalisation at UNAM was co-ordinated by H. de Witt, while the evaluation of the Universidad de Guadalajara was conducted by John Mallea.

CHAPTER 6

[1] The Steering Committee consists of the Director General of Canada's International Cultural Relations Bureau (Department of Foreign Affairs and International Trade), the Associate Director of U.S. State Department's Bureau of Educational and Cultural Affairs, and Mexico's Director General of Higher Education.

[2] There are disagreements about the methodology for calculating the economic impacts of international higher education with some organisations placing the figure between $11 billion (IIE estimate) and $13 billion (NAFSA estimate).

[3] The Commission on Colleges of the Southern Association of Colleges and Schools (2001) identifies itself as "the recognized regional accrediting body in the eleven U.S. Southern states (Alabama, Florida, Georgia, Kentucky, Louisiana, Mississippi, North Carolina, South Carolina, Tennessee, Texas and Virginia) and in Latin America for those institutions of higher education that award associate, baccalaureate, master's or doctoral degrees." The Universidad de las Americas and the Instituto Tecnologico de Estudios Superiores de Monterrey were last accredited by SACS in 1994 and 1998, respectively.

REFERENCES

Aboites, Hugo. *Vientos del Norte. TLC y Privatización de la Educación Superior en México.* México: Plaza y Valdés, 1997.

Aboites, Hugo. "Crisis de Conducción en la Universidad Pública." México, UAM-Xochimilco/RISEU, Foro:¿adónde va la Universidad Pública?, 1999. 26-27 de enero 2000 en *http://www.unam.mx/coordhum/riseu/foro.html*

Academy for Educational Development, Inc. *Developing a Process Model for Institutional and State-level Review and Evaluation of Academic Programs.* Washington, D.C.: Ohio Board of Regents, 1979.

Acosta, Silva A. "Conflicto, poder y trabajo académico en la universidad pública en México: una perspectiva desde el punto de la gobernabilidad universitaria." México, UAM-Xochimilco/RISEU, Foro:¿adónde va la universidad pública?, 1999. 26-27 de enero 2000 en http://www.unam.mx/coordhum/riseu/foro.html

Ad Hoc Working Group on Research-Intensive Universities and the Federal Government. *In the National Interest: The Federal Government and Research-Intensive Universities.* Washington, D.C.: Federal Coordinating Council for Science, Engineering, and Technology, 1992.

Adams, J. Q. "The Globalization of Engineering Licensure." In Lenn, M. P. and Campos, L. Eds. *Globalization of the Professions and the Quality Imperative: Professional Accreditation, Certification, and Licensure.* Madison, WI.: Magna Publications, 1997.

Adelman, Alan. "North America Needs its Own Academic Common Market." *Chronicle of Higher Education.* December 12, 1990, p. A36.

Adelman, Alan. "Exploring an Academic Common Market in North America." *Educational Record* (Fall 1992): 35-36.

Adelman, Alan. "Academic and student mobility in North America." *Educación Global,* 3 (1999): 31-34

Almanac of Higher Education, 1995. Chicago: University of Chicago Press, 1995.

Altbach, P.G. and McGill, P. "Internationalize American Higher Education? Not Exactly." *Change* 30 (July/August 1998): 36-39.

American Association of State Colleges and Universities. 1999a. "The Association Liaison Office for University Cooperation in Development." http://www.aascu.org/alo/about.htm

American Association of State Colleges and Universities. 1999b. "The Association Liaison Office for University Cooperation in Development." http://www.aascu.org/alo/work.htm

REFERENCES

American Association of State Colleges and Universities. 1999c. "International Higher Education Linkages Project." http://www.aascu.org/alo/ihelp/link.asp

American Association of State Colleges and Universities. 1999d. "Institutional Partnerships in Higher Education for International Development." http://www.aascu.org/alo/proposals.htm

American Council of Education. *Educating Americans for a World in Flux: Ten Ground Rules for Internationalizing Higher Education.* Washington, D.C.: ACE, 1996.

American Council on Education, la Asociacion Nacional de Universidades e Instituciones de Educacion Superior, and Association of Universities and Colleges of Canada. *Increasing North American Higher Education Cooperation, Collaboration, and Exchange: A Trilateral Effort to Study and Propose New Approaches.* Washington, D.C.: Trilateral Steering Committee, 2000.

American Federation of Labor and Congress of Industrial Organizations. *Exploiting Both Sides: US-Mexico Free Trade.* Washington, D.C.: AFL-CIO, 1991.

Anderson, Elizabeth. "International Education in Australia: Historical Trends, Current Developments, and Challenges for the Future." Pp. 286-299 in Peggy Blumenthal, Craufurd Goodwin, Alan Smith, and Ulrich Teichler, eds., *Academic Mobility in a Changing World.* London and Bristol, Penn.: Jessica Kingsley Publishers, 1996.

Anthony, Nancy Hughes and Robert J. Keyes "Canada Needs GATS'. In *The National Post,* July 26, 2002, p. 15.

Arredondo, Alvarez V. "Consolidación y Proyección de la Universidad Veracruzana Hacia el Siglo XXI." In *Programa de Trabajo 1998-2001 y Programa Operativo Annual.* Veracruz, México: Universidad Veracruzan,1998.

Arreola, C., comp. *Testimonios sobre* el TLC. México: Porrúa, 1994.

Arzac, A. 'La Fundación Fullbright en México." en http://elnet.org/trilater/guadalajara/speeches/arzac.htm (n.d.)

Ascher, B. "Is Quality Assurance in Education Consistent with International Trade Agreements?" *In International Trade in Professional Services: Advancing Liberalisation through Regulatory Reform.* Paris: OECD, 1997.

Asia Pacific Foundation of Canada. *Canada Asia Review* 1998. Vancouver: APFC, 1998.

Asociación Mexicana para la Educación Internacional and Secretaría de Educación Pública. *An International Student Guide to Mexican Universities.* México: AMPEI-SEP, 1994.

Asociación Nacional Universidades e Instituciones de Educacion Superior. "Consolidación y desarrollo del sistema nacional de educación superior." *Documento base aprobado en la XXIII Reunión Ordinaria de la Asamblea General de la ANUIES.* Cuernavaca, Morelos, febrero 1990. Revista de la Educación Superior 73 (1990).

Asociacion Nacional Universidades e Instituciones de Educacion Superior. "Programa Nacional de Superación del Personal Académico." *Revista de la Educación Superior* 86 (1993a).

Asociacion Nacional Universidades e Instituciones de Educacion Superior. "Acuerdos y Convenios entre Instituciones de Educación Superior Contrapartes de los Estados Unidos y Canadá." *Revista de la Educación Superior* 87 (1993b).

Asociacion Nacional Universidades e Instituciones de Educacion Superior. "Consideraciones Generales sobre el Proceso de Acreditación de las Instituciones de Educación Superior en México." *Revista de la Educación Superior* 88 (1993c).

Asociacion Nacional Universidades e Instituciones de Educacion Superior, Secretaría GeneralEjecutiva. "Estudio Comparativo entre las Áreas del Conocimiento de la Educación Superior en América Latina y la International Standard Classification of Education (ISCED)." *Revista de la Educación Superior* 92 (1994).

Asociacion Nacional Universidades e Instituciones de Educacion Superior. "Los Exámenes Nacionales y el Examen General de Calidad Profesional." *Revista de la Educación Superior* 95 (1995).

Asociacion Nacional Universidades e Instituciones de Educacion Superior. "Sistema Nacional de Evaluación y Acreditación de la Educación Media Superior y Superior." *Documento aprobado en la XXVIII Sesión Ordinaria de la Asamblea General de ANUIES,* Oaxaca, Mexico, 1997a.

Asociacion Nacional Universidades e Instituciones de Educacion Superior. "Evaluación y acreditación de la educación superior en México." *Revista de la Educación Superior* 101 (1997b).

Asociacion Nacional Universidades e Instituciones de Educacion Superior. *Licenciatura en Universidades e Institutos Tecnológicos: Procedencia de los Alumnos de PrimerIngreso.* México: ANUIES, 1998a.

Asociacion Nacional Universidades e Instituciones de Educacion Superior. "Aprobó la XXIX Asamblea General una Estrategia para Seguir Impulsando la Consolidación del Sistema Nacional de Evaluación y Acreditación'. *Confluencia* 6.67 (1998b).

References

Asociacion Nacional Universidades e Instituciones de Educacion Superior. *Acciones de Transformación de las Universidades Públicas Mexicanas en el Periodo 1994-1999 (versión in extenso)*. México: ANUIES, 1999a.

Asociacion Nacional Universidades e Instituciones de Educacion Superior. *Acciones ANUIES, 1998*. México: ANUIES, 1999b.

Asociacion Nacional Universidades e Instituciones de Educacion Superior. *El PROMEP. Etapas de Planeación enero de 1997-abril de 1999*. México: ANUIES, 1999c.

Asociacion Nacional Universidades e Instituciones de Educacion Superior. *La Educación Superior en el Siglo XXI: Lineas Estratégicas de Desarrollo: Una Propuesta de la ANUIES*. México, ANUIES, 2000. http.//www.anuies.mx/21

Association of Canadian Community Colleges. "Internationalisation of Colleges: An Orientation Document." Ottawa: ACCC, 1994.

Association of Canadian Community Colleges. *Internationalisation of Colleges: An Orientation Document.* Ottawa: ACCC, 1994.

Association of Canadian Community Colleges. "Trilateral Initiatives of Canadian Professions, Current Status: May 1997." (Unpublished report). Ottawa: Association of Accrediting Agencies of Canada, 1997.

Association of Southeast Asian Nations. *ASEAN Framework Agreement on Services.* Jakarta: ASEAN Secretariat, 1995.

Association of Universities and Colleges of Canada. "What is Internationalisation?" *Uniworld* (Winter/Spring 1992).

Association of Universities and Colleges of Canada. *Report on the Inventory of Canadian University Linkages with Mexico and the United States.* Ottawa: AUCC, 1994.

Association of Universities and Colleges of Canada. "Association of Universities and Colleges of Canada." http://www.aucc.ca, 1995a.

Association of Universities and Colleges of Canada. "Internationalisation and Canadian Universities." http://homes.aucc.ca/nglish/international/statement.html, 1995b.

Association Liaison Office for University Cooperation in Development and U.S. Agency for International Development. *Increasing the Relevance of Higher Education to Development: What U.S. and Mexican Public/Private Partnerships Can Do.* Washington, D.C.: ALO and USAID, 1997.

Australian Trade Commission. *Intelligent Exports.* Sydney: AUSTRADE, 1994.

Avila, Díaz A. "Canadá, el otro socio." México: Banco Nacional de Comercio Exterior, *Comercio Exterior* 44.2 (1994).

Avila, Connelly C. "Canadá: un Mercado para las Exportaciones Mexicanas." México: Banco Nacional de Comercio Exterior *Comercio Exterior* 44.2 (1994).

Azariadis, Costas and Allen Drazen. "Threshold Externalities in Economic Development." *Quarterly Journal of Economics* 105.2 (1990): 501-26.

Back, K., Davis, D. and Olsen, A. (1996). *Internationalisation and Higher Education: Goals and Strategies.* Canberra: Australian Government Publishing Service.

Bailey, T. "Jobs of the Future and the Skills They Will Require: New Thinking on an Old Debate." *American Educator* 14 (1990): 10-15, 40-44.

Banco de Mexico. *The Mexican Economy,* 1993. Mexico City: Direccion de Organismos y Acuerdos Internacionales, 1993.

Banco de Mexico. *The Mexican Economy,* 1997. Mexico City: Direccion de Organismos y Acuerdos Internacionales, 1997.

Banco de Mexico. *The Mexican Economy,* 1998. Mexico City: Direccion de Organismos y Acuerdos Internacionales, 1998.

Banco de Mexico. *The Mexican Economy,* 1999. Mexico City: Direccion de Organismos y Acuerdos Internacionales, 1999.

Baran, Paul A. and Paul M. Sweezey. *Monopoly Capital: An Essay on the American Economic and Social Order.* New York: Monthly Review Press, 1966.

Barro, R.J. "Economic Growth in a Cross-Section of Countries." *Quarterly Journal of Economics* 106.2 (1991): 407-44.

Barrow, ClydeW. "Will the Fiscal Crisis Force Higher Education to Restructure?" *Thought and Action: The NEA Higher Education Journal* 9 (Fall 1993): 25-39.

Barrow, Clyde W. "The New Economy and the Restructuring of Higher Education." *Thought and Action: The NEA Higher Education Journal* 12 (Spring 1996): 37-54.

Barrow, Clyde W. "Economic Globalization and the New Economy: The United States of America." México, *draft,* Proyecto de Investigación Trinacional sobre Globalización, TLCAN y Educación Superior, El Colegio de México A.C, 1998.

Barrow, Clyde W. "Higher Education Policies and the North American Free Trade Agreement: The United States Case." *Educación Global* 3 (1999):139-55.

Barrow, Clyde W. "NAFTA and Trilateral Cooperation in Higher Education: Policy Initiatives in the USA." *Educación Global* 4 (2000):95-120.

Barrow, Clyde W. "Globalization, Trade Liberalization, and the Higher Education Industry." In Stanley Aronowitz and Heather Gautney, eds., *Implicating Empire: Globalization and Resistance in the Twenty-First Century.* New York: Basic Books, Inc., 2002.

Bartel, A., and Lichtenberg, F. "The Comparative Advantage of Educated Workers in Implementing the New Technology." *Review of Economics and Statistics* 69.1 (1987):1-11.

Baumgratz-Gangl, Gisela. "Developments in the Internationalization of Higher Education in Europe.' Pp. 103-128 in Peggy Blumenthal, Craufurd Goodwin, Alan Smith, and Ulrich Teichler, eds., *Academic Mobility in a Changing World.* London and Bristol, PA: Jessica Kingsley Publishers, 1996.

Baumol, W.J., Blackman, S.A.B., and Wolff, E.N. *Productivity and American Leadership.* Cambridge, MA: MIT Press, 1989.

Beard, Charles A. *The Open Door at Home: A Trial Philosophy of National Interest.* New York: Macmillan Co., 1934.

Becker, Gary S. *Human Capital: A Theoretical and Empirical Analysis with Special Reference to Education,* 3rd Edition. Chicago: University of Chicago Press, 1993.

Bell, Daniel. *The Coming of the Postindustrial Society: A Venture in Social Forecasting.* New York: Basic Books, 1976.

Bernal, R.V. "Vías hacia el área de Libre Comercio de las Américas." Caracas, SELA, *Revista Capítulos* 49 (1997). http://lanic.utexas.edu/sela/capitulos/edit49.html

Bikson, T. K. and Law, S. A. *Global Preparedness and Human Resources: College and Corporate Perspectives.* Santa Monica, CA: Rand Institute on Education and Training, 1994.

Bird, B.J., and Allen, D.N. "Faculty Entrepreneurship in Research University Environments." *Journal of Higher Education* 60.5 (1989): 583-96.

Blaug, M. "The Empirical Status of Human Capital Theory: A Slightly Jaundiced Survey." *Journal of Economic Literature* 14 (1976): 827-55.

Bluestone, Barry and Harrison Bennett. *The Deindustrialization of America.* New York: Basic Books, 1982.

Bond, S. L. and Lemasson, J.P., eds. *A New World of Knowledge: Canada and Globalization.* Ottawa: International Development Research Centre, 1999.

Bond, S. L. and Scott, J. T. "From Reluctant Acceptance to Modest Embrace: The Internationalisation of Undergraduate Education." In S.L. Bond and J.P. Lemasson, eds., *A New World of Knowledge: Canadian Universities and Globalization.* Ottawa: International Development Research Centre, 1999.

Boot, M. "Winds of Change Buffet Academia." *The Christian Science Monitor,* November 16, 1992, p. 10

BORDERLINK. 1994. "Economic Profile of the San-Diego-Tijuana Region: Characteristics for Investment and Governance Decisions." http://www-rohan.sdsu.edu/dept/ciber/borderlink-1994.html

BORDER PACT. 1999. "Border Pact: Memorandum of Understanding." http://borderpact.org/bpmou.htm

Bowen, H. *The Cost of Higher Education: How Much Do Colleges and Universities Spend Per Student and How Much Should They Spend?.* San Francisco: Jossey-Bass, 1980.

Bowen, W.G., and J.A. Sosa *Prospects for Faculty in the Arts and Sciences: A Study of Factors Affecting Demand and Supply, 1987 to 2012.* Princeton: Princeton University Press, 1989.

Bradford, Neil. "Governing the Canadian Economy: Ideas and Politics." In Michael Whittington and Glen Williams, eds., *Canadian Politics in the 21st Century.* Scarborough: Nelson Thomson Learning, 2000.

Brady, R. "Fox's dream: A North American Common Market." *Business Week* (August 14, 2000, p. 56.

Brazziel, W.F. "College-Corporate Partnerships in Higher Education." *Educational Record* 62 (1981): 50-53.

Bremer, L. and M.C. van der Wende. Internationalizing the Curriculum in Higher Education. The Hague: Nuffic, 1995.

Brett, A.M., D.V. Powers, M.F. Powers, F. Betz, and C. Alsanian. *Higher Education in Partnership with Industry Opportunities and Strategies for Training, Research, and Economic Development.* San Francisco: Jossey-Bass, 1988.

British Columbia Centre for International Education. *Anticipating the Future: Workshops and Resources of Internationalizing the Post-Secondary Campus.* Vancouver: BCCIE, 1996a.

British Columbia Centre for International Education. *Developing the International Dimensions of Post-Secondary Education: A Regional Conference on Internationalizing the Curriculum.* Vancouver: BCCIE, 1996b.

Brod, Richard and Bettina J. Huber. "Foreign Language Enrollments in United States Institutions of Higher Education, Fall 1995." *ADFL Bulletin* 28.2 (Winter 1997): 1-7.

Brod, Richard. "Foreign Language Enrollments in United States Institutions of Higher Education, Fall 1998." http://www.mla.org, 2000.

Brown, S. *Productivity Through Innovation: The Role of Universities.* Ottawa: AUCC, 1999.

Brubacher, John S. and Willis Rudy. *Higher Education in Transition A History of American Colleges and Universities.* 4th ed. New Brunswick: Transaction Publishers, 1997.

Bueno, Zirión G. 1996. "La Fundación México - Estados Unidos para la Ciencia y la Colaboración en América del Norte. Ponencia." Presentada en el Panel "The Role of Foundations in North America Cooperation." Guadalajara, 1996.

Bustamante, J. "El Consejo Asesor del Tratado de Libre Comercio en América del Norte." In C. Arreola, (comp.), *Testimonios sobre el TLC.* México: Porrúa, 1994.

Business-Higher Education Forum. *America's Competitive Challenge: The Need for a National Response.* Washington, D.C., 1983.

Business-Higher Education Forum. *Corporate and Campus Cooperation: An Action Agenda.* Washington, D.C., 1984.

Business-Higher Education Forum. *An Action Agenda for American Competitiveness.* Washington, D.C.: Congressional Clearinghouse on the Future, 1986.

Business-Higher Education Forum. *Spanning the Chasm: Corporate and Academic Cooperation to Improve Workforce Preparation.* Washington, D.C., 1997.

Business-Higher Education Forum. *Beyond the Rhetoric: Evaluating University-Industry Cooperation in Research and Technology Exchange,* 2 vols. Washington, D.C., 1998.

California Postsecondary Education Commission. *Planning for a New Faculty.* Sacramento, CA, 1991.

Calvert, John and Larry Kuehn. *Pandora's Box: Corporate Power, Free Trade, and Canadian Education.* Toronto: Our Schools/Our Selves Foundation, 1993.

Cameron, D.M. "Higher Education in Federal Systems: Canada." In D. Brown, P. Cazalis, and G. Jasmin, G., eds., *Higher Education in Federal Systems.* Kingston, Ontario: Institute of Governmental Relations, Queen's University, 1992.

Cameron, K.S., and Tschirhart, M. "Postindustrial Environments and Organizational Effectiveness in Colleges and Universities." *Journal of Higher Education* 63.1 (1992): 87-108.

Campbell, Bruce, Robert Scott, and Carlos Salas. "NAFTA at Seven." In *The CCPA Monitor* (July/August 2001): 3.

Campbell, Robert M. (1999). "The Fourth Fiscal Era: Can There be a 'Post-Neo-Conservative' Fiscal Policy?" In Leslie A. Pal, ed., *How Ottawa Spends. 1999-2000. Shape Shifting: Canadian Governance Toward the 21st Century.* Don Mills: Oxford University Press, 1999.

Canada. *Inventing our Future: An Action Plan for Canada's Prosperity.* Ottawa, 1992.

Canada. "Reviewing Canadian Foreign Policy: Minutes of Proceedings and Evidence of the Special Joint Committee of the Senate and House of Commons." First Session of the Thirty-Fifth Parliament, June 7, 1994a.

Canada. "Canadas Foreign Policy: Principles and Priorities for the Future." Report of the Special Joint Committee of the Senate and the House of Commons Reviewing Canadian Foreign Policy. Ottawa: Public Works and Government Services, 1994b.

Canada. "Notes for an Address by the Honourable Andre Ouellet, Ministry of Foreign Affairs." Ottawa: Department of Foreign Affairs and International Trade, October 19, 1994c.

Canada. *Program for North American Mobility in Higher Education.* Ottawa: Human Resources Development Canada, 1995.

Canadian Bureau for International Education. Ontario's International Activities in Postsecondary Education." Synthesis (Summer 1992).

Canadian Bureau for International Education. "Economic and Social Challenges: New Educational Paradigms and Needed Attitude Changes." *Synthesis* (Autumn 1993).

Canadian Bureau for International Education. "International Education is the Best Foreign Policy." *Synthesis* (Summer 1994).

Canadian Bureau for International Education. *International Education is a Bottom Line Issue. A Strategy for Building an Internationally Competent Workforce.* Ottawa: CBIE, 1995.

Canadian Bureau for International Education. "Canada's Export Potential." *Canadian Internationalist* 9.4 (1999).

Canadian Bureau for International Education. *Canadian Internationalist* (Winter 2000a).

Canadian Bureau for International Education. "The Millenium Consultation on International Education." Ottawa: CBIE, 2000b.

Canadian Bureau for International Education. *The National Report on International Students in Canada* 1998/99. Ottawa: CBIE, 2000c.

Canadian Consulate General in New York. www.can-am.gc.ca, 2002.

Canales, JoAnn, Leticia Calzada Gomez, and Nellyda Villanueva. 1995. *The Educational Systems of Mexico and the United States: Prospects for Reform and Collaboration.* Boulder, Colorado: Western Interstate Commission on Higher Education.

Card, D., and Krueger A. "Does School Quality Matter? Returns to Education and the Characteristics of Public Schools in the United States." *Journal of Political Economy* 100.1 (1992).

Carnevale, Anthony P. *America and the New Economy: How the New Competitive Standards are Radically Changing American Workplaces.* San Francisco: Jossey-Bass, 1991.

Carnevale, A.P., Gainer, L.J., and Meltzer, A.S. *Workplace Basics: The Skills Employers Want.* Alexandria, VA: American Society for Training and Development, 1988.

Casas, R. *Un Diagnóstico sobre la Vinculación Universidad-Empresa CONACYT-ANUIES.* México: ANUIES, Biblioteca de la Educación Superior, Serie Investigaciones, 1998a.

Casas, R. "Nuevas Orientaciones de las Políticas de las Universidades en su Relación con las Empresas." en A. Mungaray y G. Valenti, *Políticas Públicas y Educación Superior.* México, ANUIES, 1998b. http://148.206.180.3/anuies/libros98/libro25/0.htm

Castaños-Lomnitz, H. "La Globalización y la Investigación Científica: El Caso de México." Caracas, CRESALC-UNESCO, *Revista Educación Superior y Sociedad* 6.2 (1995).

Cecchini, Paulo. *The European Challenge 1992: The Benefits of a Single Market.* Hants, England: Wildwood Press, 1988.

Center for North American Studies. "Duke University's Center for North American Studies." http://www.duke.edu/web/northamer, 2002.

Center for Quality Assurance in International Education. "The Impact of Globalization on Mexican Pharmacy: A Profile." *Policy and News Report* 6.2 (1997).

Centre for Higher Education Research and Development. *Globalization, Trade Liberalization and Higher Education: Research Areas and Questions.* Winnipeg: CHERD, University of Manitoba, 2002.

Centre for the Study of Living Standards. "Capital, Labour and Total Factor Productivity Tables by Province." www.csls.ca/ptables.html, 2002.

Centro Nacional de Evaluación para la Educación Superior, A.C. *Acerca del CENEVAL y los Exámenes Generales para el Egreso de la Licenciatura (EGEL).* México: CENEVAL, 1998.

Chartrand, H. H. *International Higher Education: The Peculiar Case of Canada.* Ottawa: Kultural Econometrics International, 1992.

Cheever, Jr., Daniel S. "Higher (and Higher Ed)." *The Boston Sunday Globe*, April 26, 1992, p. 75.

Chidambaranathan, S. "The Internationalisation of Knowledge through Industry/University Cooperation." *AUCC Conference on Seeking Innovation: International Cooperation Among Universities.* Ottawa: Association of Universities and Colleges of Canada, 1992.

Chmura, T.J. "The Higher Education-Economic Development Connection: Emerging Roles for Colleges and Universities." *Economic Development Commentary* 11.3 (1987): 1-7.

Church, E. "Born to be a global business leader." *The Globe and Mail.* January 7, 1999.

Clarke, T. and Barlow, M. MAI: *The Multilateral Agreement on Investment and the Threat to Canadian Sovereignty.* Toronto: Stoddart Publishing Company, 1997.

Clift, J. "International Trade in Legal Services." Paper prepared for the Third International Conference on International Trade in Services. Brisbane, Australia, 12-13 July 12-13, 1995.

Colorado Commission on Higher Education. *Report of Colorado Commission on Higher Education's Program Discontinuance Responsibility.* Denver, 1987.

Commission on the Skills of the American Workforce. *America's Choice: High Skills or Low Wages!* Rochester, NY: National Center for Education and the Economy, 1990.

Commonwealth of Australia. *Arrangement between the Australian Parties and New Zealand Relating to Trans-Tasman Mutual Recognition.* Canberra: Commonwealth of Australia, 1996a.

Commonwealth of Australia. *Skills Recognition Directory for Professional Occupations in ASEAN and Australia.* Canberra: Australian Government Publishing Service, 1996b.

Commonwealth of Australia. *Balance of Payments and International Investment Position,* Catalogue No. 5363. Canberra: Australian Bureau of Statistics, 1997.

Competitiveness Policy Council. *Building a Competitive America: First Annual Report to the President and the Congress.* Washington, D.C., 1992.

Conchello, J.A. *TLC, un Callejón sin Salida.* México: Grijalbo, 1992.

Conference Board of Canada. "Conference Board Says 'Brain Drain' is Real." *The Globe and Mail,* August 16, 1999.

Consejo Nacional de Ciencia y Tecnologia. *Reporte de Actividades Internacionales,* 1994. México: CONACYT, 1994.http://info.main.conacyt.mx/INTERNACIONALES/INDICE.htm

Consejo Nacional de Ciencia y Tecnologia. *Indicadores de Actividades Científicas y Tecnológicas,* 1996 y 1997. México: CONACYT, 1998a.

Consejo Nacional de Ciencia y Tecnologia. *PACIME,* 1991-1997. México: CONACYT, 1998b.

Consortium on North American Higher Education Collaboration (CONAHEC). 1999a. "General Trilateral Meetings on North American Cooperation in Higher Education, Research, and Training." http://elnet.org/trilater/english Consortium on North American Higher Education Collaboration (CONAHEC). 1999b. "North American Higher Education Cooperation: Implementing the Agenda." http://elnet.org/trilater/english/vancouv.htm

Consortium on North American Higher Education Collaboration (CONAHEC). 1999c. "Major Developments." *Update,* 1997-1998 (Summer 1998): 1-2.

Consortium on North American Higher Education Collaboration (CONAHEC). 1999d. "1999-2000 Members." http://conahec.org/members.htm

Consortium on North American Higher Education Collaboration (CONAHEC). "Border Pact Network." 2002. http://www.wiche/edu/conahec/english/bddesc.htm

Coombs, P.H. *A Strategy to Improve the Quality of Mexican Higher Education: A Report to the Secretary of Education from the International Council for Educationnal Development.* México: FCE/SEP, 1992.

"Cornell Faculty Panel Urges Cuts in Jobs So Pay Can Go Up." *The Chronicle of Higher Education,* December 6, 1989, p. A25.

Corporate-Higher Education Forum. *Going Global: Meeting the Need for International Business Expertise in Canada.* Montreal, 1988.

Council on International Education Exchange. *Educating for Global Competence.* Washington, D.C., 1988.

References

Council on International Education Exchange. 1999. "Work in Canada." http://www.ciee.org/work/canada.htm

Council of Ministers of Education, Canada. *Asia-Pacific Economic Cooperation (APEC) and the APEC Education Forum: Briefing note.* Toronto: CMEC, 1996.

Cowen, R. "Internationalization Dilemmas, National Development Strategies and University Systems: England in Comparative Perspective." KIEC and KCUE Conference, Seoul, Korea, 1994.

Craven, Marianne. "USIA Initiatives for North American Trilateral Exchange." 1996. http://www.bc.edu/bc_org/avp/soe/cihe/direct1/News3/textdpt2.html

Crawford, R. *In the Era of Human Capital.* New York: Harper Collins, 1991.

Croft, Patricia. "CBC Radio Interview with Chief Economist for Sceptre Investments." July 24, 2002.

Cullen, J. (1997). "Professional mobility in the European Union." Presentation at the Conference on Trade Agreements, Higher Education, and the Globalization of the Professions. Montreal, May 9, 1997.

Cuomo Commission on Competitiveness. *America's Agenda: Rebuilding Economic Strength.* Armonk, NY: M.E. Sharpe.

Davidow, W.H. and M.S. Malone. *The Virtual Corporation: Structuring and Revitalizing the Corporation for the 21st Century.* New York: Harper-Collins, 1992.

Davis, S.J. "Cross-Country Patterns of Change in Relative Wages." *NBER Macroeconomic Annual* 1992. Cambridge, Mass.: MIT Press, 1992.

Davis, Todd M., ed. *Open Doors, 1994-95: Report on International Educational Exchange.* New York: Institute of International Education, 1995.

Davis, Todd M., ed. *Open Doors, 1995-96: Report on International Educational Exchange.* New York: Institute of International Education, 1996.

Davis, Todd M., ed. *Open Doors, 1996-97: Report on International Educational Exchange.* New York: Institute of International Education, 1997.

Davis, Todd M., ed. *Open Doors, 1997-98: Report on International Educational Exchange.* New York: Institute of International Education, 1998.

DeCloet, Derek. "Official: U.S. Had Recession Last Year." *The National Post,* August 1, 2002, p. FP1.

De la Garza, Guillermo Fernandez, Bertha A. Landrum, and Barbara Samuels. *Teaming Up: Higher Education-Business Partnerships and Alliances in North America.* Boulder, CO: Western Interstate Commission on Higher Education, 1997.

De la Torre, Augusto and Margaret R. Kelley. *Regional Trade Arrangements.* Washington, D.C.: International Monetary Fund, 1992.

Deupree, J. and M. P. Lenn. *Ambassadors of U.S. Higher Education: Quality Credit-Bearing Programs Abroad.* New York: College Board, 1997.

de Wit, H. *Strategies for Internationalisation of Higher Education: A Comparative Study of Australia, Canada, Europe and the United States of America.* Amsterdam: The European Association for International Education, 1995.

Didou, Sylvie. "Las Propuestas de Cooperación Académica Europea en América Latina y México." en R. Rodríguez Gómez, (coord). *La Integración Latinoamericana y las Universidades,* UDUAL, No. 8. México, 1998a.

Didou, Sylvie, (coord). *Integración Económica y Políticas de Educación Superior.* México: ANUIES, Biblioteca de la Educación Superior, 1998b.

Didou Sylvie. *La Acreditación: Enfoques Internacionales.* México: Universidad de Colima and SEP, 1999.

Didou, Sylvie. *Sociedad del Conocimiento e Internacionalización de las Instituciones de Educación Superior en México.* México: ANUIES, 2000.

Dimancescu, D., and Botkin, J. *The New Alliance: America's R&D Consortia.* Cambridge, MA: Ballinger, 1986.

Dobbin, Murray. "A World Ruled by Corporations: More and More, Our Lives are Dominated by the TNCs', *The CCPA Monitor* (April 2001).

Dobell, R. and Neufeld, M. Eds. *Trans-border Citizens: Networks and New Institutions in North America.* Lantzville, B.C.: Oolichan Books, 1994.

Dolbeare, Kenneth M. and Linda J. Medcalf. *American Ideologies: Shaping the New Politics of the 1990s.* 2nd ed. New York: McGraw-Hill, Inc., 1993.

Druker, M., and Robinson, B. (1994). "Implementing Retrenchment Strategies: A Comparison of State Governments and Public Higher Education." *New England Journal of Public Policy* 10.2 (1994): 83-96.

Drucker, Peter. *Post-Capitalist Society.* New York: Harper Business, 1993.

Dukakis, Michael S. and Rosabeth M. Kanter. *Creating the Future: The Massachusetts Comeback and its Promise for America.* New York: Summit Books, 1988.

Dupree, A. Hunter. *Science in the Federal Government: A History of Policies and Activities to 1940.* Cambridge, MA: Harvard University Press, 1957.

Edsall, Thomas B. *The New Politics of Inequality.* New York: W.W. Norton, Inc., 1984.

El-Khawas, E. *Campus Trends,* 1992. Washington, D.C.: American Council on Education, 1992.

El-Khawas, E. *Campus Trends,* 1995. Washington, D.C.: American Council on Education, 1995.

Etzkowitz, Henry. "Entrepreneurial Science in the Academy: A Case of the Transformation of Norms." *Social Problems* 36.1 (1989): 14-28.

Executive Office of the U.S. President. *Standard Industrial Classification Manual.* Washington, D.C.: Office of Management and Budget, 1987.

Fairweather, James S. *Entrepreneurship and Higher Education,* ASHE-ERIC Higher Education Report No. 6. Washington, D.C.: Association for the Study of Higher Education, 1988.

Farell, Johnson y López del Puerto. *Le Rôle de la Technologie dans l'enseignement Supérieur en Amérique du Nord: Les Implications des Politiques en Matière d'éducation.* Boulder, Colorado: Western Interstate Commission on Higher Education, 1997.

Farquhar, R.H. *Advancing the Canadian Agenda for International Education.* Ottawa: Canadian Bureau for International Education, 2001.

Federal Reserve Bank of Boston. *New England Economic Indicators.* Boston, January, 1990.

Federal Reserve Bank of Boston. *New England Economic Indicators.* Boston, March, 1995.

Fellegi, I. P. *Brain Drain—What We Know and What We Don't* . Ottawa, 1999.

Fernández de la Garza G., A. A. Landrum y B. Samuels. *Asociaciones y Alianzas entre Instituciones de Educación Superior y Empresas en América del Norte.* Boulder, Colorado:Western Interstate Commission on Higher Education, 1997.

Finifter, D.H., Baldwin, R.G., and Thelin, J.R., eds. *The Uneasy Public Policy Triangle in Higher Education: Quality, Diversity, and Budgetary Efficiency.* New York: American Council on Education and Macmillan Publishing Co., 1991.

Finn, E. "No Alternatives?" *Canadian Forum* (December 1994).

Finn, Michael G. *Stay Rates of Foreign Doctorate Recipients from U.S. Universities,* 1995. Oak Ridge, Tenn.: Oak Ridge Institute for Science and Education, 1997.

Flint, D. "The Export of Legal Education." Address Given at the 120th Anniversary Seminar and Dinner of the International Law Association. Sydney, Australia. October 16, 1993.

Fundación Mexico Estados Unidos para la Ciencia. *Reporte de Actividades 1994-1998.* México D.F. , 28 avril 1999. http://www.fumec. org.mx/docs/reporte1.htm

Furubotn, Eirik G. and Rudolf Richter, eds. *The New Institutional Economics.* College Station, TX.: Texas A&M University Press, 1991.

Gacel, Avila J. *Internacionalización de la Educación Superior en América Latina y el Caribe: Reflexiones y Lineamientos.* Guadalajara: Organizacion Universitaria Interamericana, 1999.

Gacel-Avila, Jocelyne y Rosa Rojas. "Las Oficinas de Intercambio Académico en las Instituciones de Educación Superior en México." *Educación Global* 3 (1999a): 109-20.

Gacel-Avila, Jocelyne y Rosa Rojas. "Características de los Estudiantes Extranjeros en México." *Educación Global* 3 (1999b): 121-28.

Gacel Avila G., A. Adelman y P. Van der Donck (coord). *Educación Superior e Integración Regional en América del Norte: Primera Conferencia de Rectores de América del Norte, Memorias.* México: Universidad de Guadalajara, 1993.

Gagnon, Y. "Personal Communication to Dr. John Mallea from the Director General, International Cultural Relations Bureau, Department of Foreign Affairs and International Trade." June 26, 2000.

Ganster, P. "La Educación Superior en la Frontera Estados Unidos - México ante el TLC." México: Banco Nacional de Comercio Exterior, *Comercio Exterior* 44.3 (1994).

Ganster, P. "The US- Mexico Border Region (draft)." *In The Border Pact Report: A Region in Transition:The US-Mexico Borderlands and The Role of Higher Education,* Working Paper No. 6. Tuscon, AZ: CONAHEC, 1997.

Garavalia, B. "The Private Sector/Educational Partnership for International Competence." n C. B. Klasek, ed. *Bridges to the Future:Strategies for Internationalizing Higher education.* Carbondale, IL: Association of International Education Administrators, 1992.

Gestrin, Michael and Alan M. Rugman. "The NAFTA Investment Provisions: Prototype for Multilateral Investment Rules?" Pp. 63-77 in OECD, *Market Access After the Uruguay Round: Investment, Competition and Technology Perspectives.* Paris, 1996.

Gibson, D.V., and R.W. Smilor, eds. *University Spin-Off Companies:Economic Development, Faculty Entrepreneurs, and Technology Transfer.* Savage, MD: Rowen and Littlefield, 1991.

Gilbón, Acevedo D.M. y M.E. Gómez Más. "Desarrollo de los Centros de Lenguas Extranjera en las IES de México: Una Primera Aproximación a su Estudio." México: ANUIES, *Revista de la Educación Superior* 99 (1996).

Gill, Judith I. and Lilian Alvarez de Testa. *Understanding the Differences: An Essay on Higher Education in Mexico and the United States.* Boulder, CO: Western Interstate Commission on Higher Education, 1995.

Gilpin, Robert. *Global Political Economy: Understanding the International Economic Order.* Princeton: Princeton University Press, 2001.

Gingras, Y., B. Godin, and M. Foisy. "The Internationalisation of University Research in Canada." In S. Bond, and J.P. Lemasson, eds., *A New World of Knowledge: Canadian Universities and Globalization.* Ottawa: International Development Research Centre, 1999.

Global Alliance for Transnational Education. (n.d.). *Achieving Worldwide Access to Quality Education and Training.* Washington, D.C.: GATE.

"Globalization of Higher Education and the Professions: The Case of North America." *QAUSA* 2.3 (Winters 1993): 1-2.

Gómez Palacios, M. "Cooperación Internacional , Desafíos y Oportunidades en el Contexto del TLC." México: ANUIES, *Revista de la Educación Superior* 96 (1995).

Goodwin, Craufurd D. and Michael Nacht. *Missing the Boat: The Failure to Internationalize American Higher Education.* Cambridge: Cambridge University Press, 1991.

Government of Mexico. *The Globalization of Higher Education and the Professions: The Case of North America.* Mexico City: Ministry of Public Education, 1994.

Graham, Edward M. "Investment and the New Multilateral Trade Context." Pp. 35-62 in OECD, *Market Access After the Uruguay Round: Investment, Competition and Technology Perspectives.* Paris, 1996.

Graham, J. "Third Pillar or Fifth Wheel? International Education and Cultural Foreign Policy." Pp. 137-154 in F.O. Hampson, M. Hart, and M. Rudner, eds., *Canada Among Nations 1999: A Big League Player?* Don Mills, Ontario: Oxford University Press, 1999.

Grassmuck, Karen. "Columbia University Uses Philosophy of 'Selective Excellence' to Make Painful Cuts in Programs, Administration." *Chronicle of Higher Education,* April 25, 1990, p. 1.

Grayson, George W. *The North American Free Trade Agreement.* New York: Foreign Policy Association, 1993.

Guevara, Niebla G. y N. García Canclini (coord). *La Educación y la Cultura ante el Tratado de Libre Comercio.* México: Nexos/Nueva Imagen, 1992.

Gumport, Patricia J. (1993). "The Contested Terrain of Academic Program reduction." *Journal of Higher Education* 64.3 (1993): 283-331.

Halstead, K. *Higher Education Revenues: A Study of Institutional Costs.* Washington, D.C.: Research Associates, 1992.

Hammer, Michael and James Champy. *Reengineering the Corporation: A Manifesto for Business Revolution.* New York: Harper Collins, 1993.

Harari, M. "Some Reflections on the Future of International Education." Proceedings of the International Association of University Presidents, International Education Seminar, Bangkok, Thailand, July 24, 1992a.

Harari, M. "Internationalization of the Curriculum." In C.B. Klasek, ed., Bridges to the Future: *Strategies for Internationalizing Higher Education.* Carbondale, IL: Association of International Education Administrators, 1992b.

Harney, J.O. (1991). "Disinvestment: Higher Education's Shrinking Piece of the Pie." *Connection: New England's Journal of Higher Education and Economic Development* 6 (1991): 12-18.

Harvey, E.B. "The Alliance for Higher Education and Enterprise in North America." Paper Delivered at a Meeting of the Inter-American Organization for Higher Education, Quebec City, Canada, 1999.
http://www.northamericaninstitute.org/alliance/quebec.html

Hay, D.A. "Anti-competitive Practices, Market Access and Competition Policy in a Global Economy,' Pp. 81-100 in OECD, *Market Access after the Uruguay Round: Investment, Competition and Technology Perspectives.* Paris, 1996.

Hayward, F.M. "International Opportunities and Challenges for American Higher Education in Africa, Asia, and Latin America." Pp. 117-140 in Katherine H. Hanson and Joel W. Meyerson, eds., *International Challenges to American Colleges and Universities.* Phoenix, Arizona: American Council on Education and Oryx Press, 1995.

Head, I. L. *On a Hinge of History: The Mutual Vulnerability of South and North.* Toronto: University of Toronto Press, 1991.

Hellyer, P. *The Evil Empire: Globalization's Darker Side.* Toronto: Chimo Media Ltd, 1997.

Helpman, E. and Krugman, P. *Market Structure and Foreign Trade.* Cambridge, MA: M.I.T. Press, 1985.

Hinojosa-Ojeda, Raul. "NAFTA's Next Steps: Hemispheric and Global Implications." Pp. 87-102 in OECD, *Regionalism and its Place in the Multilateral Trading System.* Paris, 1996.

Hirschhorn, Larry. "The Postindustrial Labour Process." *New Political Science* 2 (1981): 5-47.

Holmes, J. "Export-readiness in the Canadian Education Sector." *CBIE Research No. 8.* Ottawa: Canadian Bureau for International Education, 1996.

Hong Kong Society of Accountants. *New Professional Accreditation System.* Hong Kong: HKSA, 1997.

Hornbeck, D. and L. Salamon, eds. *Human Capital and America's Future.* Baltimore: Johns Hopkins University Press, 1991.

Hufbauer, Gary Clyde and Kimberly Ann Elliott. *Measuring the Costs of Protection in the United States.* Washington, D.C.: Institute for International Economics, 1994.

Hufbauer, Gary Clyde and Anup Malani. "Economic Dimensions of Regionalism." Pp. 20-56 in Peggy Blumenthal, Craufurd Goodwin, Alan Smith, and Ulrich Teichler, eds., *Academic Mobility in a Changing World.* London and Bristol, Penn.: Jessica Kingsley Publishers, 1996.

Hufbauer, Gary Clyde and Jeffrey J. Schott, *North American Free Trade: Issues and Recommendations.* Washington, D.C.: Institute for International Economics, 1992.

Hufbauer, Gary Clyde and Jeffrey J. Schott, *NAFTA: An Assessment,* revised ed. Washington, D.C.: Institute for International Economics, 1993a.

Hufbauer, Gary Clyde and Jeffrey J. Schott, *Western Hemisphere Economic Integration.* Washington, D.C.: Institute for International Economics, 1993b.

Human Resources Development Canada. *Program for North American Mobility in Higher Education.* Important Summary Data. Ottawa, 1999.

Humphries, J. *Where the Students Are: An Analysis of the Major Competing Countries for the International Student Market.* Ottawa: Canadian Bureau for International Education, 1996.

Huntington, Samuel P. *The Clash of Civilizations and the Remaking of World Order.* New York: Simon and Schuster, 1996.

IEA. *National Competency Standards for Professional Engineers (stages 1 and 2).* Barton, ACT: The Institution of Engineers, 1993.

Industry Canada. *Education and Training Services: Part 1--Overview and Prospects. Sector Competitiveness Frameworks.* Ottawa: Industry Canada, 1998.

Institute of International Education. 1997. *Survey and Evaluation of North American Higher Education Cooperation.* Washington, D.C.: U.S. Information Agency.www.iie.org/Content/NavigationMenu/Research_Publications/Archives/l inkages.pdf

Institute for International Education. "IIE/Latin America." 1999a. http://www.iie.org/latinamerica

Institute for International Education. "Regional Educational Advising Consultancy for Mexico, Central America, and the Caribbean." 1999b. http://www.iie.org/latinamerica/reac Institute for International Education. "Country Summary for Graduate Study and Research Abroad in 2000/2001." 1999c. http://iie.org/cgi-bin/george/point.pl

Institute for International Education. "USIA Fulbright: 1999/2000 Competition Statistics." 1999d. http://iie.org/fulbright/us/stats2000.htm

Instituto Nacional de Estadística, Geografía e Informática. *Los Profesionistas en México.* México: INEGI, 1993.

Instituto Nacional de Estadística, Geografía e Informática. *Encuesta Nacional de Educación, Capacitación y Empleo,* 1995. México D.F, INEGI/ Secretaria del Trabajo y Previsión Social, 1996.

Instituto Tecnológico y de Estudios Superiores de Monterrey. "Camino a la Excelencia. La Transformación del Cuerpo Docente del Sistema Tecnológico de Monterrey de 1989 a 1995'. México, *Revista de la Educación Superior,* 94 (1996).

International Association of Students in Economics and Management. *Educating Tomorrow's Global Gusiness Leaders.* Brussels: AIESEC, 1995.

International Association of Universities. *Internationalization of Higher Education: IAU Statement-1998.* Paris: UNESCO, 1998. http://www.unesco.org/iau/tfi-statement.html

International Legal Services Advisory Committee. *Australia in Asia: Legal Education Challenges and Opportunities.* Canberra: ILSAC, 1992.

International Legal Services Advisory Committee. *Australian International Legal Education and Training: Directions, Issues and Opportunities.* Canberra: ILSAC. 1995.

International Union of Artchitects. "Proposed 1997-1999 Professional Practice Program." As Approved by the 86th Session of the International Union of Architects Council Meeting at Chandigarn, India, 1997.

Janow, Merit E. "Public and Private Restraints That Limit Access to Markets." Pp. 101-122 in OECD, *Market Access After the Uruguay Round: Investment, Competition and Technology Perspectives.* Paris, 1996.

Japan. "APEC, Best Practices in Engineering Accreditation, Recognition and Development Project: Response to Survey Questionnaire prepared by Japan Consulting Engineers." Jakarta: APEC Secretariat, 1997.

Johnson, L.G. *The High Technology Connection: Academic/Industrial Cooperation for Economic Growth.* Washington, D.C.: Association for the Study of Higher Education, 1984.

Johnston, W.B. *Workforce 2000: Work and Workers for the Twenty-First Century.* Indianapolis: Hudson Institute, 1987.

Johnston, W.B. "Global Workforce 2000: The New World Labor Market." *Harvard Business Review* 69 (1991): 115-27.

Johnstone, D.Bruce. "The Costs of Higher Education: Worldwide Issues and Trends for the 1990s." Pp. 3-24 in Philip G. Altbach and D. Bruce Johnstone, eds., *The Funding of Higher Education: International Perspectives.* New York and London: Garland Publishing, 1993.

Katz, Stanley. "The Future of Educational Exchange in North America: A View from the United States." Pp. 220-236 in Peggy Blumenthal, Craufurd Goodwin, Alan Smith, and Ulrich Teichler, eds., *Academic Mobility in a Changing World.* London and Bristol, PA: Jessica Kingsley Publishers, 1996.

Kennedy, Paul. *Preparing for the Twenty-First Century.* Toronto: Harper Collins, 1993.

Kenski, H.C. and M.C. Kenski. *A Profile of Canadian Studies in the United States.* Washington, D.C.: Association for Canadian Studies in the United States, 1991.

Kerr, Clark. *The Uses of the University, With a Postscript - 1972.* Cambridge, MA: Harvard University Press, 1977.

Kettinger, W.J., and R.D. Wertz, R.D. "The Financial Restructuring of Higher Education: Reengineering or Radical Reform?" *Journal for Higher Education Management* 9.1 (1993): 13-27.

Killian, C. "Exporting Education." *The Georgia Straight* (August 21-28, 1997).

Knight, J. "Internationalization: Management Strategies and Issues." *International Education Magazine,* (1993).

Knight, J. *Internationalizing Higher Education: A Shared Vision?*. Ottawa: CBIE, 1996.

Knight, J. and H. De Wit, eds. *Internationalization of Higher Education in Asia Pacific Countries.* Amsterdam: European Association for International Education, 1997.

Knowles, A. S. *The International Encyclopedia of Higher Education,* vol. 5. San Francisco: Jossey-Bass, 1997.

Krugman, Paul. "Europe Jobless, America Penniless?". *Foreign Affairs* 95 (Summer 1994a): 19-34.

Krugman, Paul. "Competitiveness: Does it Matter?" *Fortune* 129 (March 7, 1994b): 109-15.

Krugman, Paul. "Competitiveness: A Dangerous Obsession." *Foreign Affairs.* 72.2 (1994c): 28-44.

Krugman, Paul. *Peddling Prosperity: Economic Sense in the Age of Diminished Expectations.* New York: W.W. Norton Co., Inc., 1994d.

Laird, Sam. "Fostering Regional Integration." Pp. 169-*191 in OECD, Regionalism and its Place in the Multilateral Trading System.* Paris, 1996.

Laird, Sam. and Alexander Yeats. *Quantitative Methods for Trade-Barrier Analysis.* Washington Square, NY: New York University Press, 1990.

Lambert, Richard D. *International Studies and the Undergraduate.* Washington, D.C.: American Council on Education, 1989.

Lambert, Richard D. "Foreign Student Flows and the Internationalization of Higher Education." Pp. 18-41 in Katherine H. Hanson and Joel W. Meyerson, eds., *International Challenges to American Colleges and Universities.* Phoenix, Arizona: American Council on Education and Oryx Press, 1995.

Langfitt, T.W. "Growth by Substitution Rather Than By Accretion: Quality Versus Size and Scale." *Policy Perspectives* 2.1 (1989).

Larsen, Kurt, Rosemary Morris, and John P. Martin. *Trade in Education Services: Trends and Emerging Issues.* Paris: OECD Centre for Educational Research and Innovation, OECD Document CERI/CD/RD(2001)6.

Latapí, P. "Asimetrías Educativas ante el TLC." México, Banco Nacional de Comercio Exterior, *Comercio Exterior,* 44.3 (1994).

Latimer, J.,ed.. *Peterson's Guide to Four-Year Colleges,* 1998. Princeton: Peterson's Guides, Inc., 1998a.

Latimer, J., ed. *Peterson's Graduate and Professional Programs: An Overview, 1998.* Princeton: Peterson's Guides, Inc, 1998b.

Latin American Studies Association. *Latin American Studies in North America,* 1995-1996. Pittsburgh: University of Pittsburgh, 1996.

Lawrence, Robert Z. "Towards Globally Contestable Markets." Pp.25-34 in OECD, *Market Access After the Uruguay Round: Investment, Competition and Technology Perspectives.* Paris, 1996.

Laver, R. (1999). "Nortel's Driving Force." *Maclean's.* August 2, 1999, pp. 13-18.

Laxer, J. *False Gods: How the Globalization Myth has Impoverished Canada.* Toronto: Lester Publishing, 1993.

Laxer, J. *In Search of a New Left: Canadian Politics after the Neo-conservative Assault.* Toronto: Penguin, 1997.

Layzel, D.T., and Lyddon, J.W. *Budgeting for Higher Education at the State Level,* ASHE-ERIC Higher Education Report No. 4. Washington, D.C.: Association for the Study of Higher Education, 1990.

Lee, Thea. *False Prophets: The Selling of NAFTA.* Washington, D.C.: Economic Policy Institute, 1995.

Lemasson, J.P. "Introduction: The Internationalisation of Canadian Iniversities." In S.L. Bond, and J.P. Lemasson, *A New World of Knowledge: Canadian Universities and Globalization.* Ottawa: International Development Research Centre, 1999.

Lenin, Vladimir I. *Imperialism: The Highest Stage of Capitalism.* New York: International Publishers, 1939.

Lenn, M. P. and L. Campos, L., eds. *Globalization of the Professions and the Quality Imperative: Professional Accreditation, Certification, and Licensure.* Madison, WI: Magna Publications, 1997.

Lenn, M. P. and L. Campos, eds. *Multinational Discourse on Professional Accreditation, Certification, and Licensure: Bridges for the Globalizing Professions.* Washington D. C.: Center for Quality Assurance in International Education, 1998.

Leslie, L. and Brinkman, P. *The Economic Value of Higher Education.* New York: Macmillan Co., 1998.

Levinson, Jerome I. *The Labor Side Accords to the North American Free Trade Agreement: An Endorsement of Abuse of Worker Rights in Mexico.* Washington, D.C.: Economic Policy Institute, 1993

Lewington, J. "Steady Drop in Foreign Students Hurts Canadian Education System." *Globe and Mail,* October 9, 1995, p. A5.

Leyton-Brown, David. "Political Dimensions of Regionalization in a Changing World." Pp. 7-19 in Peggy Blumenthal, Craufurd Goodwin, Alan Smith, and Ulrich Teichler, eds., *Academic Mobility in a Changing World.* London and Bristol, PA: Jessica Kingsley Publishers, 1996.

Libertas. "Guía de Instituciones de Educación Superior en México." México, 1998. http://www.libertas.com.mx/catalogo/geografico.htm

Lindgren, A. "Brain Gain Offsets So-called Brain Drain." *The Ottawa Citizen,* November 8, 1997, pp. B1-B2.

Little, Bruce "Jobs Boom Hits Record as Economy Roars Ahead." *The Globe and Mail,* July 6, 2002a, p. A1.

Little, Bruce. "Experts at Odds on Economy's Direction." *The Globe and Mail,* July 27, 2002b, p. B6.

Little, Bruce. "Canadian Economy Takes May 'Breather'." *The Globe and Mail,* August 1, 2002c, p. B1.

Loiello, J.P. "Remarks to the Opening Plenary Session of General Meeting on Cooperation in Higher Education, Research, and Training in North America, April 28, 1996." http://elnet.org/trilater/english/guadalajara/index.htm

Logan, M. "Internationalisation: Challenges for the Next Decade." Presentation at the IMHE/OECD Conference on the Internationalisation of Higher Education in the Asia-Pacific Region, October, 7-9, 1996. Melbourne, Australia.

López, G. J. "México en la Perspectiva del Tratado de Libre Comercio." In Niebla G. Guevara y N. García Canclini (coord). *La Educación y la Cultura ante el Tratado de Libre Comercio.* México: Nexos/Nueva Imagen, 1992.

Lozoya, Thalmann J.A *La Nueva Política Mexicana de Cooperación Internacional.* México: SRE-PNUD, 1999.

MacCordy, E.L. "Managing Technology Transfer." In Richard E. Anderson and Joel W. Meyerson, eds., *Productivity and Higher Education.* Princeton: Peterson's Guides, Inc., 1992.

McCleery, R. K. "The Dynamics of Integration in the Americas: A Look at the Political Economy of NAFTA Expansion." In Donald Barry and Ronald C. Keith, eds., *Regionalism, Multilateralism, and the Politics of Global Trade.* Vancouver and Toronto: UBC Press, 1999.

McMahon, W.W. "The Relation of Education and R&D to Productivity Growth (in OECD Nations)." *Economics of Education Review* 3.4 (1984): 299-314.

McQuaig, Linda. *The Cult of Impotence: Selling the Myth of Powerlessness in the Global Economy.* Toronto: Penguin, 1998.

Mahroum, S. "Europe and the Challenge of the Brain Drain." *IPTS* 29 (1998). http://www.jrc.es/iptsreport/vol29/english/SAT1E296.htm.

Mallea, John R. "North American Cooperation in Higher Education: Optimizing Complementarities." *Proceedings of the Wingspread Conference.* Racine, WI: The Johnson Foundation, 1992.

Mallea, John R. "Human Resources Development and Higher Education in the Triad: Europe, North America and Japan." In *Proceedings of the Seminar on Education and Resource Development for the Pacific Basin. Co-partnership Strategies and Actions.* Guadalajara: Universidad Autonoma de Guadalajara, 1994a.

Mallea, John R. "The Views and Activities of Stakeholders on the Internationalisation of Higher Education." Paper delivered at the International Conference on Learning Beyond Schooling–New Forms of Supply and New Demands. Paris: OECD/CERI, 1994b.

Mallea, John R. "Monitoring an Institution's International Dimension." Paper presented at the Conference on Excellence in Education, Autonomous University of Guadalajara. 1995.

Mallea, John R. "The Internationalisation of Higher Education–Stakeholder Views in North America." In *Internationalisation of higher education*. Paris: OECD/CERI, 1996.

Mallea, John R. "Internationalisation of Higher Education and the Professions.' In *International Trade in Professional Services Advancing Liberalization Through Regulatory Reform.* Paris: OECD, 1997.

Mallea, John R. *International Trade in Professional and Educational Services: Implications for the Professions and Higher Education.* Paris: OECD, 1998a. http://www.oecd.org./els/edu/ceri/index.htm

Mallea, John R. "Globalization. NAFTA and Higher Education in Canada (draft)." México, Proyecto de Investigación Trinacional sobre Globalización, TLCAN y Educación Superior, El Colegio de México A.C., 1998b.

Mallea, John R. "Globalisation, Trade Liberalisation and Higher Education in North America." Wei Lun Lecture Series, Chinese University of Hong Kong, 1999.

Mallea, John R., Salvador Malo, and Dell Pendergrast. The Vancouver Communique Revisited: *An Assessment.* Boulder, CO: Western Interstate Commission for Higher Education, 1997.

Mallea, J., M. Harari y T. Bates. "El Procesos de Internacionalización de la Universidad de Guadalajara: Perspectivas y Propuestas'. Guadalajara, 1999. http://148.202.2.214/dimenint.htm

Malo, S. *El Proceso de Revisión de la Calidad de la Internacionalización en la Universidad Nacional Autónoma de México.* México, UNAM/Dirección General de Planeación, Documento de Trabajo, 1999.

Malo, S. y A. Velázquez (coords). *La Calidad en la Educación Superior en México: Una Comparación Internacional.* México, UNAM/Coordinación de Humanidades/M.A. Porrúa, 1998.

Mangum, Garth L. *Youth and America's Future.* Washington, D.C.: William T. Grant Foundation Commission on Work, Family, and Citizenship, 1989.

Marmolejo, F. "Redes de Colaboración en América del Norte: El Caso del CONAHEC." *Educación Global* 2 (1998).

Marmolejo, F. y F. León García. *Higher Education in the US Mexico Borderlands: A Profile.* Tuscon, AZ: CONAHEC, 1997.

Marroquín, E. J. (1990). "Sobre la Investigación para el Desarrollo Local y Regional de la Zona Fronteriza (Mex-EUA)." México: ANUIES, *Revista de la Educación Superior* 74 (1990).

Martín, Christopher. "El Programa para el Mejoramiento del Profesorado y el Consejo Británico." *Educación Global* 3 (1999): 61-68.

Martin, J. and Samels, J.E. *Merging Colleges for Mutual Growth: A New Strategy for Academic Managers.* Baltimore: Johns Hopkins University Press, 1994.

Massy, W.F., and M.C. Hulfactor, "Optimizing Allocation Strategy." Pp. 25-44 in P.G. Altbach and D.G. Johnstone, eds., *The Funding of Higher Education: International Perspectives.* New York and London: Garland Publishing, Inc., 1993.

Massy, W.F., and J.W. Meyerson, *Strategy and Finance in Higher Education.* Princeton: Peterson's Guides, Inc., 1992.

Massy, W.F., and R. Zemsky. "Faculty Discretionary Time: Departments and the Academic Ratchet." *Journal of Higher Education* 65.1 (1994): 1-22.

Mateo F., ed.. "El Comercio Transfronterizo y los Servicios Profesionales." *En Regulación de las Profesiones, Situación Actual y Prospectiva,* Memoria. México: SEP/SESIC/Dirección General de Profesiones, 1996.

Matkin, G.W. *Technology Transfer and the University.* New York: American Council on Education and Macmillan Publishing Co., 1990.

Méndez Lugo, B. "Homologación, Certificación y Acreditación en el Contexto del TLC: Asimetrías Nacionales y Vulnerabilidad del Profesionista Mexicano." Caracas, CRESALC-UNESCO, *Revista Educación Superior y Sociedad* 6.2 (1995).

Menzies, H. *Whose Brave New World? The Information Highway and the New Economy.* Toronto: Between the Lines, 1996.

Meyerson, J.W., eds. *International Challenges to American Colleges and Universities.* Phoenix, AZ: American Council on Education and Oryx Press.

Miles, M. "Services: The Interdependent Economy." Paper Presented at Japanese Service Investment in Europe, Programme of Policy Research in Engineering, Science and Technology, Manchester, England: University of Manchester, April 1995.

Mims, R.S. "Resource Allocation: Stopgap or Support for Academic Planning?" *New Directions for Institutional Research* 28 (1980): 57-72.

Ministry for Foreign Affairs and International Trade, Canada. (1994). "The International Dimension of Higher Education in Canada. A Draft Discussion Paper on a Collaborative Policy Framework." Ottawa, 1994.

Ministry of Supply and Services, Canada. *Prosperity Through Competitiveness.* Ottawa: Prosperity Secretariat, 1991a.

Ministry of Supply and Services, Canada. *Learning Well . . . Living Well.* Ottawa: Prosperity Secretariat, 1991b.

Minister of Supply and Services. *Industrial Competitiveness: A Sectoral Perspective.* Ottawa, 1991c.

Mishel, Lawrence and Jared Bernstein. *Declining Wages for High School and College Graduates: Pay And Benefits Trends by Education, Gender, Occupation, and State, 1979-1991.* Washington, D.C.: Economic Policy Institute, 1992.

Mishel, Lawrence and Ruy A. Teixeira. *The Myth of the Coming Labor Shortage: Jobs, Skills, and Incomes of America's Workforce 2000.* Washington, D.C.: Economic Policy Institute, 1991.

Mortimer, K.P., and M.L.Tierney, *The Three R's of the Eighties: Reduction, Reallocation, and Retrenchment.* Washington, D.C.: American Association for Higher Education, 1979.

Muiño, Kielman J. "Una Amplia red de Convenios: Las Relaciones Académicas y Científicas entre México y Alemania." Francfort, *Desarrollo y Cooperación* 1 (1998).

Mungaray, A. "Retos y Perspectivas de la Educación Superior de México Hacia Finales del Siglo." México: Banco Nacional de Comercio Exterior, *Comercio Exterior* 44.3 (1994).

Mungaray, A. "Concepto y Práctica del Papel de la ANUIES en la Colaboración Interinstitucional a Nivel Superior en América del Norte." México: ANUIES, *Revista de la Educación Superior* 99 (1996).

Mungaray, A. and D. Sanchez. "Transference of Courses and Degrees from a Trilateral Higher Education Perspective." Paper Presented in the Roundtable on the Impact of NAFTA on Educational Policy and Assessment in Higher Education, June 9-11, 1995. Montreal: University of Montreal, 1995.

Mungaray, A. y M. Green. *Colaboración Aacadémica México-Estados Unidos.* México: ANUIES, Col. Temas de hoy 23 (1997).

Munro, M. "Generation Debt." *Canadian Forum.* (January/February 1995).

Murphy, Kevin and Finis Welch. "Wage Premiums for College Graduates: Recent Growth and Possible Explanations." *Educational Researcher* 18 (1989): 17-27.

National Association of Foreign Student Advisors. "Creating an International Education Policy." 1999. http://www.nafsa.org/int-ed/speech.html

National Association of Foreign Student Advisors. "Toward an International Education Policy for the United States." 2000a. http://www.nafsa.org/int-ed/22200.html and http://www.nafsa.org/int-ed/policy.html

National Association of Foreign Student Advisors. "President Clinton Issues Executive Memorandum on International Education." 2000b. http://www.nafsa.org/niep/action.html

National Association of Foreign Student Advisors. "Memorandum for the Heads of Executive Departments and Agencies." 2000c. http://www.nafsa.org/int-ed/exec.memo/011900.html

National Association of Foreign Student Advisors. "NAFSA Issue Briefs: International Education Exchange." 2000d. http://www.nafsa.org/advo/issue-briefs/ed_exchanges.html

National Association of Foreign Student Advisors. "NAFSA Issue Briefs: Increase Funding for Title VI/Fulbright-Hays Programs." 2000e. http://www.nafsa.org/advo/issuebriefs/titlevi.html

National Association of Foreign Student Advisors. "NAFSA Releases International Education Policy Statement." 2000f. http://www.nafsa.org/int-ed/statement.html

National Education Goals Panel. *The National Education Goals Report: Building a Nation of Learners, 1997.* Washington, D.C.: Government Printing Office, 1997.

National Housing and Homelessness Network. "State of the Crisis, 2001: A Report on Housing and Homelessness in Canada." The CCPA Monitor (March 2002): 3.

National Science Foundation. *University-Industry Research Relationship: Myths, Realities and Potentials*. Washington, D.C.: Government Printing Office, 1982.

National Task Force on Undergraduate Education Abroad. *A National Mandate for Education Abroad: Getting on With The Task.* Washington, D.C.: Council for International Education Exchange, 1990.

New England Board of Higher Education. *Regional Conference on The Financial Crisis Facing New England Colleges: Mutual Problems and Solutions; Selected Articles and Press Clippings*. Boston, 1992.

New Zealand. (n.d.). *The Record of Learning.* Wellington: New Zealand Qualifications Authority. Newman, Frank. Higher Education and the American Resurgence. Princeton: Carnegie Foundation for the Advancement of Teaching, 1985.

Newson, Janice. "Constructing the 'Post-Industrial University': Institutional Budgeting and University-Corporate Linkages." Pp. 285-304 in P.G. Altbach and D.B. Johnstone, eds., *The Funding of Higher Education: International Perspectives.* New York and London: Garland Publishing, Inc., 1993.

Newson, Janice and Howard Buchbinder. *The University Means Business: Universities, Corporations, and Academic Work.* Toronto: Garamond Press, 1988.

Nissman, Cara. "Northern Exposure: Canadian Colleges Attract Growing Number of U.S. Students." *Boston Herald,* November 11, 2002, p. 34.

"North American Free Trade Agreement." Http://the-tech.mit.edu./Bulletins/Nafta North American Institute. "About the North American Institute." 2000. http://www.northamericaninstitute.org

NZSA. *Admissions Policy: Guidelines for Practical Experience, Mentors and Approved Training Organisations.* Wellington: New Zealand Society of Accountants, 1995.

O'Connor, J. *The Fiscal Crisis of the State.* New York: St. Martin's Press, 1973.

O'Connor, Kevin. "From the Back Bay to Bankrolls: What Massachusetts' Visionary Tradition is Doing for International Students." Pp. 113-14 in Todd M. Davis, ed., Open Doors, 1994-95: *Report on International Educational Exchange.* New York: Institute of International Education, 1995.

Ocegueda, Hernández J.M. *Integración Económica Regional y Educación Superior en México.* México: ANUIES, Temas de hoy No. 20, 1997.

Office of Technology Assessment. *U.S.-Mexico Trade? Pulling Together or Pulling Apart?*, ITE-545. Washington, D.C.: Government Printing Office, 1992.

Office of the Commissioner of Higher Education. *Issues in Montana Higher Education: A Report Requested by the Montana Board of Regents of Higher Education.* Helena, 1986.

Office of the United States President. *Economic Report of the President.* Washington, D.C.: Government Printing Office, 1993.

Office of the United States President. *Economic Report of the President.* Washington, D.C.: Government Printing Office, 1997.

Ojeda Delgado, A. (1994). 'Educación superior, economía y sociedad en el occidente de México'. México: Banco Nacional de Comercio Exterior, *Comercio Exterior*, 44 (3).

Ojeda, Gómez M. "Documento Sobre Identidad y Entendimiento Mutuo en la Región de Norteamérica: La Promoción de Intercambio Académico y la Cooperación entre Socios

Desiguales." Estados Unidos, Racine, Conferencia de Wingspread, 1992.

Okamoto, K. *Foreign Students in OECD Countries: Changing Flows and Policy Trends.* Tokyo: Ministry of Education, Science, and Culture, 1990.

Olivera Lozano, G. "Economic change in Metropolitan Mexico." México: Banco Nacional de Comercio Exterior', *Comercio Exterior* 47.3 (1997). http://www.bancomext.gob.mx

Opper, Susan, Ulrich Teichler, and Jerry Carlson. *Impacts of Study Abroad Programmes on Students and Graduates.* London: Jessica Kingsley Publishers, 1990.

Organisation for Economic Cooperation and Development. "Higher Education in a New International Setting: International Dimensions of Quality Assurance." Paris: OECD/CERI, 1993a.

Organisation for Economic Cooperation and Development. "Internationalisation: Views and Activities of Stakeholders. Preliminary Version." Paris: OECD/CERI, 1993b.

Organisation for Economic Cooperation and Development. *México, 1995.* París: OECD, 1995.

Organisation for Economic Cooperation and Development. *L'économie Fondée sur le Savoir.* Paris: OECD, 1996a.

Organisation for Economic Cooperation and Development. *Employment and Growth in the Knowledge-Based Economy.* Paris: OECD, 1996b.

Organisation for Economic Cooperation and Development. *Indicators of Tariff and Non-tariff Trade Barriers.* Paris: OECD, 1996c.

Organisation for Economic Cooperation and Development. *Measuring What People Know: Human Capital Accounting for the Knowledge Economy.* Paris: OECD, 1996d.

Organisation for Economic Cooperation and Development. *Trade Liberalisation Policies in Mexico.* Paris: OECD, 1996e.

Organisation for Economic Cooperation and Development. *Internationalisation of Higher Education.* París: OECD, 1996f.

Organisation for Economic Cooperation and Development. *International Trade in Professional Services: Advancing Liberalisation Through Regulatory Reform.* Paris: OECD, 1997.

Ortega, A. D. C. Las Profesiones en México. México: Universidad de Colima/SEP, 1999.Ortega S. "El TLC de la Zona Norteamericana y el Proceso de Modernización de la Educación Superior." *El Cotidiano* 66 (1994).

Ostry, S. "Technology Issues in the International Trading System." Pp. 145-70 in OECD, *Market Access After the Uruguay Round: Investment, Competition and Technology Perspectives.* Paris, 1996.

Ostry, S. *The Post-Cold War Trading System: Who's on First?* Chicago: University of Chicago Press, 1997.

Pal, Leslie A., ed. *How Ottawa Spends. 1999-2000. Shape Shifting: Canadian Governance Toward the 21st Century.* Don Mills: Oxford University Press, 1999.

Pallán, C. *El Intercambio Académico Internacional de México.* México: ANUIES. Temas de hoy No. 12, 1996.

Parker, L. "Industry-University Research Collaboration: An Option for Generating Revenue." Pp. 101-124 in P.G. Altbach and D.B. Johnstone, eds., *The Funding of Higher Education: International Perspectives.* New York and London: Garland Publishing, 1993.

Pastor, R.A. "NAFTA as the Center of an Integration Process: The Nontrade Issues." Pp. 176-209 in Nora Lustig, Barry P. Bosworth, and Robert Z. Lawrence, eds., *North American Free Trade*: Assessing the Impact. Washington, D.C.: Brookings Institution.

Perelman, L.J. *The Learning Enterprise: Adult Learning, Human Capital, and Economic Development.* Washington, D.C.: Council of State Planning Agencies, 1984.

Pérez, Franco L y C. Cárdenas Cabello. "La Internacionalización de los Sistemas de Educación Superior: Un Acercamiento al Caso Mexicano." *Sociológica* 13.36 (1998).

Piore, Michael J. and Charles F. Sabel. *The Second Industrial Divide.* New York: Basic Books, 1984.

Poder Ejecutivo Federal. *Programa para la Modernización Educativa,1989-1994.* México: Poder Ejecutivo Federal, 1998.

Poder Ejecutivo Federal. *Programa de Desarrollo Educativo, 1995-2000.* México: Poder Ejecutivo Federal, 1999.

Poggi, Gianfranco. *The State: Its Nature, Development and Prospects.* Stanford: Stanford University Press, 1990.

Ponton, Beatriz Calvo, Paul Ganster, Fernando Leon-Garcia, and Francisco Marmolejo. *A Region in Transition: The U.S.-Mexico Borderlands and the Role of Higher Education (The BORDER PACT REPORT).* Boulder, Colo.: Western Interstate Commission on Higher Education, 1997.

Porter, Michael E. *The Competitive Advantage of Nations.* New York: The Free Press, 1990.

Porter, Michael E. *The Competitive Advantage of Massachusetts*. Boston: Secretary of the Commonwealth, 1991a.

Porter, Michael E. *Canada at the Crossroads: The Reality of a New Competitive Environment*. Ottawa: Business Council on National Issues and Minister of Supply and Services, 1991b.

President's Council of Advisors on Science and Technology. *Renewing the Promise: Research-Intensive Universities and the Nation*. Washington, D.C.: Government Printing Office, 1992.

Rahm, D. "Academic Perceptions of University Firm Technology Transfer." *Policy Studies Journal* 22.2 (1994): 267-78.

Ramirez de la O, Rogelio. "The North American Free Trade Agreement from a Mexican Perspective." Pp. 60-86 in Steven Globerman and Michael Walker, eds., Assessing NAFTA: *A Trinational Analysis*. Vancouver: The Fraser Institute, 1993.

Ramonet, I. "Régimes globalitaires." París: Le Monde Diplomatique, 1997.

Reich, Robert B. *The Work of Nations: Preparing Ourselves for 21st-Century Capitalism*. New York: Vintage Books, 1992.

Reguly, Eric. "Hollowing Out: Canadian Big Business Wakes Up to Peril of Globalization." *The Globe and Mail,* July 1, 2002, p. B7.

Resendiz D. "La Agenda Mexicana para Mejorar la Calidad de la Educación Superior." *Revista de la Educación Superior* 105 (1998).

Rhoades, Gary. "Retrenchment Clauses in Faculty Union Contracts: Faculty Rights and Administrative Discretion." *Journal of Higher Education* 64.3 (1993): 312-47.

Rodriquez, E.M. *Building a Quality Workforce: An Agenda for Postsecondary Education*. Denver: State Higher Education Executive Officers, 1992.

Roemer, Paul M. "Increasing Returns and Long-run Growth." *Journal of Political Economy* 94 (1986): 1002-37.

Rothstein, Jesse. and Robert E. Scott. *The Failed Experiment: NAFTA's at Three Years*. Washington, D.C.: Economic Policy Institute, 1997.

Rowe, F. and DeVoretz, D. "An Estimate of the Economic Value of International Students in Canada." Vancouver: Canadian Education Centre Network, Unpublished Research Report, 1998.

Rubio, J. "Los Retos para la Educación Mexicana de Fin de Siglo." *Revista de la Educación Superior* 105 (1998).

Rubio, Luis. "Mexico and NAFTA Expansion." *NAMINEWS* 23 (Summer 1999). http://www.northamericaninstitute.org/naminews/issue23

Rudy, Willis. *Total War and Twentieth-Century Higher Learning.* Cranbury, NJ: Associated University Presses, 1991.

Ruiz, W. "El Empleo de los Profesionistas en la Frontera Norte: Efiniciones y Características." *El Cotidiano* 77 (1996).

Rush, S.C. "Productivity or Quality?" Pp. 1-14 in R.E. Anderson and J.W. Meyerson, eds., *Productivity and Higher Education.* Princeton: Peterson's Guides, Inc.

Ryan-Bacon, W. "Engineering: The NAFTA MRD and Other International Agreements." Unpublished Paper Presented to the Workshop on Internationalizing the Professions at the AUCC Conference on Internationalization: Moving from Rhetoric to Reality, November 20-22, 1996.

Safa, P. y E. Nivón. "La educación y el Tratado de Libre Comercio: de la crisis a las perspectivas." In Niebla G. Guevara y N. García Canclini (coord), *La Educación y la Cultura ante el Tratado de Libre Comercio.* México: Nexos/Nueva Imagen, 1992.

Safadi, Raed and Vera Nicholas. "Suggested Issues for Discussion." Pp. 17-27 in OECD, *Regionalism and its Place in the Multilateral Trading System.* Paris, 1996.

Salazar, Sylivia B.Ortega. "From Threat to Opportunity: A New Perspective for the Development of International Education in North America." Pp. 237-44 in Peggy Blumenthal, Craufurd Goodwin, Alan Smith, and Ulrich Teichler, eds., *Academic Mobility in a Changing World.* London and Bristol, PA: Jessica Kingsley Publishers, 1996.

Sánchez, M. D., J. Claffey y M. Castañeda (coords.). *Vinculación entre los Sectores Académico y Productivo en México y Estados Unidos: Catálogo de Casos.* México: ANUIES, Biblioteca de la Educación Superior, 1996.

Sánchez, M. D. "Transformaciones Educativas en la Frontera Durante los Noventa." En A. Mungaray y M.G. García de Léon (coord), *Desarrollo Fronterizo y Globalización.* México: ANUIES/Universidad de Sonora, Biblioteca de la Educación Superior, 1997.

Santillanez, Elizabeth J. *Higher Education's Responsiveness in Mexico and the United States to a New Economy and the Impacts of NAFTA.* Boulder, CO: Western Interstate Commission on Higher Education, 1995.

Saul, John Ralston. *Reflections of a Siamese Twin: Canada at the End of the Twentieth Century.* Toronto: Viking, 1997.

Schembri, L. L. "Canadian Exports of Business and Education Services to the Asia Pacific region." In R. G. Harris, ed., *The Asia Pacific Region in the Global Economy: A Canadian Perspective.* Calgary: University of Calgary Press, 1996.

Scott, Barbara Ann. *Crisis Management in American Higher Education.* Westport, CT: Praeger Press, 1983.

Scott, Robert E. *North American Trade NAFTA: Rising Deficits, Disappearing Jobs.* Washington, D.C.: Economic Policy Institute, 1996.

Scott, Robert E., Thea Lee, and John Schmitt. *Trading Away Good Jobs: An Examination of Employment and Wages in the U.S., 1979-94.* Washington, D.C.: Economic Policy Institute, 1997.

Schott, Jeffrey J. *The Uruguay Round: An Assessment.* Washington, D.C.: Institute for International Economics, 1994.

Schultz, T.W. "The Value of the Ability to Deal with Disequilibria." *Journal of Economic Literature* 13.3 (1975): 827-46.

Sculley, J. "A Perspective on the Future: What Business Needs from Higher Education." *Change* (March/April 1988).

Shute, J. "From Here to There and Back Again: International Outreach in the Canadian University'. In S.L. Bond and J.P Lemasson, eds., *A New World of Knowledge: Canadian Universities and Globalization.* Ottawa: International Development Research Centre, 1999.

Secretary's Commission on Achieving Necessary Skills, United States Department of Labor. *What Work Requires of Schools: A SCANS Report for America 2000.* Washington, D.C.: Government Printing Office, 1991.

Secretary's Commission on Achieving Necessary Skills, U.S. Department of Labor. *Learning a Living: A Blueprint for High Performance.* Washington, D.C.: Government Printing Office, 1992.

SESIC/Dirección General de Profesiones. "Evolución del Quehacer de la DGP." México: SESIC/DGP, *Colegios y profesiones,* Segunda época, 1999.

SESIC/ Dirección General de Profesiones. (1997). 'Reporte Ejecutivo de Avances en las Negociaciones Internacionales de los Servicios Profesionales en el Marco de TLCAN', México: Policopiado, 1997.

Silvestri, G.T. and J.M. Lukasiewicz. "Projections 2000: A Look at Occupational Employment Trends to the Year 2000." *Monthly Labor Review* 110.9 (1987): 46-69.

Skilbeck, Malcolm and Helen Connell. "International Education from the Perspective of Emergence World Regionalism: the Academic, Scientific, and Technological Dimension." Pp. 66-102 in Peggy Blumenthal, Craufurd Goodwin, Alan Smith, and Ulrich Teichler, eds., *Academic Mobility in a Changing World.* London and Bristol, PA: Jessica Kingsley Publishers, 1996.

Slaughter, Sheila. *The Higher Learning and High Technology: Dynamics of Higher Education Policy Formation.* Albany: State University of New York Press, 1990.

Slaughter, Sheila. "Retrenchment in the 1980s: The Politics of Prestige and Gender." *Journal of Higher Education* 64.3 (1993): 250-82.

Smilor, R.W., G. Kozmetsky, and D.V. Gibson, eds. *Creating the Technopolis: Linking Technology Commercialization and Economic Development.* Cambridge, MA: Ballinger Publishing Co., 1988.

Smilor, R.W. and M.D. Gill, Jr. *The New Business Incubator: Linking Talent, Technology, Capital, and Know-How.* Lexington, MA: Lexington Books, 1986.

Smith, Alan. "Regional Cooperation and Mobility in a Global Setting: The Example of the European Community." Pp. 129-146 in Peggy Blumenthal, Craufurd Goodwin, Alan Smith, and Ulrich Teichler (eds), *Academic Mobility in a Changing World.* London and Bristol, PA: Jessica Kingsley Publishers, 1996.

Smith, Thomas W. "Teaching Politics Abroad: The Internationalization of a Profession?' *PS: Political Science and Politics* 33.1 (March 2000): 65-72.

Sohn, L. B. "Model Rule for the Licensing of Legal Consultants." *The International Lawyer* (Spring, 1994): 336-351.

Southern Association of Colleges and Schools. 2002. "Commission on Colleges of the Southern Association of Colleges and Schools. http://www.sacscoc.org/index.asp

SRI International. *The Higher Education-Economic Development Connection: Emerging Roles for Public Colleges and Universities in a Changing Economy.* Washington, D.C.: American Association of State Colleges and Universities, 1986.

Stanford, Jim. *Paper Boom: Why Real Prosperity Requires a New Approach to Canada's Economy.* Ottawa: The Canadian Centre for Policy Alternatives and James Lorimer and Co. Ltd., 1999.

Stanley, D. and J. Mason. *Preparing Graduates for the Future: International Learning Outcomes.* Victoria; British Columbia Centre for International Education, 1997.

Statistics Canada. www.statcan.ca, 2001.

Statistics Canada. "Brain Drain or Grain Gain? What Do the Data Say?" Ottawa, 1998.

Steger, Manfred B. 2002. *Globalism: The New Market Ideology.* Lanham, Maryland: Rowman and Littlefield.

Stiglitz, Joseph E. *Globalization and Its Discontents.* New York: W.W. Norton & Co., 2002.

Strong, D. "We Need a National Commitment to University Education." *University Affairs* (February 1999).

Tan, J.P. and A. Mingat, *Education in Asia: A Comparative Study of Cost and Financing.* Washington, D.C.: World Bank, 1992.

Tavernier, K. "Are University Funding Systems in Need of an Overhaul?" Pp. 83-100 in P.G. Altbach and D.B. Johnstone, eds., *The Funding of Higher Education: International Perspectives.* New York and London: Garland Publishing, Inc., 1993.

Teather C. B., H.H. Tsang, and W.W.Y. Chan. "Internationalisation of Higher Education in Hong Kong." In J. Knight and H. de Wit, eds., *Internationalisation of Higher Education in Asia-Pacific Countries.* Melbourne, Australia, 1996.

Teicher, Ulrich. "Research on Academic Mobility and International Cooperation in Higher Education: An Agenda for the Future.' Pp. 338-58 in Peggy Blumenthal, Craufurd Goodwin, Alan Smith, and Ulrich Teichler, eds., *Academic Mobility in a Changing World.* London and Bristol, PA: Jessica Kingsley Publishers, 1996.

"The Alliance for Higher Education and Enterprise in North America." *NAMINEWS* 22 (Winter 1998). http://www.northamericaninstitute.org/naminews/issue22

The Globe and Mail, August 19, 1994, p. C6.

Thurow, Lester. "Planning for the New World Economy." *Planning for Higher Education* 20 (1991): 17-23.

Thurow, Lester. *Head to Head: The Coming Economic Battle Among Japan, Europe, and America.* New York: William Morrow and Co., 1992.

Tillett, A.D. and B. Lesser. *International Students and Higher Education:Canadian Choices,* Research Paper No. 2. Ottawa: Canadian Bureau for International Education, 1992.

Townsend, B.K., L.J. Newell, and M.D. Wiese. *Creating Distinctiveness: Lessons From Uncommon Colleges and Universities,* ASHE-ERIC Higher Education Report No. 6. Washington, D.C.: Association for the Study of Higher Education, 1992.

REFERENCES

Trilateral Task Force on North American Collaboration in Higher Education. "Discussion paper for the International Symposium on Higher Education and Strategic Partnerships: The Challenge of Global Competitiveness from a North American Perspective." Vancouver, British Columbia, September10-13, 1993.

Trolliet, C. "Recent Developments in the WTO on Professional Services." In *International Trade in Professional Services: Advancing Liberalisation through Regulatory Reform.* Paris: Organisation for Economic Cooperation and Development, 1997a.

Trolliet, C. "The Liberalisation of Professional Services According to the GATS." Address Presented at the Conference on Trade Agreements, Higher Education and the Globalization of the Professions: A Multinational Discourse on Quality Assurance and Competency. Montreal, May 7-9, 1997b.

Tsongas, Paul. *A Call to Economic Arms: Forging a New American Mandate.* Boston: The Tsongas Committee, 1991.

Tucker, J. G. *An Overview of the Export of Australian Legal Services.* Canberra: International Legal Services Advisory Council, 1996.

Tudiver, N. *Universities for Sale: Resisting Corporate Control over Canadian Higher Education.* Toronto: James Lorimer and Co. Ltd., 1999.

Union PanAmericana de Asociaciones de Ingenieros. "Evaluation and Accreditation of Engineering Studies." In *World Federation of Engineering Organizations (WFEO), Committee on Education and Training Journal Ideas.* 3 (January 1996).

United Nations Conference on Trade and Development. *World Investment Report,* 1998: Trends and Determinants. New York and Geneva, 1998.

United Nations Educational and Scientific Organisation. *Statistical Yearbook.* Paris: UNESCO, 1992.

United Nations Educational and Scientific Organisation. *Hacia un Programa 21 para la Educación Superior.* Paris: Conferencia Mundial sobre la Educación Superior, 1998a.

United Nations Educational and Scientific Organisation. *Panorama Estadístico de la Enseñanza Superior en el Mundo: 1980-1995.* Documento de Trabajo. París: Conferencia Mundial sobre la Educación Superior, 1998b.

United States Agency for International Development. *Agency Performance Report, 1998.* Washington, D.C.: Center for Development Information and Evaluation, 1999a.

United States Agency for International Development. "USAID Higher Education Community Partnership." 1999b. http://www.info.usaid.gov/about/highered.htm

United States Agency for International Development. "Congressional Presentation, FY 2000: Statement of the Administrator." 1999c. http://www.info.usaid.gov/pubs/cp2000/adminst.html

United States Agency for International Development. "Congressional Presentation, FY 2000: Summary of USAID Fiscal Year 2000 Budget Request." 1999d.http://www.info.usaid.gov/pubs/cp2000/cp00bud.html

United States Agency for International Development. "Congressional Presentation, FY 2000: Program Performance." 1999e. http://www.info.usaid.gov/pubs/cp2000/wpdpp.html

United States Agency for International Development. "Congressional Presentation, FY 2000: Mexico." 1999f. http://www.info.usaid.gov/pubs/cp2000/lac/mexico.html

United States Bureau of Labor Statistics. "MultifactorProductivity: Private Business Sector: Productivity and Related Indexes, 1948-97." http://stats.bls.gov/news.release/prod3.t01.htm

United States Department of Commerce, Bureau of the Census. *Census of Population and Housing, 1990.* www.census.gov

United States Department of Commerce, Bureau of the Census. *Census of Population and Housing, 2000.* www.census.gov

United States Department of Commerce, Bureau of the Census. "U.S. Trade Balance with Advanced Technology, 1989-2000." http://www.census.gov/foreign-trade/balance/c0007.html

United States Department of Commerce, Bureau of Economic Analysis. "U.S.Iinternational Trade in Goods and Services, Balance of Payments Basis, 1960-2001." http://www.bea.doc.gov/bea/di1.htm

United States Department of Commerce, Bureau of Economic Analysis. *Survey of Current Business.* Washington, D.C.: Government Printing Office, 1999.

United States Department of Education, National Center for Education Statistics. *Digest of Education Statistics, 1992.* Washington, D.C.: Government Printing Office, 1992.

United States Department of Education. "The Growing Importance of International Education: Remarks as Prepared for Delivery by U.S. Secretary of Education Richard W. Riley." http://www.ed.gov/Speeches/04-2000/000419.html

United States Department of Education. "FY 2000 Budget Summary." 1999a. http://www.ed.gov/offices/OUS/Budget00/BudgetSumm/sum-e.html#2000

United States Department of Education. "International Education and Graduate Programs." 1999b. http://www.ed.gov/offices/OPE/HEP/iegps

United States Department of Justice. *1999 Statistical Yearbook of the Immigration and Naturalization Service.* Washington, D.C.: Government Printing Office, 1999. http://www.ins.usdoj.gov/graphics/aboutins/statistics/FY99Yearbook.pdf

United States Department of Labor. *What Work Requires of Schools: A SCANS Report for America 2000.* Washington, D.C.: Government Printing Office, 1991.

United States Department of State. "Educational and Cultural Affairs: Fulbright Program." 1999a. http://e.usia.gov/education/fulbright

United States Department of State. "Building a North American Partnership: Statement Agreed by U.S. Secretary of State Madeleine K. Albright, Mexican Foreign Secretary Rosario

Green, and Canadian Foreign Minister Lloyd Axworthy, September 1999, New York, NY." 1999b. file:///C|/My Documents/Mexico/partnership.html United States Department of State. "Memorandum of Understanding on International

Development Cooperation Between the Government of the United States of America and the Government of Canada and the Government of the United Mexican States." 1999c. file:///C|/My Documents/Mexico/mou_uscanmex.html

United States Department of State. "North American Partnership: Trilateral Inventory." 1999d. file:///C|/My Documents/Mexico/inventory.html

United States International Trade Commission. *Potential Impact on the U.S. Economy and Industries of the GATT Uruguay Round Agreements.* Washington, D.C.: USITC Publication 2790, 1994.

United States International Trade Commission. *Recent Trends in U.S Services Trade.* Washington, D. C.: USITC, 1997.

United States International Trade Commission. *The Year in Trade: Operation of the Trade Agreements Program During 1997.* Washington, D.C.: USITC Publication 3103, 1998.

Universidad de Guadalajara. "Autoevaluación de la Dimensión Internacional de la Universidad de Guadalajara: Autoestudio "El Proceso de Internacionalización de la Universidad de Guadalajara: Perspectivas y Propuestas." Guadalajara, 1999. *http://148.202.2.214/dimenint.htm*

Universidad Veracruzana /Dirección de Planeación Institucional. *Guía para la Formulación de Solicitudes de Apoyo Financiero y Académico a Proyectos de Educación Superior: Fuentes Nacionales e Internacionales de Apoyo Financiero y Académico.* Veracruz: Universidad Veracruzana, s.f: 40p+anexos.

Urquidi, V. L. "México Frente a los Bloques Regionales." In C. Arreola, (comp.), *Testimonios Sobre el TLC.* México: Porrúa, 1994.

Useem, Michael. *The Inner Circle: Large Corporations and the Rise of Business Political Activity in the U.S. and U.K.* Oxford: Oxford University Press, 1984.

van der Wende, M. "Internationalising the Curriculum in Higher Education" In *Internationalisation of Higher Education.* París: OECD, 1996.

Vega, Canovas G. "¿Hacia un acuerdo de Libre Comercio?" In C. Arreola, (comp.), *Testimonios Sobre el TLC.* México: Porrúa, 1994.

Verry, D. and B. Davies. University Costs and Outputs. Amsterdam: Elsevier, 1976.

Villa-Prezelski, Carmen and Richard Navarro. *New Models and Possibilities for Academic Cooperation in North America: An Executive Summary of the WICHE/AMPEI Educational Leadership Seminar, November 8-10, 1995.* Boulder, CO: Western Interstate Commission on Higher Education, 1996.

Vogel, David. "The Power of Business in America: A Reappraisal." *British Journal of Political Science* 13.1 (1983): 19-43.

Wallerstein, Immanuel. *The World Capitalist System,* 2 Vols. New York: Academic Press, 1980.

Warner, G. "Internationalisation Models and the Role of the Universities." *The McMaster Courier* 10.14 (1991).

Warner, Mark A. "Public and Private Restraints on Trade: Effects on Investment Decisions and Policy Approaches to Them." Pp. 123-42 in OECD, *Market Access After the Uruguay Round: Investment, Competition and Technology Perspectives.* Paris, 1996.

Waters, Malcolm. 2001. *Globalization,* 2nd ed. London: Routledge.

Watts, R.L. "The Federal Context for Higher Education." In D. Brown, P. Cazalis, and G. Jasmin, eds., *Higher Education in Federal Systems.* Kingston, Ontario: Institute of Governmental Relations, Queen's University, 1992.

Weintraub, Sydney. "The North American Free Trade Agreement as Negotiated: A US Perspective." Pp. 1-31 in Steven Globerman and Michael Walker, eds., *Assessing NAFTA: A Trinational Analysis.* Vancouver: The Fraser Institute, 1993.

Weintraub, Sydney. *NAFTA: What Comes Next?* Westport, CT: Praeger, 1994.

Western Interstate Commission on Higher Education. *Exploring the Relationship: A Survey of the Literature of Higher Education and the Economy,* Working Paper No. 2. Boulder, CO, 1992a.

Western Interstate Commission on Higher Education. *The Higher Education-Economy Tie: A Sampling of Exemplary Programs in the West.* Boulder, CO, 1992b.

Western Interstate Commission on Higher Education. *Insights on the Higher Education-Economy Relationship: Interviews with the Stakeholders,* Working Paper No. 4. Boulder, CO, 1992c.

Western Interstate Commission on Higher Education. *Joined or Unconnected?: A Look at State Economic Development and Higher Education Plans,* Working Paper #5. Boulder, CO, 1992d.

Western Interstate Commission on Higher Education. *Meeting Economic and Social Challenges: A Strategic Agenda for Higher Education.* Boulder, CO, 1992e.

Western Interstate Commission on Higher Education. 1994. *Leading the Way: Leadership Perspectives on Creating Binational Programs in Higher Education; An Executive Summary of the WICHE/AMPEI Educational Leadership Seminar, May 15-17, 1994.* Boulder, CO: WICHE, 1994.

Whalley, John. *The Uruguay Round and Beyond.* Ann Arbor: University of Michigan Press, 1989.

Whitcomb, D. G. "Investment in Education." *Synthesis* (Winter 1997).

Whittington, Michael and Glen Williams, eds. *Canadian Politics in the 21st Century.* Scarborough: Nelson Thomson Learning, 2000.

Wilson, D. "What Impact will the Harmonization of Occupational Classification Have Upon North American Educational Systems?" Presentation at a Conference on Education Reform in Canada, Mexico and the United States: An Agenda for Cooperation and Research, Brown University, Providence, Rhode Island, October 17-18, 1996.

Wilson, D. "Defining International Competencies for the New Millennium." *CBIE Research.* Ottawa: CBIE, 1998.

Wirth, John D. "Advancing the North American Community." *American Review of Canadian Studies* (Summer 1996): 261-73.

Wirth, John D. and Robert Earle, eds. *Identities in North America: The Search for Community.* Stanford: Standford University Press, 1995.

Wit, H. y J. Knight. *Quality and Internationalization in Higher Education.* Paris: OECD, Programm on Institutionnal Management, 1997.

World Bank. *Higher Education: The Lessons of Experience.* Washington, D.C.: World Bank, 1994.

World Bank. *Priorities and Strategies for Education: A World Bank Review.* Washington, D.C.: World Bank, 1995.

World Bank. 1999 *World Development Indicators.* Washington, D.C.: World Bank, 1999.

World Federation of Engineering Organisations. "Special Edition on Accreditation and Professional Practice.' *Committee on Education and Training Journal Ideas* 3 (January 1996).

World Trade Organisation. "Education Services: Background Note by the Secretariat (Document 98-3691)." Geneva: Council for Trade in Services, 1998a.

World Trade Organisation. "Communication from the United States: Education Services (Document 98-4048)." Geneva: Council for Trade in Services, 1998b.

World Trade Organisation. "The Organization: Members." 2002. http://www.wto.org/english/thewto_e/whatis_e/whatis_e.htm

WPPS. "WTO Guidelines for Mutual Recognition Agreements in the Accountancy Sector. Communication from the European Community and its Member States." August 5, 1996.

Yalnizyan, Armine. "The Road from Monterrey: A Caution from Canada." In Canada Report, Social Watch, 2002. www.socwatch.org.uy/2002/eng/national%20reports/canada2002_eng.htm

York University. "North American Studies Exchange Program." 1999.http://yorku.ca/research/cpnai/univnort.htm

Young, Judy. "Oportunidades en la Movilidad Académica para Norteamerica en el Siglo XXI." *Educación Global* 3 (1999): 17-20.

Zemsky, R. and P. Oedel. "Higher Education and the Changing Nature of the American Workforce – Responses, Challenges, and Opportunities." *Education Quality of the Workforce Working Papers,* No. WP2. Philadelphia: Institute for Research on Higher Education, University of Pennsylvania, 1994.

Higher Education Dynamics

1. J. Enders and O. Fulton (eds.): *Higher Education in a Globalising World.* 2002
   ISBN Hb 1-4020-0863-5; Pb 1-4020-0864-3
2. A. Amaral, G.A. Jones and B. Karseth (eds.): *Governing Higher Education: National Perspectives on Institutional Governance.* 2002 ISBN 1-4020-1078-8
3. A. Amaral, V.L. Meek and I.M. Larsen (eds.): *The Higher Education Managerial Revolution?* 2003 ISBN Hb 1-4020-1575-5; Pb 1-4020-1586-0
4. C.W. Barrow, S. Didou-Aupetit and J. Mallea: *Globalisation, Trade Liberalisation, and Higher Education in North America.* 2003 ISBN 1-4020-1791-X

KLUWER ACADEMIC PUBLISHERS – DORDRECHT / BOSTON / LONDON

Printed in the United States
73331LV00001B/252